A Practical Guide to
Real-time Systems
Development

TWO WEEK LOAN

A Practical Guide to Real-time Systems Development

SYLVIA GOLDSMITH

PRENTICE HALL

New York   London   Toronto   Sydney   Tokyo   Singapore

First published 1993 by
Prentice Hall Europe
Campus 400, Maylands Avenue,
Hemel Hempstead,
Hertfordshire HP2 7EZ
A division of
Simon & Schuster International Group

Typeset in 10/12 Garamond
by MHL Typesetting

Printed and bound in Great Britain by
Redwood Books, Trowbridge, Wiltshire

Library of Congress Cataloging-in-publication data

Goldsmith, Sylivia.
  A practical guide to real-time systems development / Sylvia
Goldsmith.
    p.   cm.
  Includes bibliographical references and index.
  ISBN 0-13-718503-0
  1. Real-time data processing.   I. Title.
QA76.54.G65   1992
004'.33–dc20
                                                    92-19076
                                                    CIP

British Library Cataloguing in publication data

A catalogue record for this book is available
from the British Library

ISBN 0-13-718503-0 (pbk)

---

6 7 8 9 01 00 99 98 97

Contents

Preface

I have spent the last four years teaching engineers how to analyze and design structured real-time systems. At the end of each course, I am asked to recommend a book which covers all of the fundamentals of structured development, in practical terms with lots of real-time examples. I have been able to recommend a number of very good books, all covering some part of the development cycle, although sometimes not with a real-time system in mind, in degrees ranging from 'fairly practical' to 'so theoretical as to be useless' to a practising engineer. At the end of my recommendations, someone would invariably ask me why there was no book covering just what an engineer wants to know in relevant terms — this is what I have attempted to do.

This book is based on my experiences of teaching and using structured techniques, what causes most problems, both in learning and application of the techniques, and how these techniques are actually used within industry.

The book deals very much with the real world, acknowledging that you will not always be able to build a system in the most 'theoretically correct' way, due to the existence of real-world constraints such as time and money. I have tried to show how to use the flexibility of the techniques to cope with the development and documentation of a real system.

After a brief introduction, discussing the advantages of using structured techniques within a real-time system, the modelling tools used in structured development are described in detail. The syntax of each tool (data flow diagram, state transition diagram, entity relationship diagram and structure chart) is taught, together with what the tools should be used for and how they should be constructed and reviewed. In subsequent sections, I show how these tools can be used effectively from specification to code within the context of a real-time system. Each step in the development is discussed in detail, covering exactly what should and should not be attempted, and explaining the advantages of this development strategy.

There are very few new ideas in this book. The aim of the book is to present the ideas of structured development in the most useful way for people attempting to use these techniques — almost as a reference manual for real-time structured development.

A variety of examples, both in the text and in the exercises at the end of each chapter, have been worked through from specification to implementation, in an attempt to show a range of different systems in which these techniques could be of use.

The book deals very much with the basics of structured system development. There are many other areas such as estimation, quality, testing, project management and use of CASE, which although important in their own right, have only been touched on in the context of the basic development cycle. This is due to lack of space, and an unwillingness to attempt too much at one time. I have, however, attempted to show how these peripheral activities will fit in with the techniques of structured system development.

This book is aimed at anyone who wants to understand how to develop a good real-time system. This includes not just engineers, but also the people who should know what the engineers are doing, and why they are doing it, such as project managers and quality assurance engineers.

It is not aimed purely at software engineers. The analysis and the early stages of the design are independent of how the system will finally be implemented, and many of these techniques are equally applicable to hardware engineers. The techniques are ideally suited to systems where the software and hardware are being developed jointly.

Throughout this book the pronoun 'he' is intended in the generic sense to refer to 'person' (he/she) rather than to the male.

ACKNOWLEDGEMENTS

I would very much like to thank the following people for their help and support:

- Everyone at YOURDON™. In particular Alec Bruty, Rick Marden, Keith Edwards, Mike Brough, Julian Morgan, John Bowen and Anne-Marie Gwynn (for giving me the job in the first place).

- All the people I have taught over the years who often ended up teaching me as much as I taught them, for posing problems that I never would have considered left to my own devices.

- David Lee of Marconi Software for his thorough and constructive review of the manuscript.

- Dick Bolten for spotting some mistakes that had slipped through the net and Clive Cooper for his vast knowledge of teabag manufacture.

- David, for making me believe I could do it.

Sylvia Goldsmith

CHAPTER ONE

Introduction

1.1 TRADITIONAL PROBLEMS IN REAL-TIME DEVELOPMENT

Using a structured development technique is likely to involve more time, effort and therefore money in the initial development phases than more traditional approaches. So, what is the point of using such a technique?

In this chapter I will attempt to justify the use of structured development techniques by considering some of the problems encountered during development and the way in which structured methods will help.

1.1.1 Communication

In a real-time development there are often many different people involved — software engineers, hardware engineers, quality assurance and control people, the customer, the sales people, the marketing people, project management and others. They are all working towards the same goal: the cost-effective development of a working system, which fulfils its requirements. Unfortunately, all these people see that goal in slightly different terms. So when they discuss the system, or try to explain aspects of the system to one another, they all talk about it in slightly different terms. Consequently they do not understand what the other is talking about.

Consider a few of the problems caused by many software engineers' inability to communicate with hardware engineers. Imagine a situation where there is a choice between doing something in software or hardware. Traditionally, real-time systems have been developed in an environment where hardware was very important and expensive, whilst software was something brought in at the end, once the hardware was nearly finished. So, traditionally it has always been seen as easier to modify software than hardware — even though these days software development tends to cost as much, if not more, than hardware. Many people still believe that it is a lot easier to 'change a couple of lines of code' than to change anything in the hardware. It is often very difficult to explain to a hardware engineer why it is so difficult to make a requested change.

To many people, 'changing a couple of lines of code' means just that — editing a file. They do not realize that in order to make a fairly simple conceptual

1

change, you have to find the piece of code to change and investigate the repercussions of that change on the rest of the system. If the change affects the timing or the scheduling of the system, you may have to redesign or restructure other parts of the system around it. Once you have made the modification, you have to recompile, relink and retest the whole system — which can take a very long time. An effective communication tool may help people understand the potential difficulties of software modification.

Other problems occur when hardware people choose a certain processor configuration, and expect the software somehow to fit in with it. You may not understand why they have picked that configuration, and they do not understand why you want a different one — although you may both have valid reasons. This is because they understand little about how software works and you understand little about how hardware works. Again, a common communication tool may help you to see each other's point of view.

Another group of people involved in development is the Quality Assurance (QA) or Quality Control (QC) department. Although the situation is improving, and many companies now employ QA/QC engineers with programming and design experience, it is still not uncommon to find QA/QC people with no technical experience. Many QA engineers are trained to make sure you have dotted all the i's and crossed all the t's — not to make sure that a certain, perhaps very specialized, piece of equipment actually does what the customer wants it to.

If the people in the QA/QC department do not understand what the system is supposed to do, they will not understand how to test it. A QA/QC engineer does not have to understand how the program works, but should understand what it is supposed to do. QA/QC engineers who do not understand the purpose of the systems they monitor will blindly test programs to a test specification, often written by the same programmer who wrote the code.

Testing like this is dangerous. Sometimes a system will pass a QA/QC test, not because it is right, but because something fundamental has been omitted from the test specification. It may be obvious that the system is supposed to shut down when the user presses the 'off' button, but if it is not written down it will not be tested. Equally, a system may fail a QA/QC test because it does something that is not specified in the test specification, but does not affect the overall conformance of the system to its original specification. If the system was specified to the QA/QC department in non-technical terms, they would have a feeling for the system's purpose, rather than just blindly following a test specification. \

Communication with the customer is often very difficult. It is very important that you understand what the customer wants, even though many customers do not really know themselves initially. Customers may have a basic idea of what they want their system to do, but no idea of what you can do for them. Before you can reach agreement with your customer there will be a lot of discussion. Your customer says 'Can you build me this?' You say, 'No, but

I can build you this.' He then says 'It's not quite what I wanted, could you make this modification ?'— and so on.

Your customer does not understand computers, and sees the system in his own terms (e.g. teabag making equipment, mobile telephones, training simulators), whereas you see the system in your own terms (e.g. lines of code, communication nodes, processor capabilities). If you both consider the system from completely different angles, it will be very difficult for either of you to understand the other.

Even if you do not deal directly with the customer, you probably still have to deal with the people in the Sales or Marketing department, many of whom do not understand the complexity involved in building a large system. Often, marketing people sell something without consultation, then demand that you build the system in a ridiculous time-scale because they have promised delivery in three months' time. They do not understand why it will take two years to build the system.

Many marketing people see software development as some kind of black art. In one company where I worked, faced with the impossible, the marketing people would just wave their arms and say 'You software people can do anything if you put your minds to it'. This is the equivalent of giving builders enough bricks to build a wall and telling them to build a house with them — by 'putting their minds to it'. Worse still are the ones who wrote a 15 line Basic program once and think that is all there is to software development. It is up to you to make them understand how complex system development is. You need to back costing and time-scales with models explaining why their proposed development may not be possible.

Finally, you have the people in project management — who sometimes have very little experience in modern software development, and therefore find it difficult to keep track of what you are doing as they do not understand why some of it is being done. Some project managers seem to think that if you are not in front of a terminal typing in code, you are not actually doing any work. You need to make them aware of what you are doing, and why you are doing it. A development tool that would not only help them to understand, but also track the development would be useful.

The solution to all of these problems is the use of development tools that everybody involved in the development can understand. These tools should be technical enough to be successfully used for system development. However, they must also be user friendly enough for non-technical people to understand.

Increased communication should also help you understand other people's problems. All the people involved in development have their own very good reasons for wanting things done in a certain way or to certain time-scales. An appreciation of these problems will lead to the best possible compromise between what these people want and what you can provide for them.

1.1.2 System complexity

Figure 1.1 shows a typical real-time system, an automated system for teabag production. This is not a particularly complicated system, but there are still many different things involved. The system consists of the following:

1. Teabag making equipment.
2. A computer with some process control software which is connected to an operator terminal, allowing the operator to drive the system.
3. A communications node, allowing access to a remote database where all teabag making statistics are stored.
4. A fancy graphics terminal for the supervisor, so that he can keep an eye on the teabag manufacture.

Even though all the software will be inside the 'process control' box, in order to build this system, you still have to understand what all the other boxes do. You have to understand how to use the communications, how to get things into the database, how to use the teabag making equipment. However, if you try to understand every little detail initially, you will get confused very quickly.

The solution is 'Weinburg's Lump Law' which states that 'In order to understand anything, do not attempt to understand everything'. At the beginning of your development, you need to know only that you will be using certain pieces of equipment, and fundamentally what they do. For example, you may need to know that the graphics terminal will place certain icons on the screen. However, you will not need to know the character strings sent to put those icons on the screen until the coding phase. You need to know whether the teabag making equipment makes teabags at a set weight, or whether you have to send it a variable weight at the beginning of a production run. You will not need to know low level commands and protocol for the teabag boxing equipment until much later in the design.

During the early stages all you need to know is high level information.

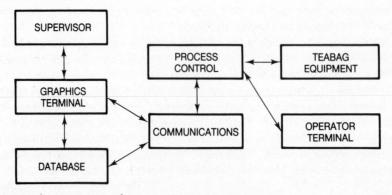

Figure 1.1   Block diagram of teabag boxing system.

When you have understood that, you can start looking at the lower levels of detail. This is easy to say, but not so easy to do. One of the tricks of analysis is knowing what is and what is not initially important, and hopefully that is one of the things that this book will help you define.

1.1.3 Different development techniques

People involved in software development tend to come from a huge range of backgrounds — you do not just get 'trained computer scientists' as in a number of other areas of engineering. As long as someone is numerate, they can end up doing software development. As these people have different backgrounds and have been trained in different ways, they will do development differently |

These days very few people, when faced with a problem, go straight to a terminal and start typing in code, without some kind of program design. Most people are fairly disciplined and have a technique for designing and building code, even if it is not a recognized technique with a name. It may just be a way of doing things that works for an individual. If you have been developing software in a certain way for some time, you are probably quite good at doing it like that. Therefore, it is silly to say 'I don't care what you've been doing for the past two or three years, or how well it's worked for you, this is the method we are going to use now.' All the good practices that have been built up over the years, based on experience, would be lost. Also, a method that is imposed on people may not fit in with the way that they like to work.

You should not attempt the wholesale adoption of a method which is completely new to you, but should try to integrate the way you currently work within the framework of a structured development method. Structured analysis and design should be flexible. A whole range of techniques is presented in this book — some of which may not be applicable or go far enough for your development. Consider the techniques as a whole, consider your own environment and decide which techniques will suit you.

This book does not define a prescriptive method — there are not a set of rules to follow. The range of developments in which you could be involved is so huge that it would be impossible to apply the same set of predictive steps to every development. In any set of steps there will be certain things that you do not need to do. A method that forces you to do things that you do not need to do is not a very good method.

Let us look at an example where not all of the development steps are needed. If a system is to be implemented across two computers, you must decide which bits of the system will go on which computer before you design the code. Processor environment modelling is a design stage that consists of examining the processor configuration and splitting work between processors. This makes sense in a multi-processor environment, but in a single processor environment, you would not need to do this. Therefore, this stage of the design would be left out.

Another area of flexibility is in the use of particular diagrams. For example, the state transition diagram is used to describe sequencing and control, and is a type of finite state machine. If you have been using finite state machines for some time with different notation, it may be easier to carry on using your finite state machine instead of the state transition diagram. If the diagram shows the same information, fits in with any other diagrams used and everyone involved in the development is familiar with the notation, there will not be any problems. However, this may cause problems with an automated toolkit, which may only support certain diagrams (although many toolkits can be configured to use different diagrams).

The techniques are very flexible and resilient to change. As a particular diagram, technique or development step will not necessarily apply to your development, the first step in any structured development process should be working out which parts of the method to use, and setting a standard for everyone involved in the development.

1.2 THE IDEAS BEHIND STRUCTURED DEVELOPMENT

1.2.1 The use of models

Models will overcome many of the problems discussed in the previous section. Building a model of something before you build the thing itself, allows you to see what that thing should look like when it is finished. The use of models is not some new radical concept of structured development. There is no branch of engineering, apart from software engineering, where models are not built. In civil engineering, electrical engineering and physical engineering models are always built first. The real thing is built on the basis of information gleaned from the model. Imagine building a house. You would not go to a builder and say 'Here's a pile of bricks, here's some money — build me a house'. You would expect the builder to produce a blueprint of the house. If you did not like the look of something on the blueprint, you would expect the builder to redraw it, to confirm that he had understood the specified changes. You would also expect stress and strain on walls to be calculated to make sure that, when the house was built, it did not fall down. Nothing like this is done as a matter of course in software developments. In many cases it seems more a matter of people crossing their fingers and hoping for the best.

There are two initial reasons for building a model. Firstly, it will give a communication tool, to ensure that what you propose to build is what the customer wants. Secondly, it will give you something concrete on which to point out errors in initial understanding of requirements. When customers ask for modifications, they are often not quite sure what they are asking you to change and neither are you. Consequently, you end up changing the wrong thing, resulting in a system with two mistakes, rather than the original one.

The cost of making a change to requirements rises exponentially as you move through the development cycle. A change at the requirements phase does not cost very much, as it probably only involves changing the documentation. On the other hand, a change after the system has been delivered to the customer will cost much more. You may have to redesign parts of the system, reimplement those parts and retest the whole system. Even changes made during design and test may require substantial redesign and reimplementation of the system. It is also very soul-destroying to put a lot of effort into developing a good system, only to deliver it to the customer and find out that it is not really what was wanted. Changes are better made as early in the development as possible.

You can also use the models in a more structured approach to estimating time-scales, costs, required processing power, etc., than is currently used in many development environments.

Before we start looking at the details of the models, let us consider them in more general terms. Figure 1.2 shows a typical diagram hierarchy used to model a system: We consider the 'data flow diagram', although most of the ideas discussed apply to all the diagrams.

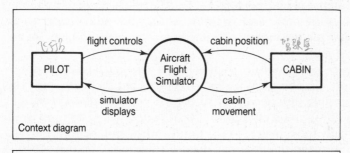

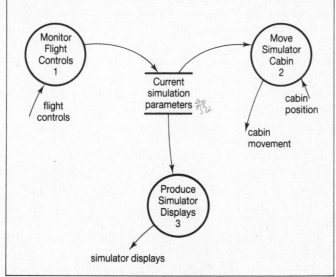

Figure 1.2 Typical diagram hierarchy.

The circle at the top of the diagram hierarchy, shown on the context diagram, represents the whole system. Any circle represents a function of the system, and can be broken into a lower level diagram containing a number of circles (i.e. a large function can be broken into many smaller functional areas). In this example the major function of the system, 'aircraft flight simulator', has been broken into a number of sub-functions, 'produce simulator displays', 'move simulator cabin' and 'monitor flight controls'.

Let us examine the characteristics of this model, and discuss why these characteristics are good to have. Firstly, the model is graphic — which is desirable for a number of reasons. A graphic representation gives a clear overview of a situation, saying something quickly without concerning you in all the depth of what is going on. Imagine having to identify a specific person from a group of people, many of whom have similarities (e.g. a number of them may wear glasses and have brown hair). Given a textual description of the specific person, you would have to read the text and think about it — it may take you a while to assimilate the information, and you could still easily pick the wrong person. Given a photograph of the specific person, it would be much easier to make the correct choice. Graphics are more user friendly, as they are much easier to assimilate than text. Also, a picture means the same in any language, which can be a major advantage over text.

However, characteristics such as how a person talked could not be shown in a photograph. Graphic gives a good overview, but there are some things that can only be sensibly described only in text. If you describe a complete system using only pictures, you would have lots of very detailed pictures at the lower levels that actually took longer to create and understand than an equivalent piece of text. I am not suggesting that you need a 'traditional' textual specification as well as a graphical model. Traditionally, 'textual specification' involves writing a huge document that describes all the functions of the system. These functional specifications often include implementation details, and tend to be very vague in some places and very detailed in others. Textual specifications are often long, boring, difficult to read and consequently not very carefully read.

The initial system description should be graphic, and text should be constructed with respect to the graphics. This gives a structured system description, in terms of text and graphics.

Figure 1.2 initially shows the overall function of the system, 'aircraft flight simulator', split into a number of smaller functions in the lower level data flow diagram. A model which allows the system to be broken into different functional areas and different levels of detail will be useful. In the aircraft flight simulator, imagine we are only interested in the production of displays. The top level data flow diagram shows how the production of displays fits in with the other functions of the system. Once this is understood, we need only consider lower level diagrams associated with 'produce simulator displays'.

It is like using a map. If I want to get to a certain address in Lincoln, initially I use a small scale map to take me from London to Lincoln. Once in

Lincoln, I can use a larger scale map to take me to the exact street. I would not start off with a street map of the whole of England to get from London to Lincoln.

Splitting the system in this way will also help when dividing the work to be done between engineers, or groups of people. We could allocate 'monitor flight controls' to one engineer, 'produce simulator displays' to another engineer and 'move simulator cabin' to another engineer. The interfaces between these areas are identified by the top level data flow diagram, and the functionality of each area by lower level data flow diagrams.

All the diagrams used have rules and guidelines associated with them, which should give you confidence in the model. If strictly adhered to, they ensure the models (and thus the systems built from them) are well structured, complete and easy to understand. Without these rules it would be possible to build a system using the diagrams described in this book that was still badly structured. Using just the diagrams without the associated rules and techniques will give you false confidence. You will think that what you are doing must be right because you are following a structured method; but the diagrams on their own are not the method — just a means of documenting the decisions arrived at using the method.

It should be possible to get a feeling for what the system will do by looking at the diagrams: realizing that something is wrong only when the end of the development has been reached should not happen. The modelling tools should be capable of modelling everything normally important in system development, to allow the whole system to be developed.

Let us consider an example where incomplete modelling has caused problems. The M25 is a ring-road around London, and is famous for being the worst motorway in Britain. The problem with the M25 is that it is incredibly busy. A motorway should be a road that gets you quickly from A to B: it is not unusual to take 2 hours to go 20 miles on the M25. The modelling of where the M25 should go was done very well, resulting in everyone wanting to use the motorway. The modelling of how many cars would use the M25 was done badly, resulting in a motorway that is too small to carry all the people that want to use it. Although it was essentially a very good idea, and some of the modelling was done very well, it failed in its aims. This happens in a lot of systems. A potentially good idea is developed into a system which is very good in many aspects, but fails owing to unconsidered areas.

Finally, the models must be user friendly — from both the customer's and the engineer's point of view. The models and the techniques must be easy for the engineer to use. Engineers have enough to worry about, without having to spend 80 per cent of their time struggling with the structured techniques, leaving only 20 per cent to build the system. This is one of the major criticisms levied at the more formal techniques, such as VDM and Z. Although theoretically they are a very good idea, as they almost guarantee error-free development, they are so difficult to use that their use normally involves an unreasonable amount of time and effort.

Using a structured technique should be like writing or driving a car —

it is difficult until you have had a little bit of practice, but once you are familiar with it, it becomes automatic. The first development may involve a long learning curve, after which it will get easier. In the long term, structured techniques should make developments run more smoothly.

The models will be shown to many potentially non-technical people. Models are used as an aid to communication, and if they do not communicate effectively, they are not fulfilling one of their major functions. It is important that the models are easy enough for the customer, the Marketing department, the QA department, etc. to understand otherwise the models are only for your benefit, and although they will help you to develop and document a well-structured system, you will not be reaping all the benefits of using structured development.

1.2.2 The diagrams

There are three diagrams, one for each aspect of system behaviour, used for modelling during both the analysis and design phases.

The data flow diagram shows the functionality of the system. It consists of circles or data transformations which represent single system functions. It shows the flow of data which enters the system passing through various functions. By examining the data entering the system, what the system does with the data and eventually the data leaving the system, we describe system functionality.

The state transition diagram shows the dynamics or the control of the system. It defines the order in which system functions have to be done, and consists of rectangles which represent the 'states' of the system. Imagine a system controlling a robot arm with three states — idle, positioning the robot arm to screw in a bolt and screwing in the bolt. These three states must happen in a particular order. For example, we would not want to go directly from positioning the robot arm to idle without screwing in the bolt. The state transition diagram allows us to represent this order in the model, and shows how to get from state to state.

The entity relationship diagram represents the information model of the system. It is a passive diagram, which means it has no flow of either data or control, but it does show all the things which play a role in our system and how all those various things connect together in the real world.

At the last stage of the design, we use the structure chart. Structure charts are widely used in program development, as they are a good way of showing the hierarchy of work to be implemented within a program.

1.2.3 The rules

At this stage we will briefly consider the rules and guidelines associated with these diagrams; more detail is given when considering the various diagrams they are associated with. The rules are generally concerned with ensuring the syntactic correctness of the diagram, while the guidelines are generally concerned with ensuring the clarity of the diagram to fulfil its aim as a communication tool. Rules and guidelines ensure the models are well structured, and will be applied either to individual diagrams, or to the model as a whole. /

Let us first consider individual diagrams. Rules are needed to define which symbols can be used where, and which symbols can be connected to which other symbols. As one of the main advantages of building models lies in communication with other people, guidelines are also needed to ensure the diagrams are as clear and meaningful as possible. It is not really difficult to draw a diagram that is syntactically correct, but it is more difficult to draw a diagram that is clear to look at.

We also have rules for the model as a whole. In any model there will be a hierarchy of diagrams which connect together. The organization of the hierarchy should be as clear as possible, and all the diagrams should fit together. If a number of diagrams are all supposed to describe the same system, it is very important that they do. As we will see later, there are areas where the diagrams overlap, and thus there are corresponding rules to ensure that overlapping diagrams describe the same system.

1.2.4 The development steps

Analysis and design are two words frequently used by people involved in systems development. Unfortunately, everybody seems to have their own definition of what they mean.

Analysis is the process of defining a problem that is to be solved. When you analyze a system you are not thinking about how you are going to implement the system (solve the problem), but what the system is supposed to do. Many of the problems in system development arise from developers not building the system the customer wants. Developers do not do this on purpose, but they sometimes dive into the design before they have worked out what the system is supposed to do. Analysis involves working out what the system should do before you start to design and implement it. The models created during analysis show what you think the system does in the real world — not how it does it.

Design involves using the model of system requirements built during analysis to create the best solution to the defined problem. Design models show firstly how to implement your solution, and secondly how that solution matches the problem, as you may not be able to build the system that the customer initially requested. For example, your customer may specify certain response times, which you find you cannot provide when you start looking at a particular design. It will be unlikely that you can give the customer everything that he initially asks for.

Analysis followed by design ensures that you understand what the customer wants before you start telling him what can be achieved. If you are only vaguely aware of your customer's requirements, you are in danger of imposing what you have managed to design on him, rather than what he wanted.

One of the ways in which we can make analysis easier is by using 'perfect technology'. During analysis, imagine implementing the system on a perfect processor, which has the following:

1. Infinite storage capacity (code and data).
2. Infinitely fast instruction speed.
3. Infinite reliability.
4. The ability to communicate with anything in the outside world.

In fact, any technology that would make your design and implementation easier.

As analysis only involves the capture of customer requirements, you should not worry about anything that may cause problems in design. Once into the design phase, we will start to consider the actual implementation technology to be used. However, perfect technology will stop you making analysis decisions based on the way in which you think you will implement the system. Until the design stages, you probably do not know enough about the implementation technology to make sensible decisions about how to implement the system. In fact, in the analysis you do not even know what you are supposed to be implementing yet, so you cannot sensibly make any implementation decisions. During the analysis stages we assume perfect technology, which will be systematically replaced with the real technology during the design phase. This will give the best possible system, in terms of both good design and meeting the customer's requirements.

Lastly, let us look at the phases of system development that we need to go through. Table 1.1 shows the 'traditional names' used in system development against the names that we use in structured development. The argument for using these special names is that they have specific defined meanings, rather than the nebulous imprecise meanings of the more traditional terms.

A system begins with an idea — perhaps someone in your marketing department, or the customer, says 'I think it would be good if you could build a system that does this'. That is what we call a statement of purpose. This is a very brief description, perhaps one or two sides of A4 paper, that gives an idea of why the system exists. On the basis of this you should be able to start working towards a requirement.

The requirement defines the system from the customer's point of view. At this stage, the system is like a black box, i.e. we feed certain stimuli and information into the system and it gives a certain response, but we do not know or care what happens between the input and the output. That is how the customer sees the system: he is only interested in what the system appears to do, not what goes on inside it. This is what we call the essential environmental model. Anything to do with analysis is called essential, because during analysis we capture the essence of the system. We specify the fundamental requirements of the system, but not how we fulfil those requirements. It is called an environmental model because we are looking at the system from its environment i.e. from the outside.

Once we know what the customer would like the system to do, we can

Table 1.1

Traditional name	Structured development name
An idea: 'We need to build something which does this'	Statement of purpose
Requirement: 'This is what the system looks like from the user's point of view'	Environmental model
Functional specification: 'This is what the system should actually do'	Behavioural model
Hardware-based design: Decide on your hardware configuration	Processor environment model
Software-based design: Decide on your software configuration	Software environment model
Program design: Implementation	Code organization model

build a functional specification. This specifies in more detail, but still from the customer's point of view, exactly what the system should do. In a traditional development, this would be provided as a textual specification. The essential behavioural model defines what the system should do in terms of data flow, state transition and entity relationship diagrams. This should be better structured than a functional specification, and because it is still an essential model, it will not say anything about how the system will be implemented. As a result of this, a behavioural model should be easier to produce and understand than a 'traditional' functional specification.

By now, we should know enough about the system to start design. Traditionally, you would first decide on your hardware configuration, i.e. your hardware-based design. You might be deciding on implementation hardware, or possibly, if the customer has specified a certain hardware configuration, you would be deciding which bits of the system will go on which processors. We call this processor environment modelling. We use the same models as during analysis to specify which requirements each processor in the system will fulfil, and the interfaces between the processors.

The next step is to look inside each processor and consider how we will make that part of the system work. You might call this software-based design, i.e. examining each processor's requirements, examining the software architecture available on each processor (operating system, input/output (I/O) routines, etc.) and deciding on the software configuration. At this stage we should also consider any requirements for concurrency by examining customer requirements, I/O rates and system timing. This is what we call software environment modelling. Again, we use the same models to describe how the programs will fit in with and use the provided software architecture, and what each program will do and how it will do it. This is the stage where we replace most of the perfect technology, and actually show how things will work.

Finally, we model the actual programs in the code organization model, which might be called program design. At this stage we define the procedures for which we write code, and how all these procedures fit together inside the program. This is modelled by the structure chart.

A different diagram is used at this stage because the data flow, state transition and entity relationship diagrams are all network models. These are good for modelling systems, but are not very good for modelling programs which tend to be fundamentally hierarchical. The structure chart is hierarchical, and so is well able to describe the program structure. As with all the other models, the structure chart is provided with supporting text, which gives the program specifications from which to write the code.

The structure chart helps you integrate the procedures within the program. The software environment model helps you integrate the programs within a processor. Finally, the processor environment model helps you integrate the processors within the system.

1.3 EXAMPLE OF STRUCTURED DEVELOPMENT

In this section we will look at the whole development process — from the initial 'idea' for the system to the code.

1.3.1 Mushroom-picking system: statement of purpose

One of the most expensive items in commercial mushroom growing is the labour force employed to pick the mushrooms, as effective mushroom picking requires experienced pickers. Once started, mushrooms grow very quickly and so it is important to pick them at just the right time, i.e. at maximum size, but not past their best.

We would like to build a system to automate the picking of mushrooms. Mushrooms will pass on a conveyor belt, whilst the system will pick off mushrooms of the appropriate size. An operator will be provided with a means of starting and stopping the system, and of varying the picked mushroom size. Statistics on the mushrooms picked should be held, in order to produce management reports.

1.3.2 Mushroom-picking system: essential environmental model

The essential environmental model shows the system from the outside

— it shows how the customer might view the system. The essential environmental model consists of the following:

1. The context diagram.
2. The event list.

The context diagram shows a single circle representing the system, a number of rectangles around the circle (terminators) which represent things to which the system has to interface, and the interfaces between the system and these things. The context diagram in Figure 1.3 shows that in the mushroom-picking system we have the following:

continuous data flow — difference
discrete data flow

1. A mushroom scanner — this passes information on the size and position of the mushrooms to the system, as they pass on the conveyor belt. The double arrowhead on 'mushroom scanner data' indicates that the information is sent continuously from the mushroom scanner. A single arrowhead, such as that on 'new mushroom size' from the operator, indicates that the information is sent at a discrete point in time.
2. A mushroom picker — the system is able to monitor the position of the mushroom picker and move it to any required position. The system can also command the mushroom picker to pick a mushroom at any time.
3. An operator — The operator has the ability to start and stop the system, and to change the size of mushrooms to be picked. The operator is also provided with a display giving information on the mushrooms which are currently being picked.

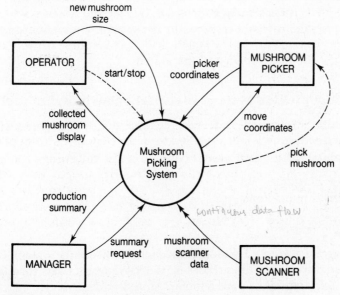

Figure 1.3   The context diagram.

Table 1.2

Event	Response
1. Operator switches on	Start scanning mushrooms Start producing operator information displays
2. Operator enters new mushroom size	Record new mushroom size
3. Scanner shows mushroom at correct size	Move picker to mushroom
4. Mushroom picker at mushroom	Stop picker and pick mushroom
5. Operator switches off	Stop scanning mushrooms Stop producing operator information displays
6. Manager requests production summary	Produce production summary

4. A manager — The manager has the ability to request a production summary, which will then be provided by the system.

The event list in Table 1.2 describes the functionality of the system in the same way in which the customer perceives it. The event column lists all the things which happen in the system's environment (i.e. outside the system), which the customer perceives will provoke a response by the system. The response column specifies what the customer thinks the system will do in response to each 'event' — therefore giving the functionality of the system.

1.3.3 Mushroom-picking system: essential behavioural model

The essential behavioural model takes a closer look at what goes on inside the system, but the behaviour is still modelled from the customer's point of view.

The essential behavioural model consists of the following:

1. Data flow diagrams.
2. State transition diagrams.
3. Entity relationship diagrams.
4. Supporting text.

The data flow diagram of Figure 1.4 models the functionality of the system. Circles represent functional areas, and lines represent the movement of data through the system. Parallel lines represent data which is stored in the system.

'Mushroom scanner data' is compared against the required 'mushroom

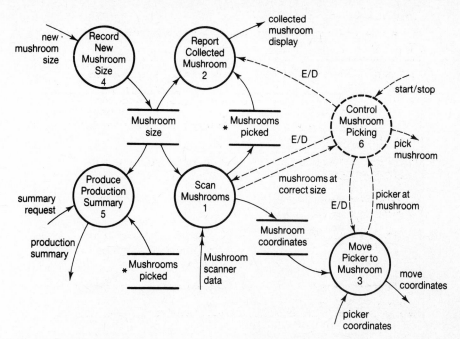

Figure 1.4   The data flow diagram.

size' inside 'scan mushrooms'. When a mushroom is found to be at the correct size, its coordinates are placed in 'mushroom coordinates', where they can be accessed by 'move picker to mushroom'. At the same time, the mushroom data is stored inside 'mushrooms picked', and mushroom information is displayed to the operator via 'report collected mushrooms'. 'Move picker to mushroom' will then drive the mushroom picker to the specified 'mushroom coordinates', via 'move coordinates', at which point the mushroom will be picked.

At any time the operator can specify a 'new mushroom size', which will be recorded by 'record new mushroom size' in 'mushroom size', where it can be subsequently used by 'scan mushrooms'. Also at any time the manager can request a production summary, which will be provided by 'produce production summary'.

The dotted circle is called a control process. This has the ability to monitor the state of the system, by examining event flows (dotted lines) which will either be set to true or false. It may also change the state of the system, by switching data transformations on and off, and sending requests to terminators, again via event flows. In this system, the control process will enable and disable (switch on and off) data transformations 'scan mushrooms', 'report collected mushrooms' and 'move picker to mushroom' in the right sequence, to ensure the correct operation of the system.

In the state transition diagram, shown by Figure 1.5, each rectangle

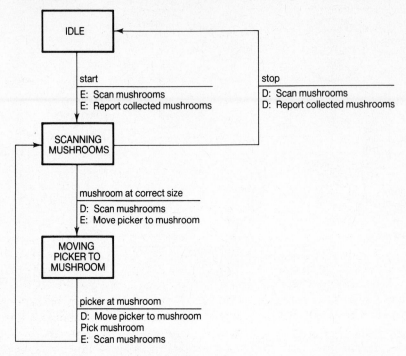

Figure 1.5   The state transition diagram.

represents a period of time over which the system does a defined thing (given by the name of the state). Lines between states, called transitions, show how the system moves between states, by defining what makes the system come out of the current state (the condition) and what it has to do to get into the next state (the actions).

The system initially waits in the 'idle' state until the operator presses 'start'. At this point the system will enable (switch on) 'scan mushrooms' and 'report collected mushrooms', which will take the system into the state of 'scanning mushrooms'.

From here two things could happen. If the operator presses 'stop', the system will disable (switch off) 'scan mushrooms' and 'report collected mushrooms', returning the system to 'idle'. Alternatively, 'scan mushrooms' could report 'mushroom at correct size'. In response to this, the system will disable 'scan mushrooms' and enable 'move picker to mushroom', which will take the system into the state of 'moving picker to mushroom'. Once 'move picker to mushroom' reports 'picker at mushroom', the system will switch it off, pick the mushroom and switch back on 'scan mushroom', to start looking for the next mushroom — this will take the system back to 'scanning mushrooms'.

The state transition diagram defines the control sequence carried out inside the control process. In fact, the control process is a shorthand notation

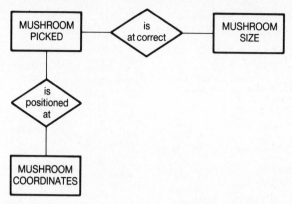

Figure 1.6   The entity relationship diagram.

of the state transition diagram, allowing aspects of control to be shown on the data flow diagram. The state transition diagram has the ability to switch the data transformations on and off, and therefore force them to happen in the right order.

In the entity relationship diagram, shown in Figure 1.6, each rectangle, or object, represents something we want to store information about in our system. Each diamond, or relationship, represents some association or mapping between connected objects, which we need to know about in our system.

A 'mushroom picked' is at a correct 'mushroom size'. The 'mushroom picked' is positioned at 'mushroom coordinates'.

1.3.4 The processor environment model

The processor environment model (PEM) shows how the essential model has been reorganized and, in some cases, elaborated, in order to fit the chosen hardware configuration. It consists of the following:

1. Top level data flow diagram, showing the system processors.
2. For each system processor:
    (a) data flow diagrams;
    (b) state transition diagrams;
    (c) entity relationship diagrams;
    (d) supporting text.

The top level PEM data flow diagram, given in Figure 1.7, shows the physical hardware configuration — each data transformation represents a physical processor in your system.

The mushroom-picking system will be implemented across two processors: one will provide the human–computer interface (HCI), the other will control the mushroom scanning and picking equipment. To arrive at this diagram, we started with the essential behavioural model data flow diagram. By examining each data transformation and deciding which processor it would be implemented

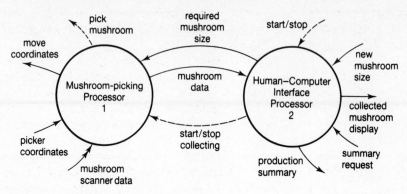

Figure 1.7   PEM — top level diagram.

on, we were able to split the data flow diagram into two halves. The interfaces between the two processors are the interfaces between the two halves of the original data flow diagram.

As the mushroom scanning and collection of information is done on the 'mushroom-picking processor', but the storage and display of this information is done on the 'HCI processor', 'mushroom data' needs to be passed from

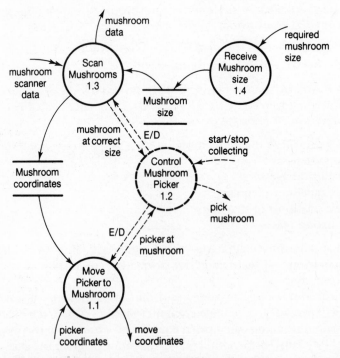

Figure 1.8   PEM — mushroom-picking processor.

processor 1 to processor 2. Also, as the operator interface is with processor 2, the operator-defined 'required mushroom size' and 'start/stop collecting' must be passed from processor 2 to processor 1.

The lower level data flow diagrams, given in Figures 1.8 and 1.9, show the data transformations, data stores and control processes from the essential model which will be implemented in this processor, together with any extra behaviour required for the split of orginal behaviour between the two processors to work. There would also be corresponding state transition diagrams, entity relationship diagrams and lower level data flow diagrams.

Notice how in Figure 1.8 the control process 'control mushroom picker' is not exactly the same as the essential control process, 'control mushroom picking' — this is because some of the work which the original control process was controlling is now in the other processor. In view of this, the essential control process has been split into two — the other half can be found in the lower level diagram for processor 2. Also notice the new data transformation 'receive mushroom size' — this has been added to model the behaviour needed to receive the 'required mushroom size' when it is sent across from the other processor.

In Figure 1.9 we find the other half of the essential control process 'control mushroom picking, called 'control human—computer interface'. As in

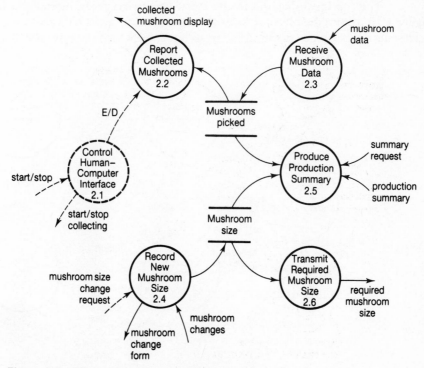

Figure 1.9   PEM — human—computer interface processor.

processor 1, we have added data transformations 'receive mushroom data' and 'transmit required mushroom size', to model communications behaviour.

These lower level diagrams show all the work to be done on the processors, as well as defining the processor interfaces, but they do not yet state how we will implement that work.

1.3.5 The software environment model

The software environment model (SEM) shows how the processor environment model for each processor has been reorganized and, in some cases, elaborated, to fit in with the chosen software architecture. The software environment model consists of the following, for each processor:

1. Top level data flow diagram, showing the processor programs (execution units) and software architecture.
2. For each execution unit:
   (a) data flow diagrams;
   (b) state transition diagrams;
   (c) entity relationship diagrams;
   (d) supporting text.

The top level diagram in the software environment model, shown by Figure 1.10, shows the physical software configuration. Each data transformation represents either a piece of the software architecture which the system will invoke

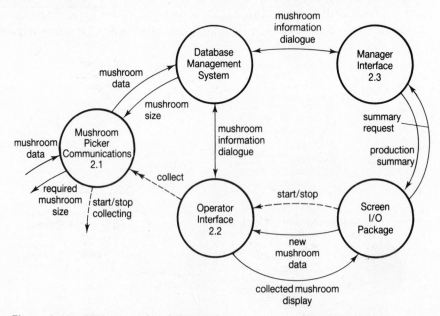

Figure 1.10 SEM — top level diagram.

for a particular area of work, or an execution unit which will have to be written to implement the application.

The human—computer interface processor contains the following:

1. Two pieces of software architecture, which are provided:
   (a) a database management system, which holds all the data on mushroom size and mushrooms picked;
   (b) a screen I/O package that provides many routines to enable communication with the operator.
2. Three execution units, which we will have to write:
   (a) 'mushroom picker communications' provides communication with the mushroom picking processor;
   (b) 'operator interface' contains all the functionality concerned with providing the operator interface;
   (c) 'manager interface' contains all the functionality concerned with providing the manager interface.

To arrive at this diagram, we decided how we would use the software architecture, and on the basis of this and concurrency requirements, split the processor environment model between execution units (more detail on how the jump from Figure 1.9 to 1.10 was made is given in following paragraphs). We have also added behaviour to show how the software architecture will be used by the execution units, and to model how the requirements modelled in previous diagrams will actually be implemented.

Lower level diagrams need not be provided for parts of the software architecture, as these represent packages being used, not programs that have to be developed. These data flow diagrams, one of which is shown by Figure 1.11,

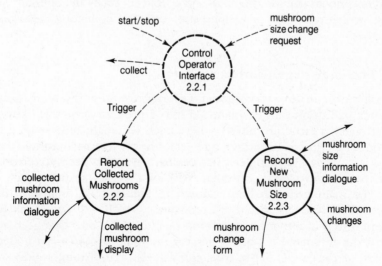

Figure 1.11   SEM — operator interface program.

show the data transformations, data stores and control processes from the processor environment model to be implemented by this execution unit, together with any extra behaviour required to make the application work. There may also be corresponding state transition diagrams, entity relationship diagrams and lower level data flow diagrams.

In the operator interface program, we have decided to implement PEM data transformations 'report collected mushrooms', 'record new mushroom size', and the PEM control process 'control human—computer interface'.

'Control human—computer interface' has been modified to become 'control operator interface', which now controls both 'report collected mushrooms' and 'record new mushroom size' — this is to impose a sequence of operation between them. In previous models, as each of these data transformations was activated by different asynchronous stimuli, they could have run concurrently. 'Trigger' is another type of event flow which can be used by a control process to switch on a data transformation — the difference between enable and trigger will be discussed in the Chapter 3.

An execution unit is seen by the operating system as a single schedulable item, within which there is a single thread of control. As there can be no concurrent behaviour within a single execution unit, only between execution units, concurrency within an execution unit has to be replaced by sequence.

Notice the way in which 'report collected mushrooms' and 'record new mushroom size' do not now directly access the data stores that they use, but have a dialogue with the database, where the data will be stored.

The manager interface program contains the PEM data transformation 'produce production summary'. The mushroom picker communications program contains the PEM data transformations 'receive mushroom data' and 'transmit required mushroom size'. It also reads a flag 'collect', set by the operator interface program, which will allow it to send start and stop collecting messages at the correct time.

1.3.6 The code organization model

The code organization model (COM) shows how the work to be done inside each execution unit is organized into a program structure. The code is modelled using a structure chart, where each rectangle represents a module (procedure, function, subroutine), and each line represents a module call. Each program is modelled in a single structure chart, which is generated from all the diagrams which describe the internal work of a single execution unit.

The main program loop, shown in Figure 1.12, is inside 'operator interface'. This will call 'get user command', which will pass back the user command (this will either be start, stop or mushroom size change request).

If the command is start, 'operator interface' will call 'set collect flag', which will set the collect flag to true, and will also start calling 'report collected mushrooms' at regular intervals. 'Report collected mushrooms' will call 'retrieve

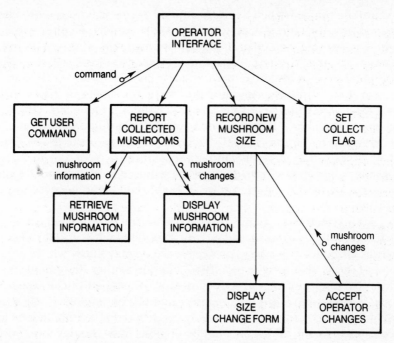

Figure 1.12   COM — operator interface program.

mushroom information' followed by 'display mushroom information', which will collect the relevant information from the database, and display it at the operator terminal.

If the command is stop, 'operator interface' will call 'set collect flag', to reset the collect flag to false.

If the command is 'mushroom size change request', 'operator interface' will call 'record new mushroom size'. This will call 'display size change form' followed by 'accept operator changes', which will put a form on the operator terminal, allowing the operator to fill in the required mushroom size change.

1.4 MAINTENANCE

Another area where the use of structured development can help is in maintenance. In a study made by Barry Boehm in 1975, it was found that a US Air Force System cost $30 per instruction to develop and $4000 per instruction to maintain over its lifetime (Boehm, 1981). Often included under the umbrella of maintenance is the task of modifying the system to make it do what it was originally meant to do. Maintenance will be difficult when a system is badly structured or badly documented, which are both problems that can be solved by structured development techniques.

It a system is badly documented or not documented at all (this happens with alarming frequency), it is very difficult for a maintenance engineer to understand how the code works, why the code does what it appears to do when the system is running, and what the system was actually meant to do in the first place. In many cases, this will lead to an engineer puzzling for days over a piece of code which is to be modified, before finally giving in and rewriting the whole thing from scratch in a way in which he or she understands. This is obviously very wasteful of development time and frustrating for engineers. Often original code is replaced before it is even used. A structured development should be 'self-documenting'. The various models built at each stage of the development not only help you to analyze, design and implement the system, but also document the decisions that have been made. If all the required models (both diagrams and supporting text) are built at each stage, there should be no need for any further documentation.

Badly structured systems cause two problems for the engineer attempting maintenance. A badly structured system rarely does what it looks like it ought to do from the code. This causes problems, as you may know which 'real world' function of the system is to be modififed, but you cannot find the piece of code that does it. Even if the system is documented, it will be difficult to understand the code; if the system is not documented it will be impossible. Badly structured systems are also difficult to modify safely, as they tend to contain dependencies between areas of code which may not be obvious from looking at a listing. This means that you could change a piece of code in one functional area that affects a number of other functional areas, without initially realizing you are doing it. Having affected those other areas, you will have to modify the code there, which in turn will affect yet other functional areas. Before long, a 'simple' modification of the code will have rippled through the whole system. Well-structured code does not suffer from this problem, and consequently should be much easier to maintain.

PART ONE

Development tools

Structured analysis and design is like anything else — before you can start, you should learn how to use the tools. If you were learning woodwork, rather than structured analysis and design, you would not expect the very first chapter to detail how to build a chest of drawers. Initially, you would learn what a hammer was and how to use it, and why it is more appropriate in some cases than a screwdriver.

In this part we will look at most of the tools required for structured analysis and design in isolation, covering the detailed syntax, rules and guidelines for use. Thus, we will cover

- the data flow diagram,
- the state transition diagram,
- the entity relationship diagram,

and all the supporting specifications and rules which bring the diagrams together into a coherent model.

The later parts will show how to use the tools as part of analysis or design. However, if you cannot use the DFD, you might understand the theory of analysis and design, but not be able to practise it effectively. As the analysis and design are expressed in terms of these diagrams, a firm understanding of the tools will make understanding the techniques of analysis and design that much easier.

At the end of this part, you should be able to understand all the diagrams, and assess whether a diagram used to model a system is good or bad, i.e. whether the tools are being used correctly. Do not worry if you cannot see the use of the tools in the context of analysis or design — that will be covered in Parts II and III.

CHAPTER TWO

Data flow diagrams

2.1 INTRODUCTION

The data flow diagram (DFD) is used to show the basic functionality of the system. The fundamental work done by any system is the transformation of inputs into outputs — everything an automated system does can be thought of in terms of turning inputs into outputs. In a simple data processing system this is fairly obvious, but even where a system physically moves pieces of equipment, it does this by measuring the position of the equipment as input data, applying an algorithm to it, then moving the equipment by sending the output data from the algorithm to it. The basic functionality of a system can be expressed purely in terms of transformations on the system data — which can be clearly represented using a data flow diagram.

2.2 DATA FLOW DIAGRAM COMPONENTS

2.2.1 Basic notation

Firstly, we will examine the basic symbols and terminology used within the DFD, which can be seen in Figure 2.1:

1. *Terminator*   such as 'scales'. This is used to show a person, piece of equipment or other system which the defined system interfaces to.
2. *Data flow*   such as 'teabag weight'.
3. *Event flow*   such as 'wrong weight'. Flows are used to pass information through the system.
4. *Data transformation*   such as 'weigh teabag'. This is used to transform input data into output data (i.e. to show the functions of the system).
5. *Data store*   such as 'teabag count'. This is used to store information.
6. *Control process*   such as 'control teabag boxing' This is used to control data transformations.

In all cases the name of the symbol describes its purpose within the DFD. These examples should give you an idea of what DFD components should look like,

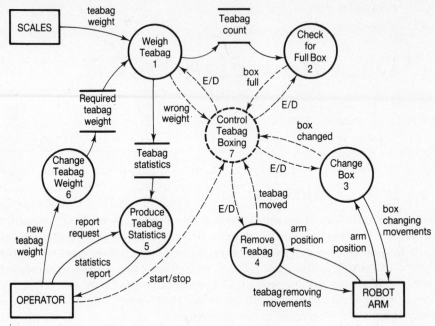

Figure 2.1   Teabag boxing system data flow diagram.

what they are used for and how to interpret them. Now let us look at the notation in more detail. We have been asked to build a system with the following statement of purpose:

1. Produce teabags at a certain weight in boxes of 40.
2. Produce statistics on the production of teabags.
3. Allow an operator to change the teabag weight.

   Teabags pass along a conveyor belt and over some scales. If they are within certain weight limits, they move along the conveyor belt and into a box. When the box is full, it is removed by a robot arm and replaced with an empty box. Any substandard teabags are removed from the conveyor belt by the robot arm before they reach the box. The system will be controlled by an operator who has the ability to start and stop the system, reset the teabag weight and request reports on weights of teabags passed through the system. The conveyor belt will not be under the control of the teabag making system.

   The DFD shown in Figure 2.1 models the system specification given for the teabag boxing system. In this diagram the weight of the teabag is sent from the scales into 'weigh teabag' which compares this weight against the 'required teabag weight'. 'Weigh teabag' keeps a count of the number of teabags it has weighed at the correct weight in 'teabag count'. It also records the weight of the teabag in 'teabag statistics', and if the teabag is too heavy or too light, it tells the control process via the 'wrong weight' event.

'Change teabag weight' will allow the operator to reset the required weight of the teabag.

'Check for full box' will monitor the teabag count until it reaches 40, when it will reset the count to zero and inform the control process that the box is full, via the 'box full' event.

'Change box' and 'remove teabag' both control the robot arm either to remove the full box and replace it with any empty one, or to remove the teabag from the conveyor belt before it has a chance to drop into the teabag box.

'Produce teabag statistics' gives reports on the weights of teabags passing through the system on request from the operator.

The control process 'control teabag boxing' ensures everything happens in the right order — it monitors 'wrong weight' and 'box full' and activates 'change box' or 'remove teabag' as appropriate. Data transformations will be activated and deactivated using the enable/disable event flow (sometimes abbreviated to E/D). 'Control teabag boxing' will also monitor the operator 'start/stop' command, to start or stop the system on request. The internal workings of a control process are described by a state transition diagram (STD) — the STD 'inside' 'control tea boxing' will be examined in Chapter 3.

2.2.2 Flows

A flow carries streams or packets of known information around the system. A flow has no inherent behaviour — its characteristics are defined firstly by the nature of what it is carrying, and secondly by whatever is producing the flow. Imagine a flow as a piece of rubber tubing which connects two things together — the thing at one end blows things down the tube and they arrive at the other end, but the tube itself does not do anything.

There are six different types of flow, differentiated by the examination of two characteristics. Figure 2.2 shows the notation and gives an example of each type of flow:

1. *Continuous data* — an analogue thermometer gives a continuous flow of temperature.
2. *Discrete data* — a computer user will login at the beginning of every session.
3. *Continuous event* — continuous event flows are analogous to flags, i.e. 'check temperature' will produce a flag which continually shows whether the temperature is too hot or not.
4. *Discrete event* — an alarm clock will give a discrete event when it is time to get up.
5. *Continuous material/energy* — an electric element in a fire continually generates heat, while it is switched on.
6. *Discrete material/energy* — every now and again, the postman delivers a letter.

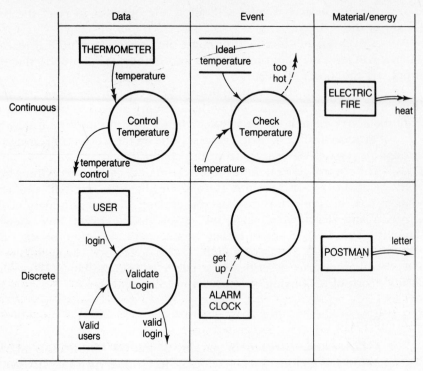

Figure 2.2   Six different types of flow.

The first characteristic, determined by what is sending the flow, is that of time duration — a flow can be continuous or discrete. Continuous or discrete is not meant in the mathematical sense, but describes how often something is sent along the flow. A continuous data flow always has data associated with it. A clock or a watch is an example of a continuous data flow, as every time you look at it, you see the time. Things are sent down a discrete flow one at a time — possibly with big indeterminate length gaps between them. Imagine waiting for a bus: the buses come one at a time, and quite often you do not know how long the gaps between them are going to be — buses flow discretely. Diagrammatically, a discrete flow is indicated by a single arrowhead showing the direction of flow, while a continuous flow is indicated by a double arrowhead showing the direction of flow.

The second characteristic of a flow is determined by what moves along the flow. Three things can be carried along flows: data, events or material/energy.

Material/energy flows carry physical things such as bricks, water or heat, whereas data flows carry information — possibly measurements of physical things such as number of bricks, water level in a tank or temperature. Diagrammatically, data flows are shown as single solid lines and material/energy flows are shown as double solid lines.

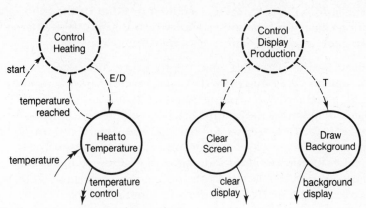

Figure 2.3   Examples of prompts.

An event flow gives information about things that are happening, or things that you would like to happen. The name of the event flow describes the event and information flowing along the event flow describes its state. Events may only take two states, e.g. on/off, true/false, start/stop. Anything which is conceptually only one bit of information can be sent down an event flow. Diagrammatically, event flows are indicated as dashed lines.

There is also a special kind of event flow, called a prompt, which has the sole purpose of switching on and off data transformations, as shown by Figure 2.3. Prompts are named either enable/disable or trigger (normally abbreviated to E/D or T) and will be discussed further in Chapter 3.

To make the data flow diagram less complicated, flows can be 'levelled', i.e. defined at different levels of detail. For example, 'address' could be composed of 'street number', 'street name' and 'town'. It would then be valid to use the flow 'address' in higher level diagrams, where not so much detail is needed, and the flows 'street number', 'street name' and 'town' in lower level diagrams.

A word of warning: owing to the lack of support from automated CASE tools, the continuous notation (i.e. the double headed arrow) and the material/energy notation (i.e. the double flow lines) are rarely seen. Often all flows are shown with single arrowheads (whether they are continuous or discrete) and material/energy flows are shown as data flows — any differentiation can be documented in the model's supporting text.

2.2.3 Transformations

2.2.3.1 *Data transformations*

Data transformations turn inputs into outputs, and thus describe the functions of the system. Consider the data transformation 'move robot arm' from Figure 2.1, which examines the current position of the robot arm, given by the flow 'current position'. Based on the required position of the robot arm, this transformation calculates 'arm movement' which is sent out to the robot arm. The following are associated with a data transformation:

1. A name — this describes what the transformation does.
2. A number — this describes the data transformation's position in the diagram hierarchy, as demonstrated by Figure 2.4. The DFD shown in 'Figure 0' describes the internal behaviour of the context transformation. Similarly, the DFDs shown in 'Figure 1' and 'Figure 3' show the internal behaviour of higher level transformations 1 and 3 respectively. There is no low level diagram to describe the internal behaviour of data transformation 2. This is because the data transformation is conceptually simple and can be fully described in supporting text.

    Conventionally the context bubble is known as transformation 0. The diagram which sits below data transformation N is known as Figure N, and the transformations within that diagram are known as $N.1$, $N.2$, etc. So the transformation 3.1 is a data transformation within Figure 3 — where Figure 3 shows the internals of data transformation 3. The internals of transformation 3.1 would be shown in Figure 3.1. There is no transformation 1.0, 2.0, etc. $N.0$ is never used as it may cause confusion — is 3.0 actually transformation 3 or the first transformation on Figure 3?

    The order in which the transformations are numbered has no significance — you cannot assume that transformation 3.1 will be done before transformation 3.2. The numbers only exist to navigate through the various levels of the model.

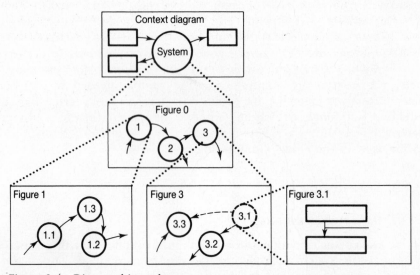

Figure 2.4   Diagram hierarchy.

3. Input(s) and output(s) — these describe what the data transformation transforms. Data transformations must have at least one input and at least one output — you cannot transform nothing into something or something into nothing — but there are no other restrictions on the number of inputs/outputs that a transformation has. A transformation could have four inputs and two outputs, or one input and six outputs. For example, the data transformation 'calculate volume and density' could receive 'length', 'breadth', 'height' and 'weight' and calculate 'volume' and 'density'.

A data transformation output can be sent to many different places. The data transformation 'calculate volume' could send the flow 'volume' to further data transformations 'calculate average volume' and 'display volume'.

There are some restrictions on the type of output a data transformation can generate. Data transformations can generate data flows (either direct or to a store), and event flows giving information, but not prompts (enable/disable and trigger). In any system, it is desirable to separate data from control, as this builds good structure into the system from an early stage. Therefore, the control process should do all the control and decision making, whilst the data transformations only do the work of the system. A data transformation which generates a prompt implies that it is trying to control the system — which is undesirable.

2.2.3.2 *Control processes*

Control processes show control on the data flow diagram, and transform input events into output events. 'Control heating', shown in Figure 2.5, monitors the 'start' event and the 'temperature too high' event. This allows it to decide when to produce the 'flash alarm' event and enable/disable the data transformation which performs the heating.

The following will be associated with a control process:

1. A name — which defines the functional area the control process controls.
2. A number — as with the data transformation, this is used to show the position in the diagram hierarchy. What is happening inside a control

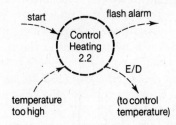

Figure 2.5   Control process.

process will normally be described by a state transition diagram (STD), as shown by Figure 2.4.

3. A state transition diagram — the control process is a shorthand way of expressing the STD, allowing aspects of control to be seen on the DFD. The link between the control process and the STD will be examined more fully in Chapter 3.

There are occasions where you may not wish to use the STD notation to express the behaviour of the control process. You may decide to use another type of notation throughout the model to describe the control behaviour, or the control behaviour may be too complex or too simple for the STD to be appropriate. Alternatives to the STDs are discussed in later chapters.

4. Input and output event flow(s) — as with the data transformation the control process must have at least one input flow and at least one output flow, but there is no maximum limit. However, there are more restrictions on the type of flow which may be processed.

Control processes may input and output event flows, but they cannot accept or generate any type of data flow. Again, this is to achieve the separation of control and data — control processes model pure control logic and can monitor/affect the state of the system using only event flows. For example, in the teabag boxing DFD, 'control teabag boxing' cannot directly examine the 'teabag count' store, to see whether the box is full. In this case, we introduce the data transformation 'check for full box', which converts the data 'teabag count' into the event 'box full'. 'Check for full box' is known as an 'event recognizer' — a data transformation whose sole purpose is to monitor data associated with an event, and produce the corresponding event flow when the data reaches the appropriate value.

2.2.4 Stores

Like a flow, a data store does not have any inherent behaviour. As a flow is like a piece of tubing, a store is like a bucket. For example, in the teabag boxing DFD, 'weigh teabag' blows 'teabag statistics' down a piece of tubing into the bucket/data store, where it stays until it is sucked up through the outgoing piece of tubing by 'produce statistics report'. You cannot assume that data in a store will be written or accessed in any particular way. The way in which data is kept or used within the store will be determined by transformations writing into or reading out of the store. These characteristics can be specified in the model's supporting text. You cannot even assume that a read on the store will be destructive (i.e. the read will 'use up' the item being read, rather than just look at it, so that it will not be available for subsequent reads) or non-destructive. However, two aspects of store access are considered for the diagram.

Firstly, is a whole data item accessed from the store? If so, there is no

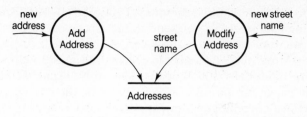

* Address = Number + Street name + Town *

Figure 2.6   Store access.

need to name the flow attached to the store — you only need to name the flow if you are accessing just part of the data item. In the left-hand side of Figure 2.6, a whole address is added to the store, and so the flow is not named. In the right-hand side, only a new street name is added to the store and so the flow is named.

Secondly, in the essential model net flow of data into or out of the data store is normally shown. Net flow describes the movement of data in conceptual rather than implementation terms. For example, to modify data in an implementation, you think of taking the data out of the store, changing it, and then putting it back in again. However, conceptually the data transformation could 'open up', look at the data in the store to see what needed changing, and write the new information over the old information, without pulling the old information into the data transformation.

In Figure 2.7(a) therefore, there is a net flow of information into the store. On the other hand in Figure 2.7(b), in order to send out the information we must pull it into the transformation in the first place. In this case the 'modify' part of the transformation makes a net flow into the store, whilst the 'report' part makes a net flow out.

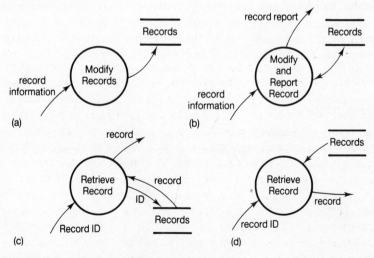

Figure 2.7   Net flow of data.

A common mistake is shown by example in Figure 2.7(c). The record ID is used to index into the data store, so you send the ID to the data store which returns the record to the transformation. However, as the store is just a piece of memory, it cannot do anything: the data transformation must look into the store and use the ID to index into the record, as shown by Figure 2.7(d).

Following this theme further, data stores cannot be directly connected to each other. Information in memory cannot spontaneously transport itself to other places in memory, no matter how perfect your technology is — data must be moved between stores via transformations.

The perfect technology of the essential model means there is no need to queue data or store data redundantly — data is only stored if it needs to be collected for later use. Considered from the transformation side, rather than from the store side, data stores are used to introduce time delays between transformations.

A discrete data flow arriving at a data transformation will spark that data transformation into action. For example, in the teabag boxing DFD, it is the arrival of the flow 'report request' which stimulates 'produce teabag statistics' to produce the 'statistics report'. Therefore, two data transformations connected by a direct data transformation will be synchronized. The data produced by one data transformation will stimulate the connected data transformation. If you do not want two data transformations to work directly one after the other, they should be connected via a store. In the teabag boxing DFD, the store 'teabag statistics' stops the system from producing a statistics report each time 'weigh teabag' produces a 'teabag statistic'.

The difference between data flows and stores is a result of the flow being an active mechanism, while the store is passive.

As well as storing data in the system we can also store events: in an event store, as shown by Figure 2.8. There are two major differences between an event store and a data store. Firstly, data stores can only store data and event stores can only store events. Secondly, whilst the data store has no inherent behaviour, an event store has a lot of associated behaviour, which will be fully discussed in Chapter 3.

2.2.5 Terminators

The terminator marks the edge of your model. It represents anything outside the system to which the system interfaces — it could be a piece of

Figure 2.8   Event store.

equipment, another system or a person. The notation for a terminator is a box containing the name of whatever or whoever is being interfaced to, such as 'scales' or 'operator' on the teabag DFD.

The name should be meaningful and describe the terminator's role with respect to the system — sometimes this means calling the terminator something other than its technical name. For instance, a terminator would be called 'printer' rather than 'Mannesman Tally' (i.e. the brand name), as 'printer' makes more sense to more people than 'Mannesman Tally'.

The same goes for interface technology: we may be communicating via an RS232, but you would never see the terminator 'RS232', because the system is interfacing via the communications link, not to it.

Generally, you will only find terminators on the context diagram, although terminators may appear on lower level DFDs. By convention, terminators are only shown on the context diagram, since it is assumed that flows which enter or leave the system can always be traced back to the context diagram, and therefore to the terminator that produced or received them.

2.3 BUILDING A DATA FLOW DIAGRAM

There are two ways of building a data flow diagram. The method used will depend upon whether you know more about the inputs or outputs of the system, or the proposed functions of the system.

2.3.1 Connectivity

Connectivity should be used when you know more about the inputs and outputs. Let us look at an example, using the following specification for a cashpoint machine:

> Customers key in their identity number to the cashpoint machine. The cashpoint machine will send the customer's account number to the bank and wait for the customer's credit limit to be returned. The amount of cash requested will be delivered by a cash dispenser and a receipt delivered.

Firstly, we identify the inputs and outputs of the system from the specification. Identifying terminators may also help, as it may give more information about the content and form of the inputs and outputs. Examining a textual specification may not give the exact inputs, outputs and terminators (especially if the specification is badly written), but it will give big hints:

Customers (*terminator*) key in their identity number (*input*) to the cashpoint machine. The cashpoint machine will send the customer's account number (*output*) to the bank (*terminator*) and wait for the customer's credit limit (*input*). The amount of money (*input*) requested by the customer (*terminator*) will be delivered (*output*) by a cash dispenser (*terminator*) and a receipt (*output*) will then be printed (*terminator*).

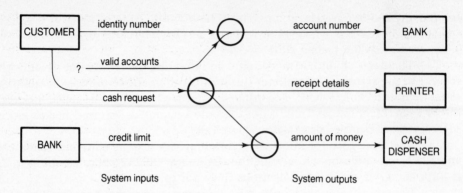

Figure 2.9 Cashpoint connectivity.

Focusing on the system, 'will be delivered' suggests some kind of output, and 'will be printed' suggests some kind of printing device. Therefore, we could translate 'will be delivered' into 'an amount of money will be delivered' and 'will be printed' into 'will be printed at a printer'.

You might ask 'Why isn't cashpoint machine a terminator?': the cashpoint machine is what we are describing, so it is what the data transformations are happening on, not something to which they interface.

Having identified potential terminators, inputs and outputs, we can construct the edges of the DFD. Next, we can mentally link up the inputs to the outputs — known as connectivity. Take any output and decide which input(s) it was generated from — alternatively, take any input and decide which output(s) it will generate, as shown by Figure 2.9.

Often trying to link the inputs and outputs in this way will lead to the discovery of other required information which has not been given in the original specification. This is one of the advantages of building a DFD to describe a system — quite often a textual specification will appear to make perfect sense until you start dissecting it to find the important pieces of information — to find that some

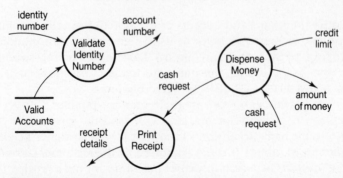

Figure 2.10 Cashpoint transformations.

are missing. In this case we know that we are given a customer identity number and presumably have to produce an account number from that — but we are not told how. Without going back to the original specifier we can only assume that we have some other information — let us call it valid accounts — that allows us to link customer account numbers to identification numbers. Every place where an input becomes an output will generate a data transformation, giving the DFD in Figure 2.10.

This DFD may not be perfect or complete (for instance, we have not specified what would happen if the customer input an invalid identification number), but we now have a firm foundation on which to start building.

2.3.2 The jigsaw approach

The jigsaw approach will be used where more is known about the functionality of the system. Consider another example, this time for an automated mail order system:

Build an automated mail order system that will provide the following functionality:

1. Accept customer order.
2. Send order dispatch note to warehouse.
3. Send invoice to customer.
4. Accept customer payment.
5. Send unsettled invoice reminders.

In this specification the functions are well defined and we can easily produce five data transformations, one for each function. Again, by focusing on the problem and examining the textual specification, we add inputs and outputs to the transformations. We can then connect the outputs of certain data transformations to the inputs of other data transformations to generate the DFD shown in Figure 2.11.

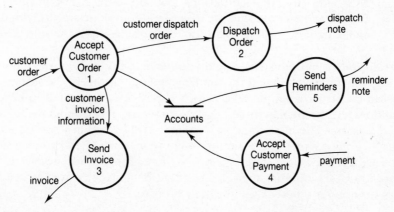

Figure 2.11　Mail order DFD.

Connecting the outputs of transformations to the inputs of others may require some thought. In this example, the flow produced by the 'accept customer order' transformation must be split into 'customer dispatch order', which goes into the 'dispatch order' transformation, and 'customer invoice information', which goes into the 'send invoice' transformation. Also, 'customer invoice information' must be stored to give the required 'account information' which is used in 'accept customer payment' and 'send reminders'.

Customers are rarely able to define the functionality of the system so clearly. This approach tends to be used more in reverse engineering, i.e. when documenting a system that has already been built, either for reimplementation or modification purposes, using data flow diagrams. In this case the functions, and the inputs and outputs to those functions, are well defined.

2.3.3 General guidelines

From a wider point of view there are other guidelines to follow which should make building DFDs as painless as possible. Firstly, do not try to incorporate everything that happens in the system all at once. Build the diagrams in steps:

1. Start off with the simple functionality of the system without worrying about things that might go wrong. Even things that are not exactly errors, but do not happen very often and are not really part of the fundamental functionality of the system (i.e. occasional maintenance procedures) should be suppressed initially.
2. Once you have a diagram describing the basic functionality, add any required functionality that is not on the diagram (such as the occasional maintenance procedures just mentioned).
3. Next, add any error conditions that should be handled.
4. Finally, when you think the diagram is complete, start tidying it up and checking it according to all the ideas discussed in the following pages.

If the diagram is built in steps, you do not have to think about the whole system at once. By concentrating on the fundamental operations of the system initially, you can construct a simple DFD which can then be extended to reflect error conditions, etc. In the first three steps, do not worry much about the 'correctness' of the diagram. The most important thing initially is to get your ideas down on paper — do not worry if the names do not seem quite right or you are not sure if you are using the right shape symbol — these problems can be sorted out later. Concentrate on modelling the functionality first. Once that is captured then you can worry about whether the diagram is correct.

2.4 CHECKING A DATA FLOW DIAGRAM

After a bit of practice, building an initial DFD should be fairly simple — building one that is correct is more difficult. The correctness of a DFD can be viewed from two angles: diagrams that are syntactically correct and diagrams that make sense.

2.4.1 Checking for syntactic correctness

There are two areas of syntax to check within the DFD:

1. Symbols should be connected and used in the correct way, e.g. stores should not be connected to one another and data transformations should not generate prompts.

   A full summary of what can or cannot be connected to what else, with what the connection implies is given in Appendix B.

2. Data transformations must comply with the rule of 'conservation of data'. This states that data transformations may not generate data from thin air, i.e. in order to produce an output there must be enough input information coming into the transformation to allow the output to be produced. Imagine a data transformation 'calculate volume', with inputs 'length' and 'width', and output 'volume'. As volume = length * width * height, this data transformation would be incapable of operating. The data transformation also needs 'height' as input.

This example is fairly straightforward: However, imagine a data transformation 'calculate wages' with inputs 'tax code', 'employee number' and 'salary scales', and output 'wages'. Can we calculate someone's wages based on tax code, employee number and salary scales? Perhaps, if we assume a set monthly salary and some correspondence between employee number and salary scales. If we do not make these assumptions, what information is actually missing? Is it hours worked or employee grade, or something we have not even thought of? The only way to find out would be to read the textual specification for the transformation or talk to the person who created the transformation.

Never make assumptions and 'correct' diagrams which have been drawn by other people unless you are absolutely sure you know what you are doing. Otherwise your misunderstanding may create a serious error later in the development.

Finally, the more conceptually complicated the function within a data transformation is, the more difficult it will be to check conservation of data. By creating simple functional units, you also make the diagram easier to check.

Syntactic checking of the DFD should be fairly easy as you follow a set of rules — a good automated toolkit will be able to do much of this checking. Coherence checking, i.e. checking how easy your model is to understand, is much more difficult, as there are no rules, only guidelines. Just because your diagram is verified by an automated toolkit does not mean it actually makes sense — the same as a program compiling does not mean it actually works. If your diagram does not make sense it will probably mislead more people than it will help. It is very important to make sure that diagrams say the same thing to everybody who reads them, otherwise they have failed as an aid to communication. The only way to check diagrams for coherence is by review. An automated toolkit does not have the intelligence to make a reasonable evaluation of whether your diagram makes sense with respect to your application. Once you have finished your diagram, get someone else to have a look at it — and if it does not say the same to them as it says to you, it is probably wrong.

2.4.2 Checking for coherence

The way in which your diagram is partitioned and named will make a lot of difference to how easy your diagram is to read. Partitioning refers to the way in which low level functions are grouped together into high level functions, and so defines the way in which the work of the system has been split up amongst the data transformations. If the system is built up from conceptually single function units, as these units themselves are easy to understand, the system should be easy to understand. On the other hand, if the system is built up of data transformations with conceptually complicated functions, which are difficult to understand, the system will be difficult to understand.

Tom De Marco said 'Partition to minimize interfaces', i.e. split the system up in such a way that the data transformations have minimal interfaces between them. In general, work involved in a single functional area will be concerned with working on the same data. If a functional area is split between a number of data transformations, the data involved will have to move between them, so increasing the interfaces within the system. Turning this around, if we have minimal interfaces, we will tend to have good functional units, which should make the system easier to understand. Also, if a data transformation is heavily connected to another data transformation, one data transformation is difficult to understand without the other. As a result of this, you cannot take just one data transformation at a time and understand it — you also have to think about everything it is connected to.

These ideas are really just statements of coupling (interface complexity) and cohesion (relationship of elements within a unit) — probably the two most basic concepts within structured development.

In the essential model you should also partition the diagram in a 'natural way', rather than reflecting the way in which you might implement the system. View the system through the customer's eyes and create data transformations which reflect what the customer thinks the system does, rather than how it does it. Imagine a system that has to make tea and coffee. This could either be modelled by two transformations:

1. 'make tea' which turns hot water and tea-leaves into tea
2. 'make coffee' which turns hot water and coffee powder into coffee

or three data transformations:

1. 'count tea-leaves' which measures the appropriate number of tea-leaves for a cup of tea
2. 'measure coffee powder' which measures the appropriate weight of coffee powder for a cup of coffee
3. 'add hot water' which turns hot water and measured coffee powder or measured tea-leaves into coffee or tea

Pulling the function 'add hot water' out of 'make tea' and 'make coffee' has two consequences:

1. It makes the DFD more complicated, and so more difficult to understand.
2. If your 'non-technical' customer does not realize that counting tea-leaves and adding hot water is how you make a cup of tea, he will never understand the diagram — all the customer is really interested in is 'will this system make tea and coffee?'

Do not worry that areas of functionality are repeated — this does not mean that the code will be written twice. The essential model states the overall functions of the system. Data transformations at this stage do not represent physical programs or areas of code, just things that the system will ultimately have to do. Common functionality can be pulled out in the design phase to ensure that lower level functions are only implemented in one place.

The naming of diagram components also makes a big difference to the clarity of DFDs (Table 2.1). To a certain extent the names on DFDs are subjective and the name given to a component may depend on who has to read and understand the diagram. However, it is better to use 'natural, real-world' terms for DFD components. A data transformation name that exactly reflects what is happening in the real world (such as 'make tea') is very difficult to misinterpret.

Some common mistakes made in DFD naming are shown in the following examples. In Figure 2.12(a), even though the DFD is correct and makes perfect sense, it does not really tell you very much. Just about every system you can think of will have something in it which processes and stores data, and given this DFD you would not have a clue even as to what kind of system you were meant to be building. If this were, for example, a banking system, it would be much better to give the diagram more specific names, as shown in Figure 2.12(b).

In Figure 2.12(c), by putting too much information into the names, we have made the diagram cluttered and difficult to read. Much of the information on the diagram is superfluous, and if required could be kept in the diagram textual specification. We could make the diagram easier to read by making the names more concise, as shown in Figure 2.12(d).

In Figure 2.12(e), the data coming in has got exactly the same name as the data going out — which suggests that we have not actually done anything

Table 2.1

DFD component	Naming convention
Data store, data flow	Stores and data flows represent things moving around the system, so should be given noun names. Occasionally they may represent commands (i.e. *withdrawal request*) and so may be given command type names. Stores and flows cannot do anything and therefore should not be given names that reflect actions (i.e. *verb* type names).
Data transformation	Transformations do something to some data and therefore should be given names:
	verb (what is being done) + *noun* (to what)
	As transformations should be single function units, they should not have names that contain and, or, if, etc. If you cannot find a good 'verb + noun' name for a transformation, it may be an indication of poor partitioning, i.e. because the transformation is doing a number of things which do not fit naturally together, there is no overall name to describe what the transformation is doing. This is not always the case — some transformations are just difficult to name.
Control process	Control processes should control some functional area, therefore should have names:
	control + function
	As with data transformations, if you cannot find a good overall name for the function, it may be that the control process is controlling too many different things.
Event flow	Event flows should be named by whatever they are modelling the state of.

to it during the transformation. Even if the actual physical form and content of a piece of data do not change on moving through a transformation, conceptually the data will have changed. The actual account number that came out of the transformation is the same as the one that went in; we have not changed its form, just compared it with valid account numbers. However, now we know that the account number is valid, we should give it a name to reflect that, as shown in Figure 2.12(f).

Large, unwieldy names tend to be generated when the system has been badly partitioned, i.e. things have been grouped together which perhaps do not belong together. In Figure 2.12(g) the data transformation is doing too many different things. Problems such as this can usually be resolved by splitting and reorganizing the work between data transformations, as shown in Figure 2.12(h).

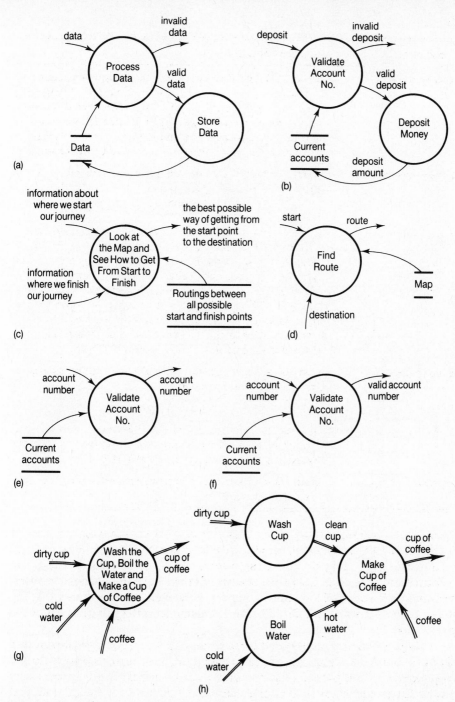

Figure 2.12 Examples of bad naming.

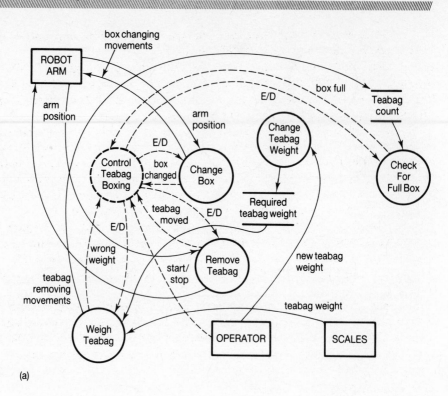

(a)

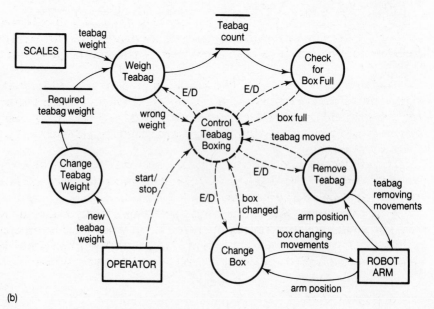

(b)

Figure 2.13 Examples of good and bad diagram layout.

Following all these heuristics on naming and partitioning should make your diagrams clear and understandable.

Size and layout also may affect the coherence of a diagram. A DFD with too much information on it is unlikely to be totally understood. Although it will be possible to understand individual transformations, all the transformations should be considered together to understand the diagram.

As a rule of thumb a diagram should have seven plus or minus two elements, where transformations and stores count as elements. However, apply your own judgement here. If a diagram looks complicated, even with less than the recommended seven elements, it has got too much on it. A diagram with too many elements can be simplified by joining elements into higher level elements, creating a levelled model. Levelling is discussed in Chapter 9.

Crossing lines and long complicated arcs may make a diagram look complicated even when it is not. Avoid crossing lines, group data transformations around the stores that they use and duplicate stores within a single DFD if it makes the diagram look tidier. Duplicated stores may be indicated by a star * inside the store.

Figure 2.13(a) shows a simplified version of our original teabag boxing system laid out in such a way as to make the diagram very cluttered and difficult to read. Figure 2.13(b) shows the same diagram laid out differently, avoiding the need for crossing lines, which makes the diagram a lot easier to read.

2.5 SUMMARY

There is only so much that you can do with a DFD: it tells you about the data transformations, something about all the data in the system and the way in which the data moves through the system — but there is quite a lot it does not show.

The DFD does not show the organization of the data. It shows that you need to store certain data, and the textual specification for a data transformation may define relationships between certain pieces of data. However, you really need another model which brings out the data more explicitly, especially if you plan to build a database.

The DFD does not show you the dynamics of the system either. A control process shows that certain things are controlled, but you cannot see how they are controlled unless you have an STD.

In conclusion, the DFD is good for showing functionality and flow of data, but is not enough to specify a whole system. There may be other aspects of the system which are important and need to be specified using either the state transition diagram (STD) or the entity relationship diagram (ERD).

2.6 EXERCISES

In all cases try to translate the text directly into a DFD. At this stage we

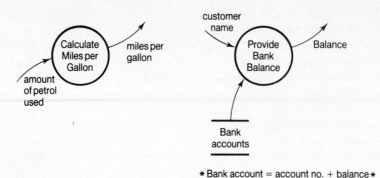

* Bank account = account no. + balance *

Figure 2.14   Exercise 5.

are not interested in implementing the system, just capturing the initial requirement.

1.   When I do the weekly wash I sort the clothes into white washing, coloured washing and things that need dry cleaning. Clothes for dry cleaning are stored away until some later date. White washing and coloured washing are washed separately, but dried together.

2.   Yearly subscriptions to the club are received from current or potential club members. New members' details are added to the club records and a 'new member's pack' is sent out. In the case of current members, a note is made that their subscription has been received, and a receipt is sent out.

3.   To make mayonnaise I use eggs, oil and seasoning. However, in the mayonnaise, I only need to use the egg yolk. To save wasting the egg white, I mix this with sugar and make meringues.

4.   The data collection system reads current temperature, humidity and light levels from weather station equipment. The current temperature and humidity are displayed at an operator screen according to some predefined format. Temperature, light levels and humidity are also stored away for future analysis.

5.   The data transformations in Figure 2.14 have conservation of data problems. Try to decide in each case what is missing.

CHAPTER THREE

State transition diagrams

3.1 INTRODUCTION

The STD is used to show the dynamics of the system, i.e. how a system behaves over time. DFDs are ideally suited to systems where there is a sequence of processing which needs to be carried out on a certain piece of data.

Figure 3.1 shows a natural flow of data running through the system, sparking transformations in the order which we would like them to happen. In many systems this may not be the case — the flow of control through the system will not always depend on some natural flow of data. Data shown coming into a data transformation may not necessarily mean that whenever that data is available, the data transformation is required. For example in Figure 3.2, we do not want to 'remove teabag' just because the arm position is available.

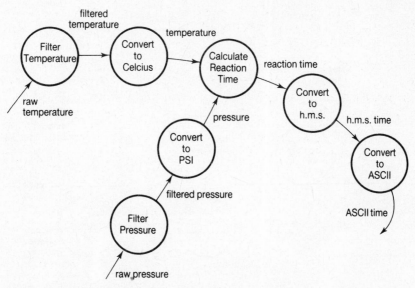

Figure 3.1   Example of DFD which does not need added control.

51

In systems like these, the processing of the data depends more on the stage in the system's sequence of behaviour. This means that we need some other way of showing which data transformations should be switched on at any given time.

In the teabag boxing system DFD, shown in Figure 3.2, there is little data flow between the data transformations. These data transformations are connected by a certain sequence in time, i.e. we want to do them in a certain time order. Therefore, we need some mechanism which allows us to switch these transformations on and off depending on what the system is doing; otherwise how will the system know when to change the box or remove a teabag?

Up until now we have shown a control process on the DFD, which has the ability to <u>monitor the status of the data transformations</u> and produce special prompt event flows (the <u>enable/disable/trigger</u> discussed briefly in Chapter 2) to switch the data transformations on and off.

This has half coped with the problem, but consider the control process in more detail and you find that all it shows is that control exists, not how the control sequencing should actually behave. What we really need is another model which tells us what causes the system to change its behaviour, i.e. if it is doing one thing, when it should stop and start doing something else. Also, having identified that the system should stop what it is doing, what it should do next, and in what order.

The model used for this is the state transition diagram.

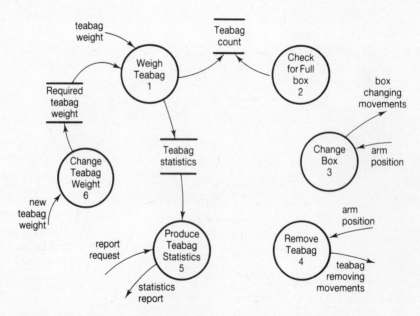

Figure 3.2 Teabag boxing system DFD without control process.

3.2 STATE TRANSITION DIAGRAM COMPONENTS

3.2.1 Basic notation

Firstly, we will consider the basic symbols and terminology used within the STD, and then we will examine an example of the STD to see how the symbols are used.

The state transition diagram in Figure 3.3 shows the basic STD symbols, and model's control of the teabag boxing system described in Chapter 2. The *state* is used to indicate a period of time over which the system is doing a certain thing; the *transition* is used to indicate the sequence in which the system passes through states; the *condition* defines what causes the system to move out of a state; and the *action* defines what the system does to enter the next state. This diagram shows the way in which we want to switch on and off those data transformations shown in Figure 3.2, and so shows the sequencing of processing required within the system.

The system starts off in the 'idle' state, where it waits for the operator to press the 'start' button. When the 'start' button has been pressed, the system switches on (enable) 'weigh teabag' and 'check for full box', which takes it into the state of 'monitoring teabag'. There are three conditions that can take the system out of this state:

1. If 'weigh teabag' indicates a teabag at the 'wrong weight', the STD will switch on 'remove teabag', which will take the system into the state of 'removing teabag'. From here, 'teabag removed' will cause the STD to switch off 'remove teabag' which will cause the system to return to the state of 'monitoring teabag'.
2. If 'check for box full' indicates 'box full', the STD will switch off 'weigh teabag' and switch on 'change box' — this will take the system into the

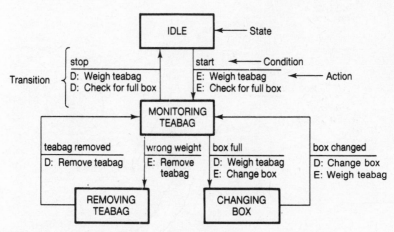

Figure 3.3 STD for teabag boxing system.

state of 'changing box'. From here 'box changed' will cause the STD to switch off 'change box' and switch on 'weigh teabag', which will return the system to the 'monitoring teabag' state.

3. If the operator presses the 'stop 'button, the system will switch off (disable) 'weigh teabag' and 'check for full box', which will take the system back to 'idle'.

Let us examine more closely the relationship between the STD and the control process. The STD describes the dynamic behaviour required of the system. The DFD control process shows how the system will make that behaviour happen. There is a direct correspondence between STD and control process — wherever a control process exists on a DFD somewhere there is a corresponding STD, and vice versa. The control process can be thought of as a 'shorthand' version of the STD which allows control to be shown on the DFD.

As the STD and the DFD control process are meant to be the same, it is important that they show the same thing. An output event flow from a control process is equivalent to an action on the STD. An input to the control process is equivalent to a condition on the STD.

The STD will change state depending on the conditions that are true within the system at any particular time. To be able to do this, the conditions must be examined, and so conditions are shown on the control process as input event flows. In effect, the control process is reading the values of system conditions.

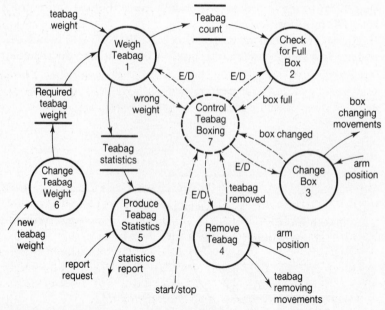

Figure 3.4 Teabag boxing system DFD with control process.

The STD changes state by making the system do something different, e.g. by telling components in the system to change state from on to off or vice versa. Therefore all actions must be output event flows to indicate control or communication to data transformations, terminators or other control processes.

On the basis of all this, wherever an STD is represented as a DFD control process, all conditions will be shown as input event flows, and all actions will be shown as output event flows.

If you do not have a condition as an input event flow, that condition will not be recognized; if you do not have an action as an output event flow, that action will never happen.

To arrive at the control process for the teabag boxing system, we have taken the STD from Figure 3.3, noted all the conditions and actions, and attached them to a control process. This control process can now be appended to the original DFD of Figure 3.2, to give Figure 3.4.

Notice that even though we may not have a data transformation to fix an event flow to, it is still an event coming in or out of the control process, e.g. the start/stop event flow — which in this case would be coming directly from the 'operator' terminator. Leaving this out could cause confusion about where the system was actually started and stopped from.

So, put all the actions and conditions on to the control process as event flows, even if they are not directly connected to the data transformations on the data flow diagram — they must be coming from or going to somewhere.

This example also shows that conditions are often generated by data transformations previously switched on, to tell the STD the state of the data transformation. For example, the 'teabag removed' condition is generated by the 'remove teabag' data transformation to tell the control process/STD that the transformation has successfully completed.

There is no limit to the number of conditions that a single data transformation can generate. For example, a data transformation which monitored temperature could produce event flows 'too hot', 'too cold' and 'much too cold', telling the STD about many different states of system temperature.

3.2.2 States

A state represents a period of time over which the system is doing a particular part of its behavioural cycle. The system enters a state by performing actions along a transition leading into that state. Once in a state, the system may continue actions switched on along the transition, and wait for any condition that might take the system out of that state.

A state may be left on a number of different conditions. For example, in the teabag boxing system, both conditions 'box full' and 'wrong weight' cause the system to leave the 'monitoring teabag' state. The system leaves by the transition containing the condition which happens first.

Firstly, let us examine the relationship between states and data transformations. Normally, the system can be doing a data transformation in a state, but there is no simple one-to-one relationship between states and data transformations. For instance, in the 'idle' state, you are not doing anything. As data transformations represent areas of work, you cannot have a data transformation which does not do anything, so there is no data transformation associated with the 'idle' state.

You can have states which represent a number of data transformations all switched on at the same time, e.g. the 'monitoring teabags' state where we have both 'weigh teabag' and 'check for full box' enabled.

Also, data transformations can be switched on across a number of different states, e.g. 'weigh teabag' is switched on in both the 'monitoring teabags'and the 'removing teabags' states. This is because whilst a teabag is being removed, the next teabag on the conveyor belt could be being weighed.

A data transformation represents a single system function, whereas a state represents what is happening in either the whole system (if the system is modelled with a single STD), or what is happening in some functional area of the system (if the system is modelled using a number of STDs). Therefore, a state represents the following:

1. A collection of functions all being carried out towards a single system purpose.
2. A record of what is happening at that time in the system, named by the net result of all the things which are going on within the area being modelled by the STD.

As states not only model what is happening in the system at that point, but also record where in the system sequence you are, states will not necessarily be the same just because you are doing the same things in them.

States are only the same if you are (a) doing exactly the same thing in them *and* (b) going to exactly the same next state on observance of exactly the same conditions.

In Figure 3.5 we will leave 'idle' on the occurrence of c1 or c2, whichever happens first. If c1 happens first, we switch on data transformation DTA, and move into the state where we are 'doing A'. In this state we wait for c3. When c3 occurs, we switch off data transformation DTA and switch on data transformation DTC. This takes us into 'state X', where we are 'doing C' and wait for c5 to occur. When c5 occurs, we switch off data transformation DTC and switch back on data transformation DTA, which returns us to the 'doing A' state.

If from 'idle', c2 were to occur, we would go through a similar sequence down the other side of the STD.

Notice that in states X and Y we are doing exactly the same thing, i.e. in each only DTC is enabled. However, when the condition c5 occurs we need to move to different destination states. Therefore, 'state X' and 'state Y' are perceived as being different system states, as the state is also remembering something about where we are in the system sequence.

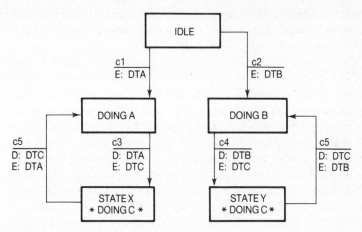

Figure 3.5 Similar states.

For states to be the same, you must be doing exactly the same thing, waiting for the same condition and when that condition occurs, be going to the same destination state. In this example the states would *only* be the same, if on recognition of c5 in both 'state X' and 'state Y', the system moved to 'idle'. It would then be correct to show a single 'doing C' state on the STD.

At any time the system can only be in one of the states shown on the STD, i.e. there is a single thread of control through an STD. What happens if a condition occurs that you are not waiting for in the current state? In the teabag boxing example, if the operator were to press the stop button whilst the system were in the removing teabag state, nothing would happen. In any state, the system will only react to conditions that are attached to that state — if we wanted the operator to be able to stop the system at this point, we would add another transition running from removing teabag to idle, initiated by the stop condition.

In a complex system there may be more than one STD. Although there is a single thread of control through a single STD there may not be single thread of control through the whole system. One STD is effectively defining one area of control or functionality — in some cases this can be seen as one area of concurrent behaviour.

A system with lots of functional areas going on at the same time, may be modelled by lots of STDs/control processes controlling those many different areas of behaviour. For example, in the teabag boxing system, one functional area concerns the monitoring of teabags going into boxes — all the work in this area is controlled by the STD which we have been examining. Another area is concerned with the production of statistics on the teabag boxing, i.e. the data transformation 'produce teabag statistics', which is not controlled by the STD. On the teabag boxing DFD, the control in this area is not complicated enough to show a control process. However, there may be a control process, with associated STD, hidden inside 'produce teabag statistics' controlling the lower level work.

Before moving on to examine conditions and actions in more detail, let us examine some special states.

3.2.2.1 *Initial states*

The initial state of the system is the state it arrives at immediately after it has been switched on. An initial state can be shown using a double headed arrow on the transition coming into the state (known as the initial transition).

The initial transition is the only transition which does not have a condition, although it may have actions.(The condition is what the system waits for to make it leave its current state. As there is no previous state to the initial state, then it makes no sense to have an 'initial condition'.) Every other state within the STD must have a condition, as it is the fulfilment of this condition which makes the system go down the transition. A transition without a condition will never be made; therefore it should not be on the STD.

Although showing the initial transition on the STD is not mandatory (normally the initial state is the one at the top of the STD), there are two cases where showing the initial transition will be useful:

1. The STD does not 'start' at the top, and you wish to indicate explicitly where to start reading it from (Figure 3.6). There is no rule that says that the top state on the STD has to be the initial state. People reading the diagrams will normally assume that they start at the top, so it is preferable to have the initial state at the top to make the diagrams easy to understand. However, there may be some reason, as in Figure 3.6, why the diagram is clearer if the initial state is not shown at the top. In this case, even though there are no initial actions , an initial transition will indicate where the flow of control on the STD starts.

2. You want to specify initial actions. In Figure 3.7 we consider the initialization of a system with a screen-based human−computer interface.

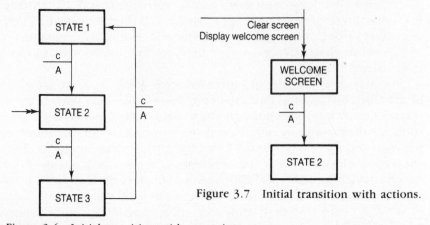

Figure 3.7   Initial transition with actions.

Figure 3.6   Initial transition with no actions.

In this kind of system, you would expect a 'welcome screen' as soon as you switch the system on. The initial actions would set up the initial display and allow user input into the system.

3.2.2.2 *Final states*

A final state has no outgoing transitions, i.e. once you get into it there is no way out, as shown in Figure 3.8. A final state will correspond to (a) the 'end' of the system sequence i.e. you have finished everything you had to do; or (b) an infinite loop that you have got stuck in.

Although case (a) is reasonable enough, case (b) is usually undesirable. Most of the STDs that we have seen so far work in sequence loops, i.e. once you have got to the last state in the diagram, you loop back to the initial state. In practical terms the only way out of a final state would be to switch the system off and then back on again — taking you back to the initial state.

As final states can creep into an STD by accident, always be on the lookout for final states, and decide which of the following applies:

1. You meant there to be a final state.
2. Some transitions have been left off your diagram by mistake.
3. You have not thought deeply enough about the sequences of behaviour within the system.

3.2.2.3 *Transitory states*

A transitory state does not strictly fit in with our definition of a system state, as it is really a cross between a state and a transition. As a result of this,

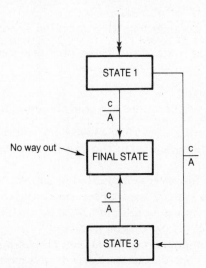

Figure 3.8   Final state.

it is difficult to explain what it is and why we need it, until we have looked at transitions in more detail.

3.2.3 Transitions

A transition is the movement of the system from one state to another. Generally the transition will consist of two parts:

1. The condition — which causes the system to make the transition.
2. The action — what the system has to do to get into the next state.

However, there are circumstances where a transition may have neither condition or action. We have already discussed the initial transition, which requires no condition, and later we will see examples of transitions which have no actions.

In the essential model, transitions take no time. Given perfect technology, the zero instruction rate means all actions can be done instantaneously. When you recognize a condition, you do all the actions specified for the associated transition and instantaneously arrive at the next state.

There is no restriction on the number of transitions within an STD. You can move from one state to any other state in the STD, as long as there is a connecting transition.

3.2.3.1 *Conditions*

Conditions are what cause the system to move from one state to the next. Within a state, imagine the system doing two things:

1. Whatever behaviour is defined for that state.
2. Looking for any conditions that might take the system out of that state.

For example, in the 'monitoring teabag' state of the teabag boxing system STD, we are doing the following:

1. Monitoring the teabag by weight.
2. Waiting for either the 'wrong weight' or the 'box full' condition to occur.

Immediately one of these conditions occurs, the system will carry out the actions associated with that condition (defined by the transition actions), and move to the next state.

A condition is any statement, however complicated or simple, that you can evaluate to be true or false. In this system, we wait for the simple condition 'box full'; however, if the system were more complicated, we might wish to wait for the condition 'box full' and (35 g < box weight < 40 g).

It is perfectly legal to state compound conditions on the condition line of the STD. However, it may make your diagrams clearer if you express the condition more simply on the STD, and hide the full detail of the condition in the project dictionary. For example, the condition 'A or B or C or D or E or F or G or H or I or J or K or L or M or N or O or P or Q or R or S or T or U or V or W or X or Y or Z' could be more clearly stated on the STD as 'alphabetic character'.

Conditions and event flows tend to be equivalent, although sometimes a condition will be caused by a number of event flows. If we consider conditions to be equivalent to event flows, conditions can come from the following:

1. Terminators.
2. Data transformations. → condition
3. Control processes.
4. Time.

Terminators

A user 'terminator' presses a start key, which causes the system to leave the 'idle' state. The condition 'start' is shown as an event flow from the user terminator. In the STD we wait for the condition 'start'.

Data transformations

A data transformation 'monitor temperature' could compare the incoming data flow 'temperature' with stored data 'required temperature', to generate the event flow 'too hot' when the temperature exceeds the required value. In the STD we wait for the condition 'too hot'.

Control processes

A system could have two control processes/STDs, 'control reaction' (controlling a reaction being carried out inside a tank) and 'control tank' (controlling the tank level). When the reaction is over, we would like to empty the tank. Therefore when 'control reaction' notices that the reaction is over, it produces the event flow 'reaction over', which 'control tank' is waiting for as a condition.

Time

As part of the perfect technology discussed previously, each system is assumed to have a clock accessible from anywhere in the system model. Therefore, in the essential model, it is legal to state conditions which are concerned with the passage of time, such as 'time to produce daily report', without showing where they will eventually come from.

Showing a 'time' data flow coming from a 'clock' terminator may sometimes make the model clearer, although the inclusion of the 'time' flow and the 'clock' is not strictly speaking necessary.

Thought of in a more abstract sense, a condition is anything that the system is able to sense and wishes to do something about.

When you build an STD, concentrate on the system you are trying to model, and make sure that your conditions and actions are appropriate to that system. With conditions, you should imagine that you are inside the system — what can you recognize happening in the outside world? There is no point in coming up with conditions that your system will not be able to recognize. Remember that your system will only have certain sensors, and these are what should be considered when thinking of recognizable conditions.

3.2.3.2 *Actions*

The action part of the transition will specify all the things the system has to do to take it into the next state.

The STD should control the system, and as such it should be almost pure logic. The STD does not do anything except examine the state of the system, and make decisions on that basis. All the work done in the system is achieved by the STD telling everything else in the system, via the actions, what to do.

In a similar way to conditions, we can think of actions in terms of output event flows, sent by control processes to the following:

1. Terminators.
2. Data transformations.
3. Timers.
4. Other control processes.

To *terminators*

Actions/event flows can be sent directly from control processes to terminators. The action takes the same name as the outgoing event flow, as shown by Figure 3.9. It will not be preceded by enable, as this is reserved purely for activating data transformations.

To *data transformations*

There are two ways of activating a data transformation from a STD, depending on the type of data transformation being activated: enable/disable and trigger.

Enable/disable is usually abbreviated to E/D: *enable* means 'switch on'; disable means 'switch off'; and for some period of time between the enable and the disable, the data transformation will be doing its job. Enable/disable is used

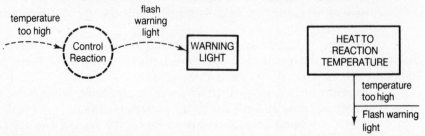

Figure 3.9   Action to terminator.

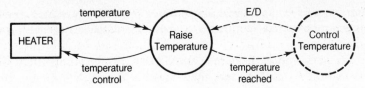

Figure 3.10   Continuous data transformation: type A.

with continuous transformations, i.e. transformations which despite perfect technology persist over time because of some kind of external influence. There are two types of transformation which may persist over time:

1. A transformation which works continuously on continuously available data, shown by Figure 3.10.
    Inside 'raise temperature' we effectively have a loop

    ```
    While temperature < > required temperature
    produce temperature control
    read temperature
    ```

    As the heater is a terminator, we cannot class it as being part of our perfect technology. This means that the amount of time it takes to raise the temperature will depend on the strength of the heater. A one bar electric fire might take 30 minutes, a three bar electric fire might take 10 minutes. It does not matter what kind of processor we implement the data transformation on, it will still take the same amount of time. If we use a one bar electric fire and a BBC Micro, the transformation will take 30 minutes; if we use a one bar electric fire and a CRAY, it will still take 30 minutes. Even if we have perfect technology, it will still take 30 minutes.

2. A transformation which does not have its data immediately available, i.e. has to wait for a discrete data input, is also continuous, as it must also persist over time.
    Figure 3.11 shows part of a DFD modelling a chess playing

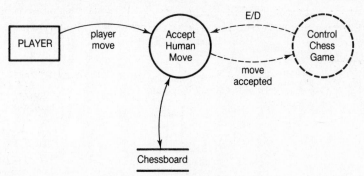

Figure 3.11   Continuous data transformation: type B.

program, between a human player and a machine. When it is the human player's turn to make a move, we enable the data transformation 'accept human move'.

At this point the human could make a move immediately, or could have a cup of coffee, and then make a move. We enable the data transformation to allow it to accept data, and let it run until that item of data is available. When the item of data arrives, it can process the data, and let the control process know, by sending the 'move accepted' event, that it has finished.

As in the previous case, the time this transformation takes depends not on the implementation processor, but on the system's environment. If the player moves immediately, the transformation will be over in seconds, whereas if the player decides to have a coffee before making the move, the transformation could be running for hours. Even with perfect implementation technology, we still could not make the human player make his move any faster. When a control process activates a continuous data transformation, it does not know how long the transformation will take (as this depends on the system's environment), and therefore when to switch the transformation off. For this reason, there will often be an event flow going from a continuous transformation to its control process, indicating that the data transformation has achieved its purpose. This is the case in both the examples given.

The second way of activating a data transformation is by use of a *trigger*, which is usually abbreviated to T. Trigger means 'switch on, do all your required work, and then switch yourself off', and is used with 'one-shot' transformations, i.e. transformations which, given perfect technology, could work in zero time.

Figure 3.12 shows another part of the chess playing system. Each time the machine or the player changes the board, we trigger 'display board' to display the board on the screen.

There will be a finite number of instructions to run inside 'display board'. If there are 500 instructions, and 1 instruction can be executed in zero time, then

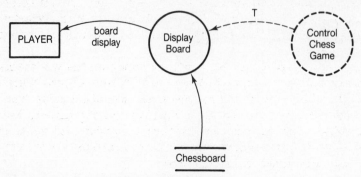

Figure 3.12 One-shot data transformation.

500 can be executed in zero time. Also, all the data the transformation needs to perform its action are immediately available from the store 'chessboard' — so there is no waiting for data involved. Therefore, with perfect technology, we could do this transformation in zero time.

Looked at another way, the time which this transformation takes to run will be entirely dependent on the speed of the implementation processor. Implemented on a BBC Micro, it would certainly take longer than on a CRAY.

Data transformations will either be one-shot or continuous. Before you activate a data transformation from an STD, you must decide what sort of transformation it is. The characteristics of a one-shot transformation are that (a) data is immediately available (either from a store, or a continuous data flow) and (b) there are a finite number of instructions. The characteristics of a continuous transformation are either that (a) data has to be waited for (from a discrete data flow) or (b) data has to act continuously on continuously available data.

The other way of looking at this is in terms of processor dependency. Imagine implementing the transformation firstly on a BBC Micro, and then in perfect technology. If the transformation takes the same amount of time no matter how you implement it, it is continuous; otherwise it will be one-shot.

Finally, let us consider transformation activation from the STD's point of view. When the STD enables a data transformation, it immediately assumes that the data transformation is switched on and running. When the STD disables a data transformation, it immediately assumes that the data transformation has stopped doing whatever it was doing.

When the STD triggers a data transformation, it immediately assumes that the data transformation has performed its function and has finished, because of the zero instruction rate provided by the perfect technology. The implications of this on the STD are shown by Figure 3.13, where DT1 is continuous, DT2 is one-shot. On condition c1 we enable DT1, but we trigger DT2. By the time we enter the next state, the triggered data transformation has finished, but the one that was enabled is still going on because it persists over time. Therefore, we are still doing DT1 in this state, but DT2 is over. DT1 will only stop when it is explicitly disabled by the control process.

Continuous transformations are switched on along the transition, but actually done in the states, whilst one-shot transformations are switched on and executed along the transition. You should never have a state where you are doing a triggered transformation.

In differentiating between continuous and one-shot transformations, we are differentiating between things which take time because of something in the outside world, i.e. things which the customer/user would expect to take time, and things which will take time because of the slowness of the implementation processor, i.e. things which the customer/user may not understand will take time. This will lead to states which reflect what the customer thinks the system does, not what the engineer thinks the system does.

We are also differentiating between data transformations whose execution time will be processor dependent, and those which will not — which may help later on in the design phases.

To timers

As discussed in Section 3.2.3.1. under 'Time', it is not necessary to show where timing information is coming from. Therefore, having an action 'set timer for 15 ms' is legal — even if no timer is shown on the DFD. However, if the timer is to be driven by a schedule, this will be shown as a data store on the DFD, e.g. a 'maintenance schedule' data store. The timer can be 'enabled' as a continuous data transformation which reads the required time from the data store schedule and compares this with the internal clock, until it produces an event flow 'time to start maintenance'.

To control process

In a system with more than one STD, an action can consist of one STD letting another STD know what state it is in. Depending on whether the receiving STD needs to know the state of the sending STD all the time, or just at a particular instant, we use either discrete or continuous event flows.

Signal is normally abbreviated to S and means 'produce a discrete event flow'. In Figure 3.14, 'control reaction' will produce the discrete event flow 'reaction over' when it notices that the reaction on the tank is over, via the action signal 'reaction over'.

Raise/lower is normally abbreviated to R/L and can be used to send continuous event flows, i.e. flags, between STDs: raise means 'set the flag to true'; lower means 'set the flag to false';

Figure 3.15 shows a flag between two control processes/STDs 'control input valve' and 'control output valve', controlling, respectively, the input valve and the output valve of the same tank.

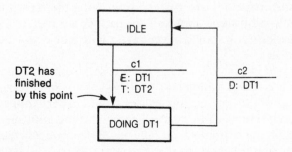

Figure 3.13 Continuous and one-shot data transformations.

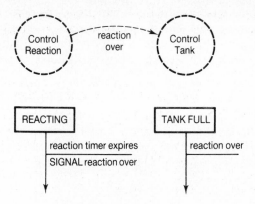

Figure 3.14   Discrete action to control process (SIGNAL).

In this system, we never want to get into the state where the input valve and output valve are both open at the same time, otherwise liquid would be draining through the tank without us being able to do anything to it. To inhibit this illegal state, we introduce the flag 'input open' which is set and reset by the 'control input valve' STD, via the raise and lower actions. At any time, the 'control output valve' STD can examine the flag to see whether it is safe to open the output valve.

These mechanisms allow us to build communications in the form of event flows between two or more STDs within the system.

Raise/lower/signal should only be used between STDs:

1. They should not be used to produce event flows and flags to terminators, i.e. the outside world. They are 'perfect technology' mechanisms and the outside world is not perfect.
2. They should not be used to set flags going into data transformations. To make the DFD easy to understand, and for good system structure, data

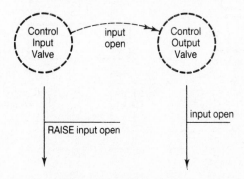

Figure 3.15   Continuous action to control process (RAISE/LOWER).

transformations should have a single function which they perform every time they are activated. If the STD sends a flag to the data transformation as well as enable/trigger, this implies the STD is telling it which of a number of different functions to perform on this particular activation.

Finally, let us examine the difference between continuous and discrete event flows. A continuous event flow will always be true or false, whereas a discrete event flow is only valid when the event happens. If you examine a discrete event flow after the event has happened, you will not know whether the event has happened or not, because the event will only be available for the split second while it is being sent. On the other hand, a flag records that the event has happened, and can be examined at any time.

3.2.3.3 *Transitory states*

Transitory states always occur after data transformations triggered to do an evaluation on the internal system state or internal system data. A transitory state can be thought of as a decision box.

Figure 3.16 shows another fragment of the chess playing system. 'Evaluate move' looks at the board each time a move has been made, and evaluates that move. The evaluation can be considered in two ways:

1. From the player's point of view we are interested in whether that move has caused the game to be won/lost/check/checkmate, etc. This information will be displayed on the screen via the 'outcome' data flow.
2. From the system's point of view, all we are interested in is whether the

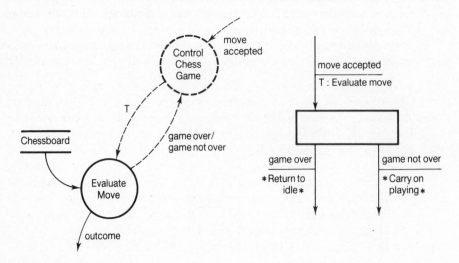

Figure 3.16 Transitory state.

game is over or not. This information will be communicated to the control process via the 'game over' event flow.

'Evaluate move' is a one-shot transformation because it satisfies the following two criteria:

1. All the data it needs is immediately available in the 'chessboard' store.
2. It will only have to go through a finite number of instructions to complete its purpose.

As the transformation is triggered, it will have finished by the time the next state is reached, so there is nothing actually happening in that state (i.e. it is not a real state). However, the destination state of the transformation depends on the outcome of the action — and so the box is required for connection of the various transitions resulting from the action. In this respect, it is just indicating a divergence in the transition — it is not a true state, because there is nothing actually happening in it. Therefore, the transitory state does not have a name because it is not a true mode of system behaviour.

Although it is not strictly correct to name a transitory state, you can name it if you find it helpful. In a system with a lot of internal decision making, i.e. a lot of transitory states, lots of empty boxes in the diagram are not very meaningful. In this case you could mark the transitory state in some other way, to show that it was different from a real state, and then give the state a name.

3.2.4 Event stores

An event store is a place where you store events. Unlike a data store, which has no inherent behaviour, an event store has lots of associated behaviour, most of which is not obvious from looking at an event store on a DFD. Event stores tell you about events that have occurred but have not been used yet.

Let us begin by discussing the inherent behaviour of the event store, then we will examine its use:

1. Only one type of event can be stored by an event store, which will queue incoming events. For example, if the event store is attached to the user stop button, every time the user presses the stop button, we add one to the event store. If the user presses the stop button four times, there will be four 'stops' in the event store.
2. You cannot look at an event store without using up the event, so reading from an event store will always be destructive. For example, if an event had happened four times when you looked into the event store, it would only show three occurrences of the event afterwards, as you would have used up one of the events by looking at it.
3. You can only access an event store via 'wait'. Wait means:

    Look in the event store
    If the event has happened

then remove it from the event store
else wait until the event happens.

Thus it causes the event store to behave like a semaphore. If the event has not happened when you 'wait' on the event store, you are effectively suspending yourself until the event happens. You cannot use an event store like a flag: you do not get stuck looking at a flag until it becomes set to true — if you look at an event store and it has not happened, you will be stuck there until it does happen. Also, you cannot use the event store as a counter. Even though event stores do count events, you cannot examine an event store to see if something has happened a number of times. For example, you cannot evaluate an event store for equality to six, you can only look at an event store to see if the event has or has not happened, using wait. If you want to see if something has happened six times, you would have to examine the event store six times.

4. 'Reset' or 'flush' can be used to clear the event store, i.e. set the value of the event store to zero or cause any processes which were waiting on the event store to stop waiting.

Figure 3.17 shows an example of event store use. The operator can initialize equipment, and then start a reaction using that equipment. As the equipment being used is external to the system, it will not be part of our perfect technology, and so will take some time to initialize. Therefore, we must ensure

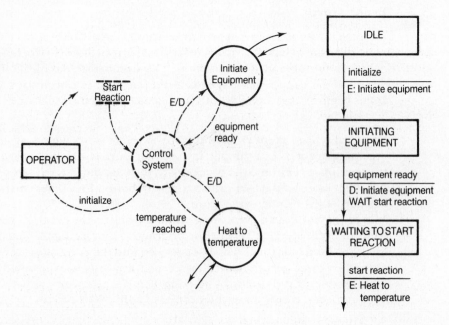

Figure 3.17 Example of event store use.

that the initialization is over before we attempt to start the reaction. By using the event store, the operator is able to press the 'initialize' and 'start reaction' buttons directly after each other, but the system does not have to take notice of the 'start reaction' button until initialization is over.

In the 'initiating equipment' state, 'start reaction' can be pressed, although 'equipment ready' is the only condition to which we want to react at that point, and so is the only condition shown on the STD. 'Start reaction' is saved in the event store, so that we can use the event when we are ready for it.

When the system is ready to start the reaction, it 'wait's on the event store as an action, entering the state 'waiting to start reaction'. If the operator has already pressed the button by this point, the event 'start reaction' will return from the 'wait' on the event store immediately. If the operator has not pressed the button, the system will stay in the state until the button is pressed.

Be careful with the use of event stores: all this behaviour is hidden on the diagram, so the event stores are open to misinterpretation. If you do use an event store remember the following:

1. They are not flags or counters.
2. Customers (or anybody else not fully aware of their hidden behaviour) will not understand what they mean.
3. You can always avoid using an event store by using flags.
4. They are probably more useful in the design stages than the analysis stages, as they often map into operating system facilities.

3.3 BUILDING A STATE TRANSITION DIAGRAM

There are two strategies for building a state transition diagram. They are not totally different strategies, but the approach you take will depend on whether you have already built the DFD for the system.

If you have already built a DFD, you can build a control process on the basis of information within the DFD and use that to help you build the STD. Remember the event flows coming in and out of the control process will define the conditions and actions on your STD.

If you have not already built the DFD, all you can do is think about the sequence of behaviour within the system that you are trying to describe.

3.3.1 The DFD control process

Let us look at the approach used when the DFD already exists. Figure 3.18 shows the DFD for a simple central heating system. The operator switches the system on, and enters the temperature at which the rooms are to be kept. The system will heat the rooms to that temperature, and will attempt to maintain that temperature, by monitoring the temperature and switching the heater back on if the temperature drops below the required level. Whenever the temperature is lower than the required level, an indication will be given to the operator.

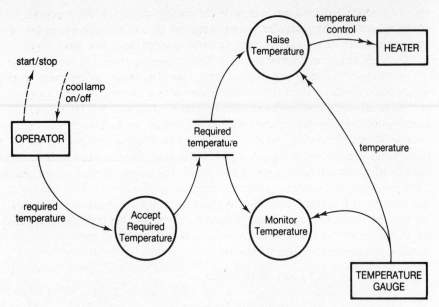

Figure 3.18   Preliminary DFD for central heating system.

The first thing we can do to help us describe the control of this DFD is build the control process:

1. Event flows from the control process to the data transformation — you may find that the data transformation does not need to be controlled, i.e. you require it always to be switched on, in which case you will not need any input from the control process.

    If the data transformation does need to be controlled, you must decide whether it is a continuous or a one-shot transformation, i.e. are you going to enable/disable or trigger the transformation.

    In our example all the data transformations are continuous: 'monitor temperature' and 'raise temperature' because they are working continuously on continuously available data, and 'accept required temperature' because it may have to wait for its input from the operator.

2. Event flows from the data transformation to the control process — are there any pieces of status information being generated from the data transformation that the control process needs to know about? For example, quite often a continuous transformation which has been enabled needs to send an event to its control process to tell the control process that it has finished.

In our example, 'raise temperature' will need to send an event flow to the control process when it has reached the required temperature, so that the control process can disable it and enable 'monitor temperature'.

'Accept required temperature' will need to send an event flow to the control process when the required temperature has been accepted by the system, so that it can be switched off and 'monitor temperature' switched on.

'Monitor temperature' will have to send an event flow to the control process to let it know when the temperature has dropped below a certain level, so that it can be switched off and 'raise temperature' switched on.

Also, remember that a data transformation may not send an enable/disable or trigger directly to another data transformation. In this example, we do not show an E/D from 'monitor temperature' into 'raise temperature': the control will be routed through the control process, i.e. 'monitor temperature' sends the event flow 'too cool' to the control process, which will in turn enable 'raise temperature'.

This routeing through the control process is to ensure the separation of control and data, i.e. data transformations which just do their jobs and do not directly attempt to control other parts of the system.

Figure 3.19 shows the original DFD with the addition of the newly created control process. Once you have sketched in the control process, you can make a list of all the possible conditions and actions that you will have on the STD.

In this example, the possible conditions are: start/stop; required temperature received; temperature reached; too cool. The possible actions are: E/D raise temperature; E/D monitor temperature; E/D accept required temperature; cool lamp on; cool lamp off.

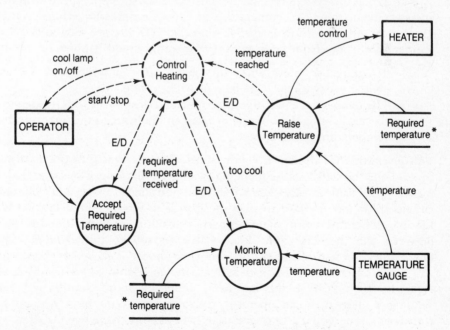

Figure 3.19   DFD for central heating system with control process.

Once you have got those you can start thinking about the sequence of events within the system.

3.3.2 System sequence

To find the sequence of events within the system, imagine using the system. Consider the example above: think about what actually happens when you use your central heating system at home, or even something a lot simpler which works on the same principle, like a thermostatically controlled iron. First of all you switch the system on and adjust the thermostat to the required temperature — as a result of this you would expect the system to start heating the room/iron up.

Now think about this with respect to your STD and DFD. On switching our system on, we expect it to allow us to input our required temperature, using the data transformation 'accept required temperature'. This takes us into the 'inputting required temperature' state.

After the required temperature has been input, in order to get the room/iron to heat up, we need to switch on the data transformation 'raise temperature'.

Having started the heating, we should not expect anything to happen now until the required heat is reached, so we can add a 'heating' state to the STD, with the condition 'temperature reached' coming out of it.

When the system reaches the correct heat, we expect it to stop heating and start maintaining the temperature, so those become our actions on the STD in terms of what we know is available on the DFD. We are now in the 'correct temperature' state: from here, one of two things could happen:

1. The operator could switch the system off — in which case we need to switch everything off to take us back to idle.
2. The temperature of the room/iron could drop — in which case we need to start heating the room/iron again and indicate to the operator that the temperature has dropped.

This gives the STD shown in Figure 3.20, which is almost finished. However, by studying the states and sequencing, we might find transitions that have been missed. For example, although we did not consider it at the time, perhaps we should allow the operator to stop the system in the 'heating' state, as well as the 'correct temperature' state. An extra transition could be added to the STD between the 'heating' and 'idle' states to reflect this. Notice that the communication with the operator 'cool lamp on/off' is shown as an event flow.

In order to activate or deactivate the cool lamp all we need is a binary signal to say 'on/off'. If this had been something more complicated, such as sending a message to an operator console, we would have needed a data transformation 'send operator message' which could have been triggered from the control process/STD.

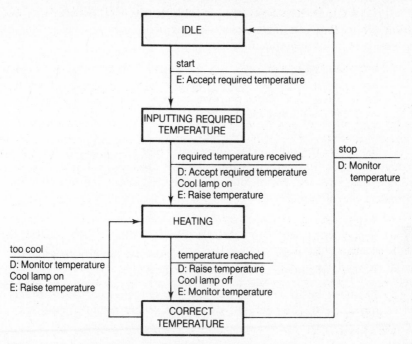

Figure 3.20   Preliminary central heating system STD.

When building an STD before the associated DFD exists, you should imagine the required sequence of system behaviour, but instead of relating conditions/actions to the DFD, create conditions/actions to make the system do what you want it to do. These can then be used to help build the DFD:

1. Always start off in the initial state: here you know exactly what has and has not happened yet in the system. Remember, in the initial state you want to do all the things that are done when the system is switched on at the mains. To get out of the initial state, imagine the first thing that you expect to happen after initialization.

2. Always think in real-world terms about the sequence of system behaviour: if you think about how you physically want to use the system, that helps you understand what you do and do not want the system to do at certain points, which in turn helps you with actions, conditions and states.

3. Initially, do not worry about the informality of the diagram. Imagine you have a system where you want to heat something up. If the DFD exists, the data transformation that does the heating will lead to an STD action 'enable: raise temperature'. If you do not have the DFD, you will not have produced the data transformation yet. In this case, the action would initially be 'start heating'. This can later be changed to 'enable: raise temperature', once the data transformation exists.

Let us consider an example of building the STD before the DFD. In this system, we are required to control a robot, which paints a car. From our customer, we have the following specification:

> Cars move along a conveyor belt and stop in front of the robot. The robot paints the car, and then scans to see if any bits have been missed. If any parts of the car have not been painted properly, the robot will touch up the paintwork. Once the robot has finished painting the car, it will indicate that it is ready for the next one.

To create the initial STD, shown in Figure 3.21, all we need to do is run through the specified sequence and map this directly on to the STD in terms of perceived actions and conditions. The specifed sequence of behaviour can be expressed as follows:

1. Car moves in front of the robot.
2. Robot paints the car.
3. Robot scans the car, and repaints bits that have been missed.
4. Robot indicates that the car is finished.

From the initial STD, we examine the sequence to make sure it is correct. For example, we have generated two states where we are painting:

1. Painting car.
2. Retouching car.

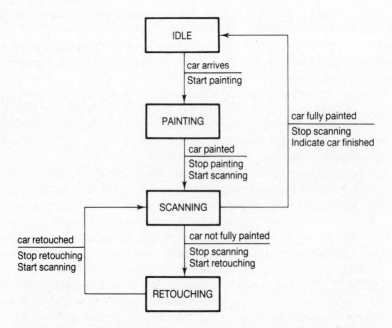

Figure 3.21 Preliminary robot control STD showing STD actions.

Could we merge these states together into a single state? This would be possible *only* if painting and retouching actually involved doing the same thing from the customer's viewpoint.

We could then use this preliminary STD to help build the initial DFD. The STD gives us the following actions:

1. Start/stop painting.
2. Start/stop scanning.
3. Start/stop retouching.
4. Indicate car finished.

The STD gives us the following conditions:

1. Car arrives
2. Car painted.
3. Car fully painted.
4. Car not fully painted.
5. Car retouched.

On the basis of these we can build the DFD shown in Figure 3.22.

The DFD is not complete yet, as we need to add data flows and stores; however, we have a good framework to add those flows and stores to. We can also now formalize the STD, by relating it to what we have created on the DFD, i.e. actions such as 'start scanning' will become 'enable: scan car'.

3.3.3 General guidelines

The basic ideas for building an STD are more or less the same as those for building a DFD. That is, start off very simply with the fundamentals of your system and then add the details.

1. Start off simply — think about the simplest sequence of system behaviour you can imagine. Do not worry about all the fine details of the system,

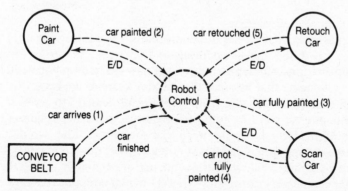

Figure 3.22 Preliminary robot painter DFD with control process.

about all the things that are not going to happen very often (e.g. maintenance loops), about system errors, and if the diagram you draw is not absolutely correct, you can worry about that later on.
2. Once you have got a basic sequence through the STD then you can start thinking about adding detail.

Think about sequences of behaviour that do not happen very often, even though perhaps they are not actually error conditions. For example, in our robot system, every now and again we may want to go through a special sequence to clean out the painting mechanisms. To model this, we could add an extra transition from 'idle' to a 'routine maintenance' state, with appropriate conditions and actions.

Also, consider any error conditions that the system should handle. For example, what would we do if the robot system ran out of paint?
3. Lastly, check that the diagram is correct. Check its syntactic correctness, that the diagram is meaningful, and that the diagram does describe the right system. It is no good having a diagram which is syntactically correct and meaningful but does not describe your customer requirements.

3.4 CHECKING A STATE TRANSITION DIAGRAM

Once you have built the STD then you need to check it. There are three things to check:

1. Check that it is syntactically correct.
2. Check that it is as easy to understand as possible.
3. Check that it describes the right system.

3.4.1 Checking for syntactic correctness

As with the DFD, we must check that symbols have been used and connected in the correct way. There are two areas of syntax to check within the STD:

1. Behavioural equivalence.
   This rule states that it does not matter how you get into a state, you must always be doing the same thing in that state. In terms of the data transformations, the same things must be switched on and switched off.

   Imagine that in the teabag boxing system, we forgot to 'disable: weigh teabag' on moving from 'monitoring teabag' to 'idle'. Although we thought we were in 'idle', we would actually be weighing teabags. More importantly, it would mean that sometimes 'idle' would be doing a different thing from what it was doing at other times (i.e. either weighing or not weighing). Following the sequence of behaviour within the system could become very confusing. An STD which contains this type of error is said to have behavioural inequivalence.

2. Transition rules.

Transitions can join any state in the state transition diagram to any other state in the same state transition, as long as this transition is expected in the real life of the system. For example, in the teabag boxing system, imagine a transition from 'idle' to 'removing teabag'. As there is no condition that takes us directly from 'idle' to 'removing teabag', it would be meaningless, because it does not show how we wish the system to operate.

Actions can be any of the following:

1. Enable/disable a continuous transformation.
2. Trigger a one-shot transformation.
3. Raise/lower a continuous event flow (flag).
4. Signal a discrete event flow.
5. Wait on an event store.
6. Flush (reset) an event store.
7. Send an event flow to a terminator.
8. Set a timer.

A common mistake with an STD is shown in Figure 3.23(a). Actions have to happen along transitions, not once you get into the state. It is doing the actions that takes you into the state. The state shown in Figure 3.23(a) should be as shown in Figure 3.23(b).

Conditions may be any expression which can be evaluated to true, and the only transition which does not have a condition will be the initial transition.

3.4.2 Checking for coherence

As with the DFD we check for careful naming and careful partitioning. Let us look firstly at naming. Naming within the STD should be easier than naming

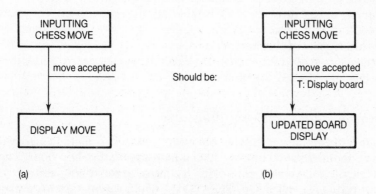

Figure 3.23 Legal transitions and states.

within the DFD, as the only name that you have to create is the state name. The condition and action names will come from names on the DFD.

In order to make the STD as meaningful as possible, try to use names from the system's subject matter. As with the DFD, use words that your customer uses to you, because then he will have more chance of understanding you.

Also, make sure that you describe the externally observable behaviour of the system and not what the system itself thinks it is doing. Imagine you are outside the system watching the sequence of behaviour, and use names that describe what you see the system doing from the outside. For example, in a central heating system, state name 'correct temperature' could describe the state a customer perceives the system to be in. Looked at from within the system, the state may well have been called 'monitoring temperature'.

Secondly, consider partitioning. The first thing to remember is that you may have a number of STDs describing the control within your system. Normally you will have one STD for each functional area. You need to strike a balance between having too many STDs and not enough. If you have a system with two major functional areas you probably want two STDs. If you only have one STD in this case, you will find that it is large, busy and probably difficult to follow. On the other hand you do not want to go too far in the other direction. It is just as difficult to understand a system where you have 15 very small STDs, as a system where you have a single, very large STD.

You may also use separate STDs to describe asynchronous or concurrent areas of behaviour. 'Concurrent' describes areas of behaviour which will be occurring at the same time, 'asynchronous' describes areas of behaviour that are likely to happen at any time. The implication of having two STDs/control processes on the same DFD is that they are both active at the same time.

With multiple STDs within a levelled system, the STDs may appear at different levels in the DFD hierarchy. In Figure 3.24(a) 'control reaction' enables 'maintain temperature' to take the system into the state of 'maintaining temperature' (the partial STD associated with 'control reaction' has not been shown). 'Maintain temperature' is further broken down in Figure 3.24(b), and a lower level control process/STD is able to move between the states of 'heating'/'cooling'/'temperature stable'. Effectively, these three states are all substates within 'maintaining temperature'.

If the STDs within the system are either too small or too large, they can be broken down or joined together.

3.4.2.1 *Joining state transition diagrams*

In this example, we expand our robot painter to include a part of the system which monitors and controls the temperature on the shop floor. The STD shown in Figure 3.25(a) is similar to that for control of the robot painting system, which has already been discussed. The STD shown in Figure 3.25(b) controls the temperature — if the temperature becomes too hot the paint will dry too quickly and not give the desired finish. This STD monitors the temperature, and if it becomes too hot attempts to bring it down, using the data transformation 'lower temperature'.

Notice the event flow 'hot' which is produced by the temperature control STD, and used by the robot control STD. This is used to communicate to the robot controller that the temperature is too hot, therefore it should not be painting — effectively it is used to inhibit the states 'painting car' and 'scanning and retouching car' whilst the temperature is in the 'too hot' state.

Merging these two STDs will give us the following possible states:

1. 'Correct temperature and waiting for car'.

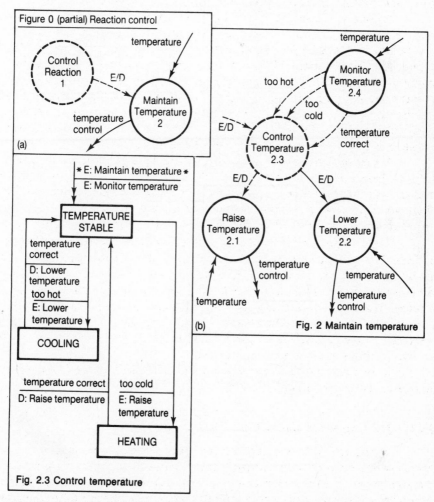

Figure 3.24 Levelled state transition diagram.

2. 'Correct temperature and painting car'.
3. 'Correct temperature and retouching car'.
4. 'Too hot and waiting for car'.
5. 'Too hot and painting car'.
6. 'Too hot and retouching car'.

However, as discussed, states 5 and 6 are illegal.

    To build the combined STD, we start with the four legal states and transfer

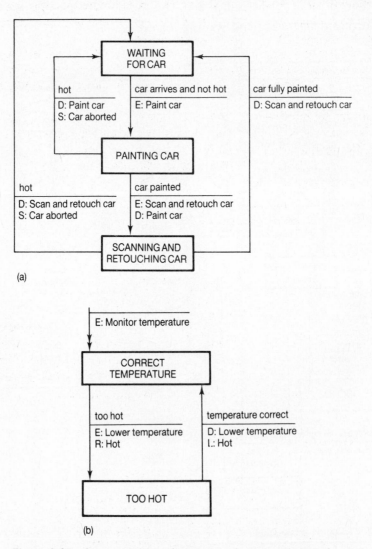

(a)

(b)

Figure 3.25   State transition diagrams to be merged: (a) robot painting system STD; (b) temperature control STD.

the transitions on to them from the original STDs. For example, let us examine the transition starting with the condition 'too hot', in Figure 3.25(b), which moved from 'correct temperature' to 'too hot' in the original temperature control STD. This transition must now run between all the 'correct temperature' states ('correct temperature and waiting for car', 'correct temperature and painting car', 'correct temperature and retouching car') and 'too hot'.

Adding all the appropriate transitions will give us the STD shown in Figure 3.26. The state 'correct temperature' has been assumed in the states 'waiting for car', 'painting car' and 'scanning and retouching car', otherwise the system would have moved to the 'too hot' state — therefore the state names do not need to reflect this, and have been left as in Figure 3.25(a).

When constructing an STD from two smaller STDs, name the combined states carefully. Having joined two halves of the system together, you may now be describing a larger, different functional area, and the names in your STD should reflect that.

Putting the two STDs together in this example has the advantage of removing the event flow 'too hot': as both areas of control are now in the same place, they no longer need to communicate across the system. However, it has the disadvantage of creating an STD which is fairly complex, and not as easy to follow as the two original STDs.

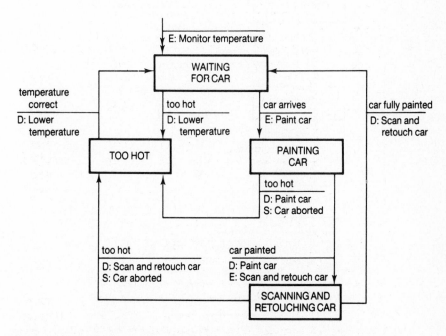

Figure 3.26 Combined robot painter and temperature control STD.

3.4.2.2 *Splitting a state transition diagram*

Figure 3.27 shows the STD for a slightly more complicated robot painter. Here, when the car arrives, the robot must position itself with respect to the car before it can begin painting. In this system, painting is done using a paint nozzle which is attached to the robot arm. Scanning the paintwork is achieved using scanning equipment which is not attached to the robot arm — so scanning can be carried out with no robot movement.

Here, we will attempt to separate the STD controlling robot movement from the STD controlling scanning and painting.

Let us firstly concentrate on the STD to control robot movement. To achieve this we need to start with the original STD and remove anything which is not concerned with robot movement. The enable/disable to 'paint car' and 'scan

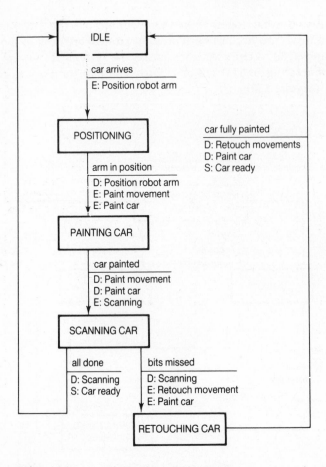

Figure 3.27 Another robot painter STD.

car' are both removed, as neither of these data transformations actually cause the robot arm to move.

The notification of the car being fully painted, 'car ready', is also removed, as this is concerned with the car being fully painted, which is nothing to do with whether the robot is moving or not.

A similar procedure can be carried out concentrating on painting and scanning, to us the STDs shown in Figure 3.28. Notice that in Figure 3.28(b) the STD is waiting for the condition 'arm in position', which is being generated by a data transformation controlled by the robot movement STD.

Again, good structure dictates that it is not desirable for a 'worker' in one area of functionality to be indicating to the controller of another area of functionality. In this case we will modify the robot movement STD such that

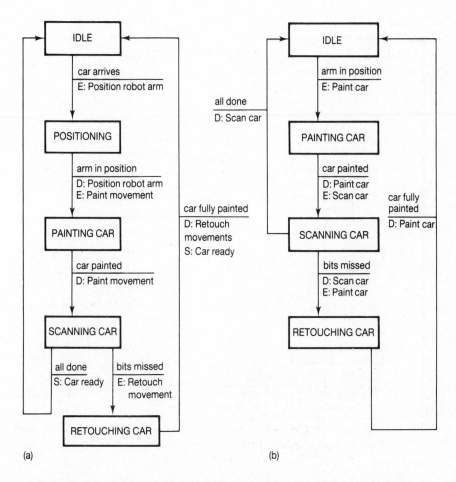

Figure 3.28 (a) Split robot movement and (b) painting/scanning STDs.

when it notices 'arm in position', it produces an event flow 'in position to paint' which can be read by the scanning and painting STD.

The same reasoning applies to the 'car painted', 'bits missed', 'car fully painted' and 'all done' conditions.

These modifications will lead to the pair of STDs shown in Figure 3.29. Although the two STDs produced are not that much simpler than the single STD we started out with, this approach may make our system more modular and easy to maintain later on. Imagine what would happen if we decided to buy a new robot movement device and therefore change the way in which it was controlled.

In the single STD solution, we would replace bits and pieces from within the single STD. In the two STD solution, we would replace the single STD concerned with robot movement — and leave the other STD just as it was.

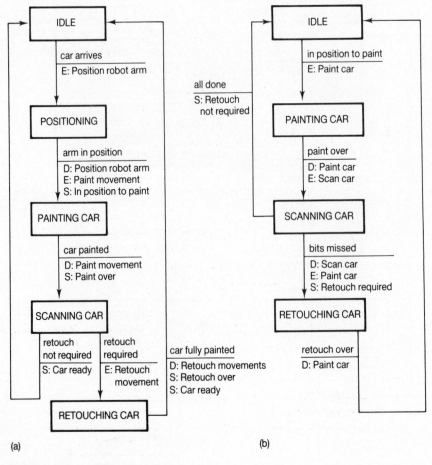

Figure 3.29 Addition of flags to STDs.

3.4.2.3 *Levelling a state transition diagram*

For an example of levelling, let us consider what the STD in Figure 3.24 would have looked like if the DFD had not been levelled (Figure 3.30). As the

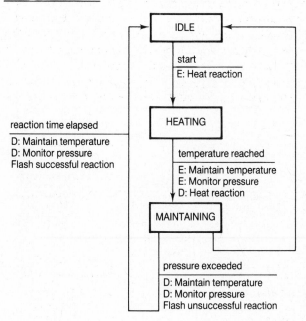

STD 1 Control reaction

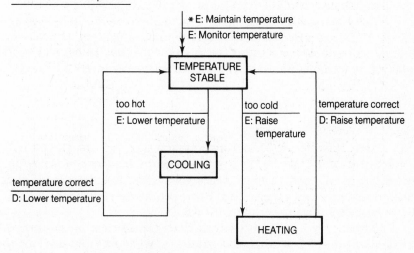

STD 2.3 Control temperature

Figure 3.30 Unlevelled control reaction STD.

Unlevelled STD

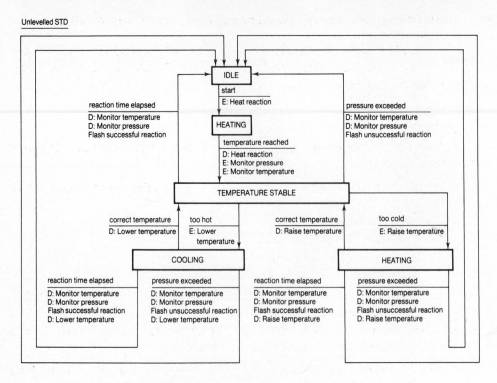

Figure 3.30   (*continued*)

STD and the DFD are so closely related, you will normally find that if the DFD is well partitioned, the STD will automatically be well partitioned.

Partitioning effort is normally concentrated on the DFD, as many people find the DFD easier to manipulate, and joining or splitting of STDs will often be done in response to splitting or joining of functionality within the DFD. However, in levelling the DFD, you are automatically levelling the STD as well.

3.5 SUMMARY

That is all you need to know about STDs. Like the DFD, there is only so much you can do with an STD — it shows the sequence of behaviour within the system, and how various pieces of system functionality (i.e. the data transformations) will be controlled. However, it completely ignores any aspects of system behaviour concerned with data.

Although you can tell what the data transformations in the system are by examining the STD actions, you cannot see what data they use, and therefore how they will do their jobs. You also cannot see how the various data transformations may be connected to each other via data. To see this you need

a DFD. The STD also contains nothing about the system information model —
this requires an ERD.

In conclusion, the STD is very good for showing sequence and control,
but it is not enough to specify the whole system. For all aspects of the system
to be described it is important to use the DFD and ERD as well.

3.6 EXERCISES

1.   Turn the STD in Figure 3.31 into a single control process and integrate it
with the given DFD.

2.   The DFD and corresponding STDs in Figure 3.32 describe a system which
must:

(a) control an experiment;
(b) allow an operator to
     (i) view the status of the current experiment,
     (ii) analyze the results of previous experiments,
     (iii) change the parameters under which the experiment is performed.

Once you have looked at the diagrams and understood what the system is
supposed to do, try to combine the two STDs for controlling the experiment and
controlling the operator functions into a single STD.

3.   This exercise carries on from Exercise 2, which should yield a single STD
for control of the whole DFD given in the exercise description. Try to split this
STD into another pair of STDs, with the following responsibilities:

(a) controlling experiment: control change of experiment parameters, and
    control display of experiment (i.e. all the things to do with the current
    experiment);
(b) controlling analysis of experiment results.

4.   The STD in Figure 3.33, which is meant to be controlling the lift system
described in the corresponding DFD contains a number of errors. Spot what they
are, and correct them.

5.   Turn the following textual description of the sequence of operation of a
washing machine into an STD.

The washing machine has two programs, a wool wash and a cotton wash.
The operator selects whether a wool wash or a cotton wash is required.

A wool wash cycle consists of a cool wash, followed by a gentle five
minute spin.

The cotton wash cycle consists of a warm wash, followed by a gentle
five minute spin.

6.   The DFD in Figure 3.34 shows the functionality required in a certain vending
machine system. A customer using the vending machine can choose between tea
and coffee.

The vending machine will accept the customer's money, via 'accept payment', and will then check whether the correct payment has been made, using either 'check payment for tea' or 'check payment for coffee'.

If the customer has made the correct payment, the appropriate drink will be dispensed, using either 'dispense tea' or 'dispense coffee'.

If the customer has not made the correct payment, any money received

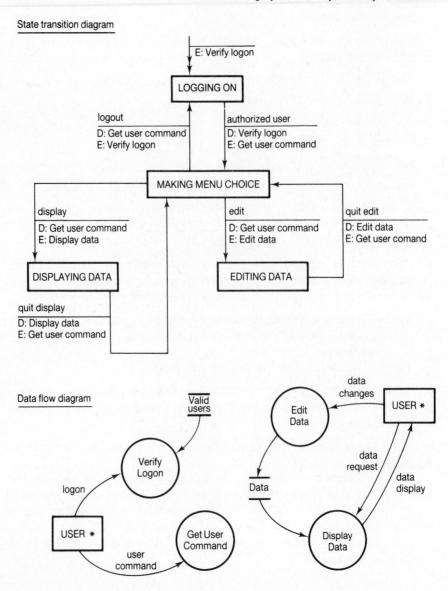

Figure 3.31   Exercise 1.

will be refunded, via 'refund money'. The customer will have to reselect the appropriate beverage, if he wishes to try again.

A control process has been added to the DFD, but only the incoming event flows have been shown. It will be good practice to work out whether a particular

Data flow diagram for experimentation system

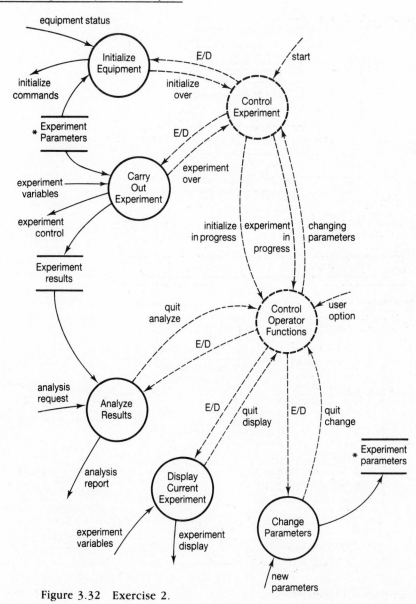

Figure 3.32   Exercise 2.

State transition diagram for control experiment

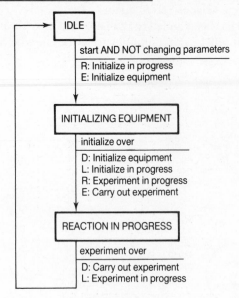

State transition diagram for control operator functions

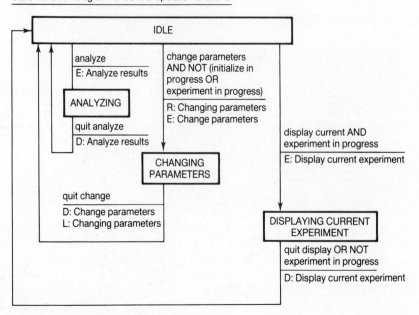

Figure 3.32 (*continued*)

State transition diagram for lift control system

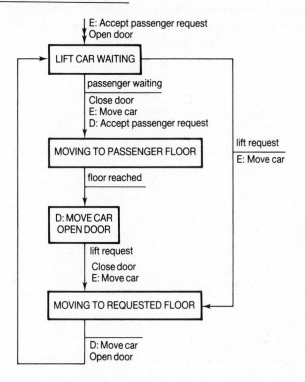

Data flow diagram for lift control system

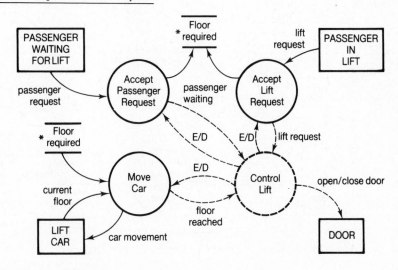

Figure 3.33 Exercise 4.

data transformation should be 'triggered' or 'enabled/disabled'. Once you have added the triggers and enable/disables between the control process and the data transformations, construct the STD which will describe the control sequence inside the control process.

7. A fan heater is to be built, consisting of a fan and a heating element. Many fan heaters are used not just to heat rooms, but also to cool rooms, by having the fan switched on without the heating element.

The fan heater will have three settings:

(a) Off.
(b) Heat — if the operator chooses to heat, the heating element is switched on first. Once it has reached a certain temperature, the fan will be switched on (we do not want to blow cold air into the room). If the heating element falls below the required temperature, the fan will be switched off until the heating element has regained the correct temperature.
(c) Cool — if the operator chooses to cool, only the fan will be switched on.

Build a pair of STDs to model this system, one controlling the fan and one controlling the heating element.

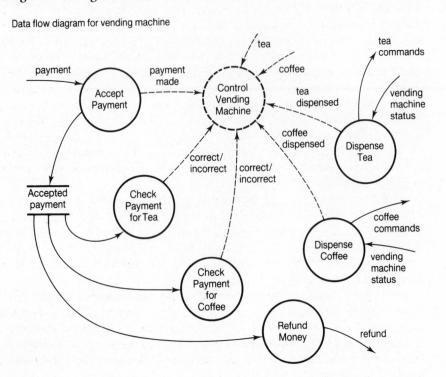

Figure 3.34   Exercise 6.

CHAPTER FOUR

Entity relationship diagrams

4.1 INTRODUCTION

A lot of real-time engineers have problems with entity relationship diagrams (ERDs), even though they are actually very simple diagrams. They do not show anything about how the system is going to work, just a simple mapping of all the information (data) in the system. Or in more real-world terms, a map of all the things in the system with which you are going to deal.

The ERD is a passive diagram, which means that it does not have a flow through it. The DFD has a flow of data moving through it, and the STD has a flow of control moving through it. These flows can help you to think not just about what the system is there for, but also how it is meant to work. For example, with the DFD, you can follow a flow from terminator input through the system, noticing the various transformations being applied to it, until it leaves the system. You can imagine animating the diagrams to understand what the system does. An ERD has no flow through it — which means you cannot start at one end of the ERD and move through it passing along the flows/transitions, like you would in a DFD/STD, and imagine what is going on.

Every box (object) in the ERD tells you about something or somebody in your system, each diamond (relationship) tells you about some connection there might be between these objects.

The essential ERD is not a map of the data storage within the system. Objects/boxes in the essential ERD do not represent data storage areas or data constructs, such as arrays or records, but the real-world things that these physical storage areas hold information about. Essential relationships do not represent the physical pointers between data storage areas, but real-world associations between things taking part in your system.

Purely because the ERD is so simple, and shows so little that can be interpreted in 'programming terms', people try to read more into it than is actually there, which can cause problems. Engineers try to show how the data is collected and stored. However, this diagram is not there to show this, but how real-world entities are connected by real-world relationships within the system, i.e. in real-world terms what the system is about.

Real-time engineers often ask what the ERD is for. Traditionally, in a real-time environment you are not that interested in the data, and a model which just shows the system data will not help very much in building the program, so why bother? The diagram is there for two reasons.

Firstly, you must not neglect data. Even in real-time systems, many problems can be caused by data not being organized in a sensible way and not being protected properly. Most programmers have experienced problems caused by a variable being corrupted, resulting in it not having the value they expected by the time it was needed. If data is organized and protected properly, the risks of corruption and misunderstanding are reduced. Certainly if you are going to build a database later on, you will need an ERD so that you can map the information in order to understand what it all is and how it connects together. The ERD helps during design when you build the physical data model within your system.

Secondly, the ERD is a very user friendly model because it does not show anything about how the developer thinks he is going to build the system.

As the ERD does not have very much to do with the code that is produced at the end of the development, but more with the data organization, it is difficult to embed implementation details in the diagrams. In contrast, it is often difficult not to embed implementation details in the DFD and STD. Since the ERD contains no implementation detail, it is a very easy diagram for the customer to understand. The developer will also often find it the easiest diagram to understand initially, especially if he has little idea what the system is about. In the past I have been presented with STDs and DFDs that have been fairly heavily implementation-biased and I have not been able to understand the fundamental purpose of the system until I have seen the ERD.

In a lot of commercial systems the ERD is the first diagram to be built, even before the analysis is started. It is easy to build without considering the implementation, so you can begin to understand the system before you start thinking in terms of how you will develop it.

So far we have two good reasons for building an ERD; however, your system may not require an ERD. Many real-time systems have a very large volume of data, but the data is not very complex. As the ERD is more concerned with the complexity of the information that may be stored, it may only have a few components on it. A diagram which is so small and holds so little information is not going to help you very much.

On the other hand, do not ignore the ERD just because you are building a real-time system — consider it, and only once you have decided that it is not really needed it should you ignore it.

Although in the essential model, the ERD does not show the data which is physically stored, it does model the things we want to store data about. As we already have data stores on the DFD, much of the information that you show on the ERD is actually already shown on the DFD. You can almost think of the DFD as the implementation of the ERD — the ERD shows the things you would like to store data about, which are stored in DFD data stores.

The ERD relationships represent connections between pieces of data in a system. These are what the data transformations use to do their jobs; for example, a data transformation which sends invoices to customers may use a relationship between customers and their addresses.

If all the information in the ERD is held in the DFD, why do we need a separate ERD? There is a lot of other information on the DFD that you do not need to know about to understand the data: for a start, all the control processes and event flows, which have nothing to do with the data in the system, but define how the system control should work. As far as the information model goes, these are spurious. Also, even though relationships are used inside data transformations, you do a lot of other things inside the data transformations as well. It is often fairly difficult to know the relationship that is being used just by looking at the data transformation name.

If all you are interested in is the actual data being used in the system, the DFD is not a very good way of representing it. We need another diagram where we can see just the data.

We have talked quite a lot in previous chapters about diagram refinement to ensure diagrams are as understandable as possible. When we refine the DFD, we aim to understand the functionality, not to make sure that the data is organized in a sensible way. We need another diagram that can be used to help refine the data — to make sure that we understand the information in the system, and that it is organized in a sensible way.

Although the ERD is not a traditional real-time tool, there are many good reasons why you might need to use it in the development of your system. There are an increasing number of real-time systems which use complex data structures, such as air traffic control systems, and the use of ERDs in this type of system is imperative. Also, a lot of expansion and upgrading in real-time systems tends to be in the area of user facilities, such as report production. If we consider the 'teabag boxing system', expansion is more likely to involve increased sophistication of the operator and management interfaces to provide useful reporting facilities, than changes to the actual teabag system control. As the generation of reports will probably involve complicated data manipulation, using ERDs early on would have helped set up the data properly from the start.

4.2 ENTITY RELATIONSHIP DIAGRAM COMPONENTS

4.2.1 Basic notation

Firstly, we will look at the symbols and terminology used within the ERD, using the ERD in Figure 4.1. A rectangular box represents an object. This is something in the system that you are interested in, and want to store information about — it represents a real-world entity within your system. Imagine that inside the object there is a table, where we store all the information we need about the

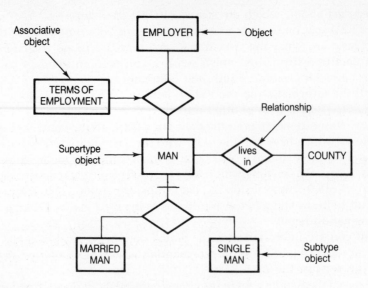

Figure 4.1   ERD example.

object. For the 'man' object in Figure 4.1, let us say we want to store the man's name, the man's age and the man's salary. These pieces of information become column headings in Table 4.1 and are known as the attributes or the data elements of the man. Every time we introduce a new man to the system, we create a row of information about him in the table. The rows are called occurrences of the object.

The subtype/supertype relationship is drawn on the diagram as an unnamed relationship (the diamond indicates a relationship), on which one of the object connections is crossed by a bar — this indicates the supertype object. In Figure 4.1 we have an overall class 'man', which can be broken down into 'married man' and 'single man'. Information which describes man in general (whether he is married or single) is kept in the supertype table, and the information which describes the particular type of man is kept in the subtype table. This information will be different depending on whether it is describing a married, or a single man. Every time we need information about a particular man, we collect a row of information from the supertype ('man') and a row of information from

Table 4.1

Name	Age	Salary
John	50	30 000
Paul	45	28 000
Ian	22	10 000

Table 4.2

Man	County
John	Kent
Paul	Surrey
Ian	Essex

one of the subtypes. That will give a complete set of information about the man.

The relationship tells us about a mapping between two or more objects in our system. Normally the relationship diamond will hold a name that describes the association between the objects which it connects.

Imagine that the relationship holds a table which shows the mapping between the objects which the relationship connects. In this example we define a relationship between the man and the county he lives in, i.e. which man lives in which county (Table 4.2).

An associative object is an object which describes a relationship, and can be thought of as a combined object and relationship. Here the relationship is absorbed into the associative object, and so the name is removed from the relationship diamond on the diagram — you should be able to tell the name of the relationship by looking at the associative object that describes it. The associative object can be identified by the arrow pointing from the object to the relationship which it is describing. 'Normal' objects connected by a relationship do not point at the relationship. If we imagine the associative object in terms of a table, we have the relationship table (which has moved out of the relationship into the associative object), followed by any information that we want to store about the relationship. In the example we define 'terms of employment' by Table 4.3; the first two columns tell us who works for whom, i.e. the 'works for' relationship. Subsequent columns tell us payroll number and number of years' service, i.e information about the working relationship.

The ERD gives the information model for the system in real-world terms — it is making a statement about what there is in the system, and the way in which these things are connected. We should be able to read these facts straight from the ERD: each set of connected components on the ERD will make one

Table 4.3

Employer	Man	Payroll number	Years' service
ABC Ltd	John	100015	25
DEF Inc.	Paul	100145	15
ABC Ltd	Ian	101065	2

statement about the system. Let us assume we are building some kind of census system, perhaps with a view to targeting people for market research. The ERD in Figure 4.1 makes the following statements:

1. A certain man lives in a certain county.
2. A man can either be married or single.
3. A man has an association with his employer which is described by his terms of employment.

The tables which we have been imagining up until this point are not part of the ERD, and will not show up on the diagram, however, they will be held in the textual support to the model.

4.2.2 Objects

An object is anything in the system which you are interested in and want to store information about. For something to be an object within your system, the following must apply:

1. It must have a name.
2. There must be information that you want to store about it.
3. It must play a functional part in your system.
4. Occurrences of the same object must be uniquely identified.

Let us consider these four characteristics in a little more detail:

1. The object's name should describe its role in the system. You do not always call an object by what it physically is — you call it by what it is doing in the system, which will tend to make the object easier to understand. We apply the same principles here as with DFD terminators, when we called the terminator 'printer', rather than 'Mannesman Tally', to ensure everyone could understand what the Mannesman Tally was there for.

    However, we can take the idea further. A single real-world thing can play more than one role in the same system. For example, a physical 'terminal' could play the roles 'programmer interface' and 'system manager interface'. The ERD will be more meaningful if we describe the role of the object. In considering a system, you are more interested in what things do with respect to that system, than what they do in general terms.

2. We need to be able to describe the object by a set of data element or attribute values — those are the column headings in our table. If the object has no attributes, there is no information that we want to store about it.

3. You do not want to store lots of information about objects which are nothing to do with your system. In a stock control system, there is little point in having an object which describes a man's wife — because we

are not interested in the man's wife. Even if we were interested in the fact that he was married, we could hold his wife's name as a column in his table, rather than as an object in her own right.

4. Occurrences of the object must be uniquely identifiable. Each row in the object 'table' gives a set of information about a particular instance of that object. For instance, the man object table holds many rows of information about men.

At some stage we may want to use information held in the object table — but if we have no way of telling one row from another, it will be very difficult for us to access specific information. If we consider the 'man' object shown in Figure 4.1, the man's name allows us to pull out a row of information about a particular man. If another man with the same name were to join our system, we would have to extend the table, perhaps to include the man's surname, so that men could still be differentiated.

As we have discussed, there are four different types of object:

1. Object.
2. Subtype object.
3. Supertype object.
4. Associative object.

However, even though there are different types of object, fundamentally all objects are the same. In the ERD an object can behave as one type of object in one relationship, and as another type of object in another relationship.

In Figure 4.2 the association between the man and his employer is described by the associative object 'terms of employment'. This associative object then becomes the supertype of the two subtype objects 'full-time contract' and 'part-time contract'.

We have discussed the fact that the DFD shows how and where we will

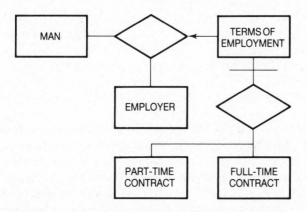

Figure 4.2 Associative subtype/supertype objects.

store the information shown on the ERD. The ERD object is directly equivalent to the DFD data store, and ERD relationships will be created and used within data transformations.

Occasionally in the essential model, an object at the edge of the ERD may represent a terminator. Although you may not want to store information about the terminator, it can help you understand the diagram if you see the real-world things which are providing or using information. As you may not want to store information about these things, they may be removed from the ERD in the implementation stages, when the ERD models the way in which the data is physically stored within the system.

This connection means that the DFD can be used to help build the ERD, or if you build the ERD first, the ERD can be used to help build the DFD.

Figure 4.3 shows segments of ERD and DFD describing the same system. There is a convention that although the DFD store and the ERD object are equivalent, the store is given a plural name, while the object is given a singular name.

Effectively, the ERD object represents the real-world thing which plays a role in the system, whereas the DFD store is the place where we actually hold information about occurrences of that object (e.g. the 'tables' of information).

4.2.2.1 *Subtype/supertype object*

Imagine an object 'employee', with attributes 'name' and 'payroll number'. If we decide to store the type of the employee's company car, we put an extra column on the employee table and give the car's type as an attribute of the employee. Some employees have company cars and some do not, so there

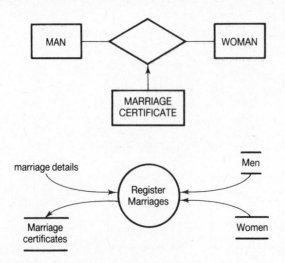

Figure 4.3   ERD/DFD connection.

will be some employees for which there is no entry under the company car column.

We do not want to imply that these employees are not really employees because they do not have all the attributes of an employee. We actually have two different types of employee — those who have company cars and those who do not. This is the kind of circumstance where we need to introduce subtype objects, as shown by Figure 4.4. The object connected to the relationship via the bar is the supertype, and the other objects are the subtypes. We show that all of the subtypes are types of supertypes.

It does not matter which way up you draw the diagram — the supertype does not have to be at the top, as long as it is next to the bar. You should consider the orientation of the diagram which will be the easiest to understand, bearing in mind that the 'employee' supertype object may be connected to a number of other objects via different relationships.

In Figure 4.4, project managers, team leaders and software engineers are all types of employee. This means that all of these types of employee have certain attributes in common, e.g. payroll number, salary, but they also have particular attributes which they do not share with the other types of employee. For example, project managers and team leaders may have company cars, which software engineers do not have. Project managers may have reserved parking spaces, which team leaders and software engineers do not have.

You can see from this example that some of the particular attributes can be shared between the different subtypes. For example, team leaders and project

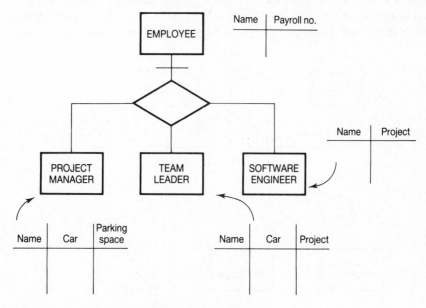

Figure 4.4   Subtype/supertype object of employee.

managers have company cars, but because the project managers also have a reserved parking space, they become a different object.

If we were to give company cars to software engineers as well, the software engineers would have the same attributes as the team leaders. This would mean two changes to the ERD:

1. As every employee now has a company car, 'car' now becomes an attribute of employee — this would not show up on the ERD, but it would appear in the diagram textual support.
2. As there is now no difference between the team leader and the software engineer, they need not be different subtypes — we could call the combined subtype 'worker'.

In summary, a supertype object represents a set of objects which have many attributes in common, but other attributes which only some of the objects have — these allow us to break down into the subtypes.

A relationship with the supertype implies a relationship with any of the subtypes. For example, as all employees earn wages, the relationship 'earns' would be between the supertype object 'employee' and the object 'wages'. Relationships with the individual subtypes are shown only if the relationship is specific to particular subtypes.

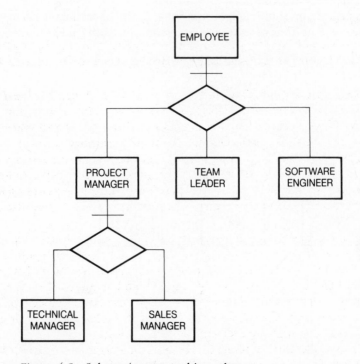

Figure 4.5   Subtype/supertype hierarchy.

Finally, a subtype object can also be a supertype object, as shown in Figure 4.5, where the subtype 'project manager' is also the supertype of 'technical manager' and 'sales manager'.

Before we leave subtype/supertype objects, let us examine two common mistakes made with them. Figure 4.6(b) shows what is often seen as an alternative to part of Figure 4.6(a), i.e. a relationship between project managers, team leaders and monthly wages, but the two diagrams are not equivalent.

Figure 4.6(a) shows a relationship between a project manager and his monthly wage, and a relationship between a team leader and his monthly wage. Figure 4.6(b) shows a three-way relationship between a project manager, a team leader and a monthly wage. If you think about this in terms of the relationship table, we have two employees matched to the same wages information.

ERD subtype/supertype relationships are also mistakenly used to show data decomposition. Imagine an ERD with supertype 'cup of tea' and subtypes 'tea', 'milk' and 'sugar'. The authors of this ERD may have thought they had said 'a cup of tea is made up of tea-leaves, milk and sugar'; what they have actually said is 'milk is a type of cup of tea, sugar is a type of cup of tea and tea-leaves is a type of cup of tea'. They have tried to use the subtype/supertype construction to show the data composition. Data compositions will be held in the model textual support, not shown on the ERD.

4.2.2.2 *Associative object*

The only place where you can store information in an ERD is inside an object. A relationship can only hold the mapping between the objects that it connects.

We can identify the relationship 'is married' between the 'man' and 'woman' objects, which holds the mapping describing which man is married to which woman. If we decide to store information about when and where they were married, we must find somewhere to put this information.

As previously stated, we cannot store information in a relationship. Also, we can only put information into an object that describes that object. Where he was married does not really describe the man (his name, age and salary would describe him) or the woman — the information is really describing the relationship.

The information must be stored in an object, which leads to a special object called an associative object, combining the relationship together with information to be stored about it. An associative object is a cross between a relationship and an object. Once created, the associative object takes over from the relationship — the first attribute columns in the associative object show the mapping between the objects which participate in this relationship, subsequent columns hold other information about the relationship.

Figure 4.7 shows the associative object 'marriage certificate'. As the associative object takes over from the relationship itself, we take the name out

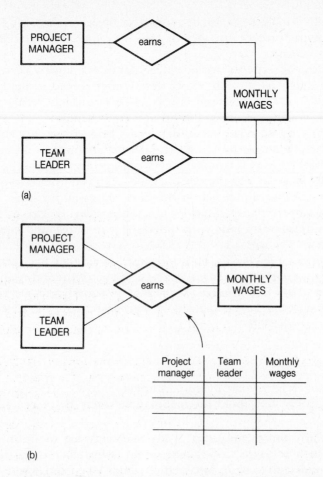

Figure 4.6 (a) Two two-way relationships; (b) Three-way relationship.

of the relationship on the diagram. Relationships described by associative objects do not have explicit names — you should be able to tell what the relationship is from the name of the associative object.

Diagrammatically, you can tell something is an associative object, rather than an object which takes part in the relationship, because the associative object points at the relationship which it is describing.

As with the subtype/supertype object symbol, the orientation of the associative object with respect to the relationship is unimportant, as long as there is an arrow coming from the associative object towards the relationship.

4.2.3 The relationship

A relationship is shown on the ERD as a named diamond connecting objects. The relationship tells us about some kind of association or mapping

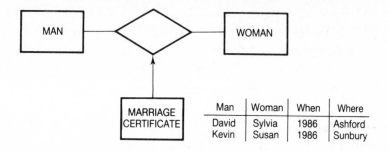

Figure 4.7   The associative object.

between objects in the system. The relationship must have a name which describes this association — if you do not give the relationship a name, you will not know how the objects are connected together.

The same objects can be connected by different types of relationship. For example, a man can be married to a woman, a man can work for a woman, a man can sit next to a woman. Diagrammatically, the 'man' and 'woman' objects will be connected by three diamonds, named 'is married', 'works for' and 'sits next to'. If we do not give the relationship a name, we do not know which of these relationships we are talking about.

Just because an object is connected by a relationship, does not mean that every occurrence of that object takes part in that relationship. For example, the 'man is married to woman' relationship defines that a man can be married to a woman — not that all the men in the system are married. The relationship shows a possible association, which may not have happened yet, and may never happen for some occurrences of the object.

So far, we have considered relationships between just two objects. As long as they are good real-world relationships, you can have relationships between many different objects. Consider the family relationship shown in Figure 4.8. In a family you can have a mother related to a father related to an aunt, related to a cousin, related to a grannie — all these objects are taking part in the same 'family' relationship.

In the binary marriage relationship a two column table held the mapping between the man and the woman. For the family relationship we have a table with one column for each object connected by the relationship.

In the real world, something can take part in different occurrences of the relationship as a different object. In one row of this table I might take part as an aunt — in another row I might take part as a cousin.

A relationship must have at least two connections to objects, however, they can be the same object. Figure 4.9 defines that a person works for another person. When constructing relationships, remember that the relationship only represents the mapping between the objects that it connects. For example, the married relationship only represents a man being married to a woman. This means

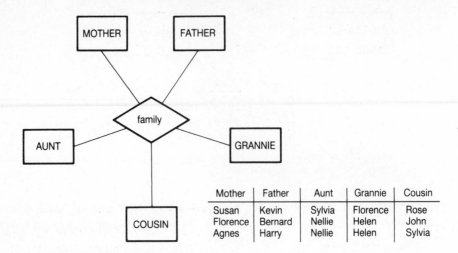

Mother	Father	Aunt	Grannie	Cousin
Susan	Kevin	Sylvia	Florence	Rose
Florence	Bernard	Nellie	Helen	John
Agnes	Harry	Nellie	Helen	Sylvia

Figure 4.8   The family relationship.

in the relationship table, we can only hold which man is married to which woman. Any other information, such as when they were married and where they were married, must be inside an object.

This is why we need the associative object — the special object which describes a relationship, discussed in Section 4.2.2.2.

Finally, if you think it will add to the meaning of the diagram, you can add the numerics of the relationship to the ERD, shown by Figure 4.10. The circle around one of each pair of numbers is called the anchor point. It shows the direction in which we read the relationship for that particular set of numbers — you always read the anchor point end first. Showing the anchor point is important, as there can be numeric relationships which are different depending on which way round you look at them. Figure 4.10 shows that one mother can have a number of children, but one child can only have one (biological) mother.

These numbers are probably more relevant in the implementation phases, when considering efficient data storage in terms of space and access times. In the essential phases they may not be important or helpful. If you do not find them useful in the essential model, it is probably better to leave them out.

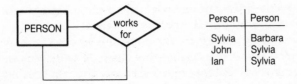

Person	Person
Sylvia	Barbara
John	Sylvia
Ian	Sylvia

Figure 4.9   Single object relationship.

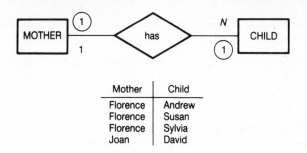

Mother	Child
Florence	Andrew
Florence	Susan
Florence	Sylvia
Joan	David

Figure 4.10   Different numeric relationships.

4.3 BUILDING AN ENTITY RELATIONSHIP DIAGRAM

When you build an ERD, you are really listening to or reading your customer's specification, and highlighting all the important things.

Quite often during specification, a customer tells you all sorts of information that you do not need to know. This may be to bulk out their specification, because they do not know what you want to know, or because in their own mind they have not really got their requirements sorted out. You have to get rid of all the information in the description that is not applicable, and concentrate on the bits that are important with respect to the customer's system. To do this, you must have a good idea of your customer's requirements.

Figure 4.11 shows two ERDs which could have been generated from the following textual specification:

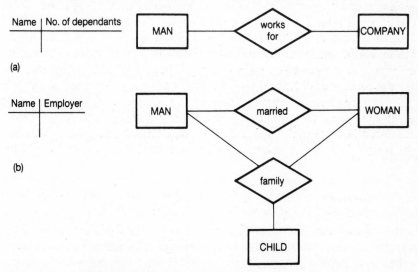

Figure 4.11   Different ERDs from the same specification (a) payroll system;
(b) census system.

A man works for a certain company. The man is married and has a number of children.

The description tells us about the 'man' object and a number of relationships that he is involved in.

In the first ERD, shown in Figure 4.11(a), we are building a payroll system. Here, although we are interested in the man's wife and children, it is only as dependants of the man — we need to know how many dependants the man has. As we do not store any information about the man's wife and children, they do not become objects in the ERD, but are stored in the 'number of dependants' attribute of the man.

In the second ERD, shown in Figure 4.11(b), we are building a census system. Here, we are equally interested in the man, his wife and his children and want to store information about all of them — so they all become objects in the ERD. On the other hand, all we need to know about the man's employment is where he works; this can be held in the 'employer' attribute of the man object.

This shows that although it is very easy to build an ERD, it is sometimes very difficult to get it right. You can start with a description, pull out all the wrong bits of information and still end up with an ERD which looks like it makes sense, but does not reflect the system that the customer thought had been explained to you.

You need a fair understanding of the customer's requirement to build the ERD, which is the reason why the ERD is built. The customer has to be sure that you understand the same system that he does — the ERD is a way of doing that. It shows you in fairly specific (but user friendly) terms which information from his description is important to his system — it gets right to the heart of the problem.

4.3.1 Building the ERD from narrative description

Let us look at how you can build an ERD on the basis of a piece of text. The ERD is dependent on the textual information taken in the context of a particular system. As well as a textual or narrative description of the system, you also need to bear in mind the underlying purpose of the system.

The customer provides us with the following piece of system specification:

Our company makes fresh milk and longlife milk. The milk is stored in a warehouse. When the main warehouse is full, it is stored in the overflow warehouse.

Further discussions with our customer reveal that fresh milk comes in cartons of 1, 2 or 4 pints, whilst longlife milk only comes in 1 litre cartons. Our customer wishes us to build a system for retrieval of milk from the warehouse on receipt of his customer orders. Our customer is very keen that the oldest milk be distributed first.

The first thing we do with this text is pick out all the nouns — these will be potential objects within our system. We then examine all these nouns in the context of our particular system to find out what relevance each noun has to our ERD. Nouns are only potential objects — it might be that information which the customer has provided in the text is irrelevant to our system. If the noun does turn out to be an object, what sort of an object will it be? It could be a supertype, a subtype, an associative object or just a plain object. The noun might be a piece of information that you want to store, but it might not be an object in its own right, it could just be an attribute of another object in the system.

On the basis of the original piece of text, I have been able to identify the following nouns/potential objects:

1. Company.
2. Fresh milk.
3. Longlife milk.
4. Milk.
5. Warehouse.
6. Main warehouse.
7. Overflow warehouse.

Let us examine each of these nouns in turn, and decide what relevance it has to our system, and therefore our ERD.

1. Company: in building our system, the company is irrelevant. This is the customer for whom the system is being built, not something that plays a functional role in the system.
2. Milk: this is obviously very important to our system. We will probably want to store quite a lot of information about milk, such as the expiry date, the quantity in stock, the farm which produced the milk.

    We should be able to use the farm and the expiry date to give us a unique identification on a particular batch of milk.

    Therefore milk will be an object in our system.
3. Fresh milk and
4. Longlife milk: these will be subtypes of milk, as they will have slightly different attributes. For longlife milk we will have one attribute 'quantity of 1 litre cartons'; for fresh milk, we will have three attributes 'quantity of 1 pint cartons', 'quantity of 2 pint cartons', 'quantity of 4 pint cartons'.
5. Warehouse: this is fairly important in our system, and we may want to store information about it, such as the temperature, the humidity and light levels.

    Therefore warehouse will be an object in our system.
6. Main warehouse and
7. Overflow warehouse: the only difference between the main warehouse and the overflow warehouse is that they are physically two different buildings; however, they appear to have all the same attributes and

therefore they will not become subtypes of warehouse. There will be an attribute of warehouse 'location' where we can indicate whether the information refers to the main warehouse or the overflow warehouse.

Once we have decided on the ERD objects, we can sometimes find verbs in the text which link those objects together — these can be used to name the relationships in the ERD. On the basis of this we can produce the ERD shown in Figure 4.12. Remember this ERD is for the particular system which we had in mind. Further discussions with our customer after production of the initial ERD may reveal misunderstandings, which may cause modification of the ERD. For example, our customer may reveal that although fresh milk and longlife milk arrive at the ultimate consumer in different-sized cartons, in the warehouse they are both stored in 10 gallon tanks. In this case they have the same attributes and can both be described by the milk object, with an attribute which holds whether the milk is fresh or longlife.

Also, we learn that main warehouses normally have slightly different characteristics from overflow warehouses. As the overflow warehouses are seldom used to any extent, the temperature and humidity control in overflow warehouses tend to be far less sensitive, and therefore we keep less information about them. In this case we would make main and overflow warehouses subtypes of the warehouse object.

Notice that if we take the information inside the object and relationship tables into account, as well as the ERD itself, both original and modified ERDs hold much of the same information — it is just that in each diagram different aspects have been emphazised to show what is important in that particular system.

4.3.2 Building the ERD from the DFD

In Section 4.2.2 we discussed the relationship between the DFD and the ERD, namely that ERD objects are equivalent to DFD data stores and terminators,

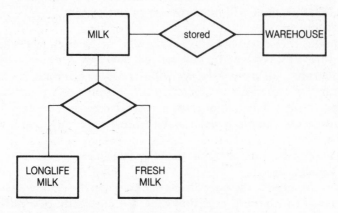

Figure 4.12   Milk warehousing system ERD.

ERD relationships are used by DFD data transformations to fulfil their purpose.

Given that this relationship exists, we should be able to construct the system ERD from an existing DFD fairly easily. Let us take as an example the DFD from our teabag boxing system, shown by Figure 4.13. Initially, we construct objects from the data stores and those terminators involved in either the production or the use of stored data within the system. Terminators which are not involved in the production or use of stored data will not appear as objects in the ERD. If they have no connection with the stored data in the DFD, there will be no relationships for them to be connected to on the ERD.

This will give us the following list of objects:

1. Operator.
2. Scales.
3. Required teabag weight.
4. Teabag count.
5. Teabag statistics.

The next step is to construct relationships between those objects which are linked by data transformations. This is not as easy as coming up with the objects themselves, as it involves examining the inner work of the data transformation (held in the model's textual support) to see how the objects are associated. Figure 4.14 shows the resulting ERD.

If the ERD is correct, we should be able to 'read' the statements which it is making.

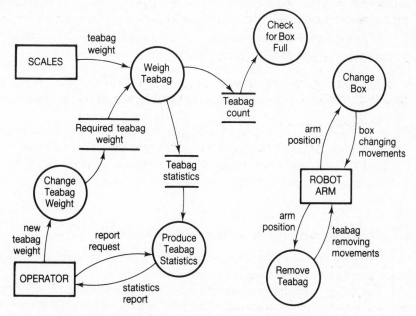

Figure 4.13 Teabag boxing system DFD.

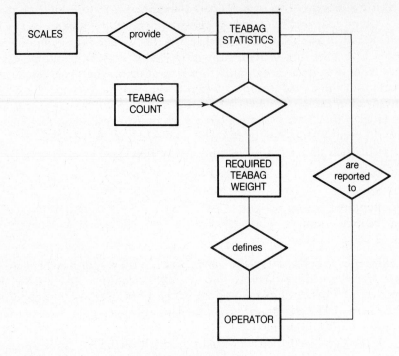

Figure 4.14 Teabag boxing system ERD.

1. 'Scales provide teabag statistics': The teabag weight is stored away in teabag statistics via 'weigh teabag'.
2. 'Teabag statistics are reported to the operator': via 'produce teabag statistics'
3. 'The operator defines the required teabag weight': via 'change teabag weight'.
4. 'The teabag count depends on the relationship between teabag statistics and required teabag weight': As 'teabag statistics' represents the 'teabag weight', 'teabag count' depends on the match between this weight and the required teabag weight, carried out by 'weigh teabag'.

4.4 Checking an entity relationship diagram

Having built the ERD, we must now check it. As there are only two basic symbols, there are not that many syntactic rules.

The ERD, especially at the essential modelling stage, is very much a semantic diagram, and so most of the checking will be concerned with ensuring that the ERD emphasizes the right aspects of your customer's system.

4.4.1 Checking for syntactic correctness

We will examine the checks that must be applied to the individual objects and relationships on the ERD, followed by the rules governing the connection of symbols.

4.4.1.1 *Object rules*

1. Any object on the ERD must have the four characteristics discussed in Section 4.2.2:
   (a) a name;
   (b) a unique identification for different occurrences of the object;
   (c) a functional role in the system;
   (d) attributes.
2. Any object symbol on the ERD must be named.

4.4.1.2 *Subtype/supertype object rules*

1. The attributes of the supertype object must be common to *all* the subtype objects.
2. All of the subtype objects must be different types of their supertype object — remember we are not showing a data decomposition.
3. (a) The bar sits between the relationship diamond and the supertype. In a single subtype/supertype construction, there will only be one supertype, but as many subtypes as are necessary.
3. (b) The subtype/supertype relationship diamond will not be named, as it is always describing the same (subtype/supertype) relationship.
4. The subtype/supertype relationship cannot be described by an associative object. The associative object gives extra information which describes the relationship, which in this case makes no sense.

4.4.1.3 *Associative object rules*

1. Any relationship which is described by an associative object need not be named, as the associative object should describe the relationship.

4.4.1.4 *Relationship rules*

1. Any relationship symbol on the ERD must be named (except the subtype/supertpe relationship, or a relationship which is described by an associative object).
2. The relationship symbol can only hold the relationship itself. Information about the relationship must be held in an associative object, which will also hold the relationship.

4.4.1.5 *Connection rules*

1. A relationship cannot be connected directly to another relationship, except via an object.
2. A relationship must have at least two connections to objects (although both connections can be to the same object).
3. An object cannot be connected to another object, except via a relationship. If we do not have the relationship diamond, we have nowhere to write the name of the relationship — so we do not know what the relationship is.

4.4.2 Checking for coherence

As previously discussed, it should not be that difficult to build an ERD which is easy to understand — it is very difficult to build implementation detail into the ERD inadvertently.

The same basic principles for clarity apply as with the DFD and STD, i.e. naming and partitioning the diagram carefully. When naming objects and relationships on the ERD, use terms from the system's subject matter. This should make your diagram easy to read and understand. If you use the same words on the ERD as the customer has used, either in his textual specification or when he spoke to you, you will both be speaking the same language.

Also, use the role of the object with respect to the particular system that you are describing, rather than the object's physical name. The role will tend to give far more information than the real-world thing's name. As a rough guideline, objects will normally have noun names, i.e. they represents things; relationships will often have verb names, i.e. they represent something that has or will happen.

Partitioning in the ERD describes how we split the information we want to store between the objects within our system. In the essential model, objects should reflect real-world entities, while relationships reflect some kind of contact or happening between those real-world things. The ERD is not supposed to be representing how you will physically store the data. Once you get into the implementation stage, you may split or join the ERD objects such that each object represents a physical storage area, but initially forget how you will ultimately store the data.

If you are in doubt about something that you have drawn on the ERD, think about the imaginary table that lives inside the object/relationship. If the table cannot be constructed to hold the information you want to store, you have probably constructed the ERD wrongly.

Imagine an ERD with three objects, 'customer', 'telephone bill' and 'calls', all connected by a relationship. We have decided that one of them is an associative object, but which one? Initially we try to make 'calls' the associative object, as 'call' depends on the relationship between the 'customer' and the 'telephone bill'. This almost sounds right until you think about the information we want to store in the respective objects:

1. Calls: call ID, length of call, call distance.
2. Customer: customer ID, address.
3. Telephone bill: this is a list of calls that the customer has made, possibly with the dates that they were made.

If 'call' is the associative object, we would expect it to hold the relationship between a customer and the telephone bill — which it does not. In fact it is 'telephone bill' which holds the relationship between 'calls' and 'customer', so this should be the associative object.

4.5 SUMMARY

In summary, the ERD is a very useful diagram as it is difficult to embed implementation detail into it, so the system is shown in very user friendly terms.

However, if you understand the fundamental purpose of your system, have a customer who is happy to look at DFD, and you are building the type of real-time system which does not have a lot of data complexity, then you may not need an ERD.

The ERD will only help you understand the functionality of your system at a fairly high level, and does not give you the ability to describe the different levels of functionality that you have with the DFD.

Also, the ERD is showing *only* the data aspects of the system — it completely ignores any control or sequencing that may be required. To model aspects of control you will always need the STD.

Even in a real-time system, the ERD may prove useful; however, it probably will not be as much use to the developer as the DFD and STD.

4.6 EXERCISES

1. Read the following piece of narrative description, and try to decide which of the given ERDs in Figure 4.15 is the best representation of that information.

Florists create wedding bouquets from real or artificial flowers (although real and artificial flowers will not be mixed in a single bouquet). There is a standard set of shapes, sizes and prices for wedding bouquets. The price of artificial flowers will be set, whilst the price of real flowers will vary according to season. Also, some types of real flowers will only be available at certain times of the year.

In each of the following exercises, try to turn the given narrative text into an ERD.

2. Incoming radar signals are matched against known radar characteristics, giving rise to incoming radar reports. Radar reports will show the radar signal to be either friendly, unfriendly or unknown. For friendly and unfriendly radars, we store the position and the known type of the radar. For unknown radars, we store the position and characteristics of the radar signal.

3. All cars have a brake pedal and an accelerator pedal, which together control the speed of the car. The brake pedal controls the brakes, either disc or drum (these work very differently), which are used to stop the car's wheels from rotating. The accelerator pedal controls the accelerator, which is used in conjunction with the car gears to control the speed of the car wheels.

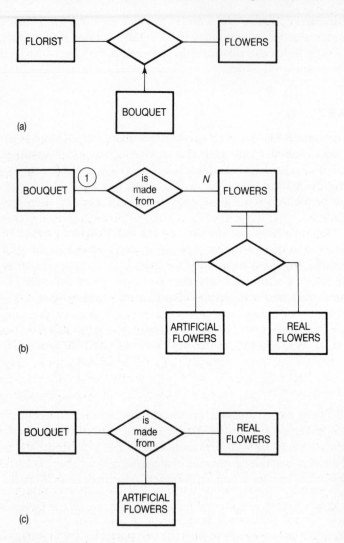

Figure 4.15 Exercise 1.

CHAPTER FIVE

Supporting textual specifications

5.1 INTRODUCTION

The textual specifications which support the diagrams are very important for two reasons. Firstly, they allow much of the checking needed to ensure model correctness and consistency. Secondly, they allow specification of low level detail not shown on the model diagrams.

So far, we have looked at all the diagrams in isolation. We now consider how the diagrams fit together and the various types of diagram support. The DFD shows the functionality of the system and is an active diagram with a flow of data moving through it. So we can see data items entering the system, and watch them passing through the various system functions and so understand what is happening in the system.

On a typical data flow diagram, such as Figure 5.1(a), there will be data transformations, data flows, data stores and possibly a control process. The diagram models not just functions (i.e. data transformations), but also some aspects of stored data (data stores), and some aspects of control (control process).

The state transition diagram shows sequencing or control in the system and is also an active diagram, this time with a flow of control. So, we can start in the initial state and follow the control through the diagram, imagining the system in animation.

There is a very close link between the STD and the DFD, which we have already discussed. The DFD control process is equivalent to the STD: input events to the control process are equivalent to conditions on the STD, output events from the control process are equivalent to actions on the STD. Given the data flow diagram in Figure 5.1(a), we know that the STD will have conditions and actions which correspond to the input and output event flows on the DFD control process. A possible STD for the DFD is shown in Figure 5.1(b).

As there is a strong link between the STD and the DFD, it is very important that an associated STD and control process say the same thing, otherwise they may describe different systems.

The entity relationship diagram describes the information model for the system. This is a passive diagram, i.e. there is no flow either of control or data

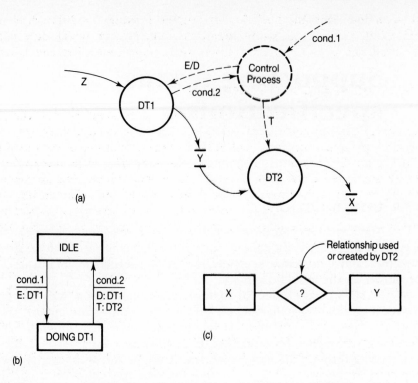

Figure 5.1 (a) Data flow diagram; (b) state transition diagrams; and (c) entity relationship diagram.

through it. You cannot start at one object and follow any kind of flow through the diagram to help you understand how the system should work. It is just a map showing all the important things in the system, which makes a number of statements about how those things interact.

There is a link between the ERD and the DFD, via the DFD data stores, which are equivalent to ERD objects. The DFD in Figure 5.1(a) implies two objects X and Y on the corresponding ERD. Also, as those objects/data stores are linked by DT2, there will probably be a relationship between them, which is either used or created by DT2. We may not be able to deduce the relationship from the name of DT2, as it may also be doing other things. The name of the relationship may only be gleaned from the internal specification for DT2.

We have a link between the DFD and the ERD, a link between the DFD and the STD, but no link between the STD and the ERD. The STD shows pure control, the ERD shows pure data, while the DFD shows aspects of control and data. We can therefore use the DFD to pull the model together, as it has areas of overlap with both of the other diagrams.

It is very important to check these areas of overlap and make sure that, in a given diagram hierarchy, we do not create overlapping, but inconsistent, diagrams. For example, if an STD waiting for a certain condition is associated with a DFD control process modelling the same system, which does not have that condition as an input event flow, then one of those diagrams is wrong.

5.2 THE PROJECT DICTIONARY

Many of the model consistency checks are done though the project dictionary. This is sometimes called the data dictionary, although, strictly speaking, the data dictionary will only hold the definitions of data used in the model, while the project dictionary holds a lot more. The project dictionary holds all the textual specifications for all of the components which make up your model, and can be seen as the firm foundation on which all the different diagrams sit.

Within every diagram, you should provide textual specifications for certain diagram components. However, where there is an overlap between diagram components (for example, the DFD data store and the ERD object), the combined component will only be described once within the project dictionary (the object specification will give a semantic description of the data, while the data store specification will give a more syntactic description of the data).

By specifying the information only once inside the project dictionary, we never have two different specifications for the same thing. The project dictionary is therefore very important in helping to provide a consistent model.

The project dictionary is also important for the specification of detail. The diagrams should only give an overview of the system. Without a corresponding textual specification, no detail can be specified. This will make checking the model very difficult, but more importantly it will make designing the system impossible. Imagine trying to check the conservation of data of a data transformation doing a complex arithmetic function, with many inputs and outputs, purely on the name of the function. Then imagine trying to implement the function, without the formula for the algorithm.

The project dictionary should hold the bulk of the system description, and its completion will require a lot of time and effort. For a complete analysis, in terms of sheets of paper, you could expect 10 per cent diagrams and 90 per cent project dictionary.

Despite its importance, the project dictionary is an area which is often ignored in development. Engineers are renowned for not doing documentation, but documentation is the only way to make sure that your system does what it is supposed to do. If all you do is draw a lot of diagrams, there are two traps that you can fall into.

First of all, you might not go into enough detail. A set of overview diagrams with no lower level detail will lead to a design based on an overview of the system. In this case, the final system might be roughly correct, but you will get a lot of it wrong because you have not fully specified requirements.

A more common problem is overspecification in the diagrams. There comes a point where it will be more long winded and difficult to specify something. Within the essential model there is a tendency for people to overspecify, especially in the diagrams. More than once, I have seen a seven level model with no textual specification, where what was needed was a three level model with some textual support.

Writing this textual support should be easier than giving a traditional textual specification, because the project dictionary is diagram-driven. It will be especially easy if you are using an automated toolkit, since most toolkits work from the diagrams. You create the diagram using the toolkit and enter the diagram into the project dictionary. The system will then go through your diagram picking off all the diagram elements and creating a pro forma for each. All you have to do is complete the pro formas in the project dictionary. If you are not using an automated toolkit, you can go through the same procedure by hand. Even though the process of producing the textual specifications is fairly easy, it is still an area where you can go very wrong. The diagrams are fairly tightly specified within the method — you can only use certain diagram components in a certain way to describe certain things. The text is not so well specified. Although for each diagram component you have to specify certain things, in most cases there is no defined method of specification. For example, the specification for a data transformation can be given in narrative text, pseudo code, formal specification language, diagrams, tables — anything you want. The only area of specification which is defined is that of data decomposition. A compound data flow must be broken down according to the syntax presented in Section 5.3.

Because of the flexibility given for most of the diagram component specifications, it is a good idea to come up with company or project standards for the project dictionary. For example, you could say all specifications are to be in a formal specification language, making your system development more or less foolproof. A formal specification language will remove errors made in further development and refinement, but is a very large overhead.

On the other hand, you may decide to use narrative text for your specifications. With a loose standard, some people will write 2 lines of text, where others might write 200 to specify the same function. This will lead to inconsistencies and gaps in the specification and will give an unprofessional look to the documentation. It is a good idea to produce standards within the development group to point engineers in the right direction when they come to write the diagram support.

5.3 DATA COMPOSITION SPECIFICATION LANGUAGE

Before we consider the supporting specifications for each diagram type, let us look at the data composition specification language. Data flows and stores on the DFD can be decomposed in the same way as the data transformations. Figure 5.2 shows a small hierarchy of DFDs. At the top level 'modify address' accepts an 'address' and writes it into the 'address book' store. At the lower level 'address' is broken into 'street number', 'street name' and 'town'.

Visually, we do not appear to have the same data coming into the top level diagram as the lower level diagram. However, 'street number', 'street name' and 'town' have been grouped into 'address' to avoid showing too much detail at the higher level. If this data breakdown is not specified somewhere, we would not be able to check that the DFD hierarchy was correct.

We need to show how a piece of compound (or non-elemental) data breaks into its component data elements. If you are using an automated toolkit, it also needs to be able to check the breakdown of data, so we need a machine-readable specification method. This is given by the data decomposition specification language.

5.3.1 Data composition

The basic symbols are = and + , where ' = ' means 'is composed of' and ' + ' means 'together with'.

address = street name + street number + town

means 'address is composed of street name together with street number together with town'.

class = instructor + students

means 'class is composed of instructor together with students'.

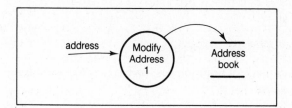

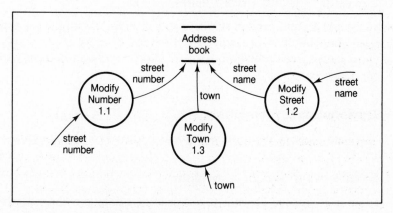

Figure 5.2   Decomposition of data.

5.3.2 Multiple data elements

Assume we wanted to specify how many students we had. To do this we would use { }.

students = {student}

means 'students is composed of a number of student'.

If we want to, we can also put upper and lower limits on the number of students. The lower limit goes at the front of the { }, the upper limit goes at the end of the { }.

students = 4{student}

means 'students is composed of at least 4 of student'. If this limit is omitted, it will default to zero.

students = {student} 18

means 'students is composed of up to 18 of student'. If this limit is omitted it will default to infinity.

students = 4 {student} 18

means 'students is composed of between 4 and 18 of student'.

students = 12 {student} 12

means 'students is composed of exactly 12 of student'.

5.3.3 Choice of data elements

The next piece of notation we have is [ ]. We use this to specify a number of different options.

instructor = [sylvia | rick | keith]

means 'instructor is composed of sylvia or rick or keith'. With the [ ], the things that you are choosing between will be delimited either by '|', as shown here, or by ';', and at any given time you can only choose *one* option from within the [ ].

5.3.4 Optional data elements

The next piece of notation we have is ( ), used to describe things which are optional.

room = walls + door + (windows)

means 'room is composed of walls together with a door possibly together with windows — some rooms will have windows, some rooms won't'. This differs from [ ], as with [ ] you are choosing one element from a number of different options. With ( ), you are choosing between including the element in the data composition or not.

5.3.5 Key data elements

Those are all the basic symbols that you will need to decompose the data, but there is one more symbol that you might find useful. When we were looking at ERD objects, we said that the object must have a unique identifier. The identifier in the object description can be shown either prefixed with @ or underlined.

man = @first-name + @family-name + age + salary

This shows that the first-name and family-name of a man can together be used to uniquely identify him.

You can use all of these symbols together. Imagine we are building a vending machine and we want to describe a cup of tea:

Cup-of-tea = water + 40 {tea-leaves} 190 + ([milk | lemon]) +
          {sugar-lump} 4

means 'cup-of-tea is composed of water together with between 40 and 190 tea-leaves (depending on how strong you want it) together with milk or lemon (the choice of which is optional, so you could have black tea) together with up to 4 sugar-lumps (as the lower limit will default to zero, this will give the option of having no sugar).

5.4 TEXTUAL SUPPORT FOR DATA FLOW DIAGRAMS

All of the components within the DFD can be given some kind of textual support, although in some cases it may not be required.

5.4.1 Data flows and data stores

Data stores and data flows are described in the same way. In the context of describing the data composition, a data store is just a data flow stopped between data transformations, rather than moving directly between them.

The data specification depends on whether it is elemental (data which has been broken down so far that we cannot break it down any more) or non-elemental (data which can be broken down further). For example, address is non-elemental data, as it can be broken into street number, street name and town; however, street number is elemental data, because it cannot be broken down any further — we could give it a range of values, but we cannot break street number into any lower level data items.

Non-elemental data decomposition is defined using the data decomposition specification language, discussed in Section 5.3.

Once non-elemental data has been broken into elemental data, the domain and the meaning of the elemental data items are specified. The domain of data values can be given in terms of either a list or a range of values. For example, street number could be in the range 1 to 250. Street name could be a list of all known street names.

We also specify the meaning of the data. For example, the meaning of street number is the position of the house in the street. We could point out significant values for the data, such as odd numbered houses will be positioned on the right-hand side of the street, even numbered houses will be positioned on the left-hand side of the street.

In the essential model you will not need to specify the physical implementation of the data. For example, you would not worry about whether you were going to store a piece of data in an array, a record or a linked list. This will not be specified until the later stages in the design. Once you have considered the implementation language, you can decide how to implement the data.

5.4.2 Data transformations

The textual support for the data transformation is called the transformation specification. The information given in the transformation specification is what would be provided as a functional specification, even if structured development was not being used.

By convention, transformation specifications are only given for data transformations at the very bottom of the model hierarchy, the rationale being that a data transformation which breaks into a lower level DFD is specified by that lower level DFD, so there is no reason for specifying it again. Also, if it is specified in text and diagrams, it has been specified twice, which introduces the danger of making inconsistent statements. On the other hand, if a customer expects textual specifications all the way down the model, you should include them.

It is important to provide the transformation specification, and to provide it in such a way that it is not open to misinterpretation. You should write the minimum amount needed to specify exactly what that transformation is supposed to do. The less you write, the less you will waffle, the clearer your specification will be, and the more people will be inclined to read it. At the essential modelling stage try not to say anything about how the transformation will be implemented, just what it will do. At the minimum, you need to describe the following:

1. The inputs to the transformation.
2. The outputs of the transformation.
3. How the input becomes the output. How you describe this is entirely up to you. You can do it in terms of tables, pseudo-code, narrative text, arithmetic formulae, pre- and post-conditions — anything you want.

5.4.3 Terminators

Although not always required, it is often helpful to describe certain aspects of terminators. If a terminator represents a piece of equipment, you might want to document how that piece of equipment works or how you expect to be able to use it from your system. If a terminator represents a person, such as the operator, you may want to note that in the implemented system you envisage the operator interacting with the system via some kind of screen and keyboard interface.

Sometimes, a single terminator on the context diagram will indicate multiple instances of the same thing. For example, in our teabag system, we may not have just one teabag scales and robot arm, but a number working in parallel, all controlled by the same operator. In this case, show only one terminator (as they all work the same and the interface to them from the system is the same), but note in the terminator specification that there will be a number of them.

There are no guidelines for information held in the terminator specification — any comments concerning the terminators can be kept there. If there is nothing to say about the terminator, the specification may not be required.

5.4.4 Event flows and event stores

Event flows and event stores can be treated similarly to data flows and stores, although as an event can only take two states, they can be described more simply.

Non-elemental event flows can be described using the data composition specification language. In Figure 5.3 a user is able to choose whether to add, modify or view an address to the address book. To avoid complicating the DFD, we have grouped all the user options together into a single event flow. This could be specified as:

User option = [view address | modify address | add new address]

Once the event flows have been broken into elemental event flows, you should describe the meaning of that event to the system. For example, 'view address' indicates that the user wishes to look at an address from the address book. In the teabag example, 'wrong weight' indicates that a teabag has passed down the conveyor belt which is either heavier or lighter than the required teabag weight, and should be removed before it gets into the teabag box.

5.4.5 Control processes

Control processes are not normally given textual specification, as the state transition diagram describes what happens inside the control process. However, where the control is very straightforward, a textual specification can be preferable to an STD.

Figure 5.4 shows the STD which describes the control process in Figure 5.3. In each case from 'awaiting user choice', we await the user choice, go into a state which represents that choice, and eventually returns to 'awaiting user choice'. This is probably more easily shown by the following structured text:

```
DO forever

    CASE user option OF

        VIEW:    Enable View Address
                 When QUIT VIEW Disable View Address

        MODIFY: Enable Modify Address
                 When QUIT MODIFY Disable Modify Address

        ADD:     Enable Add New Address
                 When QUIT ADD Disable Add New Address

    END CASE;

END DO;
```

At the other end of the scale, in cases where the control described within the control process is very complicated, it may be worth using either the state transition table described in Chapter 14, or the process activation table, described in Section 5.5.

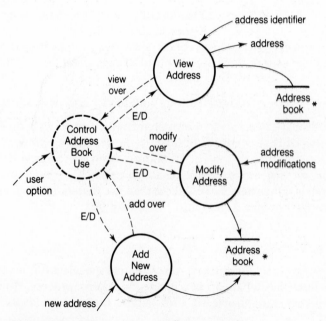

Figure 5.3   Compound event flow example.

5.4.6 Example project dictionary for teabag boxing system DFD

This is not the full project dictionary for the teabag boxing system DFD, shown in Figure 2.1, as that would take up too much space. However, it should be enough to give you a feel for what the project dictionary should contain, and what it should look like. The transformation specifications show a number of different ways of specifying a data transformation, but remember these are just some of the options. You can specify transformations using any method you choose. Note that comments can be made at any point in the project dictionary, between two '*'s, i.e. * comment *.

Data specifications
teabag weight = ELEMENTAL

    meaning = weight of teabag currently on scales
    range = 0.00 to 10.00 grams

required teabag weight = ELEMENTAL

    meaning = weight that the current batch of teabags should be at within 0.05 gram. This weight may be changed by the operator at any time.

    range = 1.00 to 3.00 grams * the range is smaller than the range for actual teabag weight, as teabag weight is catering for things to go wrong in teabag production, whereas you would never

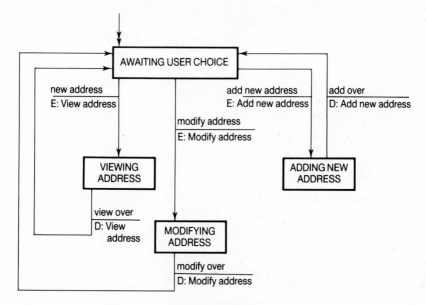

Figure 5.4   STD for control address book use.

actually be required to produce a teabag bigger or smaller than the range specified for required teabag weight *

new teabag weight * This flow allows the operator to enter the required teabag weight into the system. The value that the operator enters must be within the range specified for required teabag weight *

report request = [daily full request | daily error request | weekly full request | weekly error request | monthly full request | monthly error request]

statistics report = [daily full report | daily error report | weekly full report | weekly error report | monthly full report | monthly error report]

* The actual format and precise contents of the reports have yet to be decided; however, it is envisaged that full reports will contain all the teabag statistics, whereas error reports will only contain information on teabags at the wrong weight. *

teabag statistics = {teabag statistic}
teabag statistic = @date-time + teabag weight
date-time = current date + current time
current date = year + month + date
current time = hour + minutes + seconds
teabag count = ELEMENTAL

meaning = number of teabags in box currently being filled. * This information is used to allow the system to know when to replace a full box with any empty one. *

range = 0 to 40
0 means the box is empty
40 means the box is full

arm position = arm x + arm y + arm z + claw
* this gives the current position and state of the robot arm *

arm x = ELEMENTAL

meaning = gives the position of the arm in terms of up and down movement

range = −100 to +100
0 gives a position which is horizontal with the robot base
negative values are below the base, positive values are above the base
1 unit = 10 mm

arm y = ELEMENTAL

    meaning = gives the position of the arm in terms of backwards and
                 forwards movement

    range = −100 to +100
           0 gives a position which is vertical with the robot base
           negative values are behind the base, positive values are in
           front of the base
           1 unit = 10 mm

arm z = ELEMENTAL

    meaning = gives the position of the arm in terms of side to side
                 movement

    range = −100 to +100
           0 gives a position which is in line with the robot base
           negative values are to the right of the base, positive values
           are to the left of the base
           1 unit = 10 mm

claw = [open | closed]

    meaning = this shows whether the robot claw is open or closed

teabag removing movements = {arm movement}
* this is the sequence of commands required to make the robot arm
remove a teabag from the conveyor, and place it in the bin *

box changing movements = {arm movement}
* this is the sequence of commands required to make the robot arm
remove the full box of teabags and replace it with an empty box *

arm movement = move arm x + move arm y + move arm z

move arm x = ELEMENTAL

    meaning = gives command to robot to move the arm in the up and
                 down direction

    range = −200 to +200
           0 gives no movement
           negative values will move the arm down, positive values
           will move the arm up
           1 unit = 10 mm

    move arm y = * similar to move arm x, but for backwards and
                 forwards movement *

    move arm z = *similar to move arm x, but for side to side
                 movement *

Transformation specifications

1. Weigh teabag

INPUTS: teabag weight
required teabag weight

OUTPUTS: teabag count
teabag statistics
wrong weight

If teabag weight <> required teabag weight   teabag weight

then wrong weight: = true
else wrong weight: = false
teabag count: = teabag count + 1;
new teabag stat: = current date-time + teabag weight;
teabag statistics: = teabag statistics + new teabag stat;

2. Check for full box

* This specification is given in terms of pre- and post-conditions. The pre-condition makes a statement about the data coming into the transformation, the post-condition makes a statement about the corresponding output data, but it is not explicitly stated *how* the input becomes the output.

This method is useful, especially in essential modelling, as it allows you to specify what should happen, without allowing you to specify how. *

INPUTS: teabag count
OUTPUTS: teabag count
box full

pre-condition-1: teabag count < 40
post-condition-1: box full = false

pre-condition-2: teabag count > = 40
post-condition-2: teabag count = 0 AND box full = true

3. Change box

INPUTS: arm position
OUTPUTS: box changing movements
box changed

Change box is required to remove the box of teabags and replace it with an empty box to be filled. It will do this by using a robot arm, which has three planes of movement and a claw, which can be opened and closed to pick things up and drop them. The robot arm and its environment are described further in the terminator specifications.

Change box is able to read the current state of the robot arm (x, y, z and claw position), via the arm position data flow. It can then compare this with the required state of the robot arm, and send the appropriate commands to the robot along the data flow box changing movements.

The required sequence of movements will be as follows:

1. Move arm to teabag boxing position.
2. Close claw around box.
3. Move arm to filled box line.
4. Drop box on to filled box line.
5. Move arm to empty box line.
6. Close claw around empty box.
7. Move arm to teabag boxing line.
8. Drop box on to teabag boxing position.

Once the box has been changed, box changed should be set to true.

4. Remove teabag

INPUTS: arm position
OUTPUTS: teabag removing movements
teabag moved

Remove teabag is required to remove a teabag which is not at the appropriate weight from the conveyor belt, before it drops into the box of teabags.

The data transformation is required to go through the following sequence of robot movements, before setting the teabag moved flag to true:

1. Move arm to current teabag position.
2. Close claw around teabag.
3. Move arm to bin.
4. Drop teabag in bin.

Operation and layout of the robot are as described for data transformation 3, change box.

5. Produce teabag statistics

INPUTS: report request, teabag statistics
OUTPUTS: statistics report

This will produce a teabag statistics report on request from the operator. The operator can request a number of different reports, which are listed in the 'statistics report' entry of the project dictionary. The format and content of these reports, and further details of the system's interface to the operator have yet to be decided.

6. Change teabag weight

INPUTS: new teabag weight
OUTPUTS: required teabag weight

This will accept the new teabag weight from the operator and place it in the required teabag weight store, provided the weight given is in the appropriate range (given in the project dictionary entry for required teabag weight).

If the operator specifies a weight which is outside this range, he should be prompted for another value until a weight in the correct range is given. If the operator fails to give a weight within the correct range, the required teabag weight will remain unchanged.

Terminator specifications

Robot arm

The robot arm can be used to move things around in the teabag boxing environment. It will provide the system with the following information:

1. The position of the robot arm in three-dimensional space, as indicated in figure C1. The position of the arm provided is that at the tip of robot claw, as indicated in figure C1.
2. The state of the robot claw, which can be either open or closed.

The robot arm can be moved by sending out commands stating the desired new position and claw state.

Figure C2 shows the envisaged physical layout of the teabag boxing conveyor belt/robot environment.

[Although Figures C1 and C2 are not given, the references indicate where it would be appropriate to include diagrams as part of the project dictionary.]

Operator

It is envisaged that the operator will be positioned at some kind of terminal, which will allow him to interact with the system.

Scales

The scales are mounted on the conveyor belt, and will indicate the weight of the teabag as it passes. There is a time delay of 5 seconds between the teabag being weighed and it reaching the box of teabags.

5.5 TEXTUAL SUPPORT FOR STATE TRANSITION DIAGRAMS

If state transition diagrams are well partitioned and well named, they are unlikely to need any further textual specification.

5.5.1 States

The state name is already a high level textual description of what is happening within that state, monitoring teabag, changing box, etc. Lower level textual descriptions will be provided by specifications of data transformations enabled within the state. Therefore, the state needs no further textual description.

5.5.2 Transitions

A transition is completely described by the following:

1. The state it comes from.
2. The state it goes to.
3. The associated condition.
4. The associated action(s).

These are all shown on the STD. Therefore, no textual specification is required for the transition.

Condition and action specifications are only needed for non-trivial conditions and actions.

5.5.3 Conditions

Imagine an STD condition 'start', which corresponds to an operator terminator producing a 'start' event flow on the associated DFD. In this case, the condition is obvious and there is no point in describing it any further.

Now imagine the STD condition

(temp > 50 AND pressure > 20 AND humidity > 80) OR (temp < 10 AND pressure > 20 AND humidity < 20)

If we write the whole condition on the STD, the STD looks very busy and becomes difficult to read. Also, it is more likely that the customer thinks of the condition as 'emergency conditions', rather than in terms of its component parts. On the basis of this, we should write 'emergency conditions' on the STD, which can be broken into its component parts in the project dictionary.

5.5.4 Actions

Action specifications are only given for non-trivial actions. Imagine an STD action 'enable: heat to reaction temperature' associated with a DFD containing the data transformation 'heat to reaction temperature'. Here, there is no point in specifying the action any further. On the other hand, if there are a number of actions on the same transition, all working towards the same purpose, a long action list will be less user friendly than a single phrase describing those actions. For example, the action list:

- close windows
- close doors
- sound alarm
- evacuate personnel
- call fire brigade
- start sprinklers

could be described by 'perform fire drill'. This could be written on the STD and broken down in the project dictionary.

It may also be useful to document whether actions within the list should be performed sequentially, concurrently or in no particular order. Although this may make little difference with the 'perfect technology' of the essential model, it may be useful in the later design stages.

In cases where both conditions and actions are complex, it may be appropriate to use the process activation table (PAT), defined by Hatley and Pirbhai, to document the correspondence between conditions and actions.

Figure 5.5 shows a DFD and part of the PAT which defines the control within the control process. The first line of the PAT defines that when the conditions S2 and S3 occur simultaneously, we should enable DT1, DT2 and output S5 concurrently. The next line defines that when S1 and S3 occur simultaneously, we should enable DT1, output S4 and output S5 concurrently, followed by the enabling of DT2.

5.6 TEXTUAL SUPPORT FOR ENTITY RELATIONSHIP DIAGRAMS

Object specifications should be given for objects, supertype objects, subtype objects and associative objects. Relationship specifications should be given for relationships and the relationship part of an associative object.

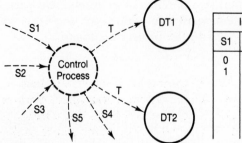

Inputs			Outputs				
S1	S2	S3	DT1	DT2	S4	S5	
0	1	1	1	1	0	1	
1	0	1	1	2	1	1	

Figure 5.5 Process activation table.

5.6.1 Objects

Although ERD objects and DFD data stores are equivalent, the data store specification defines the syntactic breakdown of the information, while the object specification defines the semantic description of the information.

An object specification gives the meaning of the object to the system, by describing the role that the object plays with respect to the system. For the 'address' object, the meaning (i.e. the reason why it is stored) is that it tells us where various people live, and so allows us to post bills or deliver orders to them.

5.6.2 Relationships

Here, we describe the meaning of the relationship to the system. If a person 'lives' at an address, the 'lives' relationship defines which person lives at which address. The numerics of the relationship (cardinality) can also be held in the relationahip specification.

Considering the relationship between the person and address, one person lives at one address, while there might be a number of different people living at the same address.

This would be shown as:

person: address $1 : 1$
address: person $1 : N$

5.6.3 Example project dictionary for teabag boxing system ERD

The partial project dictionary below describes the teabag boxing system ERD, given by Figure 4.14.

Objects

Scales: see Terminator Specification
Operator: see Terminator Specification

Teabag statistics

Teabag statistics are collected during the boxing of teabags, and allow the operator to gauge how well the system is performing. Various statistics on the number of teabags at the correct weight and information on teabags not at the correct weight will be collected, which can be formatted into a number of different reports for the operator.

Required teabag weight

Required teabag weight defines the weight that a teabag must be at before it is put into the box of teabags. Teabags which are above or below this weight will be removed from the production line and the tea will be recycled at some later date.

The value of required teabag weight may be changed by the operator at any time.

Teabag count

Teabag count is the number of correct weight teabags which have been placed by the system into the current box of teabags. Teabag count therefore allows the system to tell when a box of teabags is full, so that the box can be removed and replaced with another.

The system will put 40 teabags into a box before it is full. This number will not be configurable by the operator.

Teabag count depends on the relationship between teabag statistics and required teabag weight, as it records the number of teabags which have entered the system at the correct weight.

Relationship specifications

Provide: This relationship shows that the teabag statistics are built up from data provided by the scales.

Defines: This relationship shows that the required teabag weight is defined by the operator.

Are Reported To: This relationship shows that the teabag statistics are reported to the Operator.

Generally, relationship specifications will be a bit more interesting than this. However, in this system, most of the relationships are between 'true' objects and objects which are really terminators, which we have put in the ERD to make it more user friendly. As a result of this, all of these relationships are concerned with how the data gets in and out of the system.

Some more interesting relationship specifications are given in the exercises at the end of the next chapter.

5.7 SUMMARY OF PROJECT DICTIONARY REQUIREMENTS

1. Data stores and flows: Non-elemental: data decomposition;
                           Elemental: (a) meaning of data,
                                      (b) range of data values.
2. Data transformation: (a) Inputs/outputs;
                        (b) What turns inputs into outputs.

3. Event stores and flows: Non-elemental: decomposition;
   Elemental: meaning of event.
4. Trivial control process: Brief description of control process logic.
5. Non-trivial conditions and non-trivial actions: Decomposition.
6. Object: The meaning of the object to the system.
7. Relationship: (a) The meaning of the relationship to the system;
   (b) Numerics of the relationship.

In summary, the project dictionary is very important, both in terms of checking the model, and in being able to specify lower level detail that eventually allows you to design the system.

The project dictionary can be started as soon as you have a context diagram, and can be expanded as you build the lower level diagrams and details into the model. You can think of building the project dictionary as a background process, which is going on all through the system development.

As soon as you have a context diagram, the data-flows from the context diagram can be described in the dictionary. However, at the beginning of the development, you do not need to break data down to their lowest elemental levels. The same ideas apply to data as to the system descripton as a whole: only go into as much detail as you need to make yourself understood. The project dictionary will be continually expanded and updated throughout the design phases, and so there is no need to put all the information in right at the very beginning.

5.8 EXERCISES

In all the following examples, turn the narrative statement into a data composition specification, e.g. pasta is made from flour, salt and water:

pasta = flour + salt + water

1. Radar characteristics consist of radar frequency, radar strength and radar direction.

2. Mayonnaise is made from a number of egg yolks, oil and seasoning.

3. Seasoning consists of salt and/or pepper and, if you like it, mustard.

4. At the bank, a customer request contains the customer's account number, together with the type of request, which may be either a withdrawal, a deposit or a balance request. If the request is to deposit or withdraw, the request also contains the amount to be deposited or withdrawn.

5. A car has four wheels, between three and five doors, either electric or manual windows, and a boot lid (unless it is a hatchback).

CHAPTER SIX

Diagram integration

6.1 INTRODUCTION

Throughout previous chapters we have discussed the need for a hierarchy and for more than one type of diagram to describe a system. In the last chapter we looked at how all of these diagrams fitted together in terms of the overlap between STD and between DFD and ERD. In Chapter 3, we saw how you could take an STD, turn it into a control process and integrate it with the DFD. In Chapter 4, we saw how the ERD and the DFD were really giving the same information, but in different levels of detail, and from different viewpoints.

Now that we have looked at the details of these diagrams in isolation, we should start thinking about them in terms of a consistent model. To build a good, consistent and coherent model, the 'levelling' and 'balancing' of the model must be considered.

Levelling is the technique by which the size and complexity of the models are controlled. The aim of levelling is to partition a large model into a hierarchy of simpler pieces. This hierarchy contains both different types of diagram and different levels of diagram, all of which describe the same system, and so must be consistent. For example, a control process should be consistent with its associated STD. A DFD describing the inside of a high level data transformation should show the same functionality, but in more detail.

Diagrams modelling a system are 'in balance' when they are all consistent with each other. There are two forms of balancing:

1. Balancing different diagrams against each other, i.e. checking that an STD is consistent with the corresponding DFD, and that an ERD is consistent with the corresponding DFD.
2. Checking that each level in a DFD hierarchy describes the same system.

6.2 LEVELLING

Levelling has already been discussed in previous chapters, in the context of partitioning the system such that a single diagram does not contain too much information. While all the diagrams can be levelled, levelling is normally carried

140

out on the DFD, and the other diagrams levelled to match. This is because levelling is nearly always done on the basis of functionality (i.e. we group things together into higher level functional units), and the DFD models functionality. Also, as the DFD combines aspects of both the STD and the ERD, it is easier to see the consequences of levelling on the rest of the system from the DFD.

We have spent a lot of time thinking about how to make individual diagrams as clear and meaningful as possible. It will ease understanding, if we do not have too much information on one diagram. For instance, on a single DFD, you should have around seven elements — this was discussed in Chapter 2. If there is too much information on a single diagram, the diagram should be split up. However, if the diagram is not split in a sensible way, you will create a system modelled in a number of diagrams that are each difficult to understand, making the hierarchy as a whole difficult to understand.

Normally, a diagram will be partitioned firstly on the basis of control.

6.2.1 Levelling on control

To level on control, we collect all the data transformations controlled by a single control process, together with that control process, as shown by Figure 6.1.

A single control process controls a single functional area, thus all the data transformations it controls must be concerned with that functional area. These data transformations and the control process form a group concerned with the same functional area. Thus collecting them into a higher level data transformation will always create a single function higher level data transformation.

Figure 6.2 shows the resulting high level DFD with just four data transformations, and two lower level diagrams containing the collections of data transformations and control processes grouped from the original diagram. There are three potential problems with grouping purely on control:

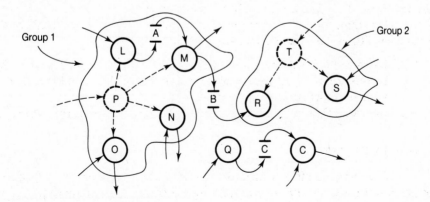

Figure 6.1   Levelling on control.

1. There may not be a control process on the DFD.
2. Once you have levelled a DFD, there may still be too many elements on the new DFD, especially if you start off with a very large DFD.
3. If the control is badly partitioned, it will cause the resultant DFD to be badly partitioned.

Consider problem 3. Imagine a large DFD, with a single control process controlling many data transformations. If too much implementation detail is embedded in a DFD, it will often result in a single control process controlling many low level data transformations on the same DFD. Effectively, this models a single program controlling the functionality of the system. In this case, grouping around the control process will yield the context diagram (i.e. a single high level data transformation).

One answer is to repartition the control process into control processes which control smaller functional areas. Alternatively, data transformations which are concerned with the same functional area could be grouped together, leaving a single control process controlling a few high level data transformations, rather than many low level functions.

However, the last solution still leaves the potential problem of an implementation-biased diagram, i.e. a 'main program loop' controlling all the functional areas of the system.

Problems 1 and 2 can be dealt with by further partitioning the DFD in terms of the use of data.

6.2.2 Levelling on data

Figure 6.3 shows a DFD which has the same flow of control as flow of

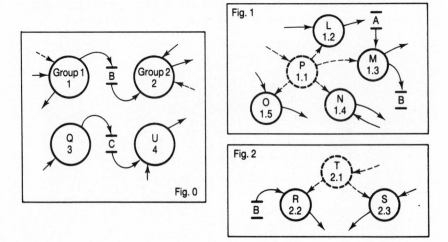

Figure 6.2 Levelled DFD hierarchy.

data, and so no control process is required. In this case, we can examine the items of data as they flow through the model, and group together data transformations into higher level functional units which process the same 'flow' of data. This gives the DFD hierarchy shown in Figure 6.4.

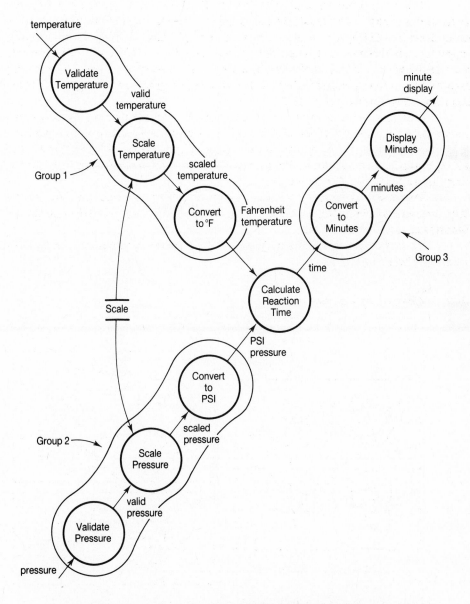

Figure 6.3   Grouping on unlevelled DFD without control process.

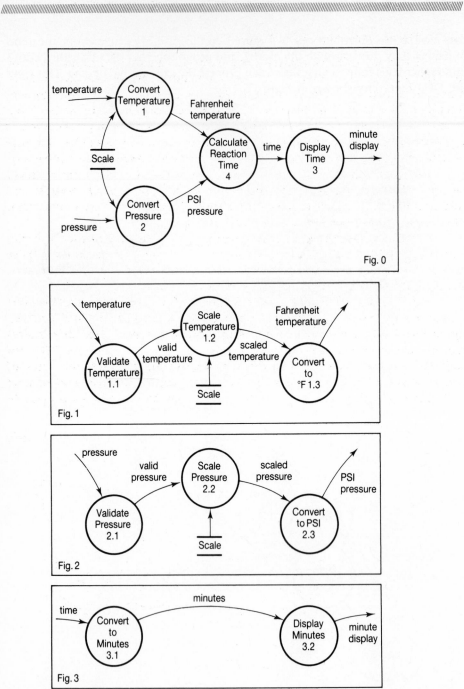

Figure 6.4   Levelled DFD hierarchy without control processes.

6.2.3 Object oriented levelling

For object oriented analysis/design/implementation, you should partition the DFD according to 'objects' or, as they manifest themselves in the DFD, functions which are concerned with the use of a particular data store or terminator. An 'object' in object oriented analysis/design/implementation is not exactly the same as an ERD object. An 'object' consists of the representation of a real-world entity (e.g. an ERD object, which is equivalent to a DFD data store or terminator), together with operations to be performed on that real-world entity.

Imagine a data store, address, representing the real-world entity 'address', together with three data transformations, 'modify address', 'display address' and 'add new address', which represent operations on address — we could group all of these things together into the 'address' object.

Similarly, imagine a heater terminator representing the real-world entity 'heater', together with data transformations, 'monitor temperature', 'raise temperature' and 'lower temperature', performing operations on the heater, which could be joined together into the 'heater' object.

In these simple examples, constructing 'object's is not difficult. However, in more complicated examples, partitioning into 'object's can cause difficulties. Figure 6.5 shows a number of data transformations, controlled by the same control process, which access more than one store. In order to break this DFD into 'object's, we may have to split the data transformations into the areas of functionality that are concerned with a particular store, as shown by the grouping on Figure 6.5. This will involve splitting the single functional area previously

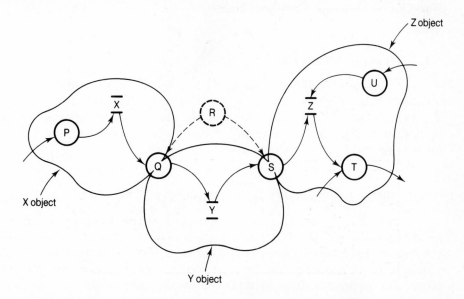

Figure 6.5   DFD split into objects.

held within a single data transformation between two objects, which may make the system more difficult to understand. Also, what will happen to the control process?

Supporters of object orientation are often a little vague when it comes to control. Even in an object oriented environment, the objects must be invoked in the correct sequence for the system to function correctly. One answer to this would be to maintain the STD, in conjunction with the objects, to describe the required control. OOD is discused more fully in section 15.4.1.

The purpose of levelling is to create a system which is well structured, and a hierarchy of diagrams which is clear and meaningful. To this end, it will sometimes be a matter of judgement as to what is most clear and meaningful — there are no hard and fast rules. However, as a general rule, 'partition to minimize interfaces', as discussed in Chapter 2. This should result in good functional units with minimal interfaces — both characteristics of a well-structured system.

Although the DFDs and corresponding STDs will always be levelled, levelling the ERD in a real-time system is often a matter of style, as real-time information models are often rather small. If the ERD is not very big, many people prefer a single ERD which describes the data model for the whole system. On the other hand, the ERD can be split to reflect the DFD hierarchy.

A single DFD within a DFD hierarchy will normally only use some of the objects and relationships shown on the ERD. The ERD can thus be partitioned into sections of ERD which are required for particular DFDs within the hierarchy. A single DFD will tend to describe a single functional area. If the ERD is partitioned with respect to the DFD, the ERD is effectively split into fragments which hold data relevant to single functional areas.

6.3 HORIZONTAL BALANCING

Checking that different diagrams describe the same system is known as horizontal balancing. We can check the DFD against the STD because there is an area in which they overlap. We can also check the DFD against the ERD, because again there is an area in which they overlap. However, the STD does not overlap the ERD, so there is nothing to check.

6.3.1 Balancing the DFD against the STD

First of all, let us look at checking the DFD against the STD. Conceptually, we are checking that the STD controls the functionality described in the DFD, and that the functionality described in the DFD is controlled by the STD. This mainly involves checking that the DFD control process shows the same input events and output events as the STD conditions and actions.

6.3.1.1 *Conditions*

Firstly, we check that conditions on the STD can be recognized using the DFD. In Chapter 3, we discussed the four places from where conditions can come into the STD:

1. Terminators.
2. Data transformations.
3. Other STD/control processes.
4. Timers.

For the STD and DFD to be in balance, you should be able to see all the conditions of the STD generated on the corresponding DFD — either by a data transformation, a terminator, a control process or a timer. Timed conditions may not show up on the DFD, but as the clock is part of your 'perfect technology' you need not worry where they will come from. Conditions from 1, 2, and 3 above will be shown on the DFD, generated as event flows by the appropriate DFD component.

If a condition specified on the STD does not come from the DFD or a timer, it will not come from anywhere else. Effectively the STD is waiting for a condition which will never be noticed, because there is nothing to make the STD aware of it.

We can also consider this the other way round. If you have an event generated on the DFD, which enters the control process, but does not appear to be used for anything on the corresponding STD, it can mean one of two things. You might be generating a condition which is not really of interest to you. In this case there is nothing missing from the STD, and the condition does not need to be generated from the DFD. Alternatively you may be generating a condition which is of interest to you, but has been ignored on the STD. Here, there is something missing from the STD.

6.3.1.2 *Actions*

Secondly, we must check that all the actions on the STD are capable of being carried out. In Chapter 3, we discussed the four places where an action can go:

1. A terminator.
2. A data transformation.
3. A control process.
4. A timer.

As with conditions, the timer action will be the only one that may not be seen on the corresponding DFD. An STD action which is not concerned with setting a timer, and cannot be carried out by communication with a data transformation, a terminator or a control process on the DFD, cannot be done. Effectively, the STD is trying to do something that it does not have the means to do.

Looking at this the other way round, if you have an event generated by the DFD control process, which does not appear as an action on the corresponding STD, it can mean one of two things. Firstly, the control process could be trying to do something that it does not need to do. In this case, the event flow does not need to be done as shown on the DFD. Secondly, the control process could be doing something it does need to do, which is ignored on the STD. Here, there is something missing from the STD.

6.3.1.3 *Data transformation control*

Finally, you should check that all the DFD data transformations which need to be performed in a certain sequence, not defined by a flow of data, are controlled by an STD.

You may want some data transformations to be active all the time, and in this case they do not need to be controlled by a control process/STD. However, if this is not the case, you should consider where the data transformation is to be active in the system sequence, and add control to the appropriate STD.

The DFD and the STD are in balance if the following hold when the STD is checked against the DFD:

1. All STD conditions are either timed or generated by the DFD, and all control process input event flows are used as conditions in the STD.
2. All STD actions are either to timers or something on the DFD, and all control process output event flows are used as actions on the STD.
3. All data transformations which need to be controlled are controlled by the appropriate STD.

Figure 6.6 shows an STD and corresponding DFD, which we will check for horizontal balancing. Firstly, we construct a control process from the STD. If the STD contains any non-trivial actions or conditions, these should be expanded, by consulting the project dictionary. This gives the control process shown in Figure 6.7.

Comparing this with the control process in Figure 6.6, there are a number of differences:

1. The STD does not control 'monitor temperature', although the control process on the DFD does.
2. The STD waits for three temperature conditions 'too hot', 'too cold' and 'temperature correct', whilst 'monitor temperature' only seems to produce the condition 'temperature correct'.

The STD and the DFD are therefore not in balance. Here, we should consider whether it is the DFD, the STD or both which are wrong, and decide on the modifications needed to put the diagrams in balance.

In this example, we could firstly modify the STD, such that immediately after it recognized the 'start' condition, it enabled 'monitor temperature'. To produce the missing conditions, we could modify 'monitor temperature'. To see whether 'monitor temperature' was actually wrong, or whether it had just been drawn incorrectly on the DFD, we would have to examine its textual description in the project dictionary. In either case, we could modify the DFD, such that

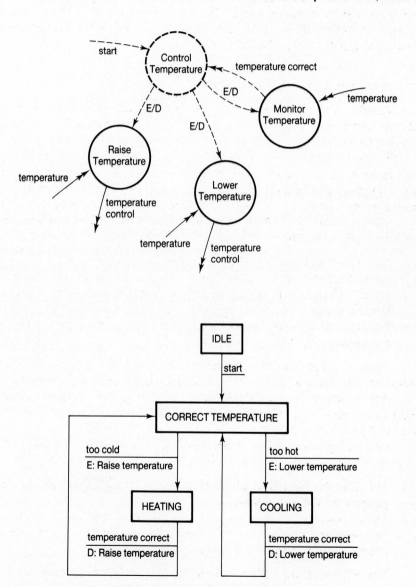

Figure 6.6   DFD/STD for horizontal balancing.

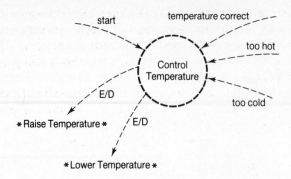

Figure 6.7   Control process for control temperature from STD.

'monitor temperature' produced all three conditions 'temperature correct', 'too hot' and 'too cold'.

6.3.2 Balancing the DFD against the ERD

Let us now consider checking the ERD against the DFD. Here, it is checked that the data and relationships defined in the ERD are used by the corresponding DFD, and that data or relationships used in the DFD have been considered in the associated ERD. Initially you should check that the ERD objects are the same as the DFD stores.

Figure 6.8 shows fragments of a DFD and an ERD which describe the same system. It is fairly simple to check visually that ERD objects correspond to DFD data stores, and that ERD relationships are used by the correct data transformations. In this example, the ERD objects 'man', 'woman' and 'marriage

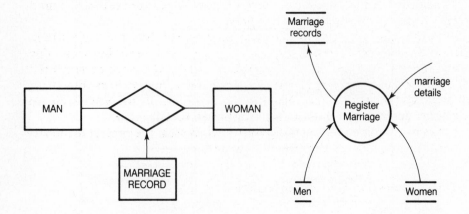

Figure 6.8   DFD/ERD fragment.

record' correspond to the DFD data stores men, women and marriage records. Also in the ERD, all three objects are connected by the same relationship, which corresponds to all three data stores being used by the same data transformation in the DFD. The implication here is that the ERD relationship is being used in the data transformation 'register marriage'.

You can also check that all the data elements in the ERD object/DFD store are created and used by some data transformation. If you store a piece of information in a data store and then do not appear to use it anywhere in your DFD, what are you storing it for? Conversely, if you use a piece of data from a data store somewhere in your DFD, and it does not appear to have been put there by anything, what are you actually using?

Firstly, you should check that every data store is both written to and read from. There are two exceptions to this:

1. Often in a diagram hierarchy, a store in a lower level diagram will appear to be just read from or just written to. However, if you look at the higher level diagram, you see that the data store is actually shared with a higher level data transformation which does not appear on the lower level diagram.
2. In something like a data logging system, you may collect data which is not used in your system. On the DFD, you will appear to be collecting lots of data which does not appear to be used. In this case, you should be certain that the data is required in another system, and not being stored for no reason.

Normally, however, you would not expect to see a data store that was either just written to or just read from. This will ensure, in fairly general terms, that data is being created and used.

More specifically, you should check that the right data is being created and used. This will involve studying the textual specifications for the diagrams and making sure that all data elements in the data stores are created and used, and that all data is used in the correct way.

In the same way, and for the same reasons, we also need to check that all the relationships on your ERD are created and used by some data transformation. Checking that relationships are used and created correctly will again involve studying the appropriate textual specifications from the project dictionary, and matching the relationships described in the ERD with the connections described in the data transformation specification.

Let us examine the following entries taken from the project dictionary of the registration system, described in Figure 6.8.

Data composition specification

men = {man}
man = mans name + date-of-birth + parents name

women = {woman}
woman = womans name + date-of-birth + parents name

marriage details = mans name + mans-date-of-birth + womans name
+ womans-date-of-birth + date + location

marriage records = {marriage record}
marriage record = mans name + womans name + date + location

Transformation specifications
register marriage

inputs   men
women
marriage details

outputs   marriage records

1. The date-of-birth of both the man and the woman must be checked to ensure that they are over 16.
2. The man's name and date-of-birth specified in 'marriage details' must be checked against 'men', to make sure that they match.
3. The woman's name and date-of-birth specified in 'marriage details' must be checked against 'women' to make sure that they match.
4. Both the man's name and the woman's name must be checked against 'marriage details' to make sure that neither of them are already married.
5. If all of these checks are successful, a new marriage record should be created consisting of the man's name, the woman's name and the date and location information from 'marriage details'.

Object and relationship specifications

Woman: Female person who lives in the parish
Man: Male person who lives in the parish and has the authority to register a marriage.
Marriage record: This gives a record of which man is married to which woman, and details of their marriage. It should allow us to prove that a man and woman have been married. Marriage describes a legal relationship between a man and a woman. If a man and a woman are married it will affect the tax that they pay, the property that they own and many other aspects of their legal and financial life.

man : woman $1 : N$
woman : man $1 : 1$

Firstly, we check the information used in the specification of 'register marriage' against the data compositions given for the inputs and outputs. The only thing which may be incorrect here is that both man and woman compositions contain details of their parents, which are not used in 'register marriage'. This can mean one of three things:

1. The data is not used anywhere and doesn't need to be stored.
2. The data is used by another data transformations, which we are not aware of.
3. Something has been missed from 'register marriage'; for example, we might want to use the parent's name to check the relationship of the two people who were marrying.

Secondly, we check the use of the information against the object and relationship specifications. There are two errors here.

The 'man' object description describes the registrar (i.e. the person who is performing the marriage) rather than the man who is being married. In all other specifications, 'man' describes the man who is being married.

The numerics of the married relationship, specified in 'marriage record', state that one man can be married to a number of women. On the other hand, in 'register marriage', if a check to see whether either man or woman has been married before shows that they have, the marriage will not be registered.

We could remove these differences by the following:

1. Adding a check to 'register marriage', to check the man's and woman's parental relationship.
2. Changing the 'man' object description, so it no longer describes the registrar.
3. Changing the numerics of the married relationship such that one man could only be married to one woman.

The diagrams would then be in balance.

6.4 VERTICAL BALANCING

Diagrams should also be balanced vertically. Here, we check that at each level in the diagram hierarchy the diagrams describe the same system. The context diagram shows the total net flow of information in to and out of the system. Even though the flows on the context diagram may decompose as we split the diagrams into more and more detail, if totally new information is added or some information shown in a composition is not used, the top level diagram must be describing a slightly different system from the lower level diagrams.

Vertical balancing is very simple: there is only one rule, which states that 'each parent bubble must have exactly the same inputs and outputs as the child diagram beneath it'.

Consider the example shown in Figure 6.9. Data transformation 1 breaks down into a lower level diagram, with data transformations 1.1, 1.2 and 1.3. We are not worried about the internal flows of data transformation 1, just the

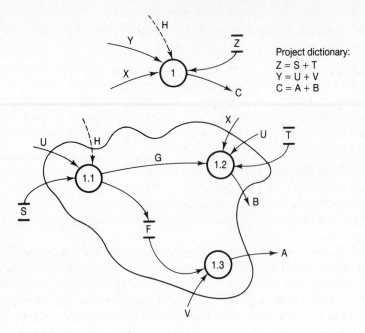

Project dictionary:
Z = S + T
Y = U + V
C = A + B

Figure 6.9   Partial DFD hierarchy for vertical balancing.

flows which come in and out of the diagram — which should be the same as the flows which come in and out of data transformation 1. A boundary drawn around the lower level diagram helps us to see the inputs and outputs of the diagram. Flows which connect data transformations such as G are internal and should be hidden within the boundary. However, we have to decide whether a store should be inside or outside the boundary.

A data store used only by data transformations inside a DFD, and not by any data transformations outside that diagram, is internal to the diagram, and therefore inside the diagram boundary. In this example, the data store F does not show up on the high level DFD, because it is hidden inside data transformation 1 (just as an internal data flow would be).

We now check that flows coming across the lower level diagram boundary are the same as flows coming in and out of the higher level data transformation. We might be able to do that just by looking at the two diagrams, but the flows may have decomposed going down the levels of the model. In this case, we will also look into the project dictionary for the data compositions to make sure that the information has decomposed correctly.

For example, in Figure 6.9, data transformation 1 accepts data flow Y. When we look at the lower level DFD, Y does not appear to be crossing the diagram boundary; therefore, the diagram appears not to be in balance. However, the project dictionary defines that Y is equivalent to U and V. As U comes into

Table 6.1

Data transformation 1	Corresponding lower level DFD
Data flow input Y	Data flow input U (1.1, 1.2) Data flow input V (1.3)
Data flow input X	Data flow input X (1.2)
Data store input Z	Data store input S (1.1) Data store input T (1.2)
Data flow output C	Data flow output A (1.3) Data flow output B (1.2)
Event flow input H	Event flow input H (1.1)

both 1.1 and 1.2, and V comes into 1.3 of the lower level DFD, Y comes into both data transformation 1 and the lower level diagram that describes it — the diagrams are in balance.

Stores can be broken down in exactly the same way as flows. Data transformation 1 takes data from the store Z. The lower level diagram accepts data from stores S and T, but not from Z. Again it appears that the two diagrams are not in balance. However, the project dictionary defines that Z breaks down into S and T. As the lower level diagram is taking information from S and T, which is equivalent to Z, the diagrams are in balance. Table 6.1 shows that data transformation 1 and its corresponding lower level DFD are in balance.

You should check that for the whole hierarchy of diagrams which describe your system, the inputs and outputs of a single data transformation are the same as the inputs and outputs of the lower level DFD which describes it. If this is true all the way up and down your model, your model is vertically in balance.

6.5 SUMMARY

Balancing the models at each stage of the development is very important. If you continue through development with unbalanced models, there is every chance that those models will be wrong. If the models are wrong, the development will also be wrong.

Allowing you to check that what you have done so far is correct is one of the most valuable benefits of using a structured technique. It does not make sense to throw away this benefit because you cannot be bothered to balance the models.

Although balancing the models can be very tedious and very time consuming, it is well worth doing, and CASE tools can be very helpful in this area. For instance vertical balancing is the kind of boring job that is very easy to get wrong because it is so simple. If you hold your diagrams and project dictionary on a machine that will automatically do this check for you, not only will the checking be much easier, but you can also rely on the validity of the check.

6.6 EXERCISES

1. Level the DFD in Figure 6.10.

2. Level the DFD in Figure 6.11 you might have to do some repartitioning of the existing data transformations.

In exercises 1 and 2, the answer should consist of a levelled DFD hierarchy.

3. Try to balance the STD in Figure 6.12 with the corresponding DFD. In areas where the two diagrams are not in balance suggest modifications that could be made to balance them.

4. Try to balance the ERD in Figure 6.13 with the corresponding DFD.

> *Partial project dictionary*
> captured radars = {captured radar}
> captured radar = frequency + strength + direction
>
> known radars = {known radar}
> known radar = frequency band + pulse width band + friendly flag
> + radar name

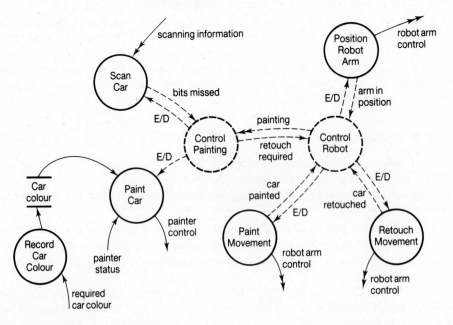

Figure 6.10   Exercise 1.

identified radars = {identified radar}
identified radar = radar name + direction + frequency + pulse width

Check radar type
INPUTS: known radars
                 captured radars
OUTPUTS: identified radars
For each radar in captured radars
     begin
     if captured radar frequency
           lies within known radar (x) frequency band
     then begin
           if known radar (x) friendly flag = false
           then begin

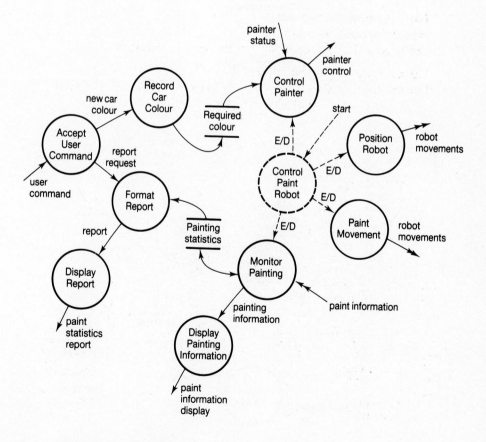

Figure 6.11   Exercise 2.

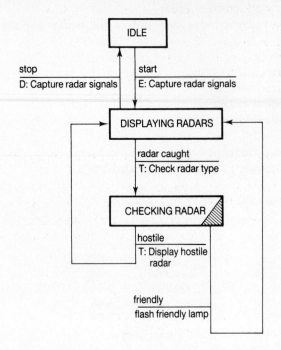

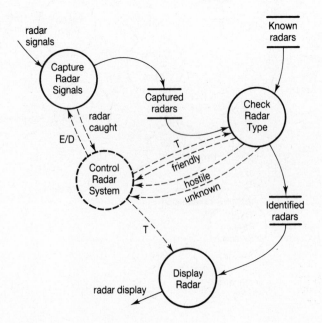

Figure 6.12   Exercise 3.

```
        create a new identified radar with
            radar name (x)
            captured radar frequency
            captured radar pulse width
            captured radar direction
        end
    end
end
```

'Captured radar:' these are the details of all the radar signals which are being picked up by the system radar receiver equipment.

'Known radar:' these are the characteristics of all the radars which the system expects to see. The frequency and pulse width combination of a radar allow us to state which type of radar is being received. The radar name is a code name for the radar, which a trained radar analyst would recognize.

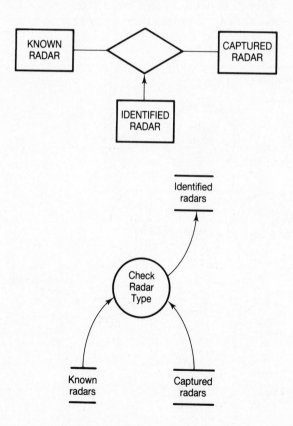

Figure 6.13   Exercise 4.

'Identified radar:' these are the details of all the radars which the system has received and has been able to identify. The identify relationship links a captured radar of a particular frequency and pulse width with a known radar name. This can be achieved by checking that the captured radar is both in the correct frequency band and correct pulse width band.

In areas where the two diagrams are not in balance suggest modifications which could be made to the diagrams, the project dictionary, or both which would balance the diagrams.

5. Check the vertical balance of the DFD hierarchy in Figure 6.14. To help with this checking, you will also need this fragment of the project dictionary:

identified radars = {identified radar}
identified radar = radar strength + radar direction + radar type +
     radar chars
radar chars = * a character string which gives the name of the radar *
radar type = * a radar will be displayed as a name (given by radar chars)
inside an icon, which will depend on the 'radar type' *
radar display = radar coords + radar chars + radar icon

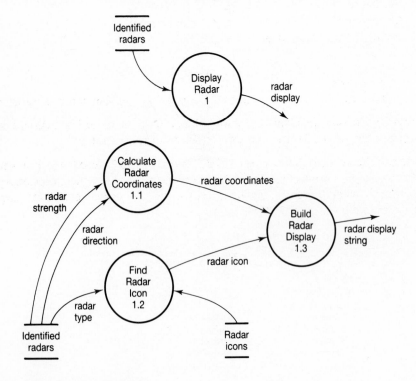

Figure 6.14 Exercise 5.

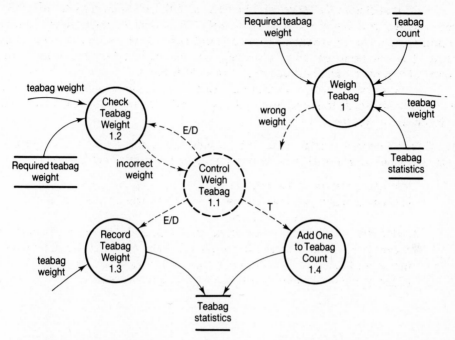

Figure 6.15 Exercise 6.

radar coords = radar x + radar y
radar display string = radar x + radar y + radar chars + radar icon

In areas where 'display radar' does not balance with its lower level DFD, suggest changes either to the DFDs, the project dictionary, or both.

6.   Check the vertical balance of the DFD hierarchy in Figure 6.15. You should be able to balance this hierarchy without reference to the project dictionary. In areas where 'weigh teabag' does not balance with its lower level DFD, suggest appropriate changes to the DFDs.

PART TWO

Analysis

In Chapter 1 the reasons for analyzing a system before it is designed were looked at. In analysis we try to discover what the system should do, before thinking about how it will do it. First of all, let us examine the ideas behind analysis and then look into the analysis procedure step by step.

Any system can be described by a network of processes and stored data. Consider a computer system, which consists of code and data. The lowest level units of your system, i.e. the machine code instructions and binary data, and the lowest level units of anybody else's system will be the same. It does not matter whether you are building a human–computer interface, a process control system or a banking system — the low level units are the same. A banking system differs from a process control system because the low level units are used by program hierarchy above them in different ways, which makes them work appropriately for that system. Therefore, the organization of the instructions within the program is what makes your program do what it does, as opposed to what somebody else's program does. This organization is very important and helps in understanding what the system does.

During analysis, we should organize the network of processes and stored data (i.e. the DFD, STD and ERD which describe the system) with respect to what the customer expects the system to do, rather than how the engineer expects to do it. If the models reflect low level units of work, rather than conceptual functions, the model for a banking system may look similar to the model for a process control system — at the very lowest level of implementation, they probably do.

Man-made systems also only do things when asked. Let us define the system's environment as anything that it is aware of or connected to in the outside world. The environment of a central heating control system might consist of the following:

1. A user control panel which would allow the user to switch on and off, set a timer and change the required room temperature.
2. A heater.
3. A temperature sensor.

This system will not do anything until something happens in the environment. When the user switches the system on, it will start monitoring the room temperature, and heating if the room is below the required temperature. Once the required room temperature has been reached (which the system will notice via the temperature sensor), the system will stop warming the room.

The central heating system will never 'just decide' to do something, without something happening in its environment to which it responds. Consider how useless a system with no interfaces would be. In many cases, the system will not be explicitly told to do something, it will have to work it out. The central heating system does not just heat up the room when the system is initially switched on. It will also heat the room if it detects that the temperature has fallen, while the system is switched on. Although this is not an explicit 'switch on' from the operator, the system still acts on information (temperature) from the system's environment.

On the basis of this, everything within an essential model should be a direct response to something happening in the system's environment. If your system has to do something which is not in response to the environment, how does the system know to do it?

Also, we should try to organize the DFD, STD and ERD to reflect how the customer perceives the system responding to customer-perceived happenings in its environment. This will make the diagrams meaningful and easy for the customer to understand.

These discussions lead to a strategy of 'outside-in' modelling. Everything which happens inside the model is dependent on things happening outside the model. Therefore, we start by modelling the system's environment on which the models of internal system behaviour are based. Initially we build models which make us concentrate on what the outside world looks like to our system. These make us aware of stimuli entering the system. By considering what the system may do on receipt of those stimuli, we can discover what we are supposed to do within the system.

The environment is modelled by a context diagram and an event list, from which the behavioural model (DFD, STD and ERD), is derived. It does not matter in which order you build the context diagram and the event list, since, as we will discuss later, they are very closely related. You might start by building a context diagram which helps you build the event list. You may find a couple of things on your event list that do not match up with your context diagram. You can then go back to your context diagram and modify it to match your event list. It will be an iterative process until the context diagram and the event list match.

CHAPTER SEVEN

The context diagram

7.1 INTRODUCTION

The context diagram is used to document the boundary between the system and its environment. It consists of a single data transformation which represents the whole system, surrounded by a number of boxes called terminators.

Terminators represent either pieces of equipment, subsystems or people in the outside world that your system has to interface to, i.e. your system's environment. An automated system normally includes more than just the computer program which drives the system. An automated central heating system could include a control panel, a boiler and a temperature sensor, as well as the computer itself.

Often a customer is not even aware of the boundary between the system and the equipment it controls. When the customer describes the system, the description may encompass many things other than the actual software and/or hardware that you ultimately develop.

The context diagram also shows the interfaces between the system and its terminators. Even though we are at the top of the system hierarchy, we show the total interface between the terminator and the system, i.e. the net flow of information.

Figure 7.1 shows the context diagram for a simple process control system. The context diagram shows the operator can start and stop the system, and that the current conditions are provided to him or her by the system. The operator

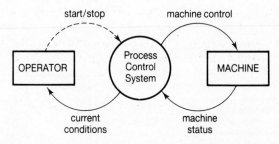

Figure 7.1   Simple process control context diagram.

cannot input any parameters to control the process control system, because there is no flow to allow this. Since a lower level DFD must have the same inputs and outputs as its parent data transformation, it does not matter how far down the model hierarchy we go: we can never introduce a flow that allows the operator to input parameters to the system. The terminator interface will depend on (a) the overall function of the system and (b) what part of that function the terminator can provide.

Assume we are building a process control system, where a furnace is heated to a certain temperature, and maintained at that temperature. An intelligent heater could be given the required temperature, and would heat and maintain that temperature. This would give the interface shown in Figure 7.2 between our system and the intelligent heater. On the other hand, with a less intelligent heater, which was not able to maintain a given temperature, we would constantly have to monitor and control the heater from within our system. This would give us the interface shown in Figure 7.2, between the system and a simple heater.

The system's requirement defines an area of work, 'maintain temperature'. With the intelligent heater, this is carried out inside the heater terminator. With the simple heater it is carried out inside our system, because the terminator is not clever enough to do it.

The interface should help us think about what's going on inside the system with respect to what is going on inside the terminator, and so describe the responsibility of our system.

Everything inside the context diagram data transformation is completely and absolutely under your control. Everything inside the context diagram data transformation is your responsibility, anything outside the boundary of the context diagram data transformation is not your responsibility (i.e. not part of your system development). The terminators are external pieces of equipment

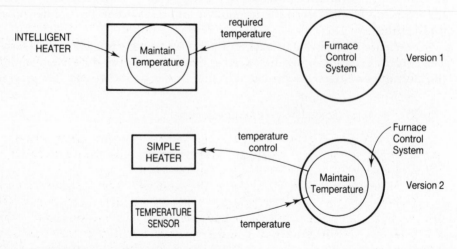

Figure 7.2   Maintain temperature positioning.

which operate in a certain predefined way, which already exist or are being built by other people. So although your system controls the terminators, it must fit in with the way in which they are defined to work.

One of the functions of the 'teabag boxing system' is to move the full teabag box from the end of the teabag conveyor belt, onto the full box conveyor belt. We have been told to use a certain robot arm to do this. Before we can decide exactly what our system must do here, we should examine the robot arm and find out how intelligent it is. i.e. how much of the overall function it can perform.

If the robot arm is very intelligent, we could send it a 'move full box' command, and it would go through the required sequence of movements automatically. In this case, we would not have to do much work in our system. However, as we have previously discussed, all we can do with this robot arm is tell it to move a certain amount in a certain direction, and to open or close its claw. Therefore, the sequence of movement commands required to move the box will have to be generated within our system. In this case, most of the work of the function is done by our system.

7.2 CONTEXT DIAGRAM COMPONENTS

7.2.1 Basic notation

As the context diagram is just a special type of DFD, the symbols and connections used in the context diagram are just a subset of those used in the DFD. The symbols which may be used are as follows:

1. Data transformation (which represents the whole system).
2. Flow.
3. Store.
4. Terminator.

These are all the symbols available to the DFD, except the control process and the prompt. The components have exactly the same meaning as in the DFD; however, the context diagram has a couple of extra rules which do not apply to a normal DFD.

7.2.2 Context diagram notation rules

A context diagram has a single data transformation, numbered implicitly, data transformation zero. You never actually write a zero in it, but it is always known as data transformation zero.

Flows between terminators are never shown. Figure 7.3 shows a system which is driven by an operator, and produces reports to a supervisor. Imagine that the supervisor is able to ask the operator to modify production control, which affects the way in which the operator drives the system. Unless they talk to each other via the system, the system will not know about the communication. If the

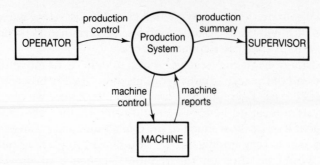

Figure 7.3   Production system context diagram.

system does not know about the communication, how can it possibly affect what the system does, and therefore the system that we are developing?

The communication will not be shown on the context diagram, because it is not relevant to our system development. If the communication between the operator and the supervisor is so important to the system that it does need to know about it, it should be routed through the system, i.e. there should be a flow 'supervisor production change' from the supervisor to the system, and a flow 'supervisor production change request' from the system to the operator.

Stores can be shown on the context diagram, but only between terminators and the system. A store on the context diagram does not necessarily represent a physical storage area. As it does on the DFD, a store represents data at rest. A direct data flow entering the system is the equivalent of a direct data flow entering any other data transformation: if the data transformation is disabled, or doing something else, it will not be able to accept the data.

Terminators do not always provide data directly to the system. If the system does not need to be ready when data is produced, and can collect the data at any time afterwards, the terminator is shown writing the data into a store. A terminator must be connected to this store so that we know where the data has come from. In this respect, a flow and a data store are almost the same. We would not show a flow on a context diagram which was not connected to a terminator, so we cannot show a store on a context diagram which is not connected to a terminator.

The other circumstance in which you might show a store on the context diagram is when the system shares some stored data with one (or more) of its terminators.

If a terminator directly accesses a store, the store access must be shown on the context diagram. Just as it is illegal for a data transformation to access an internal store of another data transformation directly, it is also illegal for a terminator to directly access a store which is internal to your system. If the store is actually within the system, we add an extra data transformation to provide the interface between the terminator and the store, as shown in Figure 7.4.

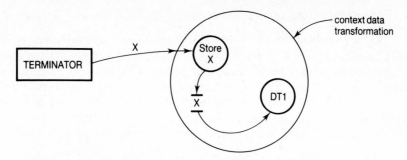

Figure 7.4   Legal store access.

7.3 BUILDING THE CONTEXT DIAGRAM

Building the context diagram involves understanding an overall functional area, understanding how a particular terminator can contribute to this functional area, and therefore understanding what is left for the system to do. This will define the interface between the system and the terminator.

Until you have identified all your terminators, and what they do, you do not know what the responsibilities of your system are, so you have no way of carrying on with your development. The strategy for building the context diagram involves the following steps:

1. Understand the purpose of the system.
2. Identify the system terminators.
3. Identify the system interface.
4. Start building the project dictionary.
5. Check the context diagram.

These five steps are considered in more detail in the remainder of this chapter.

7.3.1 Investigating the system requirements

To build the context diagram you should initially find out as much as you can about the proposed system functionality and choice of terminators.

The context diagram makes a statement about what your system will and will not do. Anything which is part of the system functionality, but which is not done by the terminator, must be done in your system. It is in your best interest to find terminators that will make the development easy for you. Finding and understanding terminators, and determining the correct interface between them and your system will involve a lot of investigation by the system development team. You will not be able to build the context diagram on day one of the development. The more effort you put into this preliminary investigation stage, the more aware you will be of exactly what you are committed to developing.

7.3.2 Identification of terminators

After understanding the overall functions of your system, you should identify your terminators. A terminator is anything that your system interfaces to. A terminator could be a person, a piece of equipment or a subsystem. Identifying terminators has already been discussed briefly in Section 2.3.

If your customer has identified that you will be controlling or interfacing to certain pieces of equipment, those will be your terminators. If we examine the following short statement of purpose, the terminators are quite easy to spot:

> The system is required to accept commands from the pilot. The system will then control the Z23 missile launching equipment on the basis of these commands and information received from the X17 navigation system.

The text specifies that the system will accept commands from the pilot, and will receive information from the X17 navigation system. Also, the system will control the Z23 missile launching equipment. Therefore, we will have three terminators:

1. Pilot.
2. X17 navigation system.
3. Z23 missile launching equipment.

Unfortunately, not many customers will be able to give you a statement of purpose which is so specific. Often, a customer will know that you need to use a certain type of equipment, but will not be more specific than that. Sometimes the customer may not even realize that you need to use a piece of equipment to fulfil some function of the system.

In both these cases it is up to you to decide on suitable equipment, based on functionality and cost. In the first case, picking a terminator involves the following:

1. Investigating the overall area of functionality that a terminator will be associated with.
2. Investigating any pieces of equipment that could fulfil that function. You should be evaluating
   (a) how much of the functional area they can perform;
   (b) how difficult it will be for your system to work with them;
   (c) how much they cost.

For example, our customer could specify a system which heats a furnace to a certain temperature, and maintains it at that temperature. We could find two pieces of equipment:

1. A simple, cheap heater with an on/off switch. To use this heater with the required functionality, we will also need a temperature sensor, so that we can monitor and control the temperature from within the system.
2. A more expensive heater, with a built-in thermostat, that will heat up to, and maintain, a given temperature. To use this heater with the required

functionality, we just need to send it the required temperature from our system.

Having investigated the various options, you should decide which heater to use, on the basis of cost and ease of development. When evaluating cost, do not just consider the actual cost of the terminator, but also the cost of extra development associated with a difficult terminator.

Let us consider costs in our example:

Option 1: cost of heater + cost of temperature sensor + cost of developing software to monitor and control temperature constantly

Option 2: cost of heater + cost of developing software to send out required temperature

In this example, option 2 would probably be cheaper than option 1 (even though the terminator is much cheaper in the first case), and would be a lot easier to develop.

In cases where customers know what they want the overall system to do, but have difficulty understanding the technology required to do it, you may have to begin with an 'expanded' context diagram. Here terminators are hidden inside the context diagram data transformation, either because nobody knows what they are, or because the customers would not understand what they were doing.

From initial discussions with our customer, we know that the teabag boxing system is meant to fill empty boxes with perfect teabags, and bin imperfect teabags. This leads to Figure 7.5, showing material flows representing teabags and boxes, which allows us to verify with our customer that we have understood his requirements.

The next step is to find out what is going on inside the material context diagram data transformation, possibly by finding out how the current manual system works:

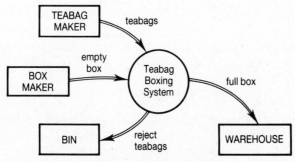

Figure 7.5 Expanded context diagram.

In the present manual system, teabags move along a conveyor belt on to some
scales.

The weight of the teabag is read by an operator, who, if the weight of
the teabag is incorrect, will pick the teabag off the scale and throw it into the
bin. If the weight is correct, the teabag will move along the conveyor belt until
it drops into the box.

Once the operator has counted 40 teabags into the box, he puts the full
box on to the conveyor belt running to the warehouse, and collects a new empty
box.

The conveyor belts are part of the teabag production and warehousing
systems, and will continue to work in the same way after the system has been
installed.

This description leads to the material DFD shown in Figure 7.6. This describes
the material processing required of the system, and should help in identifying
the equipment needed for this processing.

Examining each material transformation in turn, it is possible to split the
transformation into the 'material' part, i.e. the part concerned with the physical
teabags and equipment, and the control part, i.e. the part which will be done
in our control system:

1. Weigh teabag: to do this we need some scales from which the system
   can read the weight of the teabag.

   'Weigh teabag' contains the equipment 'scales'.

2. Place teabag in box: this will be done by the present conveyor belt system,
   so no new equipment is needed, and therefore no control is needed either.
3. Place teabag in bin: this cannot be done by the conveyor belt, so we need

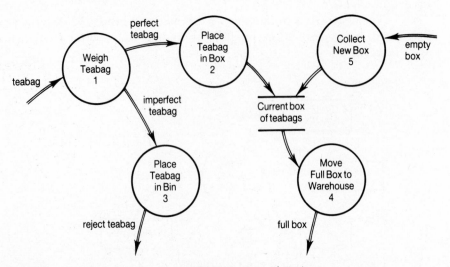

Figure 7.6   Material DFD for teabag boxing system.

another piece of equipment which will take the teabag from the conveyor belt and place it in the bin, i.e. a robot arm.

'Place teabag in bin' contains the equipment 'robot arm'.

4. Move full box to warehouse: as in 3, we need a robot arm to move the full box to the warehouse conveyor belt.

'Move full box to warehouse' contains the equipment 'robot arm'.

5. Collect new box: as in 3, we need a robot arm to collect the empty box and place it where it will be filled with teabags.

'Collect new box' contains the equipment 'robot arm'.

This identifies the new terminators 'robot arm' and 'scales' which, as in the previous example, can be chosen on the basis of functionality and cost. Joining these newly created 'terminators' to the terminators of the original context diagram, and splitting the original data transformations of Figure 7.6 into data transformations containing the identified equipment gives Figure 7.7.

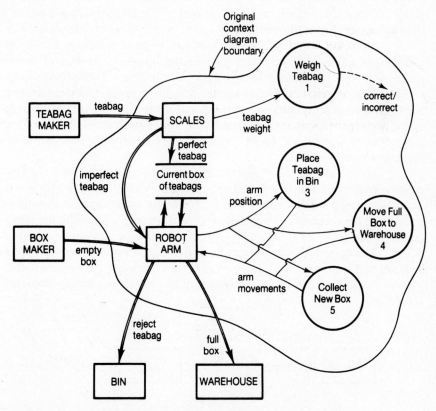

Figure 7.7   Internal expanded context diagram.

This shows the previously hidden pieces of equipment in the context of the original material requirements. Reducing the context diagram boundary, such that these pieces of equipment are now shown as terminators outside the context diagram data transformation gives the final context diagram for our system, shown in Figure 7.8. Any terminator which is not connected to the system can be removed from the context diagram, as it is not of interest in system development.

Beware of pieces of equipment which appear to be terminators, but are really just carriers of information from the real terminator.

During analysis, we are not so much interested in how information passes between the operator and the system, as in the information itself. Therefore, we are more interested in the operator than the keyboard and screen being used to communicate with the system. Although the terminal may change the form of information between the operator and the system, it does not change the essential content. The fact that the operator cannot interface directly to the system is an implementation constraint, that we suppress by means of our 'perfect technology'.

Similarly, you would not normally have a terminator representing a radio link or any other kind of communication channel. The real terminator would be whatever was using the communication channel. The communication channel is just the implementation mechanism used by the ultimate terminator as a means of communicating with the system.

Anything which passes information to your system without essentially changing it will normally be seen as a communication channel, and therefore will not be shown as the terminator. An exception to this will be pieces of equipment which work as sensors. For example, imagine a central heating system which monitors the temperature of a room and controls a heater accordingly. The terminator providing 'temperature' to the system could either be called 'temperature sensor' or 'room', as all the sensor does is pass the temperature directly to the system.

As we have already discussed, one of the steps involved in finding the context diagram boundary is understanding how intelligent our terminators are, and discovering whether they can perform any of the system functionality for us. Calling the terminator 'room' (the thing ultimately providing the temperature) is too vague to be of much help in understanding our system requirements.

The operator interfaces and communication channels which we suppress will not be forgotten about. However, as they are more concerned with how the system works than what it does, they will be considered during implementation modelling.

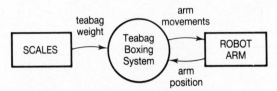

Figure 7.8   Reduced context diagram.

The only reason for showing them as terminators at this stage would be if they were part of the essential behaviour of the system. Imagine a development concerned purely with building the human—computer interface between a defined system and an operator via a defined terminal. Here, the context data transformation 'human—computer interface' would interface to terminators 'defined system' and 'operator terminal'.

7.3.3 Identification of interfaces

Once the terminators have been defined, the interface between your system and those terminators should be considered. This involves examining the function within your system that a particular terminator is associated with and considering the operation of the terminator with respect to that function.

If the terminator represents a piece of equipment, examine the type of controls the system can send it and the type of information it will send back. Evaluate how clever the terminator is and, therefore, how clever the system must be to compensate for any parts of the functional area the terminator cannot perform.

If the terminator represents a person, consider the commands and information the person will provide to the system, and the information the person will require back. Evaluate how intelligent the person expects the system to be.

This should lead to the interface between your system and the terminator. In deriving this interface, you should consider what the terminator does and mould the interface around this.

Firstly, given a system with a particular function, and a particular terminator, the interface may look very different depending on how intelligent that terminator is. Figure 7.9 shows the central heating system considered earlier in the chapter. In both (a) and (b), the terminator 'temperature sensor' communicates with a 'central heating system'. However, the interfaces shown between the terminator and the system are very different. In Figure 7.9(a), the

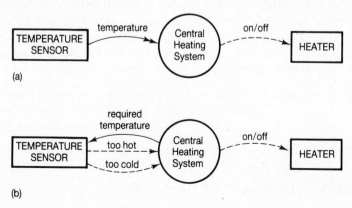

Figure 7.9   Central heating system context diagrams.

'temperature sensor' is fairly basic. The system receives the temperature constantly from the 'temperature sensor', and switches the heater on or off accordingly. In Figure 7.9(b), the 'temperature sensor' is more intelligent. Given a required temperature range by the system, it will monitor the temperature constantly, and let the system know only when the temperature becomes too hot or too cold. The system will again switch the heater on and off accordingly, but it does not have to do the work of constantly receiving and evaluating the temperature to see if it is too hot or too cold, as this is done by the intelligent sensor.

Secondly, the interface shown between your system and the terminator, must be one that the terminator can provide. In the previous example, we cannot show the unintelligent 'temperature sensor' providing the event flow 'too hot' to the system, if it is physically unable to provide anything other than a temperature reading. This would give a false idea of the amount of work required within the system, such that when the system was built, it would not function adequately with the given temperature sensor.

The whole point of building the context diagram is to show how our flexible system (at this point we are just trying to decide what the system will do) will fit in with its inflexible environment (the terminators which have already been decided upon, and work in predefined ways).

7.3.4 Starting the project dictionary

As soon as you have a diagram, you can start building the project dictionary. The context diagram requires entries for the following:

1. Terminators.
2. Flows.
3. Stores.

You could also give the statement of purpose as the transformation specification for the context diagram data transformation.

Do not feel that you have to give a lot of detail at this stage, especially in the area of flow decomposition — it is unlikely that you will be able to decompose a flow down to its elemental items. For example, consider the flow 'teabag removing movements' between the robot arm terminator and the teabag boxing system. The project dictionary entry at this stage might be:

teabag removing movements = * sequence of movements required to remove a teabag from the conveyor belt and place it in the bin *

The detail of exactly what the sequence consists of can be given at a later stage.

7.4 CHECKING THE CONTEXT DIAGRAM

Like all the other diagrams, the context diagram should be both syntactically correct and meaningful. As the behavioural model of the system will be derived from the context diagram, it is also important that it describes the customer's requirements correctly and completely.

7.4.1 Checking for syntactic correctness

The context diagram is syntactically correct if it follows all the syntax rules defined for the DFD, together with the extra rules specified in Section 7.2.2.

7.4.2 Checking for coherence

As with all the other diagrams, coherence can be checked in terms of naming and partitioning of diagram components. In the case of the context diagram, this involves checking the terminators and their interfaces.

7.4.2.1 *Naming and partitioning of terminators*

Like ERD objects, terminators do not necessarily represent physical things, but roles which those physical things play with respect to your system. This leads to a number of guidelines concerning the naming and partitioning of terminators.

1. A terminator should be named by what it does in the system, rather than by what it physically is. Imagine a naval system, required to interface to a navigation system, implemented on a DEC computer. In this case, we would call the terminator 'navigation system', i.e. the role the DEC machine is playing with respect to our system. If we were to call the terminator 'DEC computer' it could be doing just about anything, and that would not make the diagram meaningful or easy to understand.

   Naming terminators by the roles which they play will make your diagrams more helpful, both to you and your customer.

2. Just because two roles in your system are played by the same physical piece of equipment does not mean that they have to be shown as a single terminator. Imagine another naval system, interfacing to a navigation system and a missile guidance system, both implemented on the same DEC computer. As these are separate functions we show two terminators, even though they are implemented on the same physical piece of equipment. Showing the terminator as 'DEC computer' does not tell us what the computer does with respect to our system, and we may not realize it performs two functions.

   If it is important to know that both functions are implemented on the same piece of equipment, this can either be recorded in the project dictionary entry for the terminators, or as a comment on the context diagram itself.

3. If separate pieces of equipment play a single role in your system, you only need to show a single terminator.

   Imagine part of a banking system, where a card reader, a keypad and a note dispenser work together to provide the cash dispensing facility of the bank. In this case it would make the context diagram less cluttered and more clear if these pieces of equipment were represented as a single 'cash dispenser' terminator.

4. If you have multiple pieces of the same equipment, which all interface to your system in the same way and are all playing the same role, you only need to show one terminator. This idea has already been discussed in Chapter 3, when a single STD was produced where the control sequence (or STD) for several similar pieces of equipment was the same.

Figure 7.10 shows two options for indicating multiple instances of a terminator on the context diagram. Alternatively, the information could be held in the terminator entry of the project dictionary.

The context diagram should help you understand the system, and help your customer understand that you have understood the system. Within certain boundaries, whatever you do towards that end will be right.

7.4.2.2 *Naming and partitioning of the interface*

Guidelines for naming flows are the same as when building a DFD. Always name the flow by the information moving along it, not by the physical communication line which connects a terminator to the system. Imagine a weather station connected to a weather prediction system by a radio link. We will not be interested in the radio link until the implementation stages of the development. In the essential model we are more interested in the information which is passing between the weather station and the system. A flow 'radio link' will not tell us about the functional responsibilities of the system.

The interface between the context diagram data transformation and the terminator should be the whole interface (i.e. the net flow of information) between the system and whatever it interfaces to. However, putting all the detail of the interface on to the context diagram would make it look very cluttered. Therefore, the flows should be levelled to give a less crowded interface between the

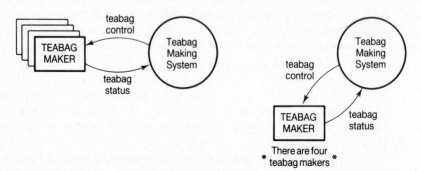

Figure 7.10   Representation of multiple terminators.

terminator and the system, whilst still giving enough information to show fundamentally how the terminator and the system work together.

At this point it is worth noting that terminators fall into two very different groups: those that represent machines and those that represent people (i.e. users of the system). Generally, when a system interfaces to a person, the interface is very different from that used when a system interfaces to a machine.

Consider the interface between a user who wishes to display a report, and the system displaying the report. The user and the system may go through the following sequence of communication:

1. System produces 'function menu' for user.
2. User requests 'report' option from menu.
3. System produces 'report menu' for user.
4. User requests 'display' option from menu.
5. System produces 'display form'.
6. User fills in: file name, display type, report sheets and various other fields.
7. System checks completed form and reports field errors to user.
8. User corrects form.
9. User requests display commence.
10. System displays report.

Essentially all that is happening here is that the user requests report to be displayed and the system displays report. If the flows representing the communication of steps 1 to 10 were shown in the context diagram, it would soon become very crowded. This would be clearer shown as two compound flows 'report display request' and 'report display', with entries in the project dictionary giving their breakdowns into steps 1 to 10.

Even though some of the low level flows within 'report display request' would go from the system to the user, the net flow of data is shown from the user to the system (i.e. the essential direction of information flow all the low level flows are trying to achieve).

In human interfaces, you will often find that several flows group into a single meaningful flow, with a decomposition in the project dictionary. This will certainly make the context diagram less crowded, and should also make it easier to understand. Initially we are unlikely to be interested in all the detail of the interface between the system and the user. On the other hand, when the system interfaces to a machine it does not need to coax information out of the machine and check every piece of information that the machine gives it (physical communication and protocol checking will be considered during design).

Normally, the system requests a piece of information, which the machine returns, or commands the machine to do something, which it will do, Therefore, interfacing with machinery implies an already minimal interface and levelling the flows within the interface does not usually help very much.

Imagine the interface between the 'teabag boxing system' and the 'robot arm' terminator, which is required to change boxes and remove teabags. Grouping the flows into 'box changing movements' and 'teabag removing movements' into 'arm movements' makes the interface look smaller, but suppresses information about what the system is doing with the robot arm.

There will also tend to be more flexibility in the interfaces between the system and people. When interfacing to a machine, the commands and protocol specified in the manual for that machine must be followed, otherwise the interface will not work. As we have already discussed, there is no point in showing an interface between a terminator and your system which the terminator cannot fit in with.

On the other hand, when interfacing to a person, information and requests can be provided in a number of different ways. In the previous operator interface example, we could decide not to provide the user with a 'display form', but to ask the user a number of questions and give him answers that he could select from the keyboard. Alternatively, we could use a mouse or a touch screen, or we may decide not to use a terminal at all. A person would be flexible enough to fit in with all of these interfaces, even though all of them require slightly different functionality from that person.

In the early analysis phases, it is unlikely that the users know exactly what the human−computer interface should look like. If they do, it is even more unlikely that they will not change their minds before you start developing it. Initially, the user is more likely to request the ability to print a particular report, than the transactions required to do it.

Specifying all the detail of the interface at this stage, will therefore cause a number of problems:

1. We have not decided firmly what the interface does yet, so defining the detail of the interface will be very difficult.
2. A lot of detail will take a lot of time to develop and document, and will cloud understanding of the fundamentals of the system.
3. The human−computer interface is an area which is very susceptible to change. Detailed analysis at this stage may be wasted when the customer changes his mind.

Normally, you can group together flows from human terminators much more easily and successfully than you can from machine terminators, although, sometimes, it will make sense to level flows to machine terminators as well.

Imagine the interface between an engine and engine management system, where valves are controlled to open and close. There are four valves in the engine which all work in exactly the same way, giving four event flows, one going to each valve instructing it to open or close. These event flows could be grouped into the compound event flow 'valve control'. The only information lost is that there are four valves. This does not make the diagram any less easy to understand, but it does remove a lot of the flows.

Whether we are considering interfaces to machines or interfaces to people, the general guidelines for levelling flows are the same. A number of lower level flows should not be grouped unless they produce a meaningful higher level flow which makes the context diagram look less cluttered. If you group lower level flows, a suitable entry should be made in the project dictionary.

However, you should avoid grouping pieces of information together which do not belong together, just to make the diagram look tidier. The diagram may look tidier, but it will also be meaningless. For instance, grouping an entire user interface into 'user commands' gives no information about what the user can do with the system.

Imagine a terminator which (wrongly) performs two functional roles, for example, a single computer which provided a navigation system and a missile control system to a naval control system. Grouping the flows 'navigation coordinates' with 'missile launch status' into 'navigation missile data' leaves a high level data flow which is, at best, meaningless and, at worse, misleading. It also hides the fact that the terminator is playing two roles and should therefore be shown as two terminators.

This leads to the next point concerning the grouping of flows connected to different terminators. Firstly, this makes the context diagram look a little odd, as shown in Figure 7.11. The temptation is to join the terminators together to tidy the diagram. Separate terminators will tend to relate to separate functional areas, and should not be joined just to tidy the diagram. By the same argument, flows related to separate terminators must also relate to different functional areas, and so will not belong to the same levelled flow.

7.4.3 Checking for completeness

Finally, before the context diagram is used to build the behavioural model of the system, you should check that it describes the right system. This will involve the following:

1. Checking the diagram against the system statement of purpose.
2. Showing the diagram to the customer or anybody who has to use the system.

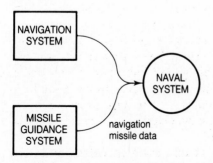

Figure 7.11   Flows from different terminators.

3. Showing the diagram to anybody who is involved in building subsystems that your system has to interface to.
4. Checking that, for pieces of equipment used as terminators, the interface defined on your context diagram between the system and that terminator is possible.

You are looking for the following:

1. Terminators and interfaces which have been forgotten.
2. Terminators and interfaces which are not really required, but which are shown on the diagram.
3. Incorrect terminators.
4. Incorrect interfaces between the system and its terminators (a very common problem which causes developers either to underestimate or to overestimate the intelligence of a terminator, leading to a system with either too much or too little functionality).

Also, once you have built the event list, you need to check that the context diagram and the event list both describe the same system — this will be covered in the next chapter.

7.5 CONTEXT DIAGRAMS FOR LARGE AND COMPLEX SYSTEMS

If, during building your context diagram, it starts to look like Figure 7.12, you may have a problem. Figure 7.12 describes part of a car control system, which has not yet been completed, as there was no room to put any more terminators. A context diagram with many terminators and/or large complicated terminator interfaces is likely to frighten and confuse both the customer and the system developer.

Large, complicated context diagrams arise either because you are developing a large, complex system or as a result of poor partitioning. The context diagram is meant to describe terminators and interfaces at a high level, giving an idea of the high level functionality of the system. We could easily join many of the terminators shown in Figure 7.12, to give the context diagram of Figure 7.13. All the detail available in Figure 7.13 will be shown in lower level DFDs and later stages of the design.

If the system under development is large and complex, partitioning will not help to reduce the complexity of the diagram. Imagine a system which interfaces to 20 terminators, all playing different roles with respect to the system. Grouping terminators will involve merging things which do not belong together, therefore either complicating or over-simplifying the system. Figure 7.14 shows the context diagram for an aircraft training simulator, which has 10 terminators, all providing different functional areas to the system.

1. Aircraft instrument displays: These are the displays on the equipment

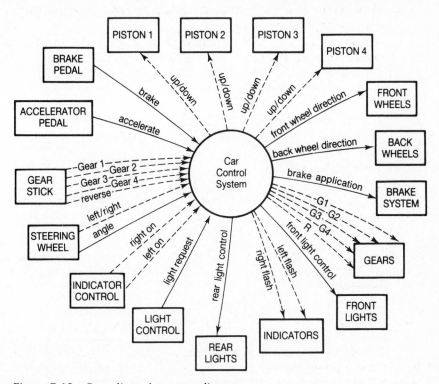

Figure 7.12 Complicated context diagram.

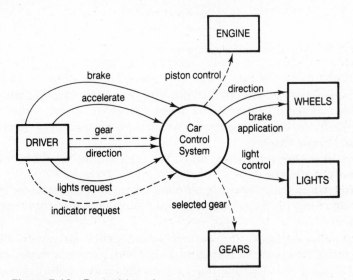

Figure 7.13 Repartitioned car control system.

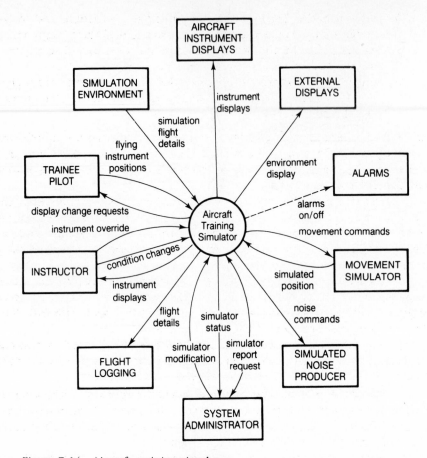

Figure 7.14   Aircraft training simulator.

inside the simulated aircraft cockpit. They mimic the displays which the pilot would see if he was flying a real aircraft.

2. External displays: this is the display which the pilot sees out of the cockpit, i.e. the terrain displays.

3. Alarms: these are the alarms which the pilot would hear if he were to fly in a real aircraft.

4. Movement simulator: this moves the cockpit of the simulator.

5. Simulated noise producer: this produces simulated engine, flight and crash noises.

6. System administrator: the system administrator is responsible for configuring the system to mimic an aircraft with particular characteristics.

7. Flight logging: this logs the flight which the trainee pilot has made, so that it can be played back and analyzed later.

8. Instructor: the instructor can monitor the simulation, and 'drive' the simulation by requesting effects such as engine failures, high winds, etc.
9. Trainee pilot: the pilot has available all the controls and displays of a real aircraft, and will wish to use them in a realistic way.
10. Simulation environment: this provides the terrain maps through which the pilot will be flying, and the airport descriptions at which the aircraft can take off and land.

In this case, there are a couple of techniques that you can use to help simplify the diagram. Firstly, you can draw a set of context diagrams describing the same system, but placing emphasis on certain parts of the system depending on to whom the diagram will be shown.

Imagine providing a context diagram for a customer, to verify that we had mimicked the aircraft controls and displays correctly. The customer would be especially interested in the terminators 'trainee pilot', 'alarms' and 'aircraft instrument displays', but would not be very interested in any of the other terminators. This is shown in Figure 7.15(a).

Figure 7.15(b) shows the context diagram produced for the developer responsible for all the aircraft displays (both internal and external). Here, the original terminator 'aircraft instrument displays' has been split into 'head-up display' and 'multi-purpose display', to give more detail.

The grouping of the other terminators in both of these diagrams may not be ideal. However, it does not matter too much, as the person at which the diagram is aimed is not interested in the other terminators.

Secondly, in a very large system, consider splitting it into a number of smaller developments. Managing a monster development is a nightmare, and most of the problems encountered with huge developments (which rarely succeed) are of a managerial rather than a technical nature.

Figure 7.16 shows a naval vessel control system, which typically will run into hundreds of man years of development. The system includes a navigation system, a missile system and an ECM (electronic counter measures) system, all of which have interfaces with the operator, specific pieces of equipment, and each other. In this example, the overall system could be split into subsystems, with a context diagram for each subsystem, as shown in Figure 7.17.

Taking each subsystem as the context, the other subsystems become terminators to that context diagram. Instead of one huge development, there are now a number of smaller developments, which can be developed almost in isolation once the interfaces have been agreed.

Notice that the interface between, for example, the ECM system and the navigation system remains the same whether we are considering the navigation system or the ECM system as the context diagram data transformation. The drawback of this approach is that you have to be absolutely sure that the subsystems have been partitioned correctly.

Finally, a word of warning. Using a structured technique will not

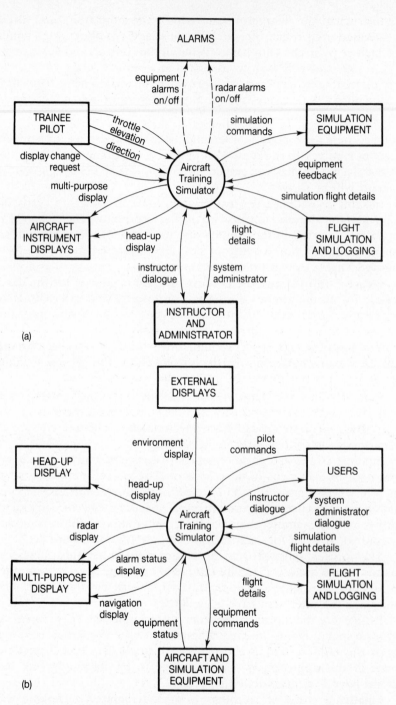

Figure 7.15 Modified aircraft training simulator: (a) for pilot; (b) for developers producing graphics systems.

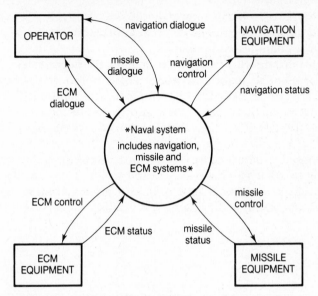

Figure 7.16   Overall naval system.

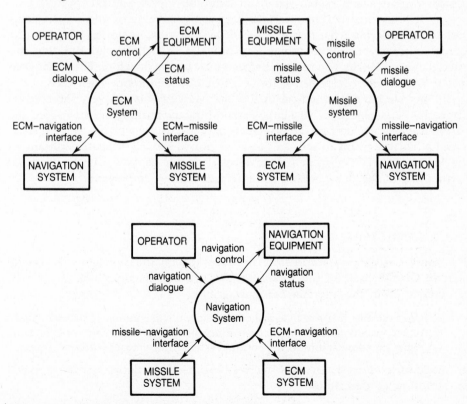

Figure 7.17   Naval system split into subsystems.

magically turn a complicated system into a simple one. If, even after careful partitioning, you end up with a complicated context diagram, it is because you are trying to develop a complicated system.

In many traditional development environments, the normal steps of top down decomposition seem to ignore anything which is too complicated to understand until it is too late. In structured development, we suppress things not because we do not understand them, but because initially we do not need to know about them, and they will not affect the early decisions that we make about the development.

One of the aims of structured analysis is to go into the design phase with a clear understanding of what you have let yourself in for. This can almost be seen as the opposite of the traditional approach, as it involves hiding detail in the bits that you do understand, and bringing out detail in the bits that you do not understand.

7.6 SUMMARY

In showing the interface between your system and its terminators, the context diagram makes a subtle statement about the responsibilities of your system.

If you construct an interface between a terminator and your system without considering what that implies the system must be doing, you may end up committing yourself to things you had not thought about. Building this interface should make you realize, before you start the development, what your system is and is not responsible for — so build the interface with care.

As we have touched on in the later part of this chapter, the context diagram is very subjective. To a large extent, how the terminators are named and partitioned depends on who the diagram is to be shown to, who has to understand it and what they want to see. As you tend not to show terminators on any of the lower level DFDs, from the developer's point of view, the naming and partitioning of the flows within the interface is more important.

7.7 EXERCISES

1.   Figure 7.18 shows four possible interfaces to a missile from a missile control system. On the basis of the following description, decide which is the best representation of the interface being described.

> Once the missile has been launched, the system will continue to provide it with directional information to steer it towards the target. The missile will detonate, either on command from the control system or on impact with the target.

2.   Build the context diagram for the 'washing machine control system' specified in the following description:

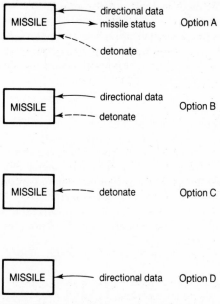

Figure 7.18 Exercise 1.

A simple washing machine could operate in the following way:

(a) A drum, where the washing is carried out, is filled with water, which is heated to a specified temperature.
(b) Once at the correct temperature, the drum goes through a sequence of rotations at different speeds and directions in order to wash the clothes.
(c) Once this sequence is over the drum is drained, and the washing is done.

The washing machine comprises:

(a) The drum — this can be sent commands to make it rotate at a certain speed in a certain direction.
(b) A heater — used to heat the water in the drum. The system is able to monitor the temperature of the heater constantly; however, is only able to heat the water while the drum is not moving.
(c) An input valve and an output valve — used to control the amount of water in the drum. An indication is also given by the drum of the water level.

The operator enters the required wash cycle, which will determine (a) the temperature of wash and (b) the sequence and speed of washing machine drum rotation.

3. Build the context diagram for the 'greenhouse atmosphere control system' described by the following description.

In order for orchids to bloom, the greenhouse temperature and humidity must be regulated to ensure that they do not go outside certain limits.

The temperature will be measured by a simple thermometer, which gives a constant reading of the temperature.

The temperature will be controlled using a heater, which has both a heating element (which only has one heat setting — so it is either on or off) and a fan which can be controlled independently. Normally, to heat the greenhouse, both the heater and the fan would be switched on. However, if the greenhouse becomes too hot, the fan can be switched on without the heating element, which will cool the greenhouse down.

The humidity will be controlled by way of vents in the greenhouse roof. The vents can be adjusted to any angle between 0° (fully shut) and 180° (fully open), and their current angle of openness can always be read.

The humidity will be measured by a simple hydrometer, which gives a constant reading of humidity levels. If the greenhouse humidity goes out of range, the vents will be adjusted by the appropriate amount.

As it takes some time for the humidity levels to drop after the vents have been adjusted, another humidity reading will not be taken for 5 minutes, to allow the change in vent positions to take effect.

The whole system should be able to be switched on and off by a gardener, using a single control.

4.   Expanding on the description given in exercise 1, build a context diagram for the following 'missile control system'.

The operator types information into the system defining the missile target, in terms of location and time.

The missile trajectory will be calculated, and at the correct time will be launched from a big gun, which has been positioned in accordance with the calculated trajectory.

Although the gun launches the missile in the correct direction, it is possible that in certain weather conditions, the missile may be blown off course.

Therefore, it is necessary to track the missile throughout its flight to ensure that it sticks to the calculated trajectory. As the missile is being tracked, a display of the current missile location will be given to the operator. Also, at any time, the operator may change the target coordinates, either because the target has moved or because a mistake has been made.

Therefore, once the missile has been launched, the system will continue to provide it with directional information to steer it towards the target. The missile will detonate, either on command from the control system or on impact with the target.

CHAPTER EIGHT

The event list

8.1 INTRODUCTION

The event list is very important as the behavioural model, i.e. the DFD, STD and ERD, is derived from it. It would be possible to build an automated toolkit, which would automatically generate the DFD, STD and ERD which describe the system, given the context diagram and the event list in a highly syntactic form.

The event list is really the pivotal point of the whole analysis phase. However, it is often ignored by people with a sparse knowledge of structured development, as it is not a diagram. Once you have built the environmental model (i.e. the context diagram and the event list), which involves studying the purpose of your system and anything your system interfaces to, building the lower levels of the essential model should be straightforward.

Before we consider building an event list, let us consider how the event list is used. This should give you an idea of why the event list is so important.

The event list is a table which holds events, responses to events and classification of events. The idea that the system work can be defined in terms of responses to things that happen in the system's environment was discussed in the introduction to Part II. Your system does not do anything unless some kind of stimulus comes from the outside world. The event list documents these stimuli and responses.

In Table 8.1 the event column is a list of everything which happens in the system's environment which causes a response from our system. The response column defines the response our system will make to the given stimuli, worded in terms of what the customer thinks the system will do. The classification column defines how the system will produce the response in terms of data transformations and state changes, thus defining how to model the response in a DFD, STD or ERD.

Let us examine a few events from Table 8.1 to see how they can be used to generate fragments of STD and DFD, ultimately combined to create the behavioural model. Event 2 states that when the operator requests a statistics report the system should provide a statistics report. The 'D' classification defines that in order to provide the response, we need a data transformation. Therefore,

Table 8.1. *Teabag boxing system event list*

Event	Response	Classification
1. Operator enters new teabag weight	Update required teabag weight	D
2. Operator requests statistics report	Provide statistics report	D
3. Operator requests start	Start weighing, counting and collecting statistics on teabags	C/D
4. Teabag at incorrect weight	Start removing teabag	C/D
5. Teabag removed	Stop removing teabag	C
6. Teabox full	Stop weighing, counting and collecting statistics on teabags and start replacing box	C/D
7. New teabox	Stop replacing box and start weighing, counting and collecting statistics on teabags	C/D
8. Operator requests stop	Stop weighing, counting and collecting statistics on teabags	C

the event prompts the generation of the data transformation 'provide statistics report'. The response becomes the name of the data transformation. The input and output of the data transformation can be found from examining the corresponding context diagram (Figure 8.8) with respect to what the data transformation has to do.

Event 4 states that when the system notices a teabag at the incorrect weight, it must start to remove it from the conveyor belt. The 'C/D' classification defines that in order to create the response, we need a change of state which involves starting a data transformation. Therefore, the event prompts the generation of the data transformation 'remove teabag' and a fragment of STD which changes state from 'idle' to 'removing teabag'. In this STD fragment, the event becomes the condition which causes the change of state, the response becomes the action which takes the system into the next state. The state names can be derived by thinking about what the system is doing.

Event 5 states that once the teabag has been removed from the conveyor belt, we need to stop trying to move the teabag. The 'C' classification defines that in order to provide this response, we need to change state; however, in this case, we will not need to start a data transformation. This prompts the generation of the fragment of STD which moves from the 'removing teabag' back to the 'idle' state. Again, the event becomes the condition which causes the change of state to happen, the response becomes the action which takes the system into the next state.

The whole event list will generate many data transformations and STD fragments, which can be joined into the DFD and STDs which model our system.

This outside-in modelling technique is known as 'event partitioning', and represents a major change from the method of top-down decomposition which many developers employ when building a hierarchy of models describing a system.

Imagine an event list with 30 events, which define 22 data transformations and 15 changes of state. From the context diagram and event list, we would generate a DFD with 22 data transformations and a number of STDs, which could be turned into control processes for integration with the DFD. This scenario is shown in Figure 8.1(a).

This DFD is too large and complicated for the top level DFD (i.e. the one directly below the context diagram), and so is levelled, as shown in Figure 8.1(b). The groups of original data transformations and control processes form the lower level diagrams for the top level DFD data transformations. If some of the original data transformations were a little complicated, we might want to decompose them into lower level DFDs. This gives the complete levelled model shown in Figure 8.2.

The advantages of this approach over top down partitioning are two-fold. Firstly, with top-down decomposition, it is difficult not to break the system down into lower level units which reflect how you think you might implement the system. In the essential model, this is exactly what we do not want to do. Using the event list, partitioned according to how the customer views the system, will ensure a system broken down into units as the customer perceives them.

Secondly, during top-down decomposition, you consider the total work of the system and group it into higher level units in your head. The event list makes you write down the total work of the system, forcing some structure into your decisions on grouping the lower level areas of work. It is much easier to make mistakes in your head than on paper.

This example should give you an idea of the purpose of the event list. Where the events come from, how they are classified and how the DFD and STDs are generated from them will be considered throughout the rest of this and the following chapters.

8.2 EVENT LIST COMPONENTS

As mentioned in the introduction, the event list does not just hold events, but is a list of events, corresponding responses and classifications.

8.2.1 The event

The event list should more properly be called the 'external' event list, as the events of interest all happen in the system's environment, i.e. externally

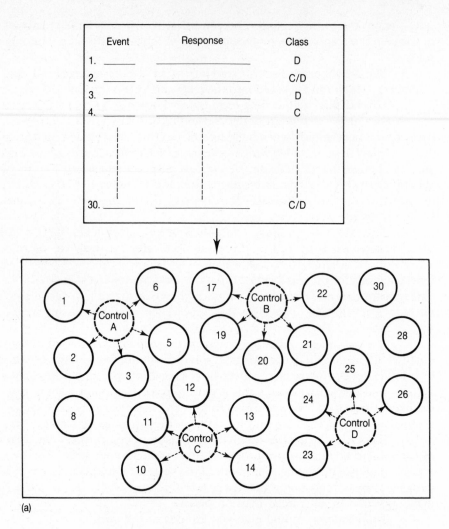

Event	Response	Class
1. ___	_____	D
2. ___	_____	C/D
3. ___	_____	D
4. ___	_____	C
30. ___	_____	C/D

(a)

Figure 8.1 Preliminary models: (a) transformation diagram.

to our system. For an event to qualify for the event list, it must have the following three characteristics:

1. It must happen in the system's environment.
2. The system must respond positively to the event.
3. The system must be able to recognize exactly when the event has happened.

Let us examine these characteristics in more detail.

First '*an event must be something that happens in the system's*

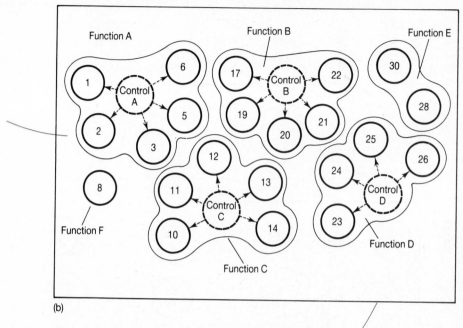

(b)

Figure 8.1 (*continued*)   (b) grouping of functionality.

environment,' i.e. inside a terminator. In order for your system to know that something has happened in a terminator, you would expect a flow coming from the terminator into the system, giving information about what was happening in the system's environment. However, it will not always be an event flow — this depends on how intelligent the terminator is.

Sometimes a terminator will not be clever enough to tell the system explicitly that an event has occurred. The terminator may only be able to pass data relating to that event to the system, from which it can derive that the event has occurred.

Figure 8.3 shows a central heating control system which will automatically heat a room once the temperature in the room drops below a certain level. The intelligent terminator 'temperature sensor' is able to tell the system that the outside temperature is too cold. In this case the terminator is able to provide the actual external event 'too cold'.

Figure 8.4 shows the same central heating control system with a temperature sensor which is not so clever. This terminator cannot tell the system that it is too cold, only the current temperature. 'Temperature' or even 'temperature arrives' is not an event — there are lots of values of the temperature that the system does not respond to (whenever the temperature is not too cold), so it does not fit in with our second criterion for being an event. The only values of temperature which interest the system are those below a certain value. We

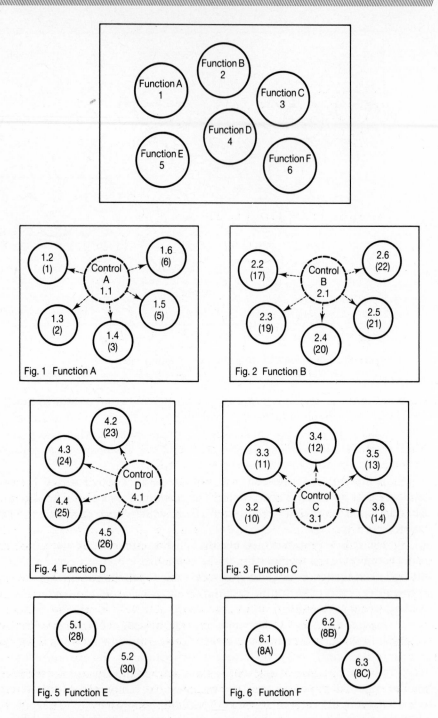

Fig. 1 Function A

Fig. 2 Function B

Fig. 4 Function D

Fig. 3 Function C

Fig. 5 Function E

Fig. 6 Function F

Figure 8.2 Levelled model.

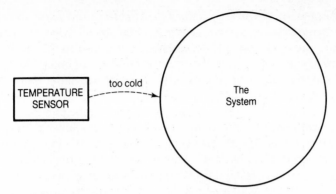

Figure 8.3   Too cold event from the terminator.

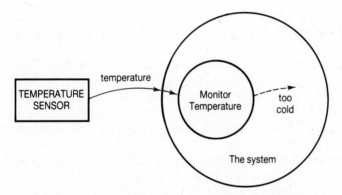

Figure 8.4   Too cold event from within the system.

are looking for the same event as in the previous example, 'too cold'. However, in this example, we do not know that the temperature has become too cold until it has been evaluated within the system and found to be lower than a certain value. Therefore, we need an 'event recognizing' data transformation within the system, which constantly monitors the temperature, and produces the event 'too cold' when the temperature drops below a certain point.

This means that the event flow 'too cold' is generated within our system, although the actual event of the temperature becoming too cold still happened in the system's environment. Just because an event flow is generated inside the system does not mean that it is not an external event. Here, the choice of terminator meant that the system cannot recognize the event until it has processed the related data.

When evaluating an external event, you should consider where the event actually happened, not where it was recognized. In our example, it did not become too cold inside the system, but inside the terminator, so the event is an external event, whether it is recognized by the terminator or by the system.

Secondly '*the system must respond positively to the event.*' There are many things happening in your system's environment, and all sorts of information being passed from the environment to your system, but not all this information promotes a positive response. There are plenty of things happening in the teabag boxing system's environment which our system does nothing about. For example, if a teabag is weighed at the correct weight, we allow it to move along the conveyor belt, which requires no action from the system. In the previous example, our system did something when the temperature dropped below a certain point. 'Temperature arrives' is not an external event, as the system does not do anything just because the temperature has arrived. 'Temperature falls' is not an event either, as the system does not do anything until the temperature drops to a certain point.

The only thing our system makes a positive response to is temperature 'too cold', so that is the only thing which should be shown in the event list. By a positive response, I mean the system responds by doing something different from what it was doing before the event occurred.

Imagine a data transformation 'check temperature', which continually monitors temperature, and eventually produces an event 'too cold'. We could argue that 'temperature arrives' is an event, because it will cause the response 'check temperature'. However, the system was already checking the temperature and will continue to do that until the temperature becomes too cold. The arrival of temperature does not cause the system to do anything different, i.e. it has not promoted any positive response, therefore 'temperature arrives' is not an external event.

The purpose of the event list is to capture the functionality of the system in terms of responses to external events. An event which the system does not make a positive response to will give an empty response column in the event list since a response that tells the system to start doing what it is already doing does not make sense. If we cannot define what the system does in response to any external event, we have nothing to record in the response and classification columns of the event list, so that event will not help to derive the behavioural model, and is of no interest.

Thirdly '*The system must be able to recognize exactly when an event has happened.*' This means that you should be able to pinpoint the exact time, or discrete piece of information that tells the system an event has occurred. The response to an event must happen immediately after the event has occurred. If the system does not know exactly when the event occurred, it will not know when to make the response. There are three points being made here:

1. The response has to happen immediately after the event has occurred. Imagine a central heating system, where the user can program the system to start heating at a specified time. The response to the event 'user enters time to start heating' is not 'start heating,' or even 'start heating at the specified time'. These responses do not describe what the system does

when the user enters the time, but what the system does some time afterwards.

The immediate response will be 'enter user specified time into heating schedule' — this information can be used later by an event-recognizing data transformation, to produce the event 'time to start heating'.

2. Events are not always indicated by information entering the system, but by the arrival of a particular time. Time must be outside your system, as it is not under your control, therefore the arrival of a particular time can be seen as something which happens in the system's environment.

3. Although it must be a discrete piece of information which tells the system an event has occurred, it may not be associated with a discrete flow. In Figure 8.3, we wait for the event 'too cold' associated with the continuous flow 'temperature'. Although the temperature arrives continually, there is a discrete value of temperature which tells the system that it has dropped below the required value. The event is not 'temperature drops', as the temperature drops continually over a period of time and the system would not know when to respond to it. The event is 'temperature starts to drop' or 'temperature drops below a certain value', to allow the system to pinpoint exactly when the event happens, and therefore exactly when to respond.

Let us examine some potential events, and evaluate whether they are external events, by asking three questions:

1. Does this happen in the systems environment?
2. Does the system respond positively to this happening?
3. Can we pinpoint this happening to a particular time?

We will consider just two terminators from the teabag boxing system. The 'scales', which produce 'teabag weight', and the robot arm, which produces 'arm position' and is sent 'box changing movements' and 'teabag removing movements'. We will consider part of the sequence of operations which this system goes through to fulfil its function, examining each step, to see whether it is an external event.

Step 1. Teabag box becomes full of teabags.
Step 2. System stops weighing teabags and starts to control the robot arm to replace the full box with an empty box.
Step 3. Robot arm removes the full teabag box.
Step 4. Robot arm provides an empty teabag box.
Step 5. System stops the robot arm, and starts to weigh more teabags.
Step 6. Teabag weighed at correct weight.

We now evaluate each event in turn answering the questions above:

Step 1. Teabag box becomes full of teabags.

Question 1: yes
Even though the teabags are being counted inside the system, and the number of teabags in the box is not even a flow which comes into the system from a terminator, the box has still become full in the outside world, not in the system.
Question 2: yes
The system responds by doing step 2 in this sequence.
Question 3: yes
We know that the event has occurred at the time when the box becomes full.

Therefore, step 1 is an external event.

Step 2. System stops weighing teabags and starts to control the robot arm to replace the full box with an empty box.

Question 1: no
Any action that involves the system doing something cannot be classed as external. Even though the results of this action will be in the environment, the action itself is carried out from inside the system.

Therefore, step 2 is not an external event.

Step 3. Robot arm removes the full teabag box.

Question 1: yes
This action is external, as the robot arm removes the teabag box outside the system.
Question 2: no
The system does not respond to the robot arm moving the full teabag box, it just carries on with the actions started in step 2.

Therefore, step 3 is not an external event.

Step 4. Robot arm provides an empty teabag box.

Question 1: yes
This action is external, as the robot arm provides an empty teabag box outside the system.
Question 2: yes
The system responds with action 5.
Question 3: yes
 We know that the event has occurred at the time when the robot arm finishes providing an empty teabag box.

Therefore, step 4 is an external event.

Step 5. System stops the robot arm, and starts to weigh more teabags.

Question 1: no
For the same reason given for step 2.

Therefore, step 5 is not an external event.

Step 6. Teabag weighed at correct weight.

Question 1: yes
This action is external, as the weight of the teabag is a real-world measurement which exists outside the system.
Question 2: no
The system makes no positive response to the teabag being at the correct weight.

Therefore, step 6 is not an external event.

A potential event must conform with all three of the criteria before it can be included in the event list. If, after applying all the criteria, you are still not sure whether something should be in the event list, try building an event list entry for it. Often, if the potential event is wrong, the entry in the event list will not make sense.

The event list in Table 8.2 treats all the steps in the previous sequence as external events, but only steps 1 and 4 have sensible entries in the response column. Steps 2 and 5 produce no entry in the response column, as they are in fact the responses to steps 1 and 4. Steps 3 and 6 produce responses which tell us to continue with what we were already doing — these will not help when building the behavioural model.

Table 8.2

Event	Response	Classification
1. Teabag box becomes full	Stop weighing and collecting teabag statistics Start replacing teabox	C/D
2. System stops weighing teabags and starts to control the robot arm	?	?
3. Robot arm removes full teabag box	Continue replacing teabox	?
4. Robot arm provides empty teabag box	Stop replacing teabox Start weighing and collecting teabag statistics	C/D
5. System stops robot arm and starts to weigh more teabags	?	?
6. Teabag weighed at correct weight	Continue weighing and collecting statistics	?

8.2.2 The response

The response defines what the system should do when a particular external event occurs. If the event list is complete, the response column should document the total functionality of the system, in terms which both the customer and the developer can understand.

One problem in developing the response column is finding a description which is not too close but not too far from the physical response of the system to the event. For example, consider event response 4 from the teabag boxing system in Table 8.1, 'teabag at incorrect weight'.

In very 'customer friendly' terms, we could describe the response as 'teabag removed into bin'. However, 'teabag removed into bin' describes the result of the system response to the event, not the system response itself. As developers, we are interested in what the system does when it notices a teabag at an incorrect weight, i.e. 'start removing teabag'. Sometime afterwards, the teabag ends up in the bin, but this happens outside the system and is not the internal response of the system to the external event. The response column should document the actions of the system, not the results of those actions.

Another response to the event 'teabag at incorrect weight' could be 'start controlling robot arm', as this is how the system gets the teabag from the conveyor belt into the bin. This describes exactly what the system does, but not in specific or customer friendly terms. This may cause two problems.

Firstly, the customer may only be vaguely aware of the function of the robot arm, and while understanding 'start removing teabag', may not realize that 'start controlling robot arm' means the same thing.

Secondly, by considering responses in implementation terms, you may generate the same implementation response to several different essential events. For example, the teabag boxing system response to 'teabox full' (event 6), 'start replacing box', could also be described by 'start controlling robot arm'. In this case the event list would be capturing the implementation detail, but not the essential functionality, which would lead to a preliminary DFD with an implementation bias.

By naming the responses to both events 4 and 6 'start controlling robot arm', we generate a single data transformation on the preliminary DFD 'control robot arm'. By naming the response to event 4 'start removing teabag from conveyor' and the response to event 6 'start replacing teabox', we will generate two data transformations in the preliminary DFD, 'remove teabag' and 'replace box'.

It is also important that the response describes what the system does at the instant when the event occurs. There are a number of points to be made about this. Firstly, if the response involves a process which persists over time, the system can only start the process at the moment when the event occurs. Consider the responses to events 2 and 4 in the teabag boxing system, given at the beginning of this chapter.

Response 2 'provide statistics report' involves the data transformation 'provide statistics report', which takes data from the 'teabag statistics' store, and sends out a 'statistics report'. As we have perfect technology, according to the rules discussed in Chapter 3, this data transformation can be done in zero time. Therefore, once the request has been received, we can provide the whole statistics report at the time the event occurs.

Response 4 'start removing teabag' involves the data transformation 'remove teabag', which interfaces with the robot arm, taking in 'arm position' and providing 'teabag removing commands'. This data transformation will persist over time, as it involves controlling a piece of equipment in the environment, outside our perfect technology. Therefore, at the moment the event occurs, the system can only start the data transformation, which will carry on for some time after the event has occurred.

Here, we are differentiating between things done entirely within the system, and things the system does within the environment. The statistics report is built up and provided by the system, whereas the teabag is removed by a piece of equipment in the system's environment over which the system has control.

Secondly, it is possible to specify a sequence of things done in response to the same event, providing they are meant to be done at the moment the event occurs, and that none of them, apart from the last in the sequence, persists over time. For example, consider a security system which monitors fire alarms:

Event	Response
There is a fire	Activate sirens
	Evacuate building
	Switch on halon gas

Although we wish all these things to happen when the event 'there is a fire' occurs, evacuating the building involves things in the system's environment, in this case people, and so it cannot all be done at the moment the event occurs. The response will have to split into two, to allow time for the building evacuation to complete, before we switch on the halon gas:

Event	Response
1. There is a fire	Activate sirens
	Evacuate building
2. Everybody out of building	Switch on halon gas

Thirdly, if an event occurs that the system is not required to respond

Table 8.3

Event	Response	Classification
User enters time to start heating	Enter user specified time into heating schedule	D
Time to start heating	Start heating	TC/D*

*See page 209.

to immediately, a valid response will be setting a flag or timer, allowing a response to be carried out later. We have already seen an example of this with the central heating system which could be programmed by the customer to switch itself on at a specified time. This gave the event list shown in Table 8.3.

Finally, the response column should not contain too much detail. Responses specified in too much detail result in the low level functional specification for the whole system being crammed into the response column of the event list.

While it is perfectly legal to have more than one response to a single event, you should only consider this if responses are concerned with different functional areas. Consider the two potential responses to the 'teabox full' event in the teabag boxing system given below:

Event	Response
Teabox full	Simple version: replace box. Detailed version: move robot arm to conveyor belt, pick up full box and move to full box conveyor belt. Move robot arm to empty box, pick up empty box and move to teabag conveyor belt. Place empty box on teabag conveyor belt.

Too much detail in the event list will not only result in a very crowded event list, but may also result in a very detailed DFD. In this example, the detailed response will result in seven data transformations (move robot arm to conveyor belt, pick up full box, move full box to conveyor belt, move robot arm to empty box, pick up empty box, move to teabag conveyor belt and place empty box on teabag conveyor belt), controlled by a control process, 'control replace box'. This preliminary DFD would be more time consuming, complicated and difficult to build than the equivalent data transformation 'replace box' generated by the simple response. The detail should be considered when the lower levels of the models are built — what is shown in the detailed response is actually the transformation specifications for the data transformation 'replace teabag'.

8.2.3 Classification

Classification of the events is very important, as it defines how the events will be modelled as components of DFDs, ERDs and STDs. A 'C' in the classification column will generate a change of state in an STD. A 'D' in the classification column will generate a data transformation in the DFD, and possibly a relationship linking objects in the ERD. If the classifications are incorrect, we may try to model changes of state in the DFD and data transformations in the STD.

There are two aspects of an event to classify:

1. Signalling mechanism: this classification shows how the system knows that the event has occurred, and can be found from the 'event' column in the event list.
2. Response type: this classification shows what the system does in response to the event, and can be found from the 'response' column of the event list.

8.2.3.1 *Classifying the signalling mechanism*

An external event occurrence can be signalled in one of two ways. Either information will flow from a terminator into the system, from which the system can derive the event (this is called a 'normal' event), or it will be time for the system to do something (this is called a 'temporal' event).

Although these classifications are not used in the generation of the behavioural model, they allow us to check that all the events defined can be recognized by the system. If an event cannot be classified as either temporal or normal, the system will not be able to recognize it, and therefore will never respond to it. Let us consider some example events, and classify the signalling mechanism.

Imagine a simple payroll system with a single terminator 'wages department', the event list for which is given below. The 'wages department' provides the data flow 'new employee details' and receives the data flow 'monthly payroll'.

Event	Response
1. Wages department enters new employee details	Add new employee details to payroll
2. Time to calculate monthly payroll	Calculate monthly payroll

A normal event is signalled by a flow passing across the system boundary which lets the system know that the event has occurred. For the first event, the arrival of the data flow 'new employee details' informs the system that 'wages department enters new employee details' has occurred, and so is classified as a normal event.

A relationship between the context diagram and the event list was hinted at earlier in this chapter. This example begins to explore that relationship. In many cases, flows coming into the context diagram will help identify events happening in the system's environment. If information comes from a terminator into the system, it is because the system needs that information, for storing, transforming and recognizing events. In this example, 'new employee details' not only tells the system about the event 'wages department enters new employee details', but also needs to be stored for later use.

In many cases, data comes into the system with the sole purpose of signalling an event. For example, in the central heating system examined in Section 8.2.1, temperature came into the system purely to let the system know that it was 'too cold'. In Section 8.3 we will examine how you can use flows coming into and out of the context diagram to help generate events.

The second event, 'time to calculate monthly payroll', is a temporal event. There is no flow entering the context diagram, which tells the system it is 'time to calculate the monthly payroll'. It may help to imagine a clock terminator on the context diagram, which is never actually shown, but is always there, continually providing time to your system.

Figure 8.5 shows what is happening inside the system. An event-recognizing data transformation reads the time at which the payroll has to be calculated from the payroll schedule. When the time coming into the system matches this time, the data transformation will produce the event flow 'time to calculate monthly payroll'. Again, the 'time' flow into the data transformation is implicit, and would not normally be shown.

Generally, all events which start with 'time to . . .' or mention time, are temporal; all others should be normal.

8.2.3.2 *Classifying the response type*

As discussed at the beginning of this chapter, there are three ways in which the system might provide a response to the outside world:

1. By transforming data — known as a 'data' type event.

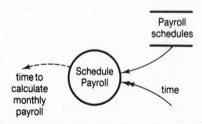

Figure 8.5   Scheduler.

2. By changing state — known as a 'control' type event.
3. By transforming data and changing state — known as a 'control/data' type event.

'Data' is an obvious name for a response which causes a data transformation; however; 'control' is not such an obvious description of a response which causes a change in state. In this context, control is meant in terms of the STD and the overall control within the system, rather than controlling something in the environment. A 'control' type event means that in order to carry out the response, the system must perform control (change state in the STD). A 'data' type event means that in order to carry out the response, the system must do some work (a data transformation).

The first mistake made in response classification is trying to classify the response type of the event column. We are not classifying the actual event here, but what the system does about it, i.e. the response column in the event list. The classification involves deciding, in terms of the diagrams used to model the system, how the system will actually provide the response. In terms of the DFD, STD and ERD, there are only two things which make anything happen in the system: a data transformation or a change of state. So modelling a response will involve a data transformation, a state change, or both.

Let us consider a few events from the teabag boxing system.

Event	Response
2. Operator requests statistics report	Provide statistics report
4. Teabag at incorrect weight	Start removing teabag
5. Teabag removed	Stop removing teabag

Event response 2 indicates that the system must 'provide statistics report'. This will involve taking teabag statistics previously stored, probably doing some calculation and formatting, and outputting the statistics to the operator. In terms of available models, this would be shown by the data transformation in Figure 8.6. Therefore, this response is provided by a data transformation, and the classification 'data'.

Event response 5 indicates that the system must 'stop removing teabag.' In order to 'stop removing teabag', the system should switch off the data transformation removing the teabag. If we switch off the data transformation in response to the event, the event is not causing the system to do the data transformation, so it is not a 'data' type response. On the other hand, the system is controlling the data transformation, in order to change the state from 'removing teabag' to 'not removing teabag' as shown by Figure 8.7. Modelled by the STD, the event becomes the condition the system waits for, and the response becomes

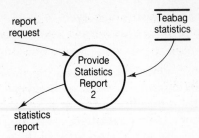

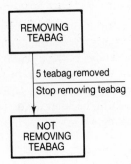

Figure 8.6 Provide teabag statistics report.

Figure 8.7 State change for removing teabag.

the action the system carries out to cause the state change. Therefore, the response is provided by a change in state, and the classification 'control'.

To recognize a control type response, think about what the system was doing before the event and what it will be doing after the response. If the system is doing something different after the response, it must have changed state.

There is sometimes a little initial confusion between control/data type events and pure data type events. When evaluating the response type, remember that you are assuming perfect technology.

Consider the data type event response 'provide statistics report'. Before the event, the system is not providing a statistics report. After the response, the system is not providing a statistics report either, because the report is provided instantaneously. Almost as soon as the event has been recognized, the data transformation which provides the response is finished. Therefore, before and after the event, the system is actually doing the same thing, and has not changed state.

On the other hand, consider the response 'start removing teabag', which involves both a data transformation and a change of state. In order to move the teabag, we monitor the current state of the robot arm, and send movement commands out to it. We can do this via the data transformation 'remove teabag', which interfaces to the robot arm via the 'arm position' and 'teabag removing movements' data flows.

As this data transformation controls something in the system's environment, outside our perfect technology, it will take a period of time to remove the teabag. Although we can switch the data transformation on when the event occurs, it will not run instantaneously, and will still be running after the response. The state of the system before the event occurred was 'not removing teabag', but after the response is 'removing teabag'. Therefore, this response requires not only a data transformation, but also a change of state, giving the classification 'control/data'.

Note that there is another event 'teabag removed', which will indicate that the data transformation 'remove teabag' has finished and needs to be switched off. Normally, data transformations which persist over time have one event associated with their enabling, and another associated with their disabling.

Reviewing what has been discussed in this section, there are two types of classification of event signalling, and three types of classification of event response, which gives six types of events overall:

1. Normal data event.
2. Normal control event.
3. Normal control/data event.
4. Temporal data event.
5. Temporal control event.
6. Temporal control/data event.

In the classification column, the following mnemonics are often used:

- Temporal: T
- Normal: −
- Data: D
- Control: C

So, a 'normal data' event would appear as 'D', a 'temporal control/data' event would appear as 'TC/D'.

8.3 BUILDING THE EVENT LIST

So far, we have discussed the identification and classification of events. The next thing to discuss is the strategy for building an event list. There are two main strategies for generating events, and it is a good idea to use both of them to ensure that you have captured all the events in your event list.

One strategy involves using the flows on the context diagram to help identify events; the other involves evaluating steps in an event scenario. Which strategy you apply first will depend on whether you build the context diagram or the event list first. If you do not have a context diagram, you should start by building an event scenario. Otherwise, it is probably easier to use the context diagram to generate events initially.

8.3.1 **Building the event list from the context diagram**

The context diagram is useful in helping to identify normal events. You can examine all the flows shown on the context diagram, and decide why they are entering or leaving the system. Consider the teabag boxing system shown in Figure 8.8, and generate events from the flows. The flows on the context diagram have been numbered to show which events they are associated with in the event list, given in Table 8.1.

This example demonstrates the many different ways in which a flow may be associated with an event. When generating events from the context diagram, examine each flow in turn. For input flows, ask the question 'Why is this flow coming into the system?' For output flows, ask the question 'What makes this flow come out of the system?'

Let us examine the input flows first. In some cases, no processing will be required on the flow to tell the system an event has occurred. In this case, the name of the event will often be almost the same as the name of the flow.

8.3.1.1 *Event flow from 'operator': 'start/stop'*

As this is really a compound event flow consisting of the event flow 'start' and the event flow 'stop', we will consider the two event flows separately.

Q: Why does 'start' come into the system?
A: It indicates that the operator wants the system to start weighing teabags, collecting statistics on teabags and filling boxes with teabags.

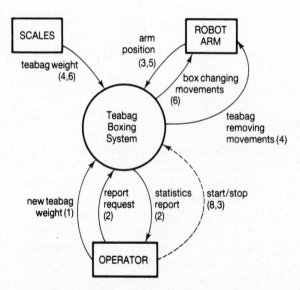

Figure 8.8   Contest diagram for teabag boxing system.

Therefore, this gives us event 3:

- *Event*: operator requests system start.
- *Response*: start weighing, counting and collecting statistics on teabags.

Q: Why does 'stop' come into the system?
A: It indicates that the operator wants the system to stop weighing teabags, collecting statistics on teabags and filling boxes with teabags.

Therefore, this gives us event 8:

- *Event*: operator requests system stop.
- Response: stop weighing, counting and collecting statistics on teabags.

8.3.1.2 *Data flow from 'operator': 'report request'*

Q: Why does 'report request' come into the system?
A: It indicates that the operator would like the system to produce a statistics report.

Therefore, this gives us event 2:

- *Event*: operator requests report.
- *Response*: provide statistics report. Note that this response also involves the output flow 'statistics report'.

8.3.1.3 *Data flow from 'operator': 'new teabag weight'*

Q: Why does 'new teabag weight' come into the system?
A: It indicates that the operator wishes to change the current required teabag weight to the value provided in 'new teabag weight'.

Therefore, this gives us event 1:

- *Event*: operator enters new teabag weight.
- *Response*: update required teabag weight.

In some cases a flow may require some processing before the event is recognized. In this case it is unlikely that the name of the event will be almost the same as the flow, although it will still be associated with the information given by the flow.

8.3.1.4 *Data flow from 'scales': 'teabag weight'*

Q: Why does 'teabag weight' come into the system?
A: It provides the weight of the current teabag to the system. If the weight is incorrect, the system must remove the teabag from the conveyor belt.

Therefore, this gives us event 4:

- *Event*: teabag at incorrect weight.

- *Response*: start removing teabag. Note that this response also involves the output flow 'teabag removing movements'.

The data flow 'teabag weight' also provides information allowing the system to recognize when the teabag box is full. Every correct teabag weight received indicates one teabag going into the box, so the system can count these until the box is full. Therefore, this also gives us event 6:

- *Event*: teabag box full.
- *Response*: stop weighing, counting and collecting statistics on teabags and start replacing box. Note that this response also involves the output flow 'box changing movements'.

'Teabag weight' shows that a single flow may advise the system of a number of events. 'Arm position' is another example of this, although the events that it generates are more obvious than those generated by 'teabag weight'.

8.3.1.5 *Data flow from 'robot arm': 'arm position'*

Q: Why does 'arm position' come into the system?
A: It indicates the position of the robot arm. This will allow the system to tell whether the robot arm movement sequences for removing a teabag from the conveyor belt and replacing the box are complete.

Therefore, this gives us events 5 and 7:

- *Event*: teabag removed.
- *Response*: stop removing teabag.

- *Event*: new box in position.
- *Response*: stop replacing box and start weighing, counting and collecting statistics on teabags.

Note that in this case we have to restart some processes which were stopped before the box was replaced. In the case of removing the teabag, the processes were not stopped, so they do not need to be started. This is a decision which has been made by the developer who feels that removing a teabag from the conveyor belt will not interfere with the monitoring of teabags going into the box, whilst replacing the box takes such a long time that it will.

In this example, we have been able to generate all the events just by looking at the system inputs. This will be the case when all the events are normal, as a normal event is always indicated by a flow entering the system. Here, looking at the system outputs will help check that we have the correct responses to the events, but it will not help to generate any further events. For example, if we look at the output 'box changing movements' and ask the question 'what makes this flow come out of the system?', the answer is 'the system recognizing that the box is full, and starting to replace the box'. This leads us to event 6 again.

Examining the output flows in a system which contained temporal events would be more useful. Imagine, in the teabag boxing system, that the statistics report was generated not on request, but every day at 4 o'clock. An event to provide the report would never be generated by examining inputs, as the input flow 'report request' no longer exists. However, asking the question 'what makes the flow "statistics report" come out of the system' would give the answer '4 o'clock'. Therefore this would generate the event:

- *Event*: time to produce statistics report.
- *Response*: provide statistics report.

All flows leaving the system are in response to events — the system will not do anything unless it receives some kind of external stimuli. However, not all input flows indicate an event. Imagine a temperature monitoring system interfacing to an operator and a temperature sensor. The temperature sensor provides the continuous flow 'temperature', used to give a continuous 'temperature display' to the operator. The event list for this system is given in Table 8.4. In this case there is no event associated with the input flow 'temperature'. 'Start' causes the system to switch on the data transformation which displays the temperature. When a temperature value arrives, the system will make no positive response to the temperature, as it is already displaying the temperature.

When using the context diagram to help generate events, remember that not all flows generate events directly. In many cases, you have to think hard about a flow before identifying the event(s) associated with it, if in fact there are any.

8.3.2 Building the event list from event scenarios

Another way of generating events is to work through event scenarios. Using an event scenario has already been discussed in the context of building an STD — think about the system in action, and consider sequences of behaviour that the system should go through.

In Section 8.2.1, we considered an event scenario for the teabag boxing system. We listed steps the system had to perform, from the teabag box becoming full, through the removal and replacement of the teabag box, until the first teabag of the new box arrived.

You should be able to evaluate each step of an event scenario as a potential

Table 8.4

Event	Response	Classification
Operator switches on	Start displaying temperature	C/D
Operator switches off	Stop displaying temperature	C

event, by considering whether that step has the three characteristics required for it to be an event.

8.3.3 General guidelines

Most customers view their systems as black boxes, into which they push information and commands. The black box responds by doing something which the customer is aware of. The event list documents the inputs and outputs of this black box in terms of events (the inputs) and responses (the outputs).

When building the event list, you should try to see the system in the same way as your customer.

As with the context diagram, you must have a fundamental understanding of what your system is supposed to do and how your terminators work, before you start to build the event list. The event list is not just a list of events, but a table containing a list of events, responses and classifications. It is easiest to consider the events and responses together. Often, you will find that events come in pairs, with one event telling the system to start something and another event later on telling the system to stop something.

Imagine a furnace control system which interfaces to a furnace. The system receives continuous 'temperature' and gives out continuous 'temperature control'. The event list contains the event:

- *Event*: time to start firing.
- *Response*: start to heat furnace.

The response 'start to heat furnace' should make us think about what will make the system stop heating the furnace. This will lead backwards to the event 'furnace at correct temperature' or 'firing over'.

There is nothing wrong with spotting a response, then trying to find the event that caused it. As a developer, you may tend to think more in terms of what the system should be doing (the responses), than in terms of what is going to make the system do something (the events). If the response is defined in essential, not implementation, terms, this will not cause any problems.

Finally, once you are familiar with building and using the event list, you may want to add some extra columns to the event list, as shown in Table 8.5. The extra columns give information relating to the response and classification.

For event 2, having identified that we require a data transformation in order to 'provide statistics report', we have also documented that the input to this data transformation will be 'statistics' and the output will be 'statistics report'.

For event 5, having identified that we require a change of state in order to 'stop removing teabag', we have also documented that the state before the event occurred was 'removing teabag', and the state after the event is 'robot arm idle'.

This extra information will be of help when building the DFDs and STDs which model the system. During analysis, you may identify extra information that you find useful, and can add columns to the event list table as appropriate.

Table 8.5

Event	Response	Classification	Data in	Data out	Initial state	Final state
Operator requests statistics report	Provide statistics report	D	Report request, statistics	Statistics report		
Teabag removed	Stop re- moving teabag	C			Removing teabag	Robot arm idle

Lastly, remember that the event list is supposed to capture the total functionality of your system. Although you have perfect technology within your system, the terminators in the systems environment will be prone to error. If there are any non-implementation-dependent errors which your system should deal with, they should be included in the event list.

We are not concerned with low level errors here, as they will be catered for later on in the development. However, things which the customer perceives may go wrong with the system should be covered, so that requirements for error recovery can be captured. For example, in the teabag boxing system, we may want to document how the system will respond to the event 'no more empty teabag boxes'. However, we probably would not document how the system responded to the event 'operator enters new teabag weight out of bounds' until later.

8.4 CHECKING THE EVENT LIST

As the event list is not a diagram or a syntactic description of the system's response to external events, there are no syntactic checks to be applied. However, it is still important to make sure that the event list is as meaningful as possible. To this end, we apply the same technique that we have used with all of the diagrams, and examine the naming and partitioning of the event list.

8.4.1 Naming in the event list

Firstly, the event and response columns should describe precisely what the events and responses are. Imagine a temperature control system, which accepts continuous 'temperature' from a temperature sensor and switches on a fan as soon as the temperature gets too high. The system waits for the event 'temperature too high'. The event should not be called simply 'temperature', or 'temperature arrives', or even 'system notices that it has to switch the fan on'. You may know what you mean when you build the event list, but is unlikely that anyone else will.

Secondly, use wording in your event and response columns that your customer is going to be familiar with. Do not document the expected implementation of the event and response, but the stimuli which the customer is aware of producing an essential response. For example, event 6 in the teabag boxing system is described as:

- *Event*: teabox full.
- *Response*: stop weighing, counting and collecting statistics on teabags and start replacing box.

This describes how the customer thinks the system will work. If we had approached this from an implementation angle, we might have come up with:

- *Event*: teabag count = 40.
- *Response*: stop monitoring teabag weight and start moving robot arm.

The two event descriptions are equivalent, but the second one describes what the system will actually do, rather than what the customer perceives the system to be doing; therefore, it is not as customer friendly.

8.4.2 Partitioning the event list

In a very large system you may have to build a very large event list. Sometimes, however, a large event list is a consequence of events and responses being considered in too much detail at an early stage. For example, consider an air conditioning system, part of whose functionality is to maintain the temperature. Considering a low level of detail, we would generate the event list shown in Table 8.6.

However, we could describe the same system in less detail with the single event:

- *Event*: operator switches system on.
- *Response*: start maintaining temperature.

Table 8.6

Event	Response	Classification
1. Operator switches system on	Start monitoring temperature	C/D
2. Temperature too high	Start lowering temperature	C/D
3. Temperature correct from too high	Stop lowering temperature	C
4. Temperature too low	Start raising temperature	C/D
5. Temperature correct from too low	Stop raising temperature	C

Here, monitoring, raising and lowering the temperature are all lower level functions of maintaining the temperature. Another way of looking at this is that 'monitor temperature', 'raise temperature' and 'lower temperature' are all lower level data transformations inside the data transformation 'maintain temperature'.

An event list which is too detailed will generate a very large, detailed preliminary model, which will be difficult to work with. This problem has already been discussed with respect to defining too much detail in the response column. An event list with around 30 to 40 events is the maximum you should attempt to work with. Otherwise, the preliminary DFD will be big enough to wallpaper your office with!

As we have just seen, it is possible to group detailed events to generate higher level events, cutting down on the number of events in your event list. However, if you have a large complicated system, which has to do many different things in response to many different events, it may not be possible to group things into higher level events.

However, it may still be possible to group events into functional areas, and consider each functional area of events separately. For example, if we consider the naval system that we discussed in the last chapter, we had three functional areas:

1. The navigation function.
2. The ECM (electronic counter measures) function.
3. The missile guidance function.

Modelling the whole naval system in a single event list might give nearly 100 events. This in turn could lead to an initial DFD with nearly 100 data transformations. However, if we consider the three areas separately, we would generate three smaller event lists, with perhaps 35 events in each. Although this is still large, it would at least be manageable.

If you partition the event list you must make sure, as we did when splitting the context diagram, that you partition into essential and not implementation functional areas.

Finally, do not group things in such a way that you have many different responses to the same event. You should avoid 'case' statements in the response column. For example, considering the operator interface of the teabag boxing system, we may group events in such a way that we end up with the following response:

- *Event*: operator gives system command.
- *Response*: if command = start
  - then start weighing teabags
  - else if command = stop
    - then stop weighing teabags
  - else if command = report request
    - then generate report request
  - else if command = new teabag weight
    - then replace required teabag weight.

Here, we have fooled ourselves into thinking we have only one event, by embedding both the event and the response into the response column.

On the other hand, do not worry about having an 'if . . . then . . . else' in the response column if you are evaluating the internal state of the system. For example, if we were to add the extra requirement that the operator could only update the required teabag weight while the system was not monitoring teabags, event 1 would become:

- *Event* 1: operator enters new teabag weight.
- *Response* 1: if not monitoring teabags then update required teabag weight.

In this case, we cannot evaluate the response until we have looked at the state of the system to see whether it is monitoring teabags. In the previous case, the information needed for evaluation of the response was all in the actual event.

8.5 SUMMARY

In summary, the event list is a very important part of the essential modelling. An incomplete or incorrect event list will lead to an incorrect or incomplete behavioural model. The event list will take a lot of time and effort to compile, but once it has been done, building the DFDs, STDs and ERDs that describe your system should be relatively simple.

Do not worry too much about the event list being absolutely perfect. Many mistakes made in the event list will become evident once you start the behavioural modelling, and there will be plenty of time for you to sort them out before they do any damage. For example, if you miss an event (and therefore, the corresponding response) from the event list, the corresponding behavioural model may contain a data transformation which is enabled, but never disabled. Or you may have a data transformation which stores data that never appears to be used. Having noticed something wrong, you can go back to your event list and see what is missing. If your event list is too detailed, you may find that you generate the same data transformation for many different responses, or that you generate a very large DFD. Both of these are mistakes which can be remedied easily by appropriate levelling.

If you get the classifications wrong, it will become obvious once you start trying to build DFDs, STDs and ERDs from them.

Concentrate on capturing the total requirements for the system in the event list. If you are not sure about whether an event should be included initially, put it in — you can always remove it at a later stage if you realize it was wrong. If you do not put it in, you run the risk of missing one of the system requirements.

8.6 EXERCISES

In order that the event lists do not get too long, and that your answer does not diverge too much from mine, I have ignored error conditions within these exercises, although you should consider them when building an event list for real.

1.   This question refers to the context diagram for the 'washing machine system', described in exercise 2 of Chapter 7. Below is a list of some possible events for this system:

   (a) Operator enters wash cycle.
   (b) Start washing according to wash cycle.
   (c) Water temperature rises.
   (d) Water temperature reaches correct level for cycle.
   (e) Water temperature falls.
   (f) Send 'cycle over' indication to operator.
   (g) Water level reached.

Based on the three criteria identified on p. 194, decide which of these are external events.

2.   Below is a partial event list for the 'washing machine control' system. Classify the events according to whether they are normal or temporal, and control or data or both.

1. Operator enters wash cycle	Start filling drum
	Store wash cycle
2. Drum full of water	Stop filling drum
	Start heating water
3. Water temperature reached	Stop heating water
	Start drum rotation sequence
4. Drum rotation sequence over	Stop drum rotation sequence
	Start emptying drum
5. Drum empty of water	Stop emptying drum
	Indicate 'cycle over'

3.   Build the event list for the 'control greenhouse atmosphere system' described in exercise 3 of Chapter 7, using both the textual description and the context diagram.

4.   Build the event list for the 'missile control' system described in exercise 4 of Chapter 7, using both the textual description and the context diagram.

5.   There follows an informal event scenario for making a telephone call. On the basis of this, build an event list for the system inside the telephone.

   Note: we are building a system to go inside the actual telephone, not the exchange.

   To make the exercise more interesting, I have given the telephone a little more functionality than it would normally have.

   (a) You have to pick up the receiver before you dial a number, otherwise the telephone will ignore you.

(b) Numbers dialled are sent by the telephone to the exchange, which will ignore all numbers after it thinks it has received a valid telephone number (e.g. if the exchange is expecting a number with seven digits, and your telephone sends it eight, it will ignore the eighth digit).

(c) The exchange will examine the line to which you are trying to connect, and will inform your telephone that it is either engaged or free.

(d) If the line is engaged, the telephone will produce the engaged tone, and wait for you to replace the receiver.

(e) If the line is free, the telephone will produce the ringing tone, and wait for:

  (i) you to replace the receiver, at which point it will inform the exchange that it no longer wishes to make the connection;

  (ii) the person you are trying to ring to answer, in which case the exchange will inform your telephone that it has connected to the called phone, and the ringing tone will cease.

(f) Once you are in a call, either:

  (i) you will replace the receiver, in which case your phone will inform the exchange that the line should be disconnected; or

  (ii) the exchange will tell your phone that the line has been disconnected from the other end, in which case your phone will give the line available tone.

CHAPTER NINE

The behavioural model

9.1 INTRODUCTION

The behavioural model consists of a hierarchy of DFDs, STDs and ERDs, together with their textual support, which describe the system's requirements. As the behavioural model is part of the essential model, it contains no implementation detail. Its purpose is to communicate to all those involved in the development (including the customer) what the system should do once it has been designed and implemented. If you imagine the context diagram at the top of the essential model hierarchy, the behavioural model gives the rest of the hierarchy, as shown in Figure 9.1.

So far, we have built the environmental model (the context diagram and event list), which describes the system requirements from the customer's point of view. We have defined that when a certain command or stimulus enters the system, the system is expected to give a certain response. This is everything we need to know about how the system should behave.

The behavioural model documents the system's requirements. The DFDs, STDs and ERDs built to model the behaviour of the system define what the customer thinks the system does. They do not show how the system does it — that is left until the implementation phase.

All the information required for the behavioural model has been captured in the environmental model. The context diagram shows the inputs and outputs of the system, and the event list defines everything the system should do and when it should do it.

We will now reorganize these two sets of information into a DFD, STD and ERD hierarchy, using the 'classification' column of the event list as an initial guide in our model building.

9.2 STRATEGY FOR BUILDING THE BEHAVIOURAL MODEL

The strategy for building the behavioural model is as follows:

1. Firstly, make sure that the event list and the context diagram are finished, correct and understood. The behavioural model is derived from the

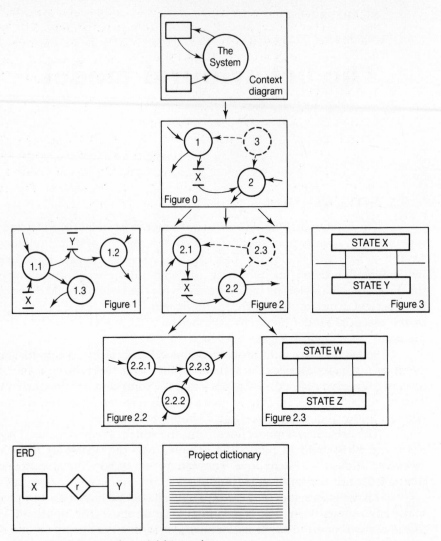

Figure 9.1   Essential model hierarchy.

environmental model, so if the environmental model is wrong, the behavioural model will also be wrong.

2. Secondly, decide what sort of system we have — called the system footprint. The system footprint will define which diagram the system will have the most of, which should be built first. This gives more insight into the system. If a system has a very large STD, but only two objects and a single relationship on the ERD, building the ERD does not tell you very much about the system. On the other hand, the STD will describe most of the behaviour of the system.

Also, the biggest diagram usually encompasses more information about the other diagrams. If the STD is bigger than the DFD, building the STD will help build the DFD, as the STD will be controlling many things which appear on the DFD. On the other hand, the DFD may not encompass all the aspects of control described by the larger STD, and so would not help build the STD.

Therefore, we build the model that we think we are going to have most of first, followed by the other models.

3. On the basis of step 2, build the DFD, STD and ERD that describe the system. The response column of the event list defines everything the system should do. This initially gives a large 'flat' model, with a single DFD describing the total functionality of the system. The models produced at this stage are called preliminary models.

4. Level all the diagrams generated by step 3 into a single hierarchy, as shown in Figure 9.1. The levelled diagrams should be balanced, to confirm that levelling has been carried out correctly.

5. Finally, fill in any lower level detail not described by the environmental model. In some cases this may involve a data transformation generated from the environmental model being broken into a hierarchy of lower level DFDs. In other cases, it will just mean giving a textual specification of what a data transformation does.

At this stage we must also complete entries in the project dictionary and check all diagrams built are correct and coherent according to all the diagram rules and guidelines discussed in Chapters 2, 3 and 4.

9.3 IDENTIFYING THE SYSTEM FOOTPRINT

Step one of the building strategy has been covered by the last two chapters. Next we identify the 'system footprint'. Imagine a three-dimensional graph, with each axis showing the amount of a certain type of diagram which is required to model a system, as represented in Figure 9.2. Here we see the footprint of a traditional real-time system, with a lot of functionality (DFD) and control (STD), but very little information model (ERD). Also shown is the footprint of a traditional business system, with lots of functionality (DFD) and a large information model (ERD), but little or no control (STD).

As technology advances, systems are becoming much larger and more complex, and the differences between real-time systems and business systems have started to disappear. Many modern systems are represented on all three axes. To know which preliminary model to build first, we establish which diagram has the longer axis. Identifying this from the event list is very easy.

Count the number of control type events and the number of data type events in the classification column of the event list. A control/data type event is counted once as a control type event and once as a data type event.

If there are more control type events than data type events, there is more

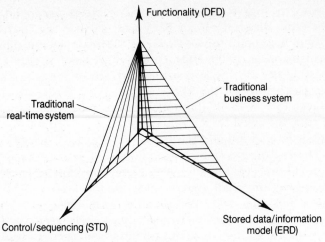

Figure 9.2 The system footprint.

control than data transformation in the system. In this case start building the behavioural model with the STD.

If there are more data type events than control type events, the situation is more complicated. The fact that there are more data type events tells us there are more data transformations than changes of state, but it does not define whether to start with the DFD or the ERD. Storage and retrieval of data is done via data transformations, so many data type events may indicate a large information model. In this case, we must also consider what the data transformations do with the data.

If most data responses are concerned with storing data and sending that data out at some later stage, a system with a lot of data storage and retrieval is indicated and the ERD is probably the best model to start with.

On the other hand, if only a few, or no, data responses are storing and retrieving data, but are more concerned with immediate data manipulation, it is probably best to start with the DFD. By immediate data manipulation, I mean the type of data transformation that receives data, processes it and sends it out immediately. For example, the data transformation 'maintain temperature', takes as input 'temperature' and immediately converts it to output 'temperature control'.

As the data used here is not stored, it will not appear on the ERD. On the other hand, data that is stored will appear on both the DFD and the ERD. If the system performs data storage and retrieval as well as the immediate data transformations, you can still start with the DFD, as the DFD and the ERD are just showing different aspects of the same information (the DFD emphasizing functionality, the ERD emphasizing stored data).

In a real-time system, it is unlikely that the ERD will be larger than the DFD. However, in a system whose purpose is to store and retrieve data, the ERD may present the system requirement in a more user friendly form.

One of the advantages of using a structured technique which has modelling tools for each aspect of system behaviour is that if you start off thinking you have a real-time system, and subsequently find more data manipulation than you at first suspected, you are not stuck with a set of purely real-time tools which give no scope for modelling the data in the system.

The event list for the teabag boxing system, described in Table 8.1 has six data type events (four control/data and two data) and six control type events (four control/data and two control). You will often find about the same amount of control events and data events. In these cases it does not matter which model you start with (either the DFD or the STD), as the system has about the same amount of functionality and control — I advise you to start with the model with which you feel happiest.

The model you feel most at ease building is probably the one that you will be best at using. If you use a model that you are not particularly happy with, you may not be very successful with it. Having not been very successful with, say, the STD, the DFD that you build with the help of that STD will probably not be very successful either.

9.4 GENERATING THE PRELIMINARY MODELS

Having decided on the system footprint, build the lower level diagrams, starting with the largest one. You should derive all the diagrams directly from the event list. Once you have built the first diagram, it can be used to help with further diagrams. For example, if you build the DFD first, followed by the STD, the DFD will define all the data transformations the STD can control.

However, do not build the first diagram on the basis of the event list, and then forget about the event list for the others. I have seen people build the DFD from the event list, and then struggle to build the STD purely on the basis of that DFD. There are two very good reasons for building all the models directly from the event list.

Firstly, having put all that time and effort into building the event list, you should get as much use out of it as you can.

Secondly, and more importantly, each diagram only shows you certain aspects of the system. An STD built on the basis of the DFD will only reflect aspects of the system which are shown on the DFD. The event list may hold other information for the STD, which will be forgotten if you do not use the event list.

9.4.1 Generating the data flow diagram

To build the DFD, you need the event list and the context diagram for the system. The event list defines all the data type events, with the response column specifying what the data transformation should achieve. The context diagram defines all the data flows between the system and its environment, which become data flows between your data transformations and the outside world.

Building the DFD involves identifying data transformations from the event list, and adding data flows to those data transformations, some of which will be provided by the context diagram, to complete the DFD.

Firstly, we build one data transformation for each data type or control/data type event in our event list. The event list for the teabag boxing system in Table 8.1 shows events 1, 2, 3, 4, 6 and 7 to have data type responses. Therefore, we build a data transformation for each of those events.

The number given to the data transformation at this stage is the number of the event that generated it, thus relating them. This helps check that this stage of the model generation has been done correctly. These numbers are likely to change when the preliminary models become a DFD hierarchy, as the number of the data transformation has to reflect its position in the hierarchy.

Next we name the data transformation from the response column, by deciding how the data transformation will provide that response. If responses are well named, it will be possible to put a phrase from the response column straight into the data transformation. Consider events 1 and 2 from our teabag boxing system.

Event 1 Response: update required teabag weight.

The data transformation needed to update required teabag weight will be doing just that — so we can call it 'update required teabag weight'.

Event 2 Response: provide statistics report.

Again, the data transformation which provides a statistics report can be called 'provide statistics report'. If the response has a pure data classification, naming the data transformation should always be that easy. It is more difficult to name data transformations with control and data in the same response. A control/data classification means the response involves not only a data transformation, but also a change of state. The data transformation name should not encompass the change of state — this will be covered by an STD. In effect, this means stripping all the control from the responses, leaving the functional area the data transformation has to perform. Consider event 3 and 6 from our teabag boxing system:

Event 3 Response: start weighing, counting and collecting statistics on teabags.

The control part of this response covers starting the functions of weighing, counting and collecting statistics on teabags. Therefore, we can strip 'start' from the response, and call the data transformation 'weigh, count and collect statistics on teabags'.

Event 6 Response: Stop weighing, counting, and collecting statistics on teabags and start replacing box.

The control part of this response covers stopping the function of weighing teabags and starting the function of replacing the box. Stopping a function does not give rise to a data transformation — only starting a function can do that. So, in this case, we strip 'stop weighing, counting and collecting statistics on teabags and start' from the response, and call the data transformation 'replace box'.

A common mistake at this stage is to show too many aspects of behaviour on a single diagram. Remember, we have three diagrams, one for each aspect of system behaviour. On the preliminary DFD, consider only the functionality of the system. Ignore the control — the preliminary DFD should not have any dashed lines on it at all. Do not worry about how the data transformation will start or stop, just think about what it does. We can worry about how it is started and stopped when we build the STD.

This stage will give a set of data transformations with names, but no data coming in and out of them, as shown in Figure 9.3. Do not worry that two of these data transformations (3 and 7) are the same — we will deal with that later in this section.

Now we add the data flows to the data transformations. Initially, we add data flows that can be seen from the context diagram. We add internal flows in the next step. There are two methods used to attach data flows from the context diagram to the data transformations.

Using method 1, start at 12 o'clock on the context diagram and work round, until you have attached each data flow entering or leaving the system to a data transformation. Figure 9.4 shows the context diagram for our teabag boxing system. Starting at 12 o'clock and working round clockwise, the first data flow is the input 'arm position'.

From the data transformations created, we consider which of them needs to use 'arm position'. Looking at each data transformation in turn, and considering its functionality leads to the conclusion that there are two data transformations.

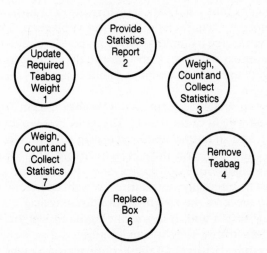

Figure 9.3   DFD without data flows.

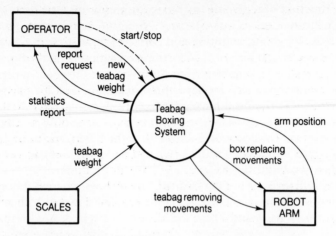

Figure 9.4   Context diagram for teabag boxing system.

'replace box' and 'remove teabag', which need to know the position of the robot arm. We therefore attach 'arm position' to both of these as an input flow.

Continuing around the context diagram in a clockwise direction, the next flow is the output flow 'box replacing movements'. Examining the data transformations created leads to this being attached as an output flow to 'replace box'.

When working around the context diagram, only consider data flows. Event flows can be added later, when we integrate the DFD and the STD. This method ensures all the data flows from the context diagram are used somewhere on the DFD. However, it does not ensure that if a data flow is used in two different data transformations, you will spot both uses.

Using method 2, you examine each data transformation in turn, and try to find the inputs and outputs they require from the context diagram. The data transformations may also be connected by internal stores, so not all required inputs and outputs appear on the context diagram. Consider the data transformations 'update required teabag weight' and 'weigh, count and collect statistics on teabag' from our teabag boxing system.

'Update required teabag weight' accepts a new teabag weight from the operator, to use as the required weight of the teabag. Therefore, we would expect an input 'new teabag weight', and an output 'required teabag weight'. Examining the context diagram shows the input data flow 'new teabag weight' from the operator. 'Required teabag weight' does not appear anywhere on the context diagram, implying that it must be internally stored data. 'Weigh, count and collect statistics on teabag' accepts and records the weight of the current teabag, compares it against the required teabag weight and, if it is at the required weight, counts it. Therefore, it will have inputs 'teabag weight' and 'required teabag weight' and outputs 'teabag count' and 'teabag statistics'. Of these, only 'teabag weight' comes from the context diagram. The others must be internally stored data.

This method ensures that you consider the inputs and outputs of each data transformation, but does not ensure that you use all the data flows from the context diagram. If you draw a boundary around the DFD which has been produced so far, shown in Figure 9.5, the input and output data flows should be the same as those of the context diagram.

Having attached all the external connections, we add data stores between transformations. If you use method 1 for attaching the external data flows, it is unlikely that you will have considered any other data which the data transformations need to fulfil their function. For each data transformation, consider any other input or output data needed, and add data stores accordingly. If you have used method 2, you may already have done this.

You may find that some data transformations take data from stores filled by other transformations. These data transformations can then be connected by the appropriate store, as shown by Figure 9.6.

At this stage, none of your data transformations should be connected by direct data flows. Data transformations connected by direct data flows happen in sequence, asynchronous data transformations must be connected by a data store. As all the data transformations generated are in response to different external events, which occur at a time determined by the environment, they must all be asynchronous with one another. As a result, you would expect them to be connected by stores.

Finally, we should tidy up the DFD to make it as coherent and easy to work with as possible. If you have two or more data transformations which are exactly the same, i.e. they have the same name, the same inputs and the same

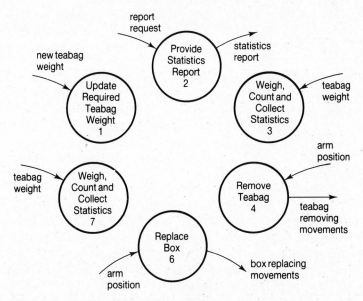

Figure 9.5   DFD with external data flows.

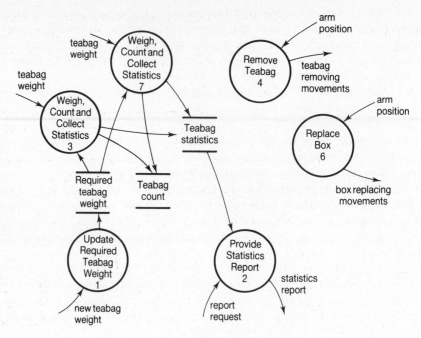

Figure 9.6   DFD with connected internal data flows.

outputs, they can be merged. In this example, we could merge '3 Weigh, count and collect statistics' and '7 Weigh, count and collect statistics' into a single data transformation. You will often find a data transformation appears more than once if you have too many events in the event list, or if you have gone into too much detail. However, sometimes you just do the same thing in more than one place in the system.

Beware of data transformations which essentially do different things, but will be implemented in the same way. In implementation terms, we could view '4 Remove teabag' and '6 Replace box' as being the same, as they are both reading the position of the robot arm and commanding it to move somewhere else. However, essentially, they provide different functions and so should not be merged. At this stage, we are concerned with the essential behaviour, not the implementation behaviour of the system.

You may also split a data transformation. An event involving more than one functional area may generate a data transformation which does a number of different jobs. For example, 'weigh, count and collect statistics on teabag' could be split into 'weigh teabag', 'count teabags' and 'collect statistics on teabags'. However, at this stage, we are more interested in the conceptual function of a data transformation than the number of lines of code it will ultimately generate. If a data transformation performs a single function, do not split it up, no matter how large and complicated that single function might be.

We now have a DFD where each data transformation has a single job, and each has inputs and outputs, but as yet they are not controlled. Control will appear when we integrate the STD built from the event list with the DFD.

9.4.2 Generating the state transition diagram

You do not really need the context diagram to build the STD, as it only defines information entering and leaving the system. The events generated by this information are fully documented by the event list.

For the STD consider only events with either a control or a control/data classification. The most difficult part of STD building is deciding whether all the control type events are concerned with the same or different functional areas. An STD models the sequence of behaviour in a particular functional area of the system. As discussed in Chapter 3, a system involved in performing a number of functions may have a corresponding number of STDs. At this stage, the events are grouped into functional areas, allowing us to build separate STDs for each functional area. It is normally easier to split the event list at this stage and build several small STDs (which could be joined at a later stage), than to build a single large STD which might then be broken down. If you identify groups of events concerned with different functional areas, you should begin by building separate STDs.

With a number of STDs, the same event can appear in more than one STD, as a single external event may have responses in more than one functional area. Consider a simplified version of the robot painter system from Chapter 3, the event list for which is given in Table 9.1.

In this example, we have two pieces of equipment, a robot arm and a painting nozzle attached to the robot arm, which together are used to paint a car. Assume that we have decided to build two STDs, one for controlling the robot arm, and one for controlling the paint nozzle. The response to event 1 is only concerned with moving the robot arm. However, the response to event 2

Table 9.1

Event	Response	Classification
1. Car arrives at robot painter	Start positioning robot arm to paint car	C/D
2. Robot arm positioned to paint car	Stop positioning robot arm Start car painting movements Start painting	C/D
3. Car painted	Stop car painting movements Stop painting	C

involves both the robot arm and the paint nozzle. Therefore, we could split this event into two:

> *Event 2A*: robot arm positioned to paint car.
> *Response 2A*: stop positioning robot arm, start car painting movements.
>
> *Event 2B*: robot arm positioned to paint car.
> *Response 2B*: start painting.

Event 2A will be considered in the group of events for controlling the robot arm, and event 2B will be considered in the group of events for controlling the paint nozzle. Event 3 should also be split in the same way. So the event list becomes as shown in Tables 9.2 and 9.3.

In our teabag boxing system, all the control type events are concerned with the single function of boxing correct weight teabags, so we construct a single STD.

Firstly, we consider the order in which the events should occur. In the teabag boxing system, we would expect the operator to switch the system on (event 3) first. Once the system is switched on, i.e. weighing and counting teabags into boxes, there are three things that could happen:

1. A teabag could arrive at an incorrect weight (event 4), in which case it would be removed (event 5), before returning to weighing and counting teabags.

Table 9.2. *Event list for control of robot painter*

Event	Response	Classification
1. Car arrives at robot painter	Start positioning robot arm to paint car	C/D
2A. Robot arm positioned to paint car	Stop positioning robot arm Start car painting movements	C/D
3A. Car painted	Stop car painting movements	C

Table 9.3. *Event list for control of paint nozzle*

Event	Response	Classification
2B. Robot arm positioned to paint car	Start painting	C/D
3B. Car painted	Stop painting	C

2. The current box could become full (event 6), in which case the box would be replaced (event 7), before returning to weighing and counting teabags.
3. The operator could switch the system off (event 8), which would take it back to the beginning of the sequence.

Having decided upon the order in which the events should happen, we can build a framework for the STD. The event describes the transition between two states. The event itself is what causes the transition to start (STD condition), while the response is what the system does to get into the next state (STD action). The connections between the events become states. The event sequence for the teabag boxing system will therefore give the STD framework shown in Figure 9.7.

Filling in the STD framework should be simple. As stated, the event becomes the condition, the response becomes the action — so these can be taken directly from the event list. The state names can be derived by considering the transitions around each state, and what the customer thinks the system is doing at that point. For the teabag boxing system, this will give the STD shown in Figure 9.8. As we have already created the DFD which this STD controls, we can replace many of the actions on the STD with prompts to data transformations on the DFD.

If the system is modelled by a number of STDs, they may need to communicate with each other using flags and signals. Applying the same development steps to the robot painter, described earlier in this section, will generate the pair of STDs shown in Figure 9.9.

Consider the original event 2:

Event 2: robot arm positioned to paint car.
Response 2: stop positioning robot arm, start car painting movements and start painting car.

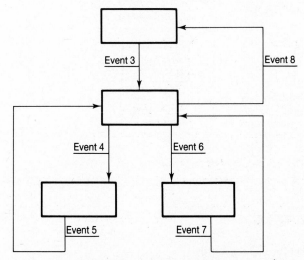

Figure 9.7   STD framework for teabag boxing system.

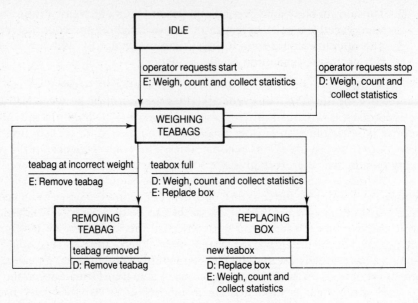

Figure 9.8 Complete STD for teabag boxing system.

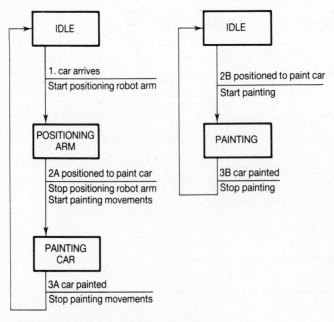

Figure 9.9 STDs for robot painter.

Although the whole response is done when the event occurs, there is an implied sequence, as we do not want to start car painting movements and painting before the robot arm has stopped positioning. The internal event 'robot arm positioning stopped' causes 'start painting', not 'robot arm positioned to paint car'; therefore, we should replace the condition 'positioned to paint car' in the paint nozzle control STD with the condition 'ready to start painting'. This new condition can be generated as a signal by the robot arm control STD. These modifications would give the STDs shown in Figure 9.10.

9.4.3 Generating the entity relationship diagram

Building the ERD from the event list is very similar to building the ERD from a textual description, discussed in Chapter4. Work through the event list, and for those data type events which are concerned with storing and retrieving data, pick out the nouns from the events and responses. Table 9.4 gives the teabag boxing system events concerned with storing and retrieving data, with nouns in UPPER CASE.

The nouns are potential objects in the system. As in Chapter 4, we consider whether they might be objects (normal, associative, subtype or supertype), attributes of objects or irrelevant to the ERD. Having decided on the objects, you can search the event list for verbs that could link the objects — these

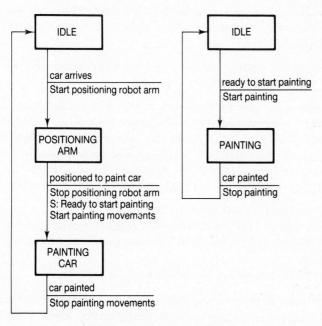

Figure 9.10   Modified robot painter STDs.

Table 9.4

Event	Response	Classification
1. OPERATOR enters NEW TEABAG WEIGHT	Update REQUIRED TEABAG WEIGHT	D
2. OPERATOR requests STATISTICS REPORT	Provide STATISTICS REPORT	D
3. OPERATOR requests start	Start weighing, counting and collecting STATISTICS on TEABAGS	C/D
7. NEW TEABOX	Stop replacing BOX and start weighing, counting and collecting STATISTICS ON TEABAGS	C/D

become relationships. In the teabag boxing example that gives the ERD shown in Figure 9.11(a).

Comparing this with the teabag boxing system ERD generated in Chapter 4 (Figure 4.14), you will notice that there are some components missing. Sometimes objects are missed as the event list is often worded actively rather than passively, which makes it easy to generate DFDs and STDs, but not ERDs. If we rephrase the response to event 3, with a view to it being used to build a passive model, we would have:

> *Response 3*: start to collect teabag weight from scales and maintain count of teabags at required weight.

Examining this response for potential objects would give the fragment of ERD shown in Figure 9.11(b), which together with Figure 9.11(a), gives the ERD we would have expected. This shows that it may be a good idea to rephrase events and responses in the passive sense before using them to generate an ERD.

By this point we have a set of flat, disorganized and largely unrelated models which together describe the system, comprising the following:

1. A single DFD, too large to show to the customer.
2. Possibly a number of STDs controlling different areas of the system, which may be loosely related to the DFD by using data transformation names in the actions.
3. Possibly an ERD describing all the data in the system.

There are still a few bits of the system model missing. The DFD built from the event list covers all areas purely concerned with functionality. The STD built from the event list covers all the areas purely concerned with control. We have not

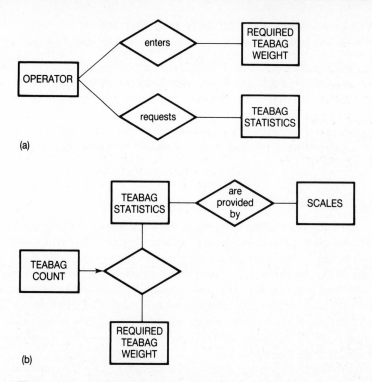

(a)

(b)

Figure 9.11   Teabag boxing system ERD: (a) ERD from active event list;
(b) ERD fragment from passive event.

yet considered the areas between functionality and control, more specifically, event recognizers. These data transformations only exist to allow the STD to monitor the state of data. Although they are data transformations, they are specifically concerned with controlling the system, not the functionality of the system. Up until this point we have been considering pure control and pure functionality; anything which contains aspects of both has yet to be modelled.

Organizing the preliminary models into a hierarchy has three advantages. Firstly, it yields a well-structured model which can be presented to a customer, and will also be a good start to a structured development.

Secondly, the merging of the data and the control (i.e. the DFD and the STD) will uncover those areas between functionality and control not thought about yet. This step should define all the event recognizers.

Thirdly, by adding aspects of control to the DFD, in the form of control processes and event flows, we can vertically balance the context diagram against the DFD. A boundary around the top level DFD in the hierarchy should show the same input and output flows as the context diagram. This is a good initial check that the preliminary models have been built correctly.

9.5 LEVELLING AND BALANCING THE MODEL

The next step is to level and balance the model. Levelling the flat model involves reorganizing the preliminary DFD into a hierarchy of smaller connected DFDs, with related STDs and ERDs. By reorganizing the model, we are in danger of introducing inconsistencies. Therefore, the final hierarchy must be balanced to make sure that all the diagrams still fit together.

As levelling has been covered in chapter 6, the details will not be discussed here, only the procedure involved in building the levelled model from your preliminary models.

9.5.1 Levelling the preliminary models

The first step in levelling the preliminary models is to integrate the STD with the DFD, to give a complete picture of the system. This will allow us to level sensibly, being fully aware of all aspects of control and data.

All the STDs should be translated into control processes, and appended to the DFD. We build one control process for each STD, turning conditions into input event flows and actions into output event flows. The method for this is discussed fully in Chapter 6. In the teabag control system, there is only one STD. Integrating this with the preliminary DFD gives the preliminary transformation diagram shown in Figure 9.12.

During this stage, event recognizers may need to be introduced. At the

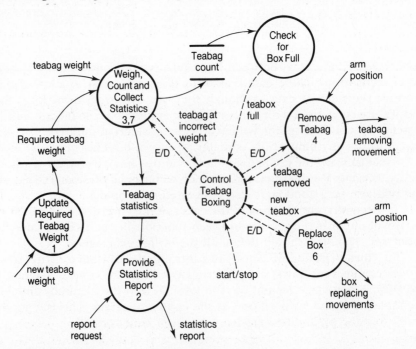

Figure 9.12 Preliminary transformation diagram.

moment 'weigh, count and collect statistics' counts correct weight teabags into the data store 'teabag count'. The control process waits for the condition 'teabox full'. This condition cannot be generated directly by the data store, therefore a data transformation, 'check for full box', is introduced. This monitors the store and generates the event 'teabox full' when the count reaches the required level.

Levelling need only be done if there is too much information on the preliminary model (i.e. more than seven plus or minus two elements on the DFD). If your preliminary model only has five data transformations and a couple of stores (although this is unlikely), it becomes figure 0 of the hierarchy. Initially, you should level on the basis of control. Group together data transformations with the control processes that control them, giving high level single function data transformations. You may also level on the basis of data, by grouping data transformations which use the same data.

To arrive at a hierarchy which is well structured, you should partition to minimize interfaces. In the teabag boxing system joining the data transformations with the control process which controls them gives us the high level data transformation 'box teabag', shown in Figure 9.13(a) and the low level DFD shown in Figure 9.13(b). At this point the data transformations assume the numbering that reflects their position in the hierarchy.

A very large model may have to be levelled more than once. Levelling a preliminary model with 50 data transformations/control processes may still yield a DFD with more than the recommended number of elements. In this case, level from the diagram produced, and keep levelling until the top level diagram has less than seven plus or minus two elements.

Finally, if appropriate, you may break up the ERD to match the levelling of the DFD, as discussed in Section 6.2.

9.5.2 Balancing the preliminary models

The levelled model should be balanced both vertically and horizontally according to all the rules defined in Chapter 6.

9.6 LOWER LEVEL MODEL DETAILS

The previous steps generate a hierarchy of DFDs, STDs and ERDs. The final step involves filling in all the lower level detail to give a complete description of all user requirements. There are three sorts of low level detail to be considered:

1. Lower level models.
2. The project dictionary.
3. Implementation constraints.

9.6.1 Lower level models

Some of the data transformations generated from the event list may perform large or complicated functions. These can now be broken down, either by connectivity or by top down functional decomposition, into lower level DFDs.

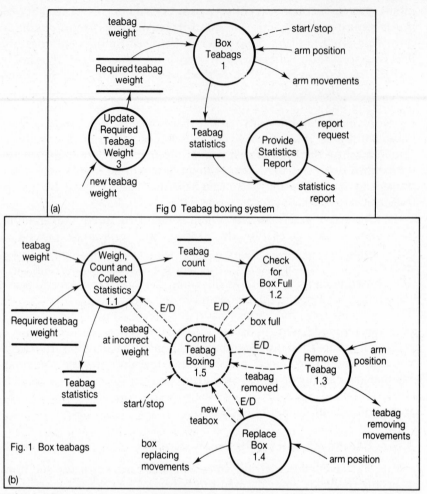

Figure 9.13   Levelled teabag boxing system.

For example, the teabag boxing system event list generates the data transformation 'replace box'. While conceptually this may be easy to understand, describing exactly how we 'replace box' may be more difficult. We could at this stage build a lower level DFD containing data transformations 'move full box to full box conveyor', 'collect empty box from empty box conveyor' and 'move empty box to filling conveyor', connected by an appropriate control process.

9.6.2 The project dictionary

You may start to provide data decompositions and specifications with the context diagram. At this stage you should complete the project dictionary for the rest of the model hierarchy. The specifications required are detailed in Chapter 5.

9.6.3 Implementation constraints

Finally, we should consider implementation constraints. These are 'requirements' which do not affect the fundamental functionality of the system, but do affect the way in which the system is designed. There are two sorts of implementation constraint: those that apply to the whole model and those that apply to particular parts of the model. Overall constraints include requirements such as the following:

1. System must be implemented on DEC equipment.
2. System must be implemented in less than 12 months.
3. System must be implemented for less than £15 000.
4. System must be implemented to run under UNIX.
5. System must be implemented with 95 per cent reliability.

These constraints do not affect the customer's functional requirements, but they do affect the way in which you design the system, and the quality of system the customer gets. If you start a design knowing that your customer has only £15 000 to spend, you may design a completely different system from the one you would have designed if you thought he had £300 000 to spend.

Overall constraints apply to the whole of the model, and cannot be noted on one particular model diagram, so they should be placed in a separate document to be kept with the model. Alternatively, they could form part of the 'transformation specification' for the context diagram data transformation.

Particular constraints can be isolated to certain parts of the model. For example, the customer may specify response time for production of the statistics report in the teabag boxing system. This can be shown as a comment on the part of the model to which it corresponds, as shown in Figure 9.14. Alternatively, it could be given as part of the transformation specification of 'provide statistics report'. When we implement 'provide statistics report', we now know that it has to run in less than 10 seconds.

There may also be customer requirements on data storage. At the moment, we appear to store all the teabag statistics we ever see. It is unlikely that we will have enough memory to do that. If the customer gives an idea of the amount of teabag data we have to store, this will help to design the system. Again, this can be shown on the model, as in Figure 9.14, or documented in the model's textual specification.

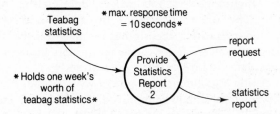

Figure 9.14   Implementation constraints on data transformations.

All implementation constraints, overall or particular, should be documented at the analysis stage. During design, you should know about any restrictions which will affect the system.

9.6.4 New versus reimplemented systems

The content of the lower level DFDs and project dictionary will probably differ, depending on whether you are building a new system or reimplementing a system which already exists. For a completely new system, the low level detail will contain any relevant information about what the customer wants, and what the terminators do. This information will come from discussions with the customer, manufacturers of equipment and builders of subsystems.

On the other hand, if you are reimplementing an existing system, there is plenty of information available from the existing system to help in the new implementation. However, the existing system may contain implementation peculiarities which compensate for the limitations of the existing implementation technology — these peculiarities should not be carried into the new implementation. When you examine the existing system, you should differentiate between what has to be done, and what has only been done because of the way in which the system had to be implemented.

We have tended to assume that you start with the essential model; on the basis of that build the implementation model; and on the basis of that, implement the system. However, if you already have an implemented system, you can use that to help build the essential model (i.e. to understand what the original system was meant to do).

Working backwards, you should be able to take a program and, possibly by way of a structure chart, convert it into a DFD, perhaps with an associated STD. This will be covered in more detail in Chapter 13. These models will describe how the program works, but not necessarily what the system does. If a system is very badly structured, what the code looks like it should do is often very different from what it does when it is run.

The next step is to examine these models (i.e. the existing implementation model) and decide which bits are only there because of the way in which the system has been implemented. For example, queues exist in many systems because the system cannot cope with the speed of incoming data. Therefore, data is stored on arrival and processed when the system has time. This would generate two data transformations, 'accept incoming data' and 'process data', with a 'queued data' store between them. The queue is caused by a limitation of the implementation technology. With perfect technology, you would be able to remove the queue and process the data as it arrived at the system, giving a single data transformation 'process data', which accepts data directly.

Everything in the existing implementation model which depends on the way the system has been implemented should be removed. This leaves an essential model which describes what the system would do, no matter how it were implemented. This existing essential model will form the basis of the new implementation. If the new system is to be a reimplementation of exactly the same requirements, the design will be carried out on this model, with a new set of implementation constraints.

If the system requirements have changed, the existing essential model can be modified to reflect these new requirements, giving a new essential model.

From this point the development will be the same as for a completely new system. However, you may be able to incorporate some parts of the old design or even old code at the appropriate stages in the system development. Using parts of the existing design or code will be a good idea if they are well structured and well written, as it will save you redevelopment time.

However, avoid using parts of the existing system which are badly structured and written, as you will probably waste more in maintenance with these than the time you would save by not writing them properly.

9.7 SUMMARY

Behavioural modelling gives an essential model consisting of an event list, a context diagram, and a hierarchy of lower level diagrams together with their supporting textual specifications, which specify exactly what the system should do. You now have enough information to go forward into the design with full confidence that you are building the right system, and you are fully aware of any constraints that the customer has placed on the design.

A word of warning — when you complete the lower levels of the system description, do not go into unnecessary detail. It may seem odd, but the biggest problem developers have in analysis is that of over-analyzing.

The essential model is not used to build the program: it is to confirm that you and your customer have got the same fundamental idea about what the system does. Low level detail should be added during the course of system design. If you generate a data transformation, even on the top level DFD, which you understand and can describe in a reasonable amount of textual specification, there is no point in breaking it down any further. The only things that need breaking into more detail are the things which you do not understand.

A complete essential model may only have three or four levels of hierarchy (including the context diagram) — this still gives potential for over 300 data transformations at the lowest level. There is no point in an eight level DFD hierarchy, with DFDs which do such trivial things that it takes you longer to understand the DFD than it would to understand a short textual description of what the DFD is meant to be achieving.

There are three very good reasons for avoiding the trap of over-analyzing:

1. Over-analyzing a system makes the analysis time-scale much greater than it should be, not leaving enough development time to design and implement the system. This will lead to engineers panicking and reverting to the bad practices used before they discovered structured development,

such as coding without design and documenting design after the code has been written, to try to get the system finished on time.

2. The bigger the essential model, the more 'baggage' there is to go through the design phases. A large model will be more difficult to understand and easier to make mistakes in than a small model.

3. It is very difficult to specify low level detail without thinking about design. Much low level detail depends on the way in which the system will be implemented. If you build a very detailed model you are in danger of attempting the analysis and the design at the same time.

9.8 EXERCISES

1. Table 9.5 lists the D and C/D type events from the missile control system. Using this and the context diagram given as the answer to exercise 4 of Chapter 7, build the corresponding data transformation for each event response.

2. From the event list of the telephone system given in Table 9.6, built as exercise 5 of Chapter 8, build an STD framework from the control type events, followed by the STD for the system.

In each of the following questions, build:

    (a) the preliminary DFD and STD;
    (b) the preliminary transformation diagram;
    (c) the levelled behavioural model;

from the event list and context diagram given. All these event lists and context diagrams have been produced as exercises in previous chapters.

Table 9.5

Event	Response	Classification
1. Operator enters target information	Calculate where and when to fire missile	D
2. Time to start positioning gun	Start positioning gun	TC/D
3. Gun aimed	Stop positioning gun Release missile Start tracking and displaying missile Start accepting target adjustments	C/D
5. Operator enters target	Accept target adjustments	D

Table 9.6

Event	Response	Classification
1. Receiver lifted	Produce 'line alive' tone Start sending input digits to exchange	C/D
2. Receiver replaced	If during call, inform exchange, otherwise stop sending digits to exchange Stop producing current tone	C
3. Exchange informs called line engaged	Produce 'engaged' tone Stop sending digits to exchange	C
4. Exchange informs called line free	Produce 'ringing' tone Stop sending digits to exchange	C
5. Exchange informs connected	Cease 'ringing' tone	C
6. Exchange informs disconnected	Produce 'line alive' tone	C

Table 9.7

Event	Response	Classification
1. Operator enters wash cycle	Start filling drum Store wash cycle	C/D
2. Drum full of water	Stop filling drum Start heating water	C/D
3. Water temperature reached	Stop heating water Start drum rotation sequence	C/D
4. Drum rotation sequence over	Stop drum rotation sequence Start emptying drum	C/D
5. Drum empty of water	Stop emptying drum Indicate 'cycle over'	C

3. The washing machine control system context diagram (Table 9.7) was built during exercise 2 of Chapter 7 (Figure A.20 in Appendix A).

4. The greenhouse atmosphere control system context diagram (Table 9.8) was built as exercise 3 of Chapter 7 (Figure A.21).

5. The missile control system context diagram (Table 9.9) was built as exercise 4 of Chapter 7 (Figure A.22).

Table 9.8

Event	Response	Classification
1. Operator switches system on	Start monitoring temperature and humidity	C/D
2. Temperature gets too high	Start lowering temperature	C
3. Temperature correct	Stop lowering or raising temperature	C
4. Temperature gets too low	Start raising temperature	C
5. Humidity incorrect	Adjust vent and stop monitoring humidity for 5 minutes	C/D
6. Time to start monitoring humidity	Start monitoring humidity	TC/D
7. Operator switches system off	Stop monitoring temperature and humidity	C/D

Table 9.9

Event	Response	Classification
1. Operator enters target information	Calculate where and when to fire missile	D
2. Time to start positioning gun	Start positioning gun	TC/D
3. Gun aimed	Stop positioning gun Release missile Start tracking and displaying missile Start accepting target adjustments	C/D
4. Operator requests fire	Send 'detonate' to missile	C
5. Operator enters target	Accept target adjustments	D
6. Tracker indicates missile fired	Stop tracking and displaying missile Stop accepting target adjustments	C

PART THREE

Design

Analysis produces an essential model which describes exactly what the system is supposed to do, together with any customer implementation constraints on that system. The aim of the design is to transform that essential model into something which can be implemented within the customer's implementation constraints.

One question that is often asked is how long should design take, in proportion to analysis? This question is impossible to answer, as it depends on many things. The amount of time spent on analysis depends on how well you know the system that is being analyzed. If you are analyzing a system which is unlike anything you have ever done, it will take a long time to understand the requirements, and the analysis will probably have to be done in a lot of detail — therefore it will take a long time. On the other hand, if you are analyzing a familiar system, it will not take long to understand the requirements — therefore, the analysis will not take very long.

The relative amount of time spent on design depends on more than just how familiar you are with the system. Let us look at two very different systems. Imagine developing a large mathematical analysis package, which has to work on masses of data to produce results. You could probably implement this as a single program in a high level language on a large number-crunching computer. This design requires us to understand the essential model and the programming language being used. To transform the essential model into a program involves introducing a hierarchy into the DFDs, and providing lower level detail of complex mathematical algorithms. Apart from this low level detail, the implemented code will be very much like the essential model.

On the other hand, imagine developing a system to be implemented across a configuration of different processors, some of which you have to specify and perhaps even build. Each processor will run under a different operating system, apart from those for which you have to write real-time kernels. There are many different asynchronous inputs to the system, which cover a wide range of concurrent functional areas. Finally, depending on the processor, different pieces of the system will be written in different high and low level programming languages. In this situation, not only do you have the problems of understanding a large essential model, and several different programming languages, but also the following:

1. You must understand the processor configuration, e.g. how much capacity and capability does each processor have, what sort of communications are available between processors, and if you are building the processor yourself, what do you want it to do.

2. You must understand the operating systems and other facilities available on each processor, e.g. how will you cope with all the asynchronous I/O and concurrent behaviour, how will you get the scheduling to work, how much of the system functionality will be fulfilled by packages already available on the processor.

In this case, transforming the essential model into a program is much more complicated and will take much longer, and the final implementation will be much more complicated than the original essential model. As with the analysis, time-scales will also depend on the experience of the people involved in the development. If they have done this kind of development before, it will not take as long as if they are working on something unfamiliar.

During analysis we assume perfect technology. One of the reasons for this is that initially we do not have enough information to make sensible design decisions, such as: (a) implementing the requirements in the best possible way using the technology that you have been given, or (b) choosing the most suitable technology to fulfil requirements. Making sensible design decisions depends on knowing exactly what your system is required to do and the exact capabilities of the technology on which intend to implement the system.

Now that we know exactly what we have to do (defined by the essential model), we can investigate the real technology being used for the implementation. During design, we will systematically replace each area of perfect technology with the real technology being used, allowing us to develop an implementation which is best suited to that technology. There are three areas of technology to consider:

1. Processors — hardware constraints. In real technology, you will be constrained to a certain implementation by

    (a) the number of processors you have;
    (b) the size and capabilities of those processors.
    (c) the possible interfaces between those processors.

2. Processors — software constraints. In real technology, you will be constrained by the type of facilities available on your processor, i.e.

    (a) the operating system;
    (b) system and library routines;
    (c) proprietary software packages.

3. Programming languages. In real technology, there is a vast range of

programming languages, offering many different capabilities and restrictions.

In developing your essential model into an implementation model, you should change it as little as possible. The essential model defines exactly want the customer wants the system to do, and so any changes will affect the customer requirements. Also, perfect technology has allowed us to develop an essential model which is perfectly structured. If you can maintain that structure throughout the design, the final implementation will also be well structured. It is also important to remember that you have requirements in terms of time and money, as well as functional requirements. There is no point is coming up with the perfect solution to your customer's requirements if he cannot afford it.

Let us briefly consider each of the design phases and how they fit together, before we consider them in detail during the rest of Section III. We have already discussed the three areas of technology that we have design around — we have one stage of design modelling for each of those areas of technology.

Firstly, processor environment modelling, where we examine all the requirements defined by the essential model, together with the physical processor

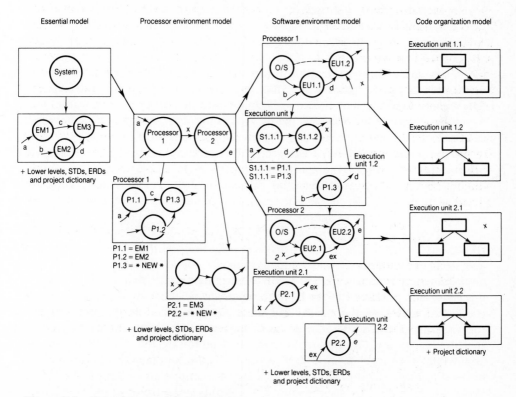

Figure P.1   Complete model structure.

configuration on which they are to be implemented, and split the essential requirements between those processors. To produce the processor environment model (PEM), we take a single DFD hierarchy (the essential model) and split it into a number of hierarchies — one for each processor within the system. Decisions on how to split the essential model will be based on processor size and capability. This gives an individual 'essential model' for each processor within the system, as shown by Figure P.1. We may also have to add extra behaviour to the model, to cope with any work caused by splitting the system across a number of processors.

Secondly, software environment modelling, where we examine all the work defined for a single processor by the PEM, together with all the resident software capabilities of that processor, and decide how that work will be implemented. This will involve deciding how to use the resident capabilities to perform certain areas of behaviour, and may also involve splitting the work within the processor into a number of different programs. To produce the software environment model (SEM), we will be taking a single DFD hierarchy defining the work to be done inside each processor (the PEM for that processor), and splitting it into a number of smaller hierarchies defining the work which will be done within each program, as shown by Figure P.1. Again, we may also have to add extra detail and behaviour to the model — it is at this stage that most of the perfect technology is removed, and we start considering how the system will do things, rather than just what it has to do.

Lastly, code organization modelling, where we examine all the work defined for a single program by the SEM, together with the programming language that we intend to implement the program in, and decide how the program will be implemented. In practice this nearly always involves translating the network structure of the DFD defining the program requirements into a hierarchy, so that it can be implemented by a hierarchical programming language. The code organisation model (COM) consists of a single structure chart for each program defined by the SEM. It is at this stage that much of the very low level program detail will be considered, as the program requirements are split between subroutines within the program.

From Figure P.1, you can see we do not produce a single hierarchy of DFDs, but a matrix. The context diagram is decomposed not just into the top level DFD of the essential model, but also into the top level DFD of the processor environment model. If we are to retain the original requirements throughout the design, it is important that we have some means of checking at each stage that the functionality of the model we have just produced is the same as the functionality of the model that it was produced from. This is done by checking that the inputs and outputs of the context diagram are the same as the inputs and outputs of the PEM (although in the PEM, the inputs and outputs may be defined in more detail). We can check that the inputs and outputs of a single processor from the PEM are the same as the inputs and outputs of the SEM which defines that processor — and so on through the entire model.

The different models are not developed from scratch at each stage, but are merely reorganizations of the previous model, with added implementation details, based on how the technology introduced at each stage forces us to carry out the implementation.

CHAPTER TEN

Processor environment modelling

10.1 INTRODUCTION

Processor environment modelling (PEM) covers three areas of the development:

1. Choosing physical processors on which to implement the development.
2. Allocation of the essential model to these physical processors. This involves considering all the requirements defined by the essential model, examining the processors available to carry out that work, and deciding which piece of work is to be done on which processor.
3. Defining the human–computer interface (HCI). Up until now HCI details have been suppressed — interfaces between the user and the system have been shown purely in terms of essential data. Now we examine the details of the HCI to be provided, as menu structures, screen layouts, flashing lights, etc., in order to continue with the design based on the physical details of the required HCI. For example, in the teabag boxing system, essentially the operator is required to input a 'new teabag weight' to update the 'required teabag weight'. In the PEM, we consider the forms and screen editing facilities provided to the operator to allow him to feed this information into the system.

These areas may be covered in any order, depending to a large degree on the type of application being developed. However, there will nearly always be a certain amount of iteration between the various stages. For example, choice of processor will depend on the capabilities of a processor, judged in respect of what you want to do on it. You could do a rough processor allocation before choosing processors, to give you a feel for the capacity and capability required. However, you might not do the final processor allocation until you knew exactly which processors you were using.

You may want to expand the details of the HCI first, to make sure you have a processor capable of coping with the needs of your HCI. On the other hand, a processor may have already been specified and the workings of the HCI may depend on whatever capacity is left on the processor after the application has been catered for.

You should consider your application and assess the most sensible order for these three steps. As long as they have all been done by the end of the PEM, the order does not matter. Processor allocation will be covered in this chapter, and expanding the details of the human– computer interface will be covered in Chapter 11.

10.1.1 Customer involvement in processor environment modelling

The details of the PEM are 'non-transparent', i.e. any decisions made during PEM affect the person either paying for (the customer) or using (the user) the system. The processors on which you decide to implement the system affect such things as the cost, the response time and convenience of access to the system. If you choose one big computer in the capital city, rather than a network of smaller machines dotted about the country, someone who has to travel 200 miles to use the system will notice the difference from just having to go into the office next door.

As the decisions made during PEM have such a large impact on the customer or user, PEM is seen as the 'changeover point' from analysis to design, and is not purely part of the design process. You still need someone to tell you what the customer's requirements are (i.e. the analyst), but you also need someone who understands the technology being used to implement the system (i.e. the designer). To make the right decisions about processors you should have enough technical knowledge to pick the right processor for the job, and also understand the customer's or user's requirements for response times, system cost, etc.

Once past the PEM stage, the decisions you make are unlikely to affect the system as your customer or user perceives it. For instance, in the software environment modelling (SEM) you may be choosing between having one big program to implement the system, or two smaller programs coordinated by the operating system. This decision will make a lot of difference to the person implementing the system, but to someone at a terminal using the system it should not make any difference.

Therefore, PEM is the last stage of the development where you need to talk to the customer in great detail, as it is probably the last stage where you make decisions that affect the customer. By the end of PEM you should know what the system will do, how much it will cost and how long it will take to build — all the things which the customer is interested in.

This is the stage where the analysis and the design come together: where you look at what the customer wants, look at what the technology can do and define the system which you are actually going to implement. The merging of requirements and technology is likely to result in approximations being made to the customer's original requirements, as the available technology may not be able to meet all the customer's requirements. In the ideal world the essential model would map on to processors in such a way that all the behaviour could be implemented. However, it is unlikely that we have access to the kind of 'perfect technology' assumed in the essential model. The best we can do is examine what the customer wants, examine the available technology and approximate a satisfactory solution.

The customer is the only person who can assess whether an approximation is satisfactory. If an essential requirement cannot be met using the available technology, you must go back with alternative solutions and let the customer decide. Imagine a case of either giving the customer a slower response time or buying a faster, more expensive processor. If the response time is very important, the customer would probably rather spend the extra money than have a slow response time. On the other hand, if the response time is not that important, the customer would probably rather live with a slower response time than spend any more money.

You must not give the customer what you can manage and let him find out about the approximations when you deliver the system. If there is any risk of the customer not accepting your approximations, the costs incurred in changing the approximations once the system has been fully implemented will be much greater than at this stage in the development.

10.1.2 Commitment to software development

It is only after processor environment modelling that we start to consider the system in terms of software. As the essential model is completely implementation-free, it says nothing about how it will be implemented. An essential model could be used to document a purely manual process. The PEM does not imply that the system will be implemented in software, as processors do not have to be computers. Part of the essential model could be allocated to a human 'processor', in which case the essential model would become an operator instruction manual. Another part of the system could be allocated to a piece of hardware, containing no software at all. In this case the essential model would act as a specification for the piece of hardware to be built.

After PEM, the method assumes the development will be carried out in software. The latter stages of the design are concerned with splitting the design into programs and, finally, program design.

Even if the whole system is not to be implemented in software, there is no reason why structured development techniques cannot be used up until the end of the PEM stage. Traditional techniques could be used from that point forward for whatever type of development you propose to carry out. This will give you a good specification for the processor you intend to build. In a system to be developed half in software and half in hardware, it will give a coherent high level description of that system (i.e. the essential model and PEM).

10.2 PROCESSOR EVALUATION

Processor evaluation involves picking processors which are big enough, powerful enough and generally well suited to your requirements.

The choice of processor(s) within the system may not be your decision. If the processor(s) on which the system is to be implemented have already been chosen, it is worth making sure that they are suitable for what you want to do. Many of the traditional problems encountered in system design are caused by people without the necessary technical knowledge picking processors which are totally unsuitable for what was to be done on them. In these cases much design effort is taken up in designing around the shortcomings of unsuitable pieces of hardware. The most common problem in real-time systems is a processor on which the system cannot run fast enough. The people who make these unsuitable choices may not consider that the money they save on the processor will probably be more than used up in trying to develop suitable software to run fast enough on a slow processor.

The following techniques can therefore be used to evaluate processors which have been imposed upon you for suitability or, in the ideal world, to pick the processor(s) which are ideal for your requirements.

Evaluating a processor and finding it unsuitable is no guarantee that the person who chose it initially will reassess their choice. However, it may lead you to suggest possible modifications to the original requirements which will make the chosen processor a more viable proposition. In the worst possible case, at least you have the satisfaction of knowing that you told them that it would not work at the beginning of the development, based on a structured assessment!

Choice of processor is very important. If you start off with the wrong processor, you may have to implement a badly structured system just to cope with the unsuitabilities of the processor. For instance, unstructured code will often run faster than structured code. If a processor is not powerful enough it may be necessary to write unstructured code, to make the system run fast enough. An unsuitable processor makes a well-structured design that much more difficult.

At this stage, you do not need to commit yourself to a particular 'brand name' processor. You cannot continue with the design unless you are aware of restrictions placed on you by the choice of processor. However, if you are aware of approximately how much memory, speed, etc., your processor will provide, you will be able to proceed with the design.

At this stage you can define a generic processor, in terms of capacity and capability, as long as you are certain you will be able to find one with those characteristics at implementation.

It may also not be appropriate to choose a particular processor when building a system with the capability to run on a number of different hardware hosts. In this case it is only desirable to define a set of characteristics which will be provided by all the foreseen hosts. In this way you will ensure that the system is designed in such a way that it will run on any of the chosen hosts.

10.2.1 Estimation of processing requirements

Before choosing processors, we should evaluate the performance and capabilities required from those processors based upon the following:

1. The essential behavioural model.
2. Environmental and implementation constraints.
3. Any knowledge of later design restrictions.
4. Concurrent behaviour.

Firstly, examine the essential behavioural model to quantify how much of a certain resource is required. To make the most accurate evaluation, work initially from the data flow diagrams at the lowest level of the essential behavioural model and evaluate each transformation in turn, as shown in Figure 10.1.

For a data transformation in a multi-processor environment it may be appropriate to identify the class of function. For example, if we were to implement the teabag making system across two processors, one which provided the user interface and one which controlled the teabag making equipment, we could class the transformations as 'equipment control' or 'user interface'.

For the data storage, it may be appropriate to identify the preferred storage medium if it is envisaged that data will be stored in different media. For example, some data may be required to be stored in non-volatile memory, while other data need only be written in volatile memory.

The estimates for all the lower level transformations within a DFD can be added together to give the estimation for the higher level data transformation. Where data transformation class or data storage medium has been identified as an aid to processor allocation, it will not be appropriate to consider total resource usage of data transformations of different classes or data storage on different media, even if they are part of the same higher level transformation. In this case, calculate the total resource usage by a particular class of data transformation — similarly for data storage media.

Estimation is very difficult. Although there are a number of techniques which may help with estimation, most techniques are no substitute for experience. If you have implemented something similar before or can find someone else who has, you can get a fairly good idea of how much CPU power and space a data transformation may need. However, if you are covering a completely new functional area, it can be very difficult to estimate how much power and space that function will require.

Secondly, consider implementation constraints. These are extra requirements, which do not affect the fundamental work done by the system, but affect the way in which the system is implemented, as discussed in the previous chapter.

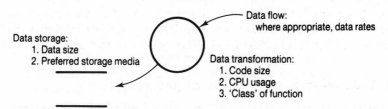

Figure 10.1   Processor evaluation.

Thirdly, consider any restrictions imposed by knowledge of what comes later in the development. These restrictions may come in two forms:

1. Later on we have to use a certain software architecture (perhaps the customer has specified that our system must run under UNIX), so we must choose a processor that supports that software architecture.
2. We may feel that something in the lower levels of the design is likely to give problems on a certain processor. In this case it is worth going into the lower levels of the design in identified problem areas (even though strictly speaking lower level design should be left until later in the development) to confirm that the choice of processor will give a solution that can be implemented.

Fourthly, it may be worth examining the system for areas of potential concurrent behaviour. A single processor can only do one thing at one time and it may be undesirable to have too many areas of concurrent behaviour within a single processor.

10.2.2 Evaluation of real-world processors

Once we have evaluated the characteristics required from processors within the system, we consider the characteristics that certain processors have in terms of capability and capacity.

When considering capability, we are deciding whether the processor is good at doing the kind of things that we would like to do in our system. For example, if you wanted to draw lots of complicated pictures on a screen, you would buy a graphics processor; if you wanted to clean the carpet, you would not buy a dishwasher.

Getting the right kind of processor should not be too difficult, but getting the right size of processor can be. Processor capacity covers: total memory usage, total CPU usage and I/O capabilities. If you estimate as discussed in the previous section, you stand some chance of picking a processor that will satisfy your requirements for capacity.

The importance of picking a processor with sufficient capacity cannot be overstressed. However, as previously discussed, this is often very difficult before the actual implementation has been carried out. If there is any doubt about the sufficiency of processor capacity, it is always better to have a processor which is slightly larger than you need, than to be stuck with a processor which is too small.

At the other end of the scale, always consider the cost of a processor against the benefits it gives you. For example, the customers will sometimes specify a response time just because they are asked to provide a figure. You may find that the only way to conform with that response time is to buy an outrageously expensive processor. As the customers are probably more worried about the cost of their system than the response time, the benefit they get from the processor is far outweighed by the cost.

10.3 PROCESSOR ALLOCATION

Processor allocation is a reorganization of the essential model which allows us to see the following:

1. For any essential requirement, which processor within the system that requirement will be implemented on — or looking at it the other way round, for every processor in the system, which essential requirements that processor will support.
2. Any behaviour added to the processor to support the allocation. For instance, if the system is split between a number of processors, extra behaviour is needed for the processors to communicate.
3. Any interfaces which are needed between the processors.

To enable us to carry out processor allocation we need the following:

1. The essential model — so that we can see all the work and data which is to be split amongst the processors.
2. Implementation/environmental constraints — any requirements such as response times, customer-specified hardware configurations, etc., that affect our choice of processor.
3. A knowledge of the available technology — if you do not know what certain processors do, you will not be able to pick one that does what you want.

10.3.1 Processor interfaces

Processor allocation involves putting every single component of the essential model on to a processor. If you allocate most of the essential model to processors, but find a couple of data transformations left over, it implies there is work to do, but no hardware to do it on — which means it will not be done. Therefore, the whole of the essential model, i.e. all the data transformations, all the stored data and all the control processes (or STDs) must be allocated to processors.

If you have a number of processors in your system, you may have to split data transformations between two or more processors. Also, essential stored data may be stored in more than one place. For example, if a data transformation which accesses a store is split between two processors, the data may be stored on both processors. The same data store on a number of processors may incur extra behaviour to ensure data is consistent amongst those processors. You also need to consider the control. A data transformation originally switched on by a control process may be split between two processors. The two halves must still be switched on by the control process in the right order, even though they are in separate processors.

There is much more to think about during allocation than which bit of work is going to be done on which processor. In allocating behaviour to processors, you should minimize the interfaces created between the processors.

When a single system is split between two processors, an interface is created. You should firstly consider the physical interface. Extra hardware may have to be bought which allows the two processors to communicate. Certainly some communications software will have to be written. Also, there is the conceptual interface — trying to coordinate two processors in such a way that they behave as one system.

For these reasons alone, interfaces should be avoided. Developing part of a system inside a single processor can be fairly easy — it is often only integrating with other processors that presents difficulties. It would be easiest to allocate the whole essential model to a single processor, creating no interfaces. In this case, the processor environment model will look exactly the same as the essential model, i.e. there will be no work to do in the processor environment modelling stage. However, there are many reasons why a single processor solution may not be possible:

1. If there are many concurrent activities within your system, it may not be a good idea to do them on the same processor.
2. There may be environmental reasons why the system cannot be in the same place — for example, either a network of terminals spread across the country, or the control of a nuclear reactor, where the operator cannot be in the same place as the actual process control.
3. You cannot find a processor that has the overall capacity and capability to support your application.

Always consider the single processor option first. If you cannot do that, try to allocate high level data transformations from the top level DFD in the essential model. If you allocate a whole high level transformation on to a processor, all the lower level diagrams that sit beneath that transformation in the DFD hierarchy will automatically be allocated on to the processor with it. As we grouped to minimize interfaces within the essential model, the deeper you go into the essential model hierarchy to split between processors, the more interfaces you will create.

Consider what happens if you split a high level data transformation between two processors. Within the essential model, the high level transformation was created by grouping lower level transformations concerned with the same functional area and common data. In that way good functional units were created with minimal interfaces.

Splitting these transformations between processors causes two problems. Firstly, all the interfaces hidden inside the transformation will be exposed, creating a large interface between the two processors. Secondly, we have a single functional area, half of which is carried out inside one processor and half of which is carried out inside another processor. Let us say that one processor is in London and the other is in Manchester. A maintenance engineer comes to look at the system in Manchester because it does not seem to be working properly. All he can see is one half of a functional area. If he is unaware of what is going on inside the processor in London, he probably thinks that half the software is missing and will maintain the system accordingly — causing all sorts of problems.

Despite all this, it is often very difficult to avoid splitting functional areas across processors; but you should try. Otherwise, processors considered in isolation will be very difficult to understand and therefore difficult to maintain.

Consider the processor allocation of the teabag boxing system, the DFD of which is shown in Figure 10.2. To assist in the implementation of this system we are given extra information regarding conditions inside the teabag factory. The operator will not be in the same area as the teabag boxing equipment, so the system will be implemented across two processors. One processor will reside with the process control equipment, and handle all the system monitoring and control of the robot arm — this is the processor which will actually box the

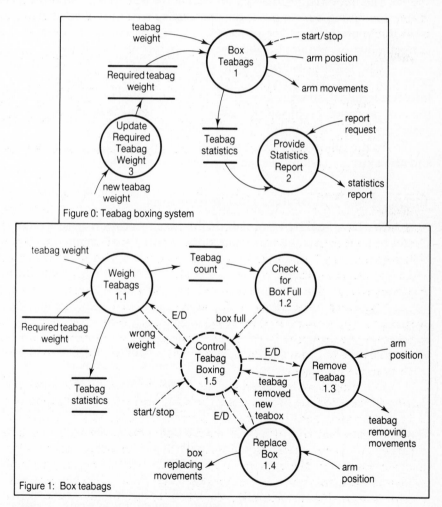

Figure 10.2   Teabag boxing system DFDs.

teabags. The other processor will handle the operator interface, and any associated functionality.

Based on this choice of processsors, and a knowledge of the capacity and capability of each of the chosen processors, the allocation in Table 10.1 has initially been made.

The 'teabag statistics' data store will be located on the operator interface processor. Firstly, there is more memory available on that processor for data storage. Secondly, the data is used to generate 'statistics reports' which form part of the operator functionality. However, this means that the part of the data transformation 'weigh teabag' which stores the data will also have to reside on the operator processor.

The 'required teabag weight' data store will reside on both processors. Within the teabag boxing processor, the teabag weight will be matched against it. In the operator interface processor, the operator may be interested in the current value of 'required teabag weight ' before he changes it.

The 'control teabag boxing' control process will also be split between both processors. The system is switched on by the operator at the operator interface terminal, so some aspects of the control need to reside there. However, the process control is physically carried out on the teabag boxing processor, so some aspects of the control need to reside there.

In the following section we will examine how these areas will be split, and any extra behaviour needed as a result of these splits.

10.3.2 Allocation of data transformations

We have already identified that the data transformation 'weigh teabag' should be split across the two processors. Firstly, we examine the work done

Table 10.1

Processor	Essential behaviour	
Operator interface	3	Update required teabag weight
	2	Provide statistics report
	1.1	Weigh teabags (part of)
	1.5	Control teabag boxing (part of)
	Stores: teabag statistics, required teabag weight	
Teabag boxing	1.1	Weigh teabags (part of)
	1.2	Check for box full
	1.3	Remove teabag
	1.4	Replace Box
	1.5	Control teabag boxing (part of)
	Stores: required teabag weight, teabag count	

by the transformation and decide which bits of that work will reside on which processor. 'Weigh teabag' is responsible for the following functionality:

1. Accept 'teabag weight' from the scales.
2. Store 'teabag weight' in 'teabag statistics'.
3. Compare 'teabag weight' against 'required teabag weight'.
4. If the teabag is at the required weight, increment the 'teabag count', otherwise produce the event flow 'wrong weight'.

Action 2 is the only action which needs to be performed in the operator interface processor, actions 1, 3 and 4 will all remain in the teabag boxing processor. On the basis of this we split the data transformation into two smaller data transformations, shown by Figure 10.3, which perform the precise areas of functionality required within each processor. A boundary round the two transformations should have the same inputs and outputs as the initial transformation which generated them. When transformations are split in this way, it is important that their original functionality is maintained.

We have also generated the internal flow 'monitored teabag weight' between the two lower level transformations, which will become part of the interface between the two processors.

10.3.3 Allocation of stored data

The two data transformations which share the data store 'required teabag weight' are situated on different processors. There are a number of options concerning where the data should be stored. Just as the data transformation represents a physical processor at the top level of the PEM, a data store indicates a physical hardware device between two processors to which each processor has memory access. Choosing to store data in this way, shown by Figure 10.4(a), depends on the availability of such a shared memory device. This option also

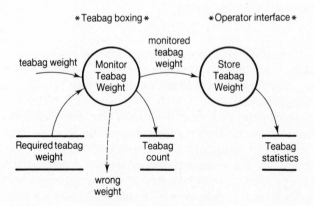

Figure 10.3   Split data transformations.

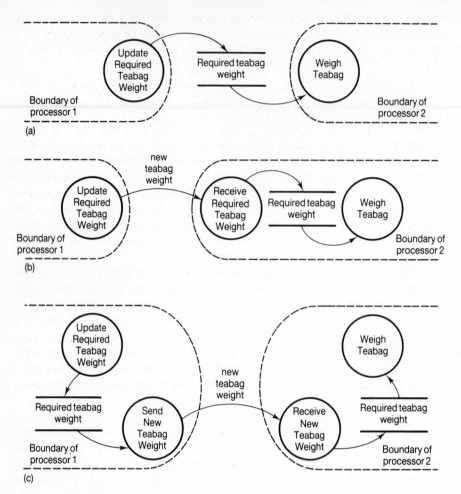

Figure 10.4   Data shared between processors.

implies the addition of 'memory management' behaviour to either one or both
processors using the data, ensuring that data is accessed in a sensible way. In our
example, this memory management could be hidden inside 'update required
teabag weight' and 'weigh teabag'.

   Figure 10.4(b) shows the data stored on only one processor. We may
choose this option if there is not enough room on one of the processors to store
all the data. Alternatively, even though the data store is shared, it may only be
read by one of the processors. For example, 'teabag statistics' will only be read
by the operator interface processor, so only needs to be stored there even though
the data transformation which fills this store is in the teabag boxing processor.

   In order for the data to get from one processor to the other, extra behaviour must be added to each processor to send and receive the data. In this case the 'send required teabag weight' behaviour can be hidden inside 'update required teabag weight', while 'receive required teabag weight' shows up as a new data transformation on the teabag boxing processor.

The final option, shown in Figure 10.4(c), shows the data store on both processors. This option would be chosen where the data is used in both processors and there is room to store the data on both processors. If the data is likely to change on one processor, the change might need to be passed to the other processor to maintain the consistency of the data. This is the case with 'required teabag weight'. The data is required and therefore will be stored on both processors within the system. However, when the 'required teabag weight' is changed by the operator in the operator interface processor, the change must be sent to the process control processor. Stores inside different processors cannot communicate directly with one another. It is necessary to add transmit and receive data transformations which take data stored inside one processor and stores it in the other.

If a data store is repeated on two or more processors, it is not necessary to repeat all the data within that store. We may have a situation where data is required for use on both processors, but there is not enough room on one of the processors for all the data to be stored. For example, we may have a system where many workstations with limited capacity are connected to a huge mainframe. People working at the workstations will be accessing large amounts of data from the mainframe and using it over prolonged periods. In this case, although the bulk of the data could be stored on the mainframe, local copies of parts of that data could be copied across into the workstations, while they were being used.

Finally, we should consider the effect reorganizing the system data has on the entity relationship diagram (ERD). If the system data is split between processors, the ERD should be split to match. This may involve objects appearing in more than one ERD where the data has been copied on to more than one processor.

10.3.4 Allocation of control processes/STDs

Wherever data transformations controlled by a single control process are split between processors, the control process must be split to match. It is undesirable to have a control process in one processor directly controlling data transformations within another processor. This would appear as 'enable/disable' and 'trigger' flows between processors on the top level PEM DFD.

Firstly, a processor should be in control of itself. If an area of work inside processor A is directly activated by a control command from processor B, processor A may be unaware of what is going on. This will make the system difficult to understand, especially if one processor is considered in isolation from the other processor.

Secondly, a more subtle point. The enable/disable and trigger used to activate data transformations are part of the 'perfect technology'. They are 'perfect' activation mechanisms which carry with them a guarantee of success. For instance, when a control process 'triggers' a data transformation, it assumes the data transformation has completed in zero time. In PEM you still have 'perfect technology', but only on a 'per-processor' basis. Inside one processor, everything is perfect. However, other processors are considered to be part of the 'real world' and therefore the 'perfect technology' does not apply. For this reason, it is not valid to use enable/disable and trigger between processors. One processor can ask for something to happen inside another processor (we shall see how that is done in the following example), but not using enable/disable or trigger.

Figure 10.5 shows the STD for the teabag boxing system, which has been modified to reflect modifications made to the original data transformations. This STD is now split into two (as discussed in Chapter 3) according to which parts of the control are to be done in each processor.

We begin by examining the teabag boxing processor. Everything within the STD which relates to the operator interface processor should either be removed or modified such that the modified STD only directly controls things inside the teabag boxing processor. The teabag boxing processor will not be directly aware of the 'start' condition recognized within the operator interface processor, so this must be relayed across from the operator interface processor. As the teabag boxing processor cannot directly control transformations within the operator interface processor (such as 'store teabag weight'), signals should be passed across to the operator interface processor STD to request activation or deactivation of data transformations within that processor. Modification of

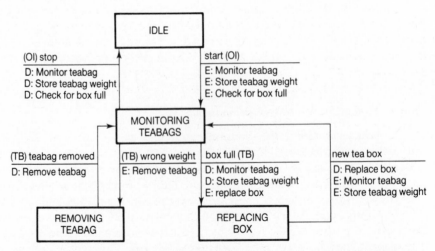

Figure 10.5 Modified STD for teabag boxing system. OI indicates condition is generated on operator interface processor and TB indicates condition is generated on teabag boxing processor.

the STD as described, gives the new teabag boxing processor STD shown in Figure 10.6(a). Starting with the same initial STD and modifying it, this time with respect to the operator interface processor, gives the new operator interface processor STD as shown in Figure 10.6(b).

Figure 10.7 shows more clearly the interfaces which have been introduced between the two halves of the STD (and therefore across the processor boundaries) to ensure the two processors still behave as halves of the same system. A boundary around these control processes will confirm that the original control process interfaces have been maintained.

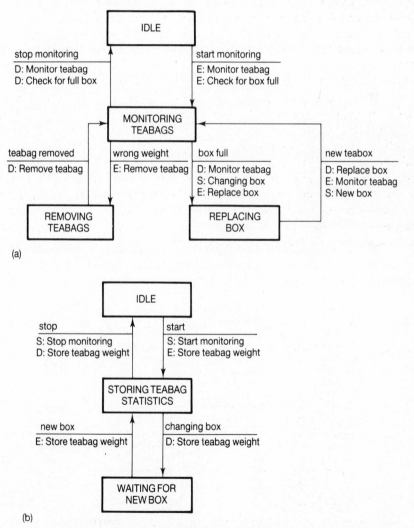

Figure 10.6 Modified (a) teabag boxing and (b) operator interface processor STDs.

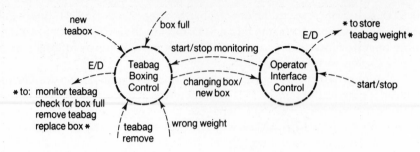

Figure 10.7   Split control process showing interface.

10.3.5 Construction of complete processor environment model

From the initial processor allocation (Table 10.1) and the discussions above concerning splitting of data transformations, data stores and control processes, we build a DFD that reflects the work required of each processor; that for the operator interface processor is shown in Figure 10.8. A boundary around these DFDs gives high level data transformations which represent the processors. By levelling and renumbering the transformations within each processor DFD to reflect the new organization of the model, we create the teabag boxing PEM, shown by Figure 10.9.

10.4 TRACEABILITY TABLES

When the essential model becomes the processor environment model, the numbers of the data transformations may change to reflect the new organization of the system. The processors on the top level PEM DFD are

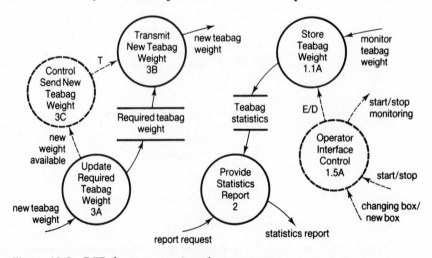

Figure 10.8   DFD for operator interface processor.

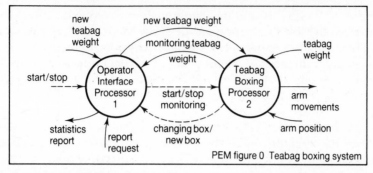

PEM figure 0 Teabag boxing system

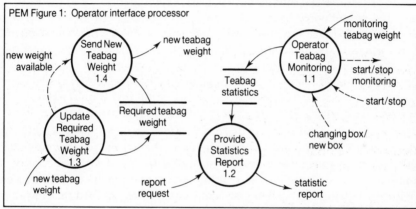

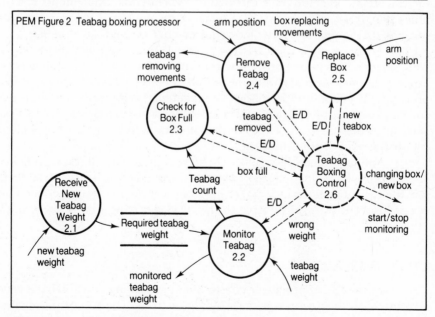

Figure 10.9   Teabag system PEM.

numbered 1, 2, 3, ..., n, and the data transformations and control processes are renumbered to reflect the processor they now reside on. For instance, in the PEM, data transformation number 1.3.2 would always be implemented on processor 1. Throughout the design, the numbers of the data transformations will change to reflect their organization with respect to the technology. If traceability through the various stages of design is to be maintained, a 'traceability table' should be built.

The traceability table has one column for each stage of the development, where all the components of the model which exist at that point (all the data transformations, control processes and data stores), should be listed.

Consider traceability between the essential model and the PEM. For each essential model entry in the table, there should be a corresponding PEM entry. If an essential data transformation does not have a corresponding PEM data transformation, we have effectively 'lost' some of the functionality of the system during the development, i.e. one of the requirements will not be implemented. Similarly, if a PEM component is not generated by an essential model component, we have added something which is not the result of a requirement, i.e. we have designed something into the system which does not need to be there.

The traceability table therefore serves two purposes. Firstly, it acts to check, in going from one model to the next, that all the requirements have been met and nothing spurious has been added to the design. Secondly, it gives traceability through the model, making system maintenance easier. If a customer identifies a change to a particular requirement, we can find that requirement in the essential model and trace through to the code that implements it. From the other side, if we wish to modify a piece of the code, we can trace that back to the essential model to see which requirements we may be affecting.

There is not necessarily a one-to-one mapping between model components. If a control process within the essential model is split across three processors, one essential model control process will map on to three PEM control processes. If a data store from the essential model is repeated on two processors and extra data transformation behaviour is added to maintain the data, an essential data store may map on to a couple of data stores and the associated data transformations within the PEM.

Building traceability tables can be very important. If traceability between code and models is lost, much of the advantage of using a structured technique (i.e. the ease of maintenance and the use of the model as system documentation) is also lost. The traceability table for the teabag boxing system is given in Table 10.2

10.5 SUMMARY

At the end of processor environment modelling you will have generated a hierarchy of diagrams as shown by Figure 10.9. The top of the hierarchy is equivalent to a hardware configuration diagram, with each data transformation

Table 10.2

Essential model		Processor environment model	
1.1	Weigh teabag	1.1.1	Store teabag weight
		2.2	Monitor teabag
1.2	Check for box full	2.3	Check for box full
1.4	Replace box	2.5	Replace box
1.3	Remove teabag	2.4	Remove teabag
2	Provide statistics report	1.2	Provide statistics report
3	Update required teabag weight	1.3	Update required teabag weight
		1.4	Send new teabag weight
1.5	Control teabag boxing	2.6	Teabag boxing control
		1.1.2	Operator interface control
Teabag statistics		Teabag statistics — on operator interface	
Required teabag weight		Required teabag weight — on operator interface and teabag boxing	
Teabag count		Teabag count — on teabag boxing figure	

or store representing a physical processor within the system. This top level diagram shows the processors, and any interfaces required between processors, or between processors and the outside world. External interfaces should be maintained from the context diagram, i.e. if you were to draw a boundary around the top level PEM, you should find the same inputs and outputs as the context diagram.

For each processor shown at level 0, there will be a hierarchy of DFDs, STDs and ERDs that specify the requirements of each processor. During processor environment modelling, we maintain much of our 'perfect technology'. We investigate the capacity of each processor during processor allocation, only to confirm the allocation of approximately the right amount of work and data to each processor. Therefore the lower levels of PEM show what will be done on the processors, not how it will be done — exactly how will be discussed during software environment modelling in Chapter 12. Effectively, the essential model has been split into a set of mini essential models, one for each processor in the system.

We should now be able to take any processor from the top level PEM

DFD, together with its lower level diagram hierarchy, and develop that processor in isolation from the other system processors, knowing that the interface between the processor and the rest of the system has been correctly defined.

10.6 EXERCISES

As stated during the chapter, sometimes you will carry out processor allocation first, sometimes you will build in the details of the HCI first. Exercises 4, 5 and 6 rely on the HCI already being completed, and follow on from exercises 1, 2, 3 and 4 of Chapter 11.

In exercises 1 and 2, you are initially presented with a fragment of an essential model. You are then presented with the processor configuration on which that essential model is to be implemented, and asked to provide some parts or all of the processor environment model.

1. Exercise on splitting data transformations. The data transformation shown in Figure 10.10 is taken from a DFD to describe a banking system. A customer may check their balance by providing a 'balance request', which includes the customer account number. This can be used to index into the 'accounts' store and provide the customer 'balance'.

In the implementation, the customer 'balance request' will actually be made at a 'cashpoint' machine. So customers may check their balance at the cashpoint machine, but all the bank account records will be held within the bank. In this system there will be two processors:

(a) Inside the cashpoint machine, to provide the customer interface.
(b) Inside the bank, to hold all the bank account records.

Consider the way in which the data transformation will be split between the processors, and draw the two data transformations that will result from this split.

2. Exercise on splitting control. The STD and DFD of Figure 10.11 show part of a system which will collect and display information on request. This system is to be split between two processors, one which will provide the data collection functionality, and another which will provide the operator interface functionality. The collected data will be stored in a separate memory area which may be shared between the two processors.

The processor allocation is to be done according to Table 10.3. Produce

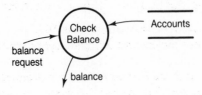

Figure 10.10 Exercise 1.

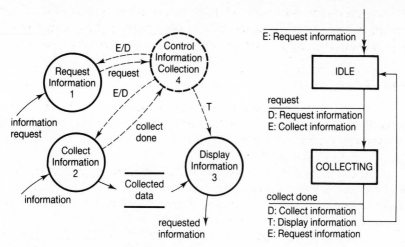

Figure 10.11   Exercise 2.

Table 10.3

Processor	Essential behaviour	
Operator interface	1	Request information
	3	Display information
	4	Control information collection (part)
Data collection	2	Collect information
	4	Control information collection (part)
Shared memory	Store: Collected data	

the STDs and control processes that will be generated within the PEM from the essential STD/control process number 4.

3. This exercise concerns the greenhouse atmosphere control system, discussed in exercise 2 of Chapter 11. It has been decided to implement the system across three processors:

(a) One responsible for temperature control.
(b) One responsible for humidity control.
(c) One responsible for providing the human–computer interface.

The allocation table for this configuration is given in Table 10.4.

Build the processor environment model and the traceability table for this allocation.

4. This exercise concerns the washing machine control system, discussed in exercise 1 of Chapter 11. It has been decided to split this system between two processors:

Table 10.4

Processor	Essential behaviour
Temperature control	1.3 Monitor temperature
	1.1 Control temperature (part)
	Required temperature
Humidity control	2.1 Control humidity (part)
	2.3 Monitor humidity
	2.4 Adjust vent
	Required humidity
HCI	1.1 Control temperature (part)
	1.2 Display temperature
	2.1 Control humidity (part)
	2.2 Display humidity
	3 Modify temperature
	4 Modify humidity

(a) One responsible for the human–computer interface.
(b) One responsible for the actual control of the washing machine drum and heater.

Firstly build an allocation table for the configuration, and then use this to build the processor environment model.

5. This exercise concerns the missile control system, discussed in exercises 3 and 4 of Chapter 11. This system will be spread across three processors:

(a) The missile itself will contain a small processor, which will allow it to communicate with the base station. It is envisaged that some intelligence will be placed within the missile to allow it to 'steer' itself.
(b) The gun will contain a small processor. It is envisaged that given target information, the gun will be able to aim itself and fire the missile. This 'stand alone' capability will enable the gun to be used more easily in other systems.
(c) A large processor will be located at the base station, responsible for the operator interface and any remote control of the gun and missile which may be required.

Figure 10.12 shows the envisaged hardware configuration.
For the missile control system, construct:

(a) A processor allocation table.
(b) The processor environment model.
(c) The traceability table.

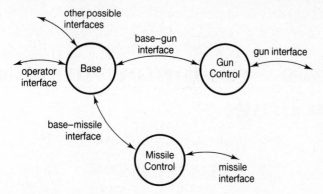

Figure 10.12   Exercise 5.

CHAPTER ELEVEN

Human−computer interface modelling

11.1 INTRODUCTION

Developing a user friendly human−computer interface (HCI) is a very difficult job — some companies employ psychologists to decide what the HCI should do. In this chapter I do not tell you how to develop an HCI, but how to model the HCI you have decided upon, and some general tips on how to get from the essential HCI to the PEM HCI are also given.

Before we consider HCI modelling, let us discuss why the HCI is so important, and why we consider it separately and differently from any other of the system interfaces. In the eyes of the customer, the HCI is often the most important system interface. In the eyes of the developer, the HCI is probably the interface involving most work and the most difficult to get right.

11.1.1 The customer's view of the HCI

It is important to model the HCI early, and in some detail. Many users are only aware of what the system does via the HCI, and they see it as being the major part of the system. A customer will not be satisfied with a requirements specification until it contains details of the HCI. It is probably the area where the customer has most idea about what the system should do, and often new areas of functionality will emerge when the customer starts to discuss the HCI.

A system built for a particular market, rather than a particular customer, will not be saleable unless it has got a good HCI, no matter how good the functionality is. You have only got to go into the electrical department of a store, into a hifi or even a computer shop, to see that what a system looks like is often more important than what the system actually does. Some hifi shops are very keen on showing you all the flashing lights and buttons you can play with, but less likely to encourage you to listen to the equipment.

It is very important that the system looks good as well as performs well. First impressions encourage the customer to buy a system, so in order to capture a market you have to make sure that your HCI is what the customer wants to see.

Many of the currently popular CASE tools that supposedly help with structured development are little more than drawing packages, which implement little of the checking and configuration management that would be so useful. Unfortunately, developers are so impressed with the wonderful HCIs that they choose them over other CASE tools, which , although they may have a less friendly interface, are functionally superior.

At this stage, you should differentiate between the customer and the operator. The customer is the person ordering the system, but will not necessarily be the person using the system. When defining the HCI, it is important to talk directly to the person who will be using the system, i.e. the operator. Many mistakes in HCIs are a result of the developer having no idea of the operator's environment.

I was once involved in building the HCI to a radar system for an aircraft. When testing the radar system, I would put it on the bench in front of me at eye level and stare straight at it. Without even thinking about it, I was building the system as if the pilot were constantly viewing the system at eye level. When I was invited to see the aircraft into which the system was to be installed, it was a revelation to me. I got into the cockpit of the plane, and at first I could not even see my piece of equipment because there were so many other displays and controls for the pilot to use. I eventually found the display on a level with my right elbow. It was so different from the way that I had imagined it: first of all it was much further away from the pilot than I had realized; secondly, the pilot had to look at it at an angle; and, finally, he was not going to be staring at it all the time because most of the time he would be flying the plane — he would just look down at it every now and again. All of these things put a whole new perspective on the HCI.

11.1.2 The developer's view of the HCI

When the system interfaces to a person, it is very different from interfacing to a machine. Most machines come with a manual, which specifies the interface between the system and the machine. If you develop the interface according to the manual and it does not work, either the interface between the system and the machine has been written incorrectly, or the piece of equipment is not working properly. Both of these things can be checked and corrected relatively easily.

On the other hand, the interface between the system and a person is much more subjective. People do not come with manuals specifying the correct way to interface to them. One person will be perfectly happy with an interface that another person cannot make any sense of. You cannot say that a particular interface is right or wrong just because a certain person understands it. Building an HCI will always be a matter of compromise. If you gear the whole system to the likes and dislikes of one particular person, it is unlikely that this will suit everybody else. The best that you can normally do is to develop an HCI which suits most people most of the time, but not all people all of the time.

Also, the system interface to a person tends to be much larger than to a piece of equipment. When the system talks to equipment, it will be via a minimal set of commands. The system tells the equipment to do something and expects it to be done; the system asks for a piece of information and expects to receive that information. When the system talks to a person, it is not that simple:

1. The system has to be polite to the person.
2. It is unlikely that a person will understand what the system means first time round, so requests for information and actions have to be fully explained.
3. It is much more likely that a person will make mistakes than a machine, and the mistakes will be of a different nature. Whereas a machine may have problems with low level communications, people are likely to provide the wrong information completely. As a result, the system has to check all inputs to the system and try to steer the user back on course when he makes mistakes.

In terms of our models, this creates a big difference between the essential HCI and the PEM HCI. In the essential model for the teabag boxing system (see Figure 2.1), we showed an essential flow 'new teabag weight' from the operator into the context diagram data transformation, to allow the operator to change the required weight of the teabag.

Considering the HCI, we realize that the operator does not just put the information straight into the system. The operator may log on, choose from a menu and then complete a form to change the required teabag weight. A lot of dialogue will pass between the system and the operator to ensure the correct information enters the system.

As we will see later on in this chapter, there is a huge difference between the simple diagram describing the HCI in the essential model and the much more complicated realization of the HCI in the PEM.

11.2 STRATEGIES FOR MODELLING THE HCI

The details of the PEM HCI should be gathered from the user of the system. Consider an example of this from the teabag boxing system. In the essential model, the operator provided a 'new teabag weight', which was recorded by the data transformation 'change teabag weight' as the 'required teabag weight'. The customer should be able to verify the system on the basis of this essential model. The next step is to show the essential model to the operator, explain that the 'new teabag weight' is to be input, and discuss the interface.

Imagine that in this particular system, the operator has no idea of what computers are capable of, and therefore does not know what he would like the computer to do. If we are automating a manual system, we should discover how the operator currently lets the equipment know the 'new teabag weight'. It will be easier for the operator to learn to use the system if it appears similar to the current system. Currently, the operator is given a blue 'weight change request' form. Information from the form is punched on to a card, which the operator feeds into the system. On the basis of this, we can provide the following interface:

> The operator indicates to the system that he would like to perform a required weight change. The system will present the operator with a form with the same layout as the 'weight change request' form — this will make transferring the data as easy as possible.

Presented with this HCI, the operator could request that the system check the order of magnitude of figures input to the system. This would lead to the final interface:

> The operator presses a key at a terminal indicating that he wishes to input some 'new teabag weight' information. The system provides the operator with a form. The operator types into the form from the keyboard, and the system checks the form as it is filled in. Any mistakes made will be indicated to the operator, who can then correct them. When the operator has filled in the form to his own satisfaction, he will indicate to the system that the form has been completed, via another key at the terminal.

Once we have an idea of the HCI required by the operator, we can model the behaviour to help us verify the HCI with the customer and the operator, and also to allow us to develop the interface through to code. The HCI model developed will be much larger than the original essential model, as it contains much more work. There are three strategies for deriving the model showing HCI behaviour:

1. Top down functional decomposition.
2. Event partitioning.
3. Translating menu structures into DFD hierarchies.

The strategy to use will depend on the complexity and type of HCI required. The following sections show how each method could be used to generate the model for the 'change teabag weight' HCI.

11.2.1 Top down functional decomposition

Using top down functional decomposition, on the basis of discussions with the operator, we could break the original data transformation 'update required teabag weight' into the following:

1. Produce form display.
2. Accept and verify form fields.
3. Store required teabag weight.

This gives the DFD and corresponding STD shown in Figure 11.1, which would become the DFD beneath the original data transformation 'update required teabag weight' in the PEM.

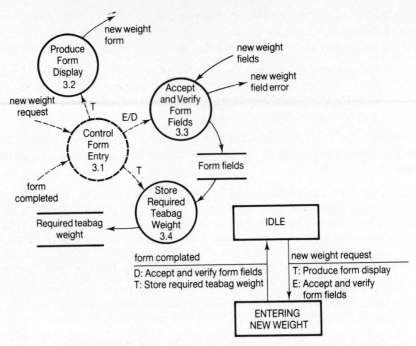

Figure 11.1   Update required teabag weight — functional decomposition.

This method can be used if the HCI is not too complicated, and you feel confident about top down decomposition, without breaking the system into 'implementation' units. At this stage we are still modelling the requirements of the HCI, i.e. what it will do, not how we will make it do it.

If the HCI is expected to be more complex, it might be better to develop it using one of the other strategies, which will guarantee a well-structured system.

11.2.2 Event partitioning

In previous discussions we decided that the operator would indicate that he wanted to make a teabag weight change, at which point he would be given a form to fill in. The form would be checked as it was filled, and mistakes could be corrected until the operator was satisfied with the contents of the form. The details of this interface are shown between the operator and the system in Figure 11.2. In this figure, we regard the system, which was decided upon during analysis, as a terminator, which receives the essential flow 'new teabag weight' from the HCI. The operator interfaces to the HCI using flows which model the actual interface required.

This gives a new context diagram describing the HCI, from which we can build an event list (Table 11.1). This should be fairly easy, as everything in

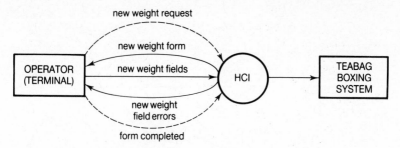

Figure 11.2   The HCI–operator interface.

Table 11.1

Event	Response	Classification
1. Operator requests to update required weight	Provide new weight form Start accepting new weight fields	C/D
2. Operator enters new weight field	Verify new weight field	C/D
3. Operator indicates form completed	Store required teabag weight Stop accepting new weight fields	C/D

the HCI is by its very nature event-driven, i.e. the operator makes a request, the system responds, the operator does something wrong, the system responds, the operator makes a correction, the system responds.

The context diagram and the event list form the environmental model for the HCI, which are used to derive the DFD and STD describing the behaviour of the HCI, shown in Figure 11.3. There are three advantages to this approach.

Firstly, the system and the HCI are connected by the essential (smallest and simplest) interface, and are therefore as loosely coupled as they can be. In many unstructured systems, the HCI and the system are very tightly coupled. In practice, this means that a function and the HCI which allows use of that function are often mixed up together in the same piece of code.

If you want to change the HCI, either because it is wrong, or in the light of new technology (perhaps the customer wants to change from black and white to colour monitors), it is often difficult to differentiate between the code which implements the HCI and the code which implements the system functionality. In this situation it is normally easier to scrap the whole system and start again, even though the fundamental functions of the system are not being changed. If the system and the HCI are as loosely coupled as possible, it will be much easier to change one without affecting the other.

Secondly, modelling the system and the HCI as parallel systems will make

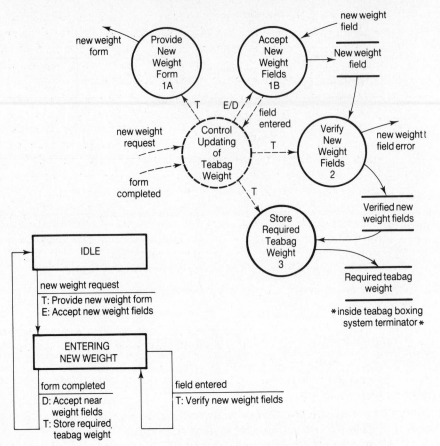

Figure 11.3 'Update required teabag weight' — behavioural model.

parallel development much easier than building the HCI and the system together. If the system and the HCI are presented as separate systems, one group of people can work on the essential system functionality, while another group can work on the HCI. This would make sense if the system functionality involved low level process control type work, while the HCI was implemented on an advanced workstation with many programmer facilities. The development engineers involved in both sides of the system would require very different skills and experience.

Once the essential interface between the operator and the system has been defined, development of the HCI can start. If the HCI is particularly important, you could model that before you model the behaviour of the system.

Thirdly, as we have already discussed, if the HCI and the system are developed as separate, loosely coupled systems, it should be easy to change the HCI without changing the whole system. There are two situations where this might be of help:

1. Many companies build fundamentally the same system over and over again, but with different interfaces for different clients. If the system is built as a separate item, it will be easy to substitute one HCI for another. This results in us building the system only once, but building a different interface based on particular clients' requirements.

2. The other situation involves a customer who has a system which you built perhaps 10 years ago. As technology in the field of HCI advances, the customer may return requesting a new system. If the customer is still involved in the same business as 10 years ago, he may want a system with the same fundamental functionality, but a completely new HCI. You may have to reimplement the system on a different machine, but the requirements of the system (i.e. the essential model) remain unchanged. Only the HCI and the lower levels of the design will have changed. If you modelled the HCI and the system separately, there will be no need to re-analyze the system — you will be able to use the original essential model.

11.2.3 Menu structures

The final strategy, of starting with a menu structure and changing that directly into an STD and DFD hierarchy, is only applicable if the HCI involves either a menu structure or a sequence of screens.

Consider how the STD can be used to model screen sequences. In an STD the system enters a state, and waits for a condition to occur, whereupon it carries out some actions which take it into the next state.

Imagine using a HCI: a system displays a screen at a terminal and waits for some input to the terminal, whereupon it responds by changing the screen (and probably doing some other things that do not show on the screen).

The states of the STD are analogous to the screens of the HCI. The conditions are analogous to the user input and the actions are analogous to the system response to user input.

Therefore, it should be easy to model a screen sequence using an STD. For example, imagine the intelligent payment machines in some car parks. You enter your parking ticket and the machine displays the parking fee. The machine is capable of giving change, and will decrement the amount payable each time a coin is entered. Once the parking fee has been paid, the machine issues a receipt and, if appropriate, change. This is modelled by the STD shown in Figure 11.4. In STDs which model screen sequences, transitory states represent things which happen 'inside' the system, and therefore do not represent screens.

We can take this idea a little further and apply it to whole menu structures. Imagine the operator within the teabag boxing system requires the HCI to be menu-driven. At the top level menu the operator has four choices:

1. Start system.
2. Stop system.

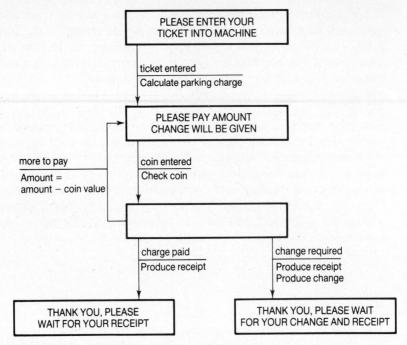

Figure 11.4   Example of a screen sequence.

3. Change teabag weight.
4. Reports.

If we imagine each of these choices giving rise to a condition within an STD which models this interface, this would give the STD in Figure 11.5. Here, the menu choices which give rise to lower level screens are modelled as states, otherwise a choice is modelled by a transition which returns to the original state. We can use this to generate the associated DFD, which models the required interface to the teabag boxing system.

The models detailing the HCI must become part of the PEM before development can continue. Therefore Figure 11.5 must be merged with the model describing the processor allocation for the teabag boxing system for the PEM to be complete. Figure 11.6 shows the operator interface processor DFD from the previous chapter (Figure 10.9), which has been merged with Figure 11.5 to produce a model of the behaviour organized with respect to the chosen operator interface.

'Change teabag weight' of Figure 11.5 can be provided by '1.3 update required teabag weight' of Figure 10.9, 'provide statistics reports' can be provided by '1.2 provide statistics report' of Figure 10.9; and the operator start/stop

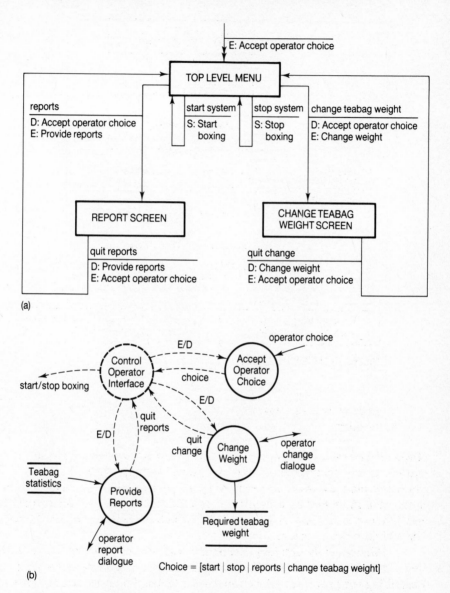

Figure 11.5   Teabag boxing operator interface: (a) operator interface STD;
(b) operator interface DFD.

command can be routed through the operator interface to '1.1 operator teabag
monitoring' of Figure 10.9, as 'start/stop boxing'. This will give the new PEM
for the operator interface processor shown in Figure 11.6, which includes details
of the HCI.

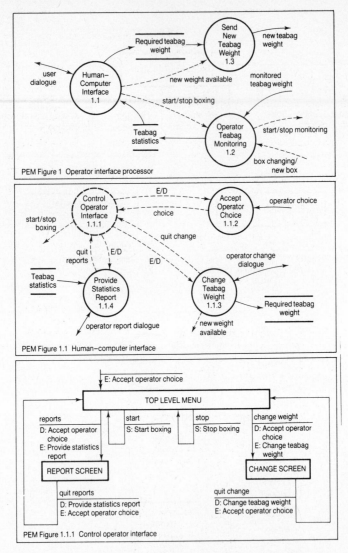

Figure 11.6   Modified operator interface processor PEM.

11.3 SUMMARY

As there is so much difference between the essential and the PEM HCIs, and it is so important to get it right, developing the HCI often involves a lot of time and effort. If you are not absolutely sure that you are building a suitable HCI for your customer, you could waste a lot of money developing an HCI which the customer wants changing as soon as he is presented with it. Also, there are often differences between what the customer thought was wanted and what is found to be wanted once it has been tried out.

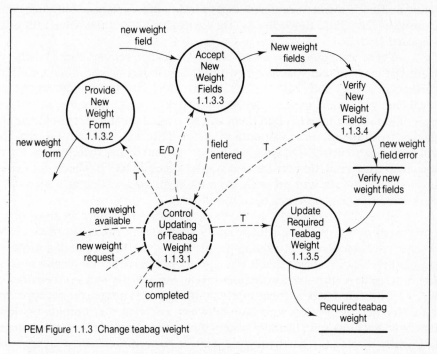

PEM Figure 1.1.3 Change teabag weight

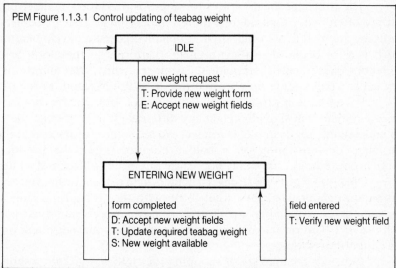

Figure 11.6 (*continued*)

To avoid this waste, consider building prototypes before you do any 'real' development. You can then try the prototype out on the customer to make sure that what you are building is what the customer really wants. There are many products available these days that help build HCI prototypes. Many packages help build displays, menu structures and windowing systems. Although these prototypes have little functionality, they will give a customer some idea of the proposed HCI.

There are some aspects of prototyping that require care. Firstly, the prototype and the real system are two different things — you should not build a prototype and let that grow into the system. The prototype should only be used to validate your initial ideas. If the customer does not like the initial prototypes, most of the work that went into them will be wasted. Prototypes should be built quickly, with the minimum amount of effort. This will tend to mean that they will not be particularly well structured or documented, and therefore should not be used as the foundation for the real system. Once an HCI has been chosen, the development should start properly from the beginning, taking into account the ideas which your prototypes have tested.

Secondly, everybody should be made aware that they are dealing with a prototype and how that differs from the real system. I have heard more than one story where sales or marketing people have quite happily sold a prototype to a customer, not realizing that it was a prototype. A lot of non-technical people do not seem to realize that a computer producing a display on a screen does not necessarily mean that it is doing anything. If your sales people do not appreciate the difference in development time between a system that outputs randomly generated data to a screen, and a system which has to collect, correlate, analyze and finally display the data, they will expect rather unrealistic delivery times.

The other 'problem' with prototypes is that, for a number of reasons, they are often better than the real thing. They often go faster, because they are not doing any real processing, or are implemented on a development machine which is a lot better than their ultimate platform, so they look better. This sometimes leads to very disappointed customers, when, after months of waiting, they get the real system only to find that it is 'not as good' as the prototype.

If you build a prototype which does not look and behave exactly like the real system, you should explain any differences, in terms that the customer can understand. For example, if you were to tell some customers that the system you were demonstrating on a colour monitor would be produced on a monochrome monitor, they may not realize this means a black and white version.

Finally, a word of warning: customers tend to assume that you know more than you do about what they want to do with the HCI, in the same way that you sometimes assume that the customer knows more about what you can do with the HCI. This means that they sometimes trust your judgement on the HCI more than they should.

Consider the analogy of shopping for clothes. I go into a shop, tell the assistant that I want a dress and my size. The assistant finds me a number of dresses in that size for me to try on. The assistant has had to make a snap judgement on the kind of person that I am, so that he or she can find me some dresses that look like they might suit me — the kind of clothes that you wear nearly always say something about the kind of person that you are. The problem is that he or she does not know me very well, and all he or she has to go on is what I am wearing at the time — which may give the wrong impression of the clothes that I normally wear.

As soon as one of the dresses fits, and looks reasonable, the assistant tells me it suits me and I buy it. It is not until I get home that I realize that although it fits and looks all right, it is not the kind of dress that I can ever imagine myself wearing. If I gave a lecture wearing a leopard skin miniskirt and fishnet stockings, I doubt that anyone would take me seriously.

It is not the assistant's fault that I bought the wrong dress, it is my own fault for putting my faith in the 'expert', who was only an expert at selling clothes that fit and seem to look right. I never actually told the assistant exactly what I wanted — just my dress size.

It is the same with users — they will say 'I want a system that does this, that and the other', and expect you to tell them what they need. If you suggest a seven level menu with forms, flashing lights and buttons, they will probably say that it is just what they need — but they will not really think about whether it is what they need or not. It is not until the system is installed and they start trying to use it that they find the only thing they actually want to do is seven menu levels down, and they have to make eight choices and wait 15 minutes to use the system. Everything else you have given them is more or less superfluous.

It is often difficult, but try to discover exactly what the user wants before suggesting things, otherwise you may develop a system which, although it works to specification, is completely unsuitable.

11.4 EXERCISES

1. This exercise concerns the HCI to the washing machine control system, specified in exercise 4 of Chapter 10. After going through the essential model with the customer, the customer now realizes that there is no way of knowing what stage of the wash cycle the washing machine is in.

Therefore a new requirement has been introduced for the system to control a panel of coloured lights, which indicate where the washing machine is in its cycle:

(a) No lights on indicates cycle over (or not yet begun).
(b) Red light on indicates filling drum with water and heating water.
(c) Yellow light on indicates washing.
(d) Green light on indicates emptying drum of water.

Modify the essential model of the washing machine control system, to incorporate these new requirements.

2. This exercise concerns the HCI to the greenhouse atmosphere control system, specified in exercise 3 of Chapter 10. After the success of the initial greenhouse atmosphere control system, it has been decided to create a more sophisticated version, which has the following additional capabilities:

1. The gardener is able to set the required temperature and humidity levels, using two dials, one for temperature and one for humidity.
2. The gardener is given a constant display of temperature and humidity values, whenever the system is switched on, at a small digital display.

Modify the original 'control greenhouse atmosphere' essential model, to take account of these new requirements.

3. This exercise concerns the HCI to the missile control system, specified in exercise 5 of Chapter 10.

(a) By using either top down decomposition, or via an event list and context diagram, model the HCI behaviour of 'accept target adjustment' described below:

Once a missile is in flight, the operator is able to change the specified target, and time of arrival of the missile.

Once a request to adjust the missile target has been made, the operator would expect to be given a 'target adjustment screen', comprising the following:

(i) Current missile target information.
(ii) Current missile location.
(iii) Target adjustment form.

When the operator has completed the target adjustment form, he needs to be told whether the new target information is feasible, i.e. once the missile is in flight, it may not be possible to reach a certain target at a certain time.

Therefore, the operator will be given a display which shows if the specified target can be reached at the specified time, and if not, when the target can be reached. The operator can then either confirm or abort the change. Confirming the change will update the 'missile schedule' with the required change, and aborting the change will take the operator back to the 'target adjustment screen', enabling him to try different target information.

(b) Integrate this behaviour into the original essential model.

4. This exercise concerns the HCI to the missile control system, specified in exercise 5 of Chapter 10. The HCI to the missile control system will be fairly complicated. First of all, before an operator can access the system, he must go through a tight logon procedure — it is very important that only authorized users are allowed to launch and direct missiles. Once into the system, the operator may perform operations on the missile schedule and the current missile.

If the operator chooses to work on the schedule, he may perform one of the following:

(a) View the schedule.
(b) Create a new schedule entry.
(c) Edit an existing schedule entry.
(d) Delete an existing schedule entry.

If the operator chooses to work on the current missile, he may perform one of the following:

(a) View the location of the current missile.
(b) Fire the current missile.
(c) Adjust the target of the current missile.

(a) The interface will be from a terminal with an attached keyboard, and should be menu driven. Build a menu structure for the required HCI.
(b) Produce the STD/DFD which models the required HCI.
(c) Integrate this HCI with the original essential model for the missile control system, given as the answer to exercise 10.5.

CHAPTER TWELVE

Software environment modelling

12.1 INTRODUCTION

The processor environment model describes what should be done in each processor. Software environment modelling considers what the operating system, I/O routines and other facilities available on the processor allow. On this basis, we can decide how to implement the behaviour defined within the PEM. Before we go any further, let us look at some definitions:

1 *Software architecture*. The software architecture of a processor can be thought of as a layer between the application and the processor, which allows the application to use the processor. It consists of any system services and library routines available on a processor, for use by the application. Basic items of software architecture will include operating systems and database management systems (DBMSs), but the software architecture can also include I/O packages, graphics packages and calculation packages — anything the application uses to fulfil its purpose.

Although basic items of software architecture are normally bought in, software architecture extends to include any packages and facilities seen as library routines which you write yourself.

2. *Execution* and *data storage units*. Execution units are units of processing within the chosen software architecture; data storage units are units of data within the chosen software architecture. For example, a data storage unit within a DBMS will be a database table.

The name by which you currently know an execution unit depends on which operating system you are familiar with — you could be used to calling them programs, tasks or processes. An operating system sees each execution unit as something it can schedule separately. Concurrent activity within a processor is achieved by the operating system swapping between execution units, such that they appear to be running at the same time. As the operating system sees the execution unit as a single schedulable item, there cannot be concurrency within a single execution unit (i.e. there is a single thread of control running through an execution unit); however, there may be concurrency between execution units.

There are three stages to software environment modelling (SEM):

1. Pick or evaluate a software architecture. If the software architecture has been defined, you should find out what the application can do with it. If no software architecture has been defined, one should be chosen on the basis of the behaviour required within each processor.
2. Remove all perfect technology. Once a processor's software architecture has been defined, you can find all you need to know about exactly how your processor can be used. This allows the removal of perfect technology, which is replaced with the real implementation technology. Removal of perfect technology may imply additional behaviour in the model, showing how the system will be implemented on the defined software architecture.
3. Allocate the PEM to execution units and data storage units. In the PEM, we took the essential model (which showed what we wanted to do), and the processor configuration (which gave us some idea of how we would do it), and split the model between the available processors. In SEM, we are doing much the same thing but on a smaller scale. Here we take the PEM (which again shows us what we will do), and the software configuration (defined by the software architecture), and split the model amongst the available execution units and storage units.

Software environment modelling will produce a hierarchy of DFDs for each processor. Data transformations on the top level DFD of each hierarchy represent either execution units or part of the software architecture, as shown by Figure 12.1. This diagram shows how the execution units will use the software

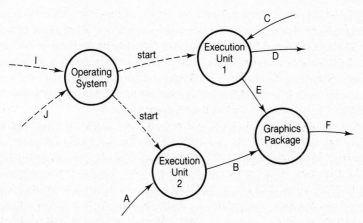

Figure 12.1   SEM — top level DFD.

architecture. In this example, we have two pieces of software architecture, the operating system and a graphics package, being used by two execution units. Notice that even though 'operating system' accepts and generates only event flows, it is not shown as a control process. Conventionally, pieces of software architecture are always shown as data transformations.

Pieces of software architecture can be thought of as 'internal terminators'. Terminators are things in the system's environment to which the system interfaces and uses to fulfil part of its functionality. As developers, we are only interested in the interface, as the terminator is not part of our system.

Pieces of software architecture are things in the software's environment to which the software interfaces and uses to fulfil part of its functionality. However, they are not really part of the application development. Again, as developers, we are only interested in the interface.

On the basis of this, data transformations which represent software architecture will not normally be broken down into lower level DFDs, as we only need to know how to interface to them, not how they work. However, software architecture that you are developing and execution units will always contain a lower level DFD hierarchy which defines the behaviour of each unit.

12.2 SOFTWARE ARCHITECTURE EVALUATION

The first stage of software environment modelling involves either choosing a software architecture, on the basis of the system's functional requirements, or evaluating a software architecture which has already been chosen.

The amount of work involved in implementation (crudely, the amount of code that you will have to write) will depend on the facilities available within the software architecture, and how well those facilities match the system's requirements.

Imagine a system requirement to draw circles on a terminal providing the user interface. If the software architecture contained a graphics package that drew circles of a certain radius, centred at a certain point on the screen, you could call the given software architecture facility as a procedure from within your code. If, on the other hand, your graphics package was much more basic, only allowing you to draw a straight line between two given points, the code to create the circle at the operator interface would be more complicated.

Given that much of your code will depend on the facilities provided by the software architecture, you should choose or understand your software architecture before you design the system. In the ideal world you would always start by examining the behaviour specified by the PEM, and finding a software architecture that did that type of thing. Practically, you are often not given a choice of software architecture — the customer is quite likely to specify, for instance, what operating system he would like you to use. Also, having identified the need for software architecture with certain capabilities, you may not be able to find one that does exactly what you want.

If you are lucky enough to be able to choose your own software architecture, there are a number of factors to consider:

1. *Functional suitability of software architecture.* The most obvious consideration is to find a software architecture which does what you want to do in the system, otherwise it may take a lot of work to make the software architecture do what you want it to. In our previous example, the amount of work involved in writing a system call to 'draw circle' is negligible compared to the amount of work involved in writing a routine that constructs a circle out of small sections of straight lines.

   When considering such items as graphics packages and calculation packages, it should not be difficult to decide whether they have the right functionality. However, it is not so easy to evaluate from the PEM whether a certain operating system is suitable. You should consider how many execution units the software architecture will support with respect to how many you will need, i.e. how much concurrent activity do you envisage within the system, and how much does the operating system support. Also how will those execution units be activated and how can they communicate — will it be possible for execution units to activate one another directly, or will activation have to be done explicitly via the operating system? What sort of scheduling does the operating system support, can execution units be given priorities, is the scheduling pre-emptive (interrupt-driven) or time sliced? In a real-time system, it may be important to have a particular type of scheduling to make your system work.

2. *Software architecture flexibility.* You should also consider the ability of the software architecture to accommodate changes in system requirements. For a maintainable system, do not just think about what your system does today, think about what it might have to do in the future.

   Imagine there are five concurrent areas of activity within your system, so you buy an operating system that supports five concurrent processes. If the customer specifies an extra processing requirement for the system that had been forgotten about, you have a system with six concurrent areas of activity, but an operating system that will only support five. The customer may be upset if, at this early stage, you cannot cope with what appears to be a fairly small change in requirements. You will have to fit six concurrent areas of activity into five concurrent processes. This will be possible, but will result in a very messy design.

   In a multi-processor system, it may also be worth having the same software architecture on many of the processors. This will allow areas of system functionality to move between processors, without having to rewrite them to work under a different software architecture.

3. *Cost of software architecture*. There are many different costs involved in software architecture, although not all of them may be relevant to your particular development.

In obvious financial terms, there is the cost of the software architecture. If you build 1000 units of a system using a certain piece of software architecture, paying a separate licence fee for each unit will amount to a large production overhead.

You should also consider the cost in time and effort implied by the use of a particular software architecture. Software architectures can be large and complicated, and it may take many months for an engineer to use one competently. In terms of time and effort, it may cost a lot to use a software architecture that development engineers are unfamiliar with.

On the other hand, unless you are very experienced in this area, be wary of building software architecture. Many pieces of software architecture are not that difficult to design and write, but are very difficult to test and maintain.

Imagine testing an operating system. It is often difficult to test low levels of code, as you have to examine the program counter, the stack — things which may be difficult to access. Also, the number of paths through an operating system makes it virtually impossible to test every aspect of its operation. Often, pieces of software architecture are only tested doing the kind of things that they will be doing most of the time. As soon as you expand the system, which may involve the operating system doing something else, you will be using untested code. Although an operating system may not be difficult to develop initially, it can cost a lot in maintenance, as every change to the system may involve a change to the operating system. Even though a commercially available system may look expensive, and may not do exactly what you want, it may be cheaper than the development and extra maintenance effort involved in building your own.

Having said all this, sometimes you have no choice but to develop your own software architecture, as what you want cannot be bought.

Finally, you should consider the amount of space and time an architecture uses on a processor. Many real-time systems do not use database management systems, as they use too much processing time. In many embedded systems, developers are forced into writing their own 'operating systems', as commercially available operating systems use too much space.

In summary, if you have the luxury of choosing your own software architecture, make sure it is compatible with the software's functional requirements. The software architecture will have quite an impact on your development time, and therefore the cost of the system. It is unlikely you will ever be able to find the 'perfect' software architecture, satisfying all the criteria discussed here. For example, a software architecture which is infinitely maintainable is likely to be large and expensive. Decide which is the most important factor in your particular development, and make that the major consideration, whilst fitting in with the other factors as best you can.

Finally, if you have been presented with a software architecture, it is still worth evaluating to see how effectively you can use it. If you do not know what your software architecture can do before you design your system, you may waste a lot of time and effort designing around problems that do not exist, writing facilities which are already available, or producing a design which is unimplementable within the software architecture that you have to use.

A company that I once worked for sent me on a course that taught me how to use VMS system services from Pascal. After the course, I would often see people who had not been on the course writing versions of routines that were already available in the VMS system services, because they were not familiar with the operating system that they were using. You should always investigate your software architecture before you design your system and design the system around it to make the best use of the available services.

If you are developing a system to run on a number of different platforms, beware of coupling the system too closely with a particular software architecture, as this will make porting the system difficult. If the system is to run under a number of known software architectures, you can define a generic software architecture, covering the common facilities of all the proposed software architectures. Designing the system around this generic software architecture should make porting from one platform to another as painless as possible, whilst still making use of the available system facilities.

12.3 REMOVAL OF 'PERFECT TECHNOLOGY'

Once we have evaluated the software architecture of a processor, we can define precisely how things within that processor will work and we have enough information to replace all the perfect technology with real technology. Perfect technology suppressed all the problems caused by imperfect technology, which made the system conceptually simpler. Removing the perfect technology will expose all of these potential problem areas, which can now be solved within the bounds of the defined software architecture. Most of what is traditionally called design is carried out during SEM. Five major problem areas have been hidden by the zero instruction rate, the infinite processor capability and the enable/disable and trigger of our perfect technology.

1. Process activation — data transformations have either been activated by the perfect technology mechanisms 'enable/ disable' and 'trigger', or by

mechanisms available within the operating system, and how we make an execution unit run at the required time.

2. Continuous data and processing — the zero instruction rate and infinite processing capability meant that it was feasible for us to accept and process data continually. In real technology, a single continuous data transformation would use up all of the processing power of the processor, leaving us no time to do anything else.

3. Discrete data arrival — we have not considered in any detail how information will move in and out of the system. For discrete data, which is liable to arrive asynchronously, we have always assumed we would be able to accept and process the data when it arrived.

4. Concurrent behaviour — perfect technology allowed us to do as many different things at the same time as we wanted. In real technology, we can only do one thing at a time within a single processor. If we want to do more than one thing at a time, we must simulate concurrent activity between execution units.

5. Data security — perfect technology gave data access so fast that there were never any problems of contention between data transformations which read and wrote to shared data areas.

12.3.1 Process activation

In the essential model, data transformations were activated by the arrival of discrete data, enable or trigger. In the SEM, execution units can only be activated by the mechanisms available within your chosen software architecture. Each different operating system will have its own type of activation mechanism for execution units, and you must examine your operating system to see what is available. In the unlikely event that your operating system supports the enable/disable, trigger and discrete data activation of perfect technology, these activations can be retained within the SEM; otherwise they will have to be replaced with whatever is available.

One of the most common mechanisms supported by operating systems is the interrupt/resume mechanism. When a data transformation is 'enabled', it is switched on from the beginning. When a data transformation is 'disabled', it forgets where it is in its sequence of behaviour and the next time it is 'enabled', it starts from the beginning (i.e. disable followed by enable will reset a data transformation). When an operating system 'interrupts' an execution unit, the execution unit's environment (its stack, program counter and any other information it uses) is saved. When the operating system 'resumes' the execution unit, it is able to recreate the environment such that the execution unit does not realize that it has been interrupted. In effect, execution units can be interrupted every now and again, but will not be aware of the fact.

Only the top level PEM DFD represented the physical hardware configuration. Lower level DFDs defined the behaviour within a processor. The top level SEM DFD represents the software configuration and only data transformations at this level represent execution units. Lower level DFDs show the required behaviour of each execution unit (i.e. the required program behaviour). Therefore, we only show the kind of activation mechanisms provided by the operating system on the top level DFD. The lower level DFDs reflect activation mechanisms that are more likely to be available within a programming language.

Activation within most programming languages is achieved by one procedure calling another procedure. When the called procedure has finished it passes control back to the calling procedure. This is equivalent to 'trigger' if the call is without parameters, and similar to a data transformation passing discrete data to another data transformation if the call is with parameters. Also, many programming languages and software architectures have I/O procedures which can be called by your program, returning control to the program once the requested I/O has been completed. This is equivalent to 'enabling' a data transformation which waits for external data. Therefore, in the lower level DFDs, you only need to replace those activations which your programming language will not support.

12.3.2 Continuous processing and data

Imagine an essential model STD which receives the condition 'start monitoring' and enables 'monitor temperature' to take the system into the state of 'monitoring temperature'. 'Monitor temperature' continuously accepts a temperature value and continuously places it into a 'temperature record' store. Inside 'monitor temperature', essentially there is an infinite loop:

```
Forever do
 - read temperature
  - place it in temperature record
```

In the implementation, it is unlikely that we want to spend all our processing power continuously collecting data, especially as the data may not change often. Using real technology, processing takes time, and we now evaluate how much time we can afford to spend collecting and storing data. In this implementation, the data transformation 'monitor temperature' becomes 'sample temperature,' which collects and samples a single temperature at each activation.

Figure 12.2 shows the new data transformation 'sample temperature' with a fragment of its controlling STD. The STD has all the conditions and states of the essential STD, but rather than enable 'monitor temperature' to run continuously, it triggers 'sample temperature' to run once. This gives rise to the extra condition 'time = last-time + sample-interval', causing 'sample temperature' to be activated every sample interval.

The sample interval depends on the power of the processor and the information being sampled. If you spend too much time sampling temperature,

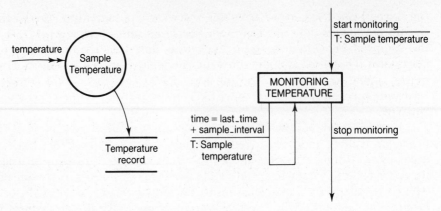

Figure 12.2   Sample temperature.

you may not have any time left to do anything else. The sample interval should also be appropriate to the rate of change of the information being sampled. Imagine a temperature capable of rising 1 degree every 15 ms, where you want to notice a change of 10 degrees. If the temperature is only sampled every four hours, changes will be missed. On the other hand, if the temperature can only rise 1 degree every four hours, it would be a waste of time sampling it every 15 ms.

Another example of a continuous data transformation is 'check for full box' from the teabag boxing system. This continually checks the 'teabag count' store, to see if the current teabox is full. Within the implementation model, this should be triggered, such that it only checks for a full box when 'monitor teabag' has increased the 'teabag count'.

12.3.3 Discrete processing and data

Discrete data is defined as data which arrives every now and again. Without perfect technology, discrete data may cause two problems:

1. The system may not always have time to process the data as it arrives.
2. In the essential model, data transformations always had to wait for discrete data as they did not know when it was going to arrive. In the implementation, it is likely that you will have more to do in your processor than wait around in a single data transformation just in case a piece of asynchronous data arrives.

Consider the first problem with respect to 'monitor teabag' from the teabag boxing system. This data transformation accepts 'teabag weight' and checks it against 'required teabag weight'. If a teabag is at the required weight, it increases the 'teabag count', otherwise it sets the flag 'wrong weight'. Finally it sends the 'monitored teabag weight' to the operator interface processor. In the essential model, this processing was done infinitely fast. Every time a 'teabag weight' arrived, we knew it would be processed before the next 'teabag weight' arrived, so there was never any problem with data coming into the system too fast. In real technology, the processing will take time, and if the system is still processing the previous 'teabag weight' when the next one arrives, data may be lost. Initially, we should examine how fast data arrives at the system and how quickly the data is processed:

1. If the processing is always completed before the next 'teabag weight' arrives, the essential data transformation will work, even with real technology, and so need not be changed for the SEM.
2. Assume that the system cannot always send the 'monitored teabag weight' to the operator interface processor before the next 'teabag weight' arrives. Here, although we cannot process all the 'teabag weight's as they arrive, we could queue them and process them later.
3. If processor environment modelling has not been done very well, the processor may not be powerful enough to process all the 'teabag weight's, even if they are queued. The best solution in this case is to buy a bigger processor. As that may be out of the question, either the amount of processing on each 'teabag weight' will have to be cut down or some 'teabag weight's will have to be ignored.

   In some systems this situation will occur by design, as it may not be necessary to process all the data arriving at the system. Imagine a radar system in a very busy environment. If all the radar data coming into the system were processed, the radar display would be so busy that an operator would find it almost impossible to interpret. If radar data is not going to be displayed on the operator screen, there may be no point in processing it.

Whether data is thrown away by design or accident, always ensure that the least important data is thrown away. In situation 2 above, the length of the queue was dictated by how much data you thought would have to be queued before it could be processed. In situation 3, it is dictated by how much data it is sensible to queue given the rate at which you can process that data. Once the queue is full, each time a new data item arrives, a decision should be made as to whether it should be kept or thrown away. You could throw the latest or the earliest data away, do some pre-processing on the arriving data to assign it a priority or use some other strategy to determine which data is kept.

In this particular system, 'teabag weight' is checked as it arrives, and placed into a queue for sending to the operator interface processor. This will be modelled by the two data transformations 'check teabag weight' and 'send teabag weight' connected by the 'teabag weight' data store. This is still an essential model, as we are 'checking teabag weight' and 'sending teabag weight' at the same time.

This leads to the second problem with discrete data: if something arrives asynchronously, unless the system is waiting for it all the time, it may be missed.

If the behaviour described above is implemented on a single processor, we must swap between the two data transformations, sending teabag weight most of the time, and only checking teabag weight when there is some data available.

In real technology discrete data flows split into a data flow and the stimulation (i.e. event flow) which indicates the data is coming. This stimulation will either be a system interrupt or some kind of timing information. There will always be something that allows the system to know that data is about to arrive.

Figure 12.3 shows how we might use an operating system with the

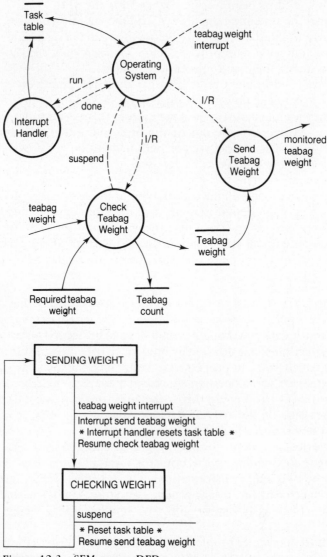

Figure 12.3   SEM queue DFD.

interrupt/resume mechanism and a task table to specify the order of execution unit activation required to implement the queue. When the operating system receives an interrupt, it interrupts the current execution unit and activates the appropriate interrupt handler, which is able to modify the task table. When the interrupt handler is done, the operating system resumes the execution unit at the top of the task table. The associated STD shows the control carried out using an operating system.

'Send teabag weight' will be running when the teabag weight interrupt arrives. The operating system will interrupt 'send teabag weight' and activate the interrupt handler. This will modify the task table, unsuspending 'check teabag weight', which will be at the top of the task table, and return control to the operating system. The operating system will resume 'check teabag weight', which will accept and check the arriving 'teabag weight', before suspending itself, at which point the operating system can resume 'send teabag weight'.

Using many modern software architectures, much of this behaviour would be hidden. Even in real-time development, there are very few engineers these days who actually have to resort to writing their own interrupt handlers.

'Check teabag weight', which would be 'triggered' in the essential model, now gives rise to the state 'checking weight'. As everything within real technology takes time, you no longer have instantaneous data transformations and transitions. In the essential model, instantaneous movement from state to state meant that conditions could not occur on transitions; in the SEM, they can. Consider the following example. Figure 12.4 shows two STDs, one which controls car painting and one which controls temperature monitoring. They are connected by the event flow 'hot', set when it is too hot for car painting, which stops the car painting STD from painting the current car.

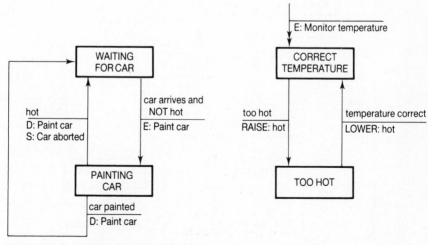

Figure 12.4 Connected pair of STDs.

Imagine that each STD is implemented within separate execution units, and that the temperature monitoring execution unit has just noticed the 'too hot' condition, but has not yet set the 'hot' flag. At that point, the operating system notices a 'car arriving' interrupt, interrupts the temperature monitoring execution unit and swaps in the car painting execution unit. This execution unit will examine the 'hot' flag, which is set to false, even though it is too hot, and will 'enable: paint car', with disastrous consequences. There are two ways of ensuring that this error condition does not occur:

1. You can merge the two STDs (i.e. implement them within the same execution unit) which removes the need for the flag, and so removes the problem, as shown in Figure 12.5.
2. You can make the transition uninterruptible, so the flag is always set before the execution unit is interrupted. The implementation of uninterruptible code will depend on your operating system; however, it can be noted on the STD as a comment.

12.3.4 Concurrent behaviour

Concurrent behaviour describes two or more areas of behaviour which are required to happen at the same time. In the previous section, 'checking teabag weight' and 'send teabag weight' were required to act concurrently.

As most single processors can only do one thing at a time, concurrent behaviour within the essential model will have to be simulated within the SEM by swapping between execution units. This implies a software architecture which supports a number of execution units which the operating system can swap between.

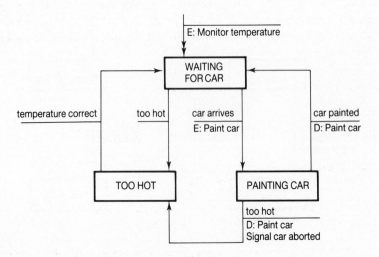

Figure 12.5 Merged STDs.

There are two reasons for implementing concurrent behaviour. Firstly, there may be a user requirement to do more than one thing at one time. For example, in a mathematical analysis package, the user may expect to carry out calculations on one set of data, whilst manipulating another set of data on the screen. Secondly, where there is a lot of asynchronous I/O, the system may spend a lot of time waiting for data to come in or go out. While the system is waiting for I/O, it is not using any processing power, so a lot of processing time is wasted. Processing time could be fully utilized by running another execution unit whilst the first execution unit waits for I/O. Figure 12.6(a) shows two execution units, under an operating system which does not allow execution units to run at the same time. Here, execution unit A stops in the middle to wait for I/O. When the I/O is done, execution unit A runs to completion and only then does execution unit B start running. In an architecture that allowed two execution units to run at the same time, as shown in Figure 12.6(b), execution unit B could be started while execution unit A was waiting for its I/O. In the second case, execution units A and B have completed in a shorter time — showing that concurrent architectures can save time.

Although this is an obvious advantage in a real-time system, you must also be aware of the disadvantages of using a concurrent architecture. Firstly, although most large, modern operating systems support simulated concurrency easily, with some smaller, more basic operating systems, simulated concurrency is more difficult to achieve. It can also be difficult to ensure that execution units are run in the required order — a problem which becomes worse under maintenance, when new execution units are inserted into the original system.

Secondly, every time you swap between execution units an overhead is incurred. When execution unit A is interrupted, we save its environment, as we discussed in Section 12.3.1. This takes a little time, and is known as context switching. A lot of swapping between execution units can use more time in context switching than is saved by utilizing I/O waits. The execution may also be slowed down as a result of resources (e.g. memory) being tied up by suspended execution units.

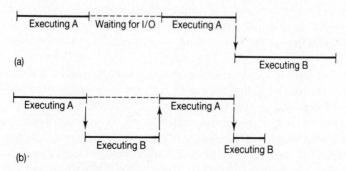

Figure 12.6 Time savings in a concurrent architecture: (a) non-concurrent architecture; (b) concurrent architecture.

As there are drawbacks involved in using a concurrent architecture, you should only consider making areas of behaviour concurrent in the implementation if there is a user requirement (required concurrency) or there is an overall time saving (desirable concurrency). If two areas of behaviour cannot happen at the same time, there is no point in trying to run them concurrently. Separate execution units in this case would make the design more complicated and use context switching overheads unnecessarily.

Imagine a chess playing system, where one data transformation accepts a move from the player and stores it in the 'chessboard' data store. Another data transformation reads the move from the 'chessboard', and displays it on a chessboard display. These two data transformations can never run at the same time, because the player will not make a move until he has seen the previous display, and we do not want to change the display while the player is trying to make a move. In fact, we will always want these data transformations to be sequential. The easiest way to ensure this is to put them both in the same execution unit and have the program call them one after the other.

On the other hand, imagine a radar receiver system, where one data transformation displays radars on the screen from a 'radar' store. Another data transformation accepts radar information from the environment, and records it in the 'radar' store. In this case, although we cannot display a radar until it has been accepted, we can display one radar whilst another one is being accepted. Therefore these data transformations could run concurrently, and if there are I/O waits involved in accepting or displaying the data, it would probably make the system faster if they were concurrent. In this case each data transformation would become a separate execution unit.

12.3.5 Data security

In the teabag boxing system the 'required teabag weight' store is filled by 'receive new teabag weight' and used by 'monitor teabag'. Imagine what would happen in real technology if 'receive new teabag weight' was half way through updating the store when 'monitor teabag' decided to read it — 'monitor teabag' would not get a very sensible value for 'required teabag weight'. Where data stores are shared between execution units, it is important that data is accessed in a sensible way. This will involve introducing extra behaviour into DFDs to ensure data security.

Security of data is also important within execution units. Even in a real-time system, the amount of global data within the system makes more difference to the number of errors that you have than the complexity of the code. If data is accessible to everything within a program, you are likely to get program errors caused by data corruption. Unfortunately, data corruption errors do not always manifest themselves as such. Many puzzling bugs have been caused by data which has been initialized, and then mistakenly overwritten before it was used.

A reasonable amount of data security can be provided by building an access layer between the application and the data. Instead of the application accessing the data directly, data access is performed by routines which are called by the application with requests for specific items of data. An access layer can also include locking mechanisms to prevent access to areas of data which are currently being used. An access layer also means that the application can remain ignorant of the physical structure of the data. For example, data stored in an array can be reorganized into a record structure, and only the routines in the access layer would have to change, rather than every access within the application.

A database management system provides such an access layer. Although it may be too much of an overhead for a real-time system, consider writing a couple of routines to provide an access layer, or there may already be some routines available within your software architecture.

12.4 SOFTWARE ALLOCATION

Software allocation is a reorganization of the PEM which shows the following:

1. For any given PEM requirement, how that requirement will be implemented — whether by the software architecture or within an execution unit. Looking at this the other way round, which PEM requirements each execution unit should implement.
2. Any behaviour added to the PEM to implement the required behaviour on the given software architecture.
3. How the execution units will use the software architecture — shown by the execution unit/software architecture interfaces, and how the execution units will interface to each other.

To carry out software allocation, we need the following:

1. The processor environment model, which shows the essential requirements of each processor, together with any implementation information which is relevant now we no longer have perfect technology (e.g. information on I/O rates and throughputs).
2. A knowledge of the software architecture available on each processor.

The following steps are involved in software allocation:

1. Allocate PEM behaviour to software architecture.
2. Remove common areas of processing from the PEM.
3. Allocate data transformations and control processes to execution units and data stores to data storage units.

After step 2, SEM is analogous to PEM. In PEM essential work is split amongst physical processors, here essential work is split amongst physical execution units and data storage units.

Within step 3, allocation of data and processing can be done in any order, but it is often worth considering the data storage before splitting the processing between execution units. As we have already discussed, we will sometimes introduce extra data transformations to model the data handling, which should be considered when splitting the processing between execution units.

12.4.1 Execution unit interfaces

Execution unit allocation involves for each PEM component either replacing it with part of the software architecture or putting it inside an execution unit or data storage units. Like PEM, all data transformations, control processes and stores must be allocated, otherwise part of the system functionality will not be implemented. As there may be a number of execution units, model components may be split across more than one execution unit, creating execution unit interfaces. Where this happens, as in PEM, you must consider the physical and conceptual interface.

Firstly, depending on the software architecture, execution unit interfaces may be difficult to implement. Some operating systems easily support many execution units and provide facilities for those execution units to communicate. Other operating systems have virtually no facilities for execution unit communication, in which case you will have to build your own execution unit communication routines.

Secondly, it is not a good idea to split a single functional area between two different execution units. This implies a large interface between the two execution units, which is undesirable. It also introduces problems with understanding and maintenance of 'half' a functional area discussed in Chapter 10.

Partition to minimize interfaces, as we have been doing all the way through the modelling. Always consider putting whole functional areas into single execution units initially. Unfortunately, concurrent areas of activity within a single functional area cannot be implemented within a single execution unit, and this will cause functional areas to be split between execution units.

12.4.2 Allocation to software architecture

In PEM, we allocated work on to 'bare' processors. We considered the capabilities and the capacity of the processor, but did not consider how the behaviour would be implemented. In SEM, the software architecture will implement some of this behaviour. Therefore, we should match the PEM against the software architecture and use the software architecture to implement as much of the required behaviour as it can.

Figure 12.7(a) shows the PEM for the operator interface processor of the teabag boxing system. Assume that as well as an operating system, we have the following pieces of software architecture:

1. A DBMS which holds all the processor teabag data.

2. An intelligent I/O package, which handles all I/O with the teabag boxing processor, and is clever enough to place arriving 'teabag statistics' directly into the database, and send 'required teabag weight' out of the database on request.

We can use the DBMS to hide the data stores 'required teabag weight' and 'teabag statistics', and we can replace the data transformations 'send new teabag weight'

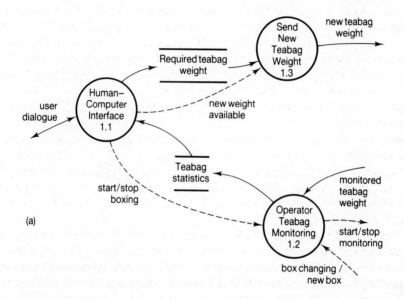

(a)

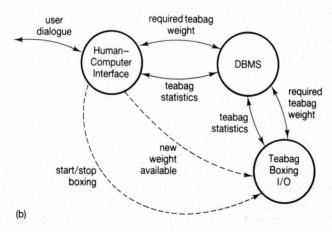

(b)

Figure 12.7 Allocating to software architecture: (a) PEM operator interface processor; (b) operator interface processor — allocation to software architecture; (c) operator interface processor — allocation to software architecture version 2.

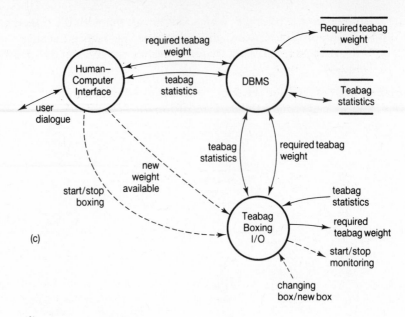

Figure 12.7 (*continued*)

and 'operator teabag monitoring' with the I/O package. This will give us the DFD shown in Figure 12.7(b). In this figure accesses to stores have been replaced by two-way data flows to the DBMS. This indicates that the system will no longer just take the data out of the store, but will request and then receive the data from the DBMS. Also, the data stores themselves and external interfaces with the teabag boxing processor have disappeared. This is a matter of style. Some people would argue that as the interface to the software architecture is the limit of your software's cogniscence, there is no point in showing further than that. Other people would argue that, as developers, it helps to know what the software architecture does — Figure 12.7(c) gives another valid version of the DFD with the external interfaces shown.

12.4.3 Removal of common processing

By considering functions in essential terms, we ignore the fact that some of our data transformations contain common areas of processing. We now start to think in terms of implementation functions, and pull out the common areas of behaviour, to avoid designing and implementing the same behaviour twice.

Two separate transformations were used in the teabag boxing system for moving the robot arm (Figure 12.8a), even though much of their implementation functionality was the same. In SEM the common area of processing 'move robot arm' is pulled out, to give the modified data transformations shown in Figure 12.8(b).

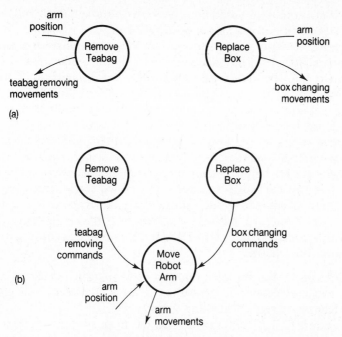

Figure 12.8   Common areas of behaviour: (a) essential behaviour;
(b) implementation behaviour.

12.4.4 Allocation of processing to execution units

A system with too many execution units may be difficult to implement
and may give rise to large context-switching overheads. Processing should be split
between execution units on the basis of concurrency. If there are no concurrent
areas of behaviour within the PEM, the easiest implementation is with all the
behaviour inside a single execution unit. Concurrent areas of behaviour can be
found by examining the DFD.

Firstly, disconnected areas of behaviour, or those connected only by data
stores, will be asynchronous, and therefore have the potential for concurrency.
Within the teabag boxing system shown by Figure 10.9, 'receive new teabag
weight' and 'monitor teabag' are connected by the store 'required teabag weight'.
Here, there is no reason why the system could not 'receive new teabag weight'
and 'monitor teabag' at the same time. Therefore, these data transformations are
allocated to different execution units.

Connected areas of behaviour will be connected by direct data flow or
by a control process. A direct data flow between transformations specifies that
they should be sequential; therefore concurrency is unlikely. However, data
transformations which sequentially process a stream of data may be concurrent.
In this case, a data transformation could be processing the last data item while
the next data item is being accepted (this is sometimes called a pipeline). Therefore,

these two data transformations could be concurrent, although the behaviour that they describe is sequential for a single occurrence of X.

If data transformations are connected by STDs, examination of the STDs will show concurrent behaviour. Separate STDs at the same level of model hierarchy normally implies those areas of behaviour are concurrent. Within the PEM operator interface processor, the data transformations 'human —computer interface' and 'operator teabag monitoring' both contain STDs which communicate via the event flow 'start/stop boxing'. Both of these STDs will be active at the same time (i.e. the system provides an HCI and a teabag boxing interface at the same time), and therefore should be held within separate execution units. Within a single STD required concurrency is the most obvious behaviour.

If two or more data transformations are enabled at the same time or one data transformation is enabled while another one is triggered, there may be concurrent activity. Figure 12.9 shows the PEM STD from the teabag boxing processor, 'control teabag boxing', which has been modified according to earlier discussions within this chapter:

1. From Section 12.3.2: the continuous transformation 'check for box full' is now triggered each time the teabag count is increased. This gives rise to the transitory state 'Checking for box full'.
2. From section 12.3.3: 'monitor teabag' has been split into 'check teabag weight' and 'send teabag weight'. Also the original continuous transformations are now triggered each time a teabag weight arrives. This gives rise to the transitory state 'Checking teabag weight'.
3. From Section 12.4.3: the removal of the common processing 'move robot arm' has led to 'enable: remove teabag' becoming 'trigger: remove teabag' followed by 'enable: move robot arm', and 'enable: replace box' becoming 'trigger: replace box' followed by 'enable: move robot arm'.

The STD has become much more complicated than the one it represents within the PEM. Normally, removing perfect technology makes the model much more complicated — which is one of the reasons for beginning with perfect technology.

In the 'removing teabag' state, 'move robot arm' is enabled at the same time as 'check teabag weight', 'send teabag weight' and 'check for box full' are triggered. Therefore 'move robot arm' is concurrent with these three data transformations.

Data transformations may also be triggered concurrently. A comment 'do concurrently' on the STD action list indicates that all the actions within that list should be in separate execution units.

Desirable concurrency is a little more difficult to spot. Consider the transitory state 'checking teabag weight' in Figure 12.9. On the condition 'not (wrong weight)', the system should 'T: send teabag weight' and 'T: check for box full'.

Firstly, consider whether it is possible to do these data transformations at the same time. In this example 'check for box full' and 'send teabag weight'

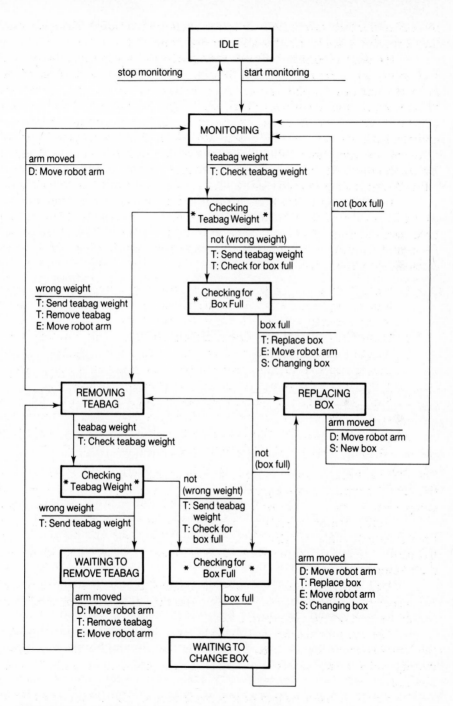

Figure 12.9 Required concurrency within an STD.

could be done at the same time. Secondly, consider whether there are any I/O waits within either data transformation, and whether we could use this wasted processing time in the other. In this example, 'send teabag weight' does have I/O waits in, and it would be worth putting 'send teabag weight' into a separate execution unit.

There is one further reason for putting areas of behaviour into separate execution units. If a processor has no concurrent behaviour, putting all the behaviour into a single execution unit will create a very large program. In an operating system which cannot support many execution units easily, the disadvantages of having a huge program would be far outweighed by the disadvantages of implementing a concurrent architecture where it was not needed.

However, a single large program does have disadvantages. Firstly, development of smaller programs is often easier. Secondly, small programs covering single functional areas give more flexibility. In terms of replacement and reusability of code, whole programs are usually easier to deal with than parts of programs. Many modern operating systems cope happily with multiple execution units and in this case it is worth considering execution units which implement single functional areas, even if they are not concurrent.

12.4.5 Allocation of data to data storage units

Essential ERD objects reflect real-world entities, relationships reflect the real-world associations between those objects. Since building the essential ERD, it has only been reorganized with respect to how the data stores representing objects and data transformations containing relationships were split between DFDs and processors.

The implementation ERD shows how data is physically stored, with objects reflecting data storage units and relationships reflecting the physical connections between data storage units (e.g. a relationship could represent pointers between data storage units).

Data structures should be as simple as possible — using complicated data structures makes a program difficult to read and maintain. Consider a data structure used to hold a noughts and crosses board, i.e. a 3 by 3 matrix. The most natural and obvious structure is a 3 by 3 array, with each element representing a single board square. Implementing this as a linked list could cause two problems.

Firstly, arrays are normally much easier to implement and understand than linked lists. Secondly, as the board cannot be naturally modelled using a linked list, how would the squares be ordered in the list? Would we have 1,1 > 1,2 > 1,3, ..., or 1,1 > 2,1 > 3,1, ..., or some other ordering? If the code was written according to one ordering, and maintained assuming another, maintenance would be very difficult.

Although many contemporary real-time systems contain databases, building a database is a very large subject which I do not intend to discuss in any depth. The ERD gives a relational database model, which maps almost directly into a relational database. In a relational database, data is stored in tables, and the relationships between these tables are given in terms of data. The mapping between an ERD and a relational database is shown by Figure 12.10. Although the associated overheads may rule out the use of a database in a real-time system, it is worth considering how a database would be constructed, to help organize the data from the ERD. The essential ERD shows the most understandable organization of data, but may not be feasible, in terms of storage space and access time.

A relationship could either be implemented as a separate table or as a foreign key. In Figure 12.10, the 'is married' relationship is shown as a separate table. However, we could merge the 'man' and 'is married' tables together, giving a table with columns 'man_name,age,salary,woman_name'. In this table, 'woman_name' is known as a foreign key, i.e. a piece of information which really belongs to another object, but which allows the access of related information. Which of these implementations we used would depend on the following:

1. The numerics of the relationship.
2. How the relationship was used.
3. How much time and space was available in the processor.

For example, using the foreign key, we can find the man's wife's name from within the man table, without having to access into a separate 'is married' table. This data could be accessed slightly faster, but the table may make it difficult to find the name of a woman's husband. Also, if we consider a man who is married to a number of different women, a foreign key on the man table would mean storing all the man's details for every woman that he is married to, which uses a lot of space.

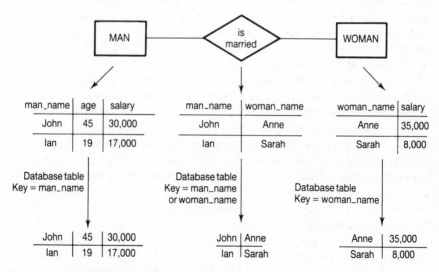

Figure 12.10   ERD to relational database.

If man and wife information is always accessed at the same time, both man, woman and is married could be combined into a single table, with columns 'man_name,man_age,man_salary,woman_name,woman_salary'. From this table, given the man's name, we can access all his information from the same table. On the other hand, given the woman's name, making access on her information may be difficult, as she has been hidden within the man table.

A pseudo-database can be constructed by implementing the ERD as a series of tables (arrays). A simple access layer can then be built between the data and the application to provide data security.

Even something like this may be too much of an overhead for some real-time systems. At the end of the day, if you cannot afford to spend the space and processing power, you will have to live with the fact that your system is constantly at risk from badly organized, unprotected data.

12.4.6 Construction of the SEM

SEM diagrams should comply with the diagram rules discussed in Chapters 2−4, which ensure a well-structured design. Also as the models now describe a real software architecture, only capable of doing certain things, they should not contain anything which is not implementable by the software architecture. For example, you will not be able to implement a SEM with one execution unit sending a direct data flow to another execution unit, unless your software architecture can support that.

Imagine an essential DFD with two data transformations, DT1 and DT2, connected by a direct data flow, Y. This implies that DT1 and DT2 share the data Y, and are synchronized, i.e. DT1 sparks DT2 into action by the provision of the data Y. In some operating systems, if DT1 and DT2 were separate execution units, this could be implemented. For example, UNIX will support the direct activation of one execution unit from within another in this way, as shown by Figure 12.11. A system call from within EU1 activates EU2 and passes the data Y. Here the SEM looks almost the same as the PEM.

However, other operating systems do not allow execution units to activate each other. Activation is always via the operating system (O/S), which may use a task table specifying the order of activation. The implementation of these data transformations in a more basic operating system might be modelled by Figure 12.12. Here when the operating system notices that X is about to arrive at the system, it activates EU1. When EU1 has finished, it puts Y into the data store and informs the operating system. The operating system then reads the task table

Figure 12.11   Implementation of DFD with sophisticated O/S.

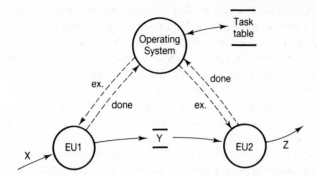

Figure 12.12 Implementation of DFD with basic O/S.

and activates EU2. In this version, EU1 explicitly passes control back to the operating system and you have to initialize the task table to define the order of execution unit activation.

The net result of Figures 12.11 and 12.12 is exactly the same. However, in Figure 12.12, you explicitly use the operating system, whereas in Figure 12.11, you do not.

The SEM shows how you will use the software architecture to achieve the behaviour described in the PEM — something that you need to know in order to write your code. In the first case it is easy to implement the required behaviour directly — which is reflected in the simple diagram. In the second case, it is more difficult to implement the required behaviour and the diagram is correspondingly more complicated.

You often have to choose whether to show the software architecture on the model. Normally, only show the software architecture if it is visible to the execution units using it. In Figure 12.11, EU1 thinks it is directly activating EU2, and the code inside EU1 would reflect this. Even though swapping between the execution units is handled by the operating system, EU1 does not realize that it is handing control back to the operating system, and so the operating system is not shown. In Figure 12.12 EU1 explicitly returns control to the operating system. Also, as developers we should be aware that we have to set up the task table. Therefore, the operating system is shown.

Sometimes, only part of a software architecture needs to be shown. If a software architecture contains facilities that are not used, it is confusing if those facilities are shown on the SEM.

Let us build the SEM for both teabag boxing system processors.

12.4.6.1 *Operator interface processor SEM*

We have already allocated most of the work to be done within the operator interface processor to the software architecture, which gave the DFD in Figure 12.7(b). From this, the only part of the original behaviour left to implement is the data transformation 'human−computer interface', the lower levels of which can be found in Chapter 11, Figure 11.6. Assume an operating system with sophisticated I/O facilities which are invisible to a programmer.

Examining the hierarchy of behaviour within 'human−computer interface' according to the discussions of Section 12.4.4, the only possible area of concurrent behaviour is where 1.1.3.4 'verify new weight field' is triggered, whilst 1.1.3.3 'accept new weight field' is enabled. However, we should not let the operator enter field values whilst those fields are being checked (this was not a problem in perfect technology, as the field could be checked instantaneously), so the data transformations remain sequential. Therefore, 'human−computer interface' is allocated to a single execution unit, giving the traceability table shown in Table 12.1 and the SEM shown by Figure 12.13.

The lower levels of the execution unit are the same as the lower levels of the PEM human−computer interface, except they access data via the DBMS, rather than directly. Also, the STD 'control updating of teabag weight' has been modified in line with the discussions in the previous paragraph. As we have made very little change to the organization, the numbers of the data transformations within the SEM are the same as within the PEM.

12.4.6.2 *Teabag boxing processor SEM*

We have removed much of the perfect technology from the teabag boxing processor, and also discussed some common areas of functionality, giving us the model in Figure 12.14, but we have not yet discussed the software architecture.

Within this processor, the software architecture is much more basic:

1. A robot arm control package — given a series of movement commands, it will make sure that the robot arm arrives at the right place and set a flag once the robot arm is there.
2. A very basic operating system, which will support a number of execution units, ordered by a task table, but has little in the way of I/O facilities.

Assume the software will be written in a low level language, with few I/O facilities. The data transformation 'move robot arm' can be allocated to the robot

Table 12.1

Processor environment model	Software environment model
Teabag statistics, required teabag weight	DBMS
1.2 Operator teabag monitoring	Teabag boxing I/O
1.3 Send new teabag weight	
1.1 Human−computer interface	1.1 Operator interface

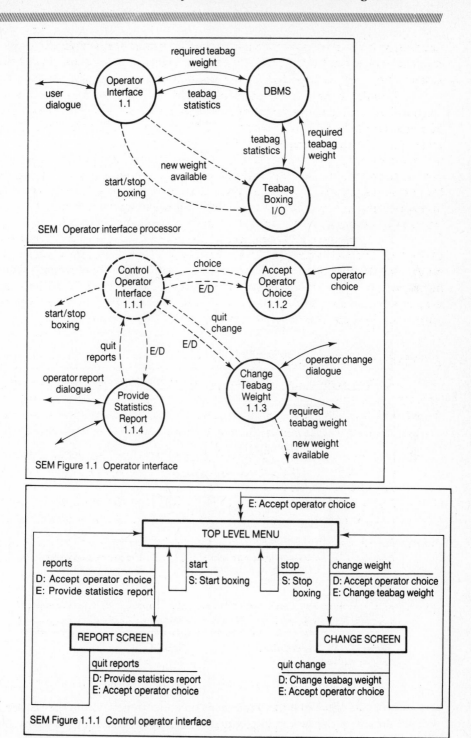

Figure 12.13 **Operator interface processor SEM.**

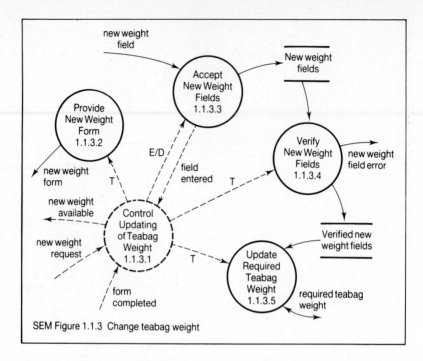

new weight
field

Accept
New Weight
Fields
1.1.3.3

New weight
fields

Provide
New Weight
Form
1.1.3.2

E/D

field
entered

T

Verify
New Weight
Fields
1.1.3.4

new weight
field error

new weight
form

T

new weight
available

Control
Updating
of Teabag
Weight
1.1.3.1

T

Verified new
weight fields

new weight
request

Update
Required
Teabag
Weight
1.1.3.5

required teabag
weight

form
completed

SEM Figure 1.1.3 Change teabag weight

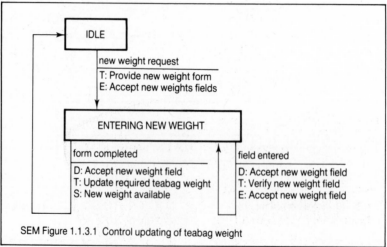

IDLE

new weight request
_____
T: Provide new weight form
E: Accept new weights fields

ENTERING NEW WEIGHT

form completed
_____
D: Accept new weight field
T: Update required teabag weight
S: New weight available

field entered
_____
D: Accept new weight field
T: Verify new weight field
E: Accept new weight field

SEM Figure 1.1.3.1 Control updating of teabag weight

Figure 12.13 (*continued*)

arm control package. From the discussions on concurrency within the last section, we split the rest of the system into concurrent areas of behaviour shown by Figure 12.15. This gives three execution units:

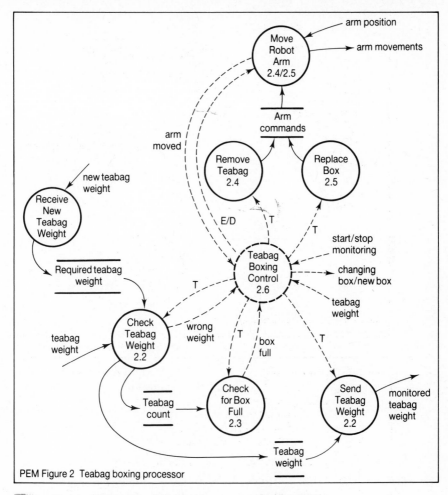

PEM Figure 2 Teabag boxing processor

Figure 12.14 Teabag boxing processor — modified PEM.

1. Receive new teabag weight.
2. Send teabag weight.
3. Teabag boxing control.

As there are no I/O facilities available from the operating system, we build an
I/O package which can be used by any of the execution units to communicate
with the operator interface processor. It will be very basic and consist of two
routines, one to output and one to accept bytes of data.

The 'start monitoring' and 'stop monitoring' signals are received
asynchronously from the operator interface processor, which can only send one
piece of information at a time. 'Receive new teabag weight' will be expanded
to receive all the incoming data from the operator interface processor:

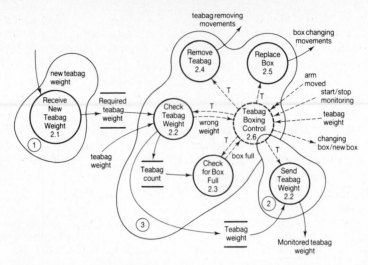

Figure 12.15   Split of teabag boxing processor into concurrent areas of behaviour.

Table 12.2

Processor environment model	Software environment model
2.1 Receive new teabag weight	2.1 Receive operator interface (part) *I/O package*
2.2 Monitor teabag	2.2.4 Check teabag weight 2.3 Send teabag weight *I/O package*
2.3 Check for box full	2.2.4 Check for box full
2.4 Remove teabag	2.2.3 Remove teabag *Robot arm control*
2.5 Replace box	2.2.2 Replace box *Robot arm control*
2.6 Teabag boxing control	2.2.1 Teabag boxing control 2.2.6 Send changing box 2.2.7 Send new box 2.1.1 Control incoming data (part) 2.1.2 Check incoming data (part) *I/O package*

1. New teabag weight.
2. Start monitoring.
3. Stop monitoring.

The traceability table for this allocation is given in Table 12.2.

The next problem is to work out how to use the operating system to run the execution units in the specified order. By examining how the functionality controlled by the original teabag boxing STD (Figure 12.14) has been split between execution units, we are able to split the original STD, as shown within Figure 12.15.

'Receive operator interface' has the highest priority, as the system should always be ready to collect the data sent from the operator interface, otherwise it may be lost. After that, 'teabag boxing' will have the next highest priority, with 'send teabag weight' running as a background task. Higher priority execution units suspend themselves when they have nothing to do, or are waiting for data to arrive, allowing the lower priority execution units to run.

The interrupts entering the system will be as follows:

1. Teabag weight arriving (from the scales). The interrupt handler will 'unsuspend' the 'teabag boxing' execution unit, which will be waiting for the arrival of 'teabag weight', by modifying the task table.
2. Operator interface data arriving. The interrupt handler will 'unsuspend' the 'receive operator interface' execution unit, by modifying the task table.

This will give the complete SEM shown in Figure 12.16.

The 'teabag boxing' execution unit moves from 'idle' to 'monitoring' when 'monitor' becomes true, i.e. when the system is started from the operator interface. The execution unit waits in 'monitoring' to receive 'teabag weight'. This is implemented by the execution unit suspending itself on entering the state, to be unsuspended by the operating system when 'teabag weight' is available.

When it is woken by the operating system, the execution unit will check the 'monitor' flag, to confirm that teabag boxing is still required by the operator, and will 'check teabag weight' and carry out all subsequent actions.

12.5 SUMMARY

As has been demonstrated in the teabag boxing example, designing a system with a software architecture which is ideally suited to your application (as with the operator interface processor), should not be too difficult and the amount of difference between the SEM and the PEM will be quite small. In some cases the SEM may even be simpler than the PEM, if much of the behaviour can be allocated to the software architecture.

On the other hand, designing a system with a software architecture which provides little help (as with the teabag boxing processor) is much more difficult. Not only is a lot of effort involved in developing a system which retains the required behaviour, but the models produced are likely to be large, complicated and a long way from the original PEM.

However, by the end of this stage you will have considered exactly how everything will work, and the design you have developed will be implementable.

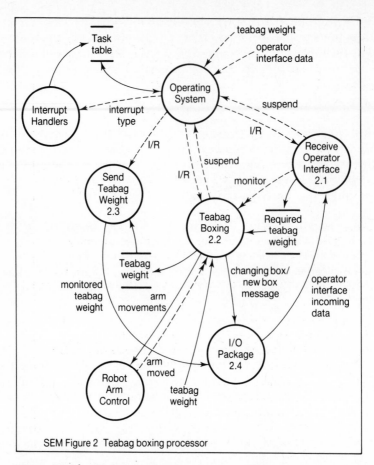

Figure 12.16   Teabag boxing processor — SEM.

It should now be a fairly simple step to take the model of each execution unit and turn that into a working program.

During SEM the design will also start to reflect what is important to you in implementation terms, i.e. whether it is more important to save space or time. With perfect technology, we only considered whether the models were well structured and easily understood. Now we also have to worry about how much time and space a certain way of doing things will take. Your final design will often depend on your objectives. For example, if you were designing a system to run very fast, but with lots of space, you would probably not do things in the same way as if you had lots of time but not much space.

12.6 EXERCISES

1.   This exercise concerns the washer control processor of exercise 4 of Chapter 10. The physical interfaces of the processor are as shown in Figure 12.17. The

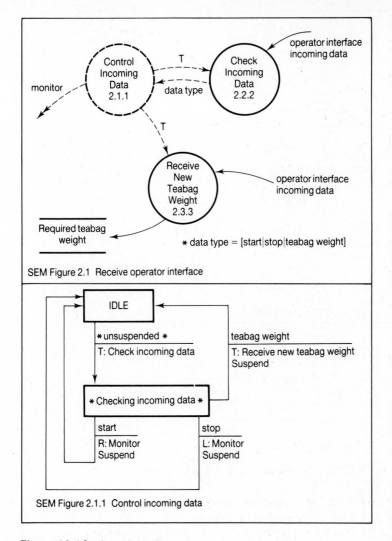

SEM Figure 2.1 Receive operator interface

SEM Figure 2.1.1 Control incoming data

Figure 12.16 (*continued*)

temperature value will change significantly every 30 seconds. The water level will change significantly every second.

Each sensor or piece of equipment of the washing machine has its own port, which can be either read from or written to, as appropriate — these ports give a direct link to the appropriate piece of equipment.

Communication with the operator interface is a little more complicated, as the communications must be sent and received.

The system is to be implemented on a very simple software architecture capable of supporting only a single execution unit and the following system services:

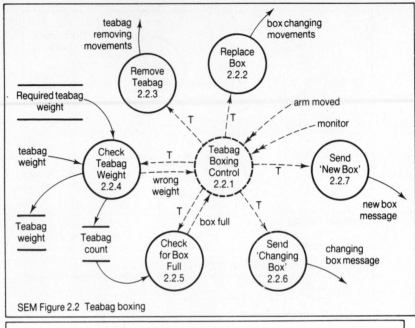

SEM Figure 2.2 Teabag boxing

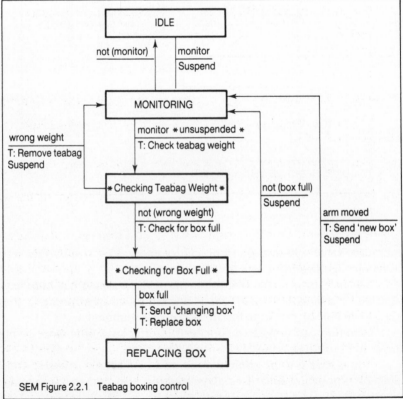

SEM Figure 2.2.1 Teabag boxing control

Figure 12.16 (*continued*)

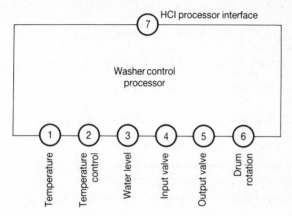

Figure 12.17   Exercise 1.

(a) For communication with the washing machine:

```
PUT (port-no, command)
GET (port-no, data)
```

(b) For communication with the operator interface processor:

```
SEND (command)
RECEIVE (data)
```

(c) `WAIT ( N )`

This command will cause the program to suspend itself for N milliseconds.

Build the software environment model for the washing machine control processor, comprising:

(a) top level DFD which shows how the execution unit interfaces to the software architecture;
(b) lower level DFD and STD, documenting the behaviour of the execution unit.

2.   This exercise concerns the temperature control processor of the greenhouse control system, described by exercise 3 of Chapter 10. As an added complication, we must now consider the fact that there is not just one temperature sensor and heater in the greenhouse, but a number, in the configuration of Figure 12.18(a). Monitoring the temperature involves reading all the temperature sensors to take account of localized changes in temperature.

Raising and lowering the temperature involves controlling all the heaters in an intelligent way to ensure that the greenhouse is kept at the same temperature.

For example, temperature variations will be greater nearer the door of the greenhouse, and sometimes it will be necessary to heat only in that area.

Taking account of this new information, we can modify the PEM as shown by Figure 12.18(b).

Here:

temp = temp 1 + temp 2 + temp 3 + temp 4
fan on/off = fan 1 on/off + fan 2 on/off + fan 3 on/off
heater on/off = heater 1 on/off + heater 2 on/off + heater 3 on/off

(a) Temperature readings are available constantly, but liable to change only every 30 seconds.
(b) As the fan and heater are very effective, the temperature should be checked more frequently when it is being raised or lowered, every 5 seconds:
(c) Commands from the gardener to switch the system on and off will be received as interrupts by the operating system.
(d) A new required temperature is likely to be sent to the system at any time.

The system is to be implemented using the following software architecture:

(a) A basic operating system, which will support a number of execution units — these may communicate via stores. Scheduling will be done on the basis of execution unit priority. The execution unit priorities may not be changed whilst the system is running; however, execution units may be made runnable/unrunnable by interrupt handlers, and may suspend themselves indefinitely or for a number of milliseconds.
(b) Simple I/O routines allowing communication with the heaters (including the fans) and temperature sensors:

```
Put (char, device name)
Get (char, device name)
```

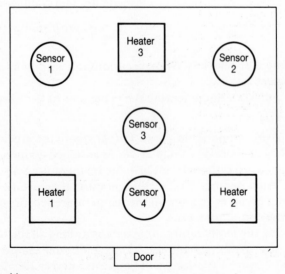

(a)

Figure 12.18 Exercise 2.

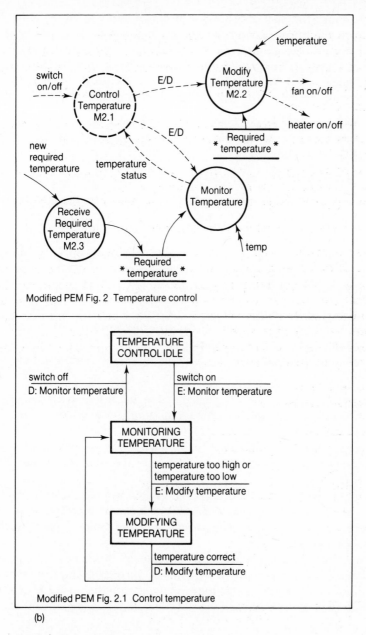

Modified PEM Fig. 2 Temperature control

Modified PEM Fig. 2.1 Control temperature

(b)

Figure 12.18 (*continued*)

Build the software environment model for this processor.

3. This exercise concerns the humidity control processor of the greenhouse control system, described in exercise 3 of Chapter 10. This system will be

implemented on the same sort of processor, using the same software architecture as the temperature control processor (except in this case, the 'put' and 'get' routines can be used to communicate with the humidity sensors and vents).

Humidity sensors are placed at the same points as temperature sensors, and there are eight vents spaced equally along the length of the greenhouse.

The PEM to support this will remain unchanged, except that:

vent angle = vent angle 1 + ... + vent angle 8
vent adjustment + vent adjustment 1 + ... + vent adjustment 8
humidity = humidity 1 + ... + humidity 4

Build the software environment model for this processor.

4. The following software architecture has been chosen for the missile control system described in exercise 5 of Chapter 10. The software architecture consists of:

(a) A database management system — it is envisaged that the missile schedule will be held in the database.

(b) A sophisticated operating system which allows

(i) up to 128 execution units;

(ii) an execution unit to activate another execution unit directly;

(iii) shared data between execution units;

(iv) scheduling is performed by time slicing between all active execution units.

(c) A security package — this package will be called with an operator identification, and will return a flag indicating whether that is an authorized operator.

(d) A package which will handle all I/O with the operator (i.e. will get characters from the operator keyboard and put characters on the operator screen).

(e) A tracking package, which will receive raw missile location data, and provide a processed missile location which can be accessed by any other package or execution unit. The package will also indicate when the missile has been detonated.

(f) An intelligent missile communication package. When this package is sent an initial missile target, it will send this to the missile and from that point continuously send the missile location data, until the missile is detonated. The package can also be used to send other commands to the missile once it is in flight.

(g) A package to allow communication with the gun — this package will expect to be passed the gun position and will return a flag once the gun has successfully fired the missile.

(a) Build a model of the defined software architecture.

(b) Allocate as much of the PEM to this software architecture as possible.

(c) Split the remaining behaviour into execution units on the basis of concurrency.

(d) From (a), (b) and (c) build the software environment model for this processor, consisting of:

   (i)   top level DFD which shows how the execution unit interfaces to the software architecture;

   (ii) lower level DFD and STD to show the internal behaviour of any execution units where the behaviour is different from the PEM, DFD and STD which generated them;

   (iii) traceability table.

CHAPTER THIRTEEN

Structure charts

13.1 INTRODUCTION

The structure chart is used to show the organization of code within a program. So far, we have modelled system behaviour in terms of DFDs, STDs and ERDs. Although these diagrams are arranged into a hierarchy, each individual diagram is a network, which makes them ideal for modelling natural behaviour.

A program normally has a hierarchical structure (i.e. the main program calls lower level routines, which in turn call even lower level routines) for which these modelling tools are not really suitable. The structure chart has the same overall hierarchical structure as a program, making it easy to translate a structure chart into code. We build one structure chart for each execution unit within the system.

13.2 STRUCTURE CHART COMPONENTS

Even where full structured development techniques are not being used, structure charts are still widely used to develop and document programs. As a result of this, many different 'varieties' of structure chart exist showing basically the same thing — the structure of work carried out inside a program. The various structure charts differ in how much and what sort of information is shown on the diagram as opposed to within the diagrams supporting specification. For example, the structure charts documented in this chapter show parameters passing between modules. Other structure charts do not show parameters on the diagram, but keep them in the supporting specifications, as it is sometimes felt that parameters clutter the diagram. Other varieties of structure chart have symbols which allow more of the control logic to be shown on the diagram, whereas in our version, the control logic is hidden within the supporting specification.

As these diagrams are fundamentally the same, it does not matter which 'variety' you use. Be careful though — as with software environment modelling, there is no point in showing something on the structure chart which cannot be implemented in the programming language. For example, if your programming language does not support the passing of parameters, do not show module calls with attached parameters.

Also, unless everybody involved in the same project uses the same variety of structure chart it may be difficult for one person to read another's structure chart. Before you start using structure charts, you should agree a standard defining which symbols will and which will not be used.

13.2.1 Basic notation

Firstly, we will look at the basic symbols and terminology used within the structure chart. Figure 13.1 shows the structure chart for the program which implements the 'teabag boxing' execution unit from the teabag boxing processor of our teabag boxing system. A module is shown as a box, with a name which describes what that module does. Modules are connected by module calls, which may have associated couples, which represent parameters passed between modules.

Within the teabag boxing program, 'box teabags' calls 'monitor teabag'. This in turn calls 'get teabag weight', which returns with the parameter 'teabag weight'. 'Monitor teabag' then calls 'validate teabag weight', passing it the 'teabag

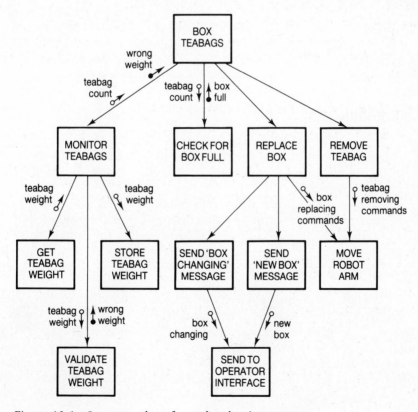

Figure 13.1   Structure chart for teabag boxing system.

weight', which returns with the flag 'wrong weight'. Next 'monitor teabag' calls 'store teabag weight', passing it the 'teabag weight'and finally it returns 'wrong weight' and 'teabag count' to 'box teabags'. 'Box teabags' examines 'wrong weight' to decide whether to call 'check for box full' or 'remove teabag'. If it decides to call 'check for box full', it passes 'teabag count' and receives back the flag 'box full', on the basis of which it may decide to call 'replace box'.

The top module, 'box teabags', represents the main program loop. The structure chart shows all the lower level modules the program calls and how they all fit together. Each module also has a supporting specification explaining exactly what happens inside the module.

13.2.2 Modules

A module is a collection of instructions treated as a unit by the programming language being used — it could be a procedure, a subroutine or a function. In a well-structured program each module will have a single function. In this respect a module is like a data transformation, and should be given a simple, meaningful name which reflects what it does when it is called.

The structure chart gives an overview of the purpose and organization of the program. Although you can tell what each individual module does from the structure chart (by its name and parameters), it is not meant to show you how each individual module works. This information (the module's algorithm and internal data) is held in the module's supporting specification.

13.2.3 Module calls

Each structure chart models a single execution unit. As an execution unit has a single thread of control running through it, it follows that there will be a single thread of control within a structure chart, i.e. only one module will be active at any given time.

In Figure 13.1, 'box teabags' calls 'monitor teabag'. Control is passed to 'monitor teabag ' when it is called by 'box teabags' (the main program loop). Once 'monitor teabag' has finished, it passes control back to the calling module, 'box teabags'. Within the structure chart control will always be returned to the top module. In a program, the final 'end' statement is always in the main program loop.

The flows of control and data through a structure chart are often different, whereas in the DFD the flows of control and data are often the same. For example, in Figure 13.2, 'provide statistics report' calls 'format statistics', which calls 'display statistics', which passes data 'statistics display' out of the structure chart (i.e. outputs data from the program). However, once all of these modules have finished, control will eventually be passed back up to 'provide statistics report'.

A single module may be called by many higher level modules; however,

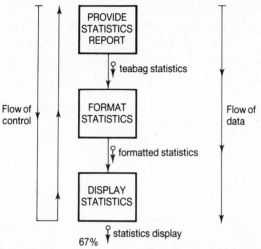

Figure 13.2   Flow of control versus flow of data.

it should only appear once on the structure chart. In the teabag boxing program, 'move robot arm' is called from 'replace box' and 'remove teabag', but appears only once. If the same module appears twice on a structure chart, the module may be implemented twice in error. This is a waste of effort, and there is a chance that both modules will be written slightly differently. 'Move robot arm' might perform one way in one part of the program, and in a different way somewhere else. In Section 13.2.5, we will look at some ways of connecting modules to avoid the mess caused by modules called from many other modules spread across the structure chart.

A module call on the structure chart does not define how many times that module is called. Considering the teabag boxing program, 'box teabags' may call 'monitor teabag' many times during the program, but it may not call 'remove teabag' at all. Information on when and why these modules are called is held in the supporting specification of 'box teabags'.

Finally, you cannot rely on the left to right sequence of module calling. If we consider the modules called by 'monitor teabag', the teabag boxing program will always call 'get teabag weight' followed by 'validate teabag weight' followed by 'store teabag weight'. However, in many real-time systems, the control logic is very complicated and it is impossible to place modules in the structure chart in the order that they will always happen. Examining the modules called from 'box teabags', we cannot guarantee that 'monitor teabag' will always be followed by 'check for box full' — sometimes it will be followed by 'remove teabag'. Where possible, construct the structure chart such that the modules appear in the correct left to right sequence, as that is the way people will naturally read them.

13.2.4 **Data**

There are two reasons for showing data shared between modules, whether in shared data or passed as parameters, on the structure chart. Firstly, they will help you understand what the program does. Secondly, they will help you evaluate whether the program is well structured. Coupling within the program is one of the fundamental measures of a good design, and as we will discuss later in this chapter, the amount and type (i.e. data or control) of coupling between modules is a good indication of how well structured code is.

13.2.4.1 *Couples*

Modules communicate using couples. Couples are very much like data and event flows, but are called couples as they allow the coupling (the size and complexity of the interface) between modules to be seen. In the teabag boxing program, 'monitor teabag' calls 'validate teabag weight', passing the data couple 'teabag weight'. Once 'validate teabag weight' has finished, it returns control to 'monitor teabag' with the control couple 'wrong weight'.

The arrow on the couple symbol shows the direction in which the couple is being passed. The data couple, where the circle on the end of the arrow is not filled in, shows that data is being passed. The control couple, where the circle on the end of the arrow has been filled in, shows that status information is being passed. Control couples differ from event flows, as they may hold many different status values, where event flows are limited to true or false. A 16-bit status word, represented by 16 event flows, could be passed by a single control couple.

As its name suggests, the control couple is used to control the program. If a module decides what to do next on the basis of received information, the information is passed in a control couple. For example, the code inside 'monitor teabag', which receives the control couple 'wrong weight' would be:

```
CALL VALIDATE TEABAG WEIGHT (teabag weight:wrong weight)
IF wrong weight = FALSE
 THEN teabag count: = teabag count + 1
```

Subroutine calls in my brand of pseudo-code are shown in capital letters. Input parameters are separated from each other by commas (as are output parameters), and from output parameters by a colon:

```
SUBROUTINE NAME (input_1,input_2:output_1,output_2)
```

If there are no output parameters, the colon after the input parameters is not required.

In the given example the module does something different depending on whether 'wrong weight' was true or false. On the other hand, if a module receives information and processes it in the same way, no matter what the value, the information is passed via a data couple. For example, no matter what the value of 'teabag weight', 'monitor teabag' will always validate and then store it.

Whether you show couples coming in or out of the bottom of your structure chart, i.e. sending or receiving data from outside the program, is up to you. Both versions of 'display statistics' shown in Figure 13.3 are equally valid. In applications where the device interfaces are liable to change, or the hardware is being developed as well as the software, it is often very useful to see the physical input or output the program has to deal with.

13.2.4.2 *Shared data*

As well as couples being passed as parameters, they can also be held as shared data. Figure 13.4 shows two different ways of indicating shared data. Figure 13.4(a) shows common or global data. Here, 'monitor teabag' writes into 'teabag count' and 'check for box full' reads out of it. As this is a global data store, 'replace box' can access the store, even though it is not connected to it (i.e. it is not supposed to access any data from within the store) — which means there is a danger of the data being corrupted.

Figure 13.4(b) shows private data, which could indicate data-hiding capabilities or scope rules provided by your programming language or your software architecture. Here, 'monitor teabag' and 'check for box full' can both access 'teabag count', but as the data is only visible to them, no other modules can access, or corrupt, the data.

Data which is shared between execution units can also be shown using the shared data notation.

13.2.5 Further notation

As well as the basic module, call and couple notation, there are many other symbols available. As mentioned earlier, there are many varieties of structure chart, and much of the variety comes from the number of additional symbols used to give extra information on the structure chart. As well as the notation covered here, there are other symbols sometimes used on structure charts which,

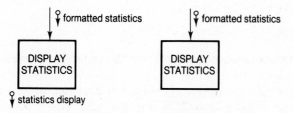

Figure 13.3 Couples passing out of the structure chart.

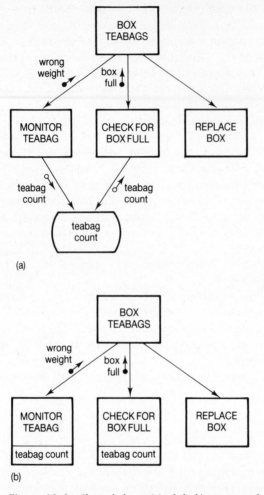

Figure 13.4 Shared data: (a) global/common data; (b) privately shared data.

because there are so many of them, are not covered — that does not mean you
should not use them if you understand them and you find them helpful.

13.2.5.1 *Library module*

The library module symbol indicates a call to a library procedure. As
library modules already exist, there will not be any modules called from a library
module symbol and there will not be a supporting specification. The symbol has
two further uses:

1. The library module symbol can show calls to modules within the software
   architecture. For example, we could modify the teabag boxing structure

chart, as shown in Figure 13.5(a), to show calls made into the software architecture.

2. The library module symbol can represent the same module called a number of times in a single structure chart, as shown by Figure 13.5(b). Here, 'send to operator interface' is called by both 'send "box changing" message' and 'send "new box" message'. However, the diagram has been drawn in such a way that it would be difficult to connect both modules to 'send to operator interface'. Therefore, only one of the module calls is shown to a normal module, 'send message to operator interface' (this is the one which will have the supporting specification, from which the code can be written). Subsequent calls to 'send to operator interface' are

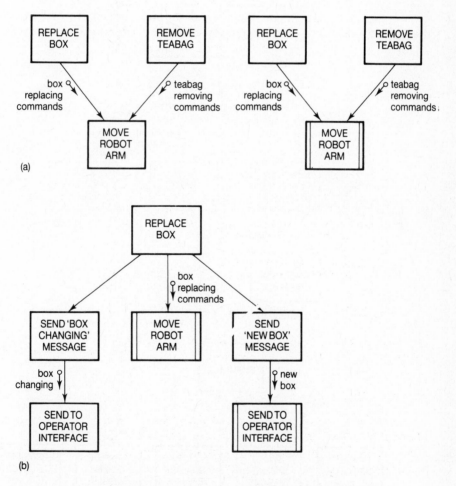

(a)

(b)

Figure 13.5   Library module uses: (a) as software architecture; (b) as repeated module.

shown using the library module symbol, which will stop the module being written twice.

13.2.5.2 *Connector*

If we have not been able to connect calling modules together, either because they are on separate sheets or because it would involve crossing lines, we use the connector symbol shown by Figure 13.6. In this example, STOI within the connector symbol stands for 'send to operator interface', i.e. the name of the module being connected to.

13.2.5.3 *Selection/transaction centre*

Figure 13.7 shows the top levels of the structure chart which implements the operator interface on the operator interface processor of the teabag boxing

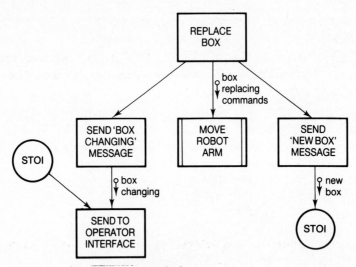

Figure 13.6   Connector symbol.

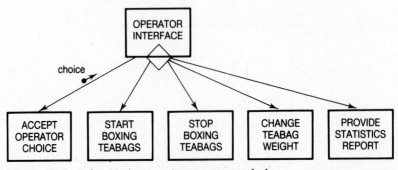

Figure 13.7   Selection/transaction centre symbol.

system. The diamond shape is called either a selection symbol or a transaction centre and indicates that modules connected to it are called in a mutually exclusive way. At any cycle through the 'operator interface' module, we would either call 'start boxing teabags', 'stop boxing teabags', 'change teabag weight' or 'provide statistics report'. The code within 'operator interface' may look like this:

```
CALL accept operator choice (:choice)
CASE choice OF
      start  : CALL start boxing teabags
      stop   : CALL stop boxing teabags
      change : CALL change teabag weight
      report : CALL provide statistics report
END CASE
```

A transaction centre/selection symbol always indicates a case statement (or equivalent) in the code.

13.2.5.4 *Repetition*

The repetition symbol shown in Figure 13.8 indicates 'produce payroll' calls 'get employee details' and 'calculate salary' a number of times. The code inside 'produce payroll' may look like this:

```
FOR each employee
    BEGIN
    CALL get employee details(employee number:salary data)
    CALL calculate salary (salary data:salary)
    END
CALL print payroll (payroll data:)
```

13.2.5.5 *Recursion*

If the programming language which you are using allows it, a module can call itself, as shown by Figure 13.9.

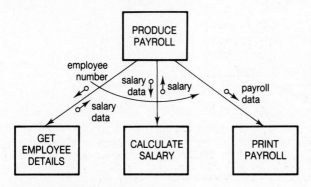

Figure 13.8   Repetition symbol.

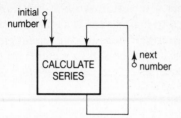

Figure 13.9   Recursion symbol.

13.2.5.6 *Inclusion*

The 'hat' on 'get validated teabag weight' in Figure 13.10 indicates that it is not a separate subroutine which can be called from 'monitor teabag', but a block of code inside 'monitor teabag'. The symbol is used to give more meaning to the structure chart, firstly by showing that 'get teabag weight' and 'validate teabag weight' together produce 'get validated teabag weight', and also by showing that one of the responsibilities of 'monitor teabag' is to 'get validated teabag weight'.

13.2.5.7 *Dialogue couple*

A couple with arrows going both ways indicates that a parameter is passed down to the module, modified and then passed back up. This could also be shown by Figure 13.11(b).

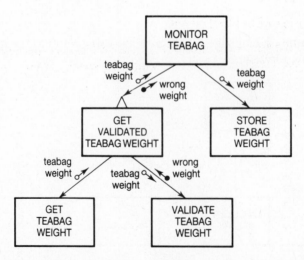

Figure 13.10   Inclusion symbol.

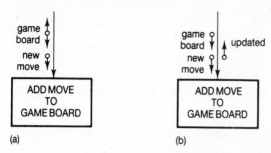

Figure 13.11   Dialogue couple symbol.

13.2.5.8 *Content coupling*

In Figure 13.12, the module call from module X is deliberately going into module Y, indicating that module X magically leaps to the middle of module Y, rather than calling it. The code within these two modules may look like this:

```
MODULE X     MODULE Y

^^^          ^^^

^^^          ^^^

GOTO L1      ^^^

^^^          LABEL 1:

^^^          ^^^
```

I am not suggesting that you should write your program in this way. However, if, for whatever reason, code does contain jumps like this, it is a good idea to document them. Otherwise the code will be impossible to understand.

13.3 SUPPORTING SPECIFICATIONS

As the structure chart is to aid development, as well as give an overview of the program, all its elements should have supporting specifications.

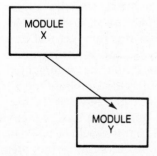

Figure 13.12   Content coupling.

13.3.1 Data specifications

Couples (passed directly or via shared data areas) hold the same information as DFD flows and are specified in the same way. However, for the implementation, the physical structure of the data should also be given. For example, in the teabag boxing textual specification, given in chapter 5, the robot 'arm position' was specified as:

arm position = arm x + arm y + arm z + claw
arm x = ELEMENTAL
meaning = gives the position of the arm in terms of up and down
         movement
range = − 100 to + 100
         0 gives a position which is horizontal with the robot base
         negative values are below the base, positive values are above
         the base
         1 unit = 10 mm

We now elaborate, specifying that arm position is held in a record structure with fields arm x, arm y, arm z and claw:

```
ARM POSITION = RECORD
  ARM X : BYTE
  ARM Y : BYTE
  ARM Z : BYTE
  CLAW : BOOLEAN
```

13.3.2 Module specifications

Modules represent areas of work within a program, i.e. they 'implement' data transformations. Modules should therefore be specified in the same way as data transformations, but, as with couples, in physical terms.

The only data transformations which required specification were those at the bottom of the DFD hierarchy. High level data transformations were just collections of lower level data transformations grouped into higher level functional units, for the purpose of understanding. Within the structure hierarchy, a high level module not only groups lower level modules together for understanding, but also controls the modules beneath it. For example, in the teabag boxing program, 'monitor teabags' groups together 'get teabag weight', 'validate teabag weight' and 'store teabag weight', and is also responsible for calling those modules in a specific order. This should be documented in the supporting specification for 'monitor teabag'. Therefore, module specifications exist for every module in the structure chart, not just those at the bottom.

Modules are generated from SEM data transformations, which already have supporting specifications, so module specifications should be based on those. However, the specifications should become more physical, as they define the implementation.

The module specifications serve two purposes and may be written in two parts. Firstly, they allow the programmer to write the code, and secondly they allow the code to be maintained.

Before the module is implemented, the module specification defines what the module should do, without much detail on how it will do it. Too much detail within the module specification means that the person writing the code will not have anything interesting left to do. Even if you code the module yourself, there may be a difference between how you thought you would implement the module and how you actually do it.

The initial specification will not be detailed enough to allow maintenance of the code. After implementation, the specification should be extended to explain how the module has been implemented. Anybody should be able to pick up the specification in the future to understand what the module does and how it works. Similarly to transformation specification, you have a choice of specification method for the module:

1. Pseudo-code.
2. Text.
3. Diagrams.
4. Program definition language.
5. Tables.
6. Any other appropriate method.

The complete module specification should contain the following:

1. A description of the module's input and output data.
2. A description of the algorithm used within the module.
3. A description of the internal data used by the module.

13.4 BUILDING A STRUCTURE CHART

Structure charts are created in different ways depending on whether you are developing a new system or maintaining an existing system. When developing a new system, the structure chart is generated by manipulation of the SEM DFD hierarchy. This is discussed in the next chapter. When maintaining an existing system, the initial structure chart models the existing code, and therefore is generated from that code.

Structure charts are often used outside structured development, as they are a good way of showing what a program does. Packages are available for some programming languages that build structure charts automatically from a piece of existing code. Consider building a structure chart from existing code. The following piece of pseudo-code describes a program used to produce a monthly payroll.

```
PRODUCE MONTHLY PAYROLL
begin
```

```
for employee : = 1 to no_of_staff do
 begin
 GET EMPLOYEE DETAILS (employee:salary, tax_code,paid)
 if paid = monthly then
  begin
  CALCULATE MONTHLY WAGES (salary,tax_code:stops,wages)
  PRODUCE PAYSLIP (employee,stops,wages)
  NOTIFY BANK (employee,wages)
  end
 end
end

CALCULATE MONTHLY WAGES (salary,tax_code:stops,wages)
begin
CALCULATE TAX (salary,tax_code:tax)
CALCULATE PENSION (salary:pension)
stops : = tax + pension
wages : = salary - stops
end
```

The main program, and therefore the top level module, is called 'produce monthly payroll'. Within the main program, there are four subroutine calls, to:

```
GET EMPLOYEE DETAILS
CALCULATE MONTHLY WAGES
PRODUCE PAYSLIP
NOTIFY BANK
```

Therefore the top level module will call four lower level modules with these names. The parameters specified in these module calls define the couples to be passed between the modules.

```
GET EMPLOYEE DETAILS (employee:salary,tax_code,paid)
```

defines that 'produce monthly payroll' calls 'get employee details' with a data couple 'employee', and is returned data couples 'salary' and 'tax-code', and the control couple 'paid'.

Subroutine 'calculate monthly wages' is broken down further, and calls subroutines:

```
CALCULATE TAX (salary,tax_code:tax)
CALCULATE PENSION (salary:pension)
```

giving the structure chart shown in Figure 13.13.

Taking the names of the subroutines and parameters from the pseudo-code as the names of the modules and couples, produces a structure chart which is easy to read. However, some real programming languages place restrictions on the number of characters subroutine and variable names can have, making

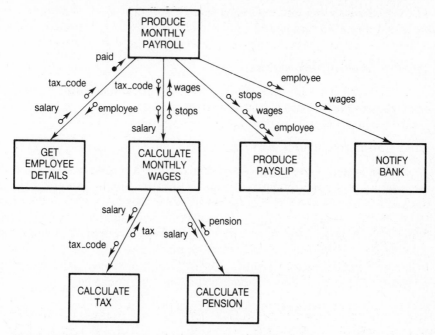

Figure 13.13 Produce monthly payroll — structure chart.

it impossible to call a subroutine GET EMPLOYEE DETAILS. In this case, you have two choices:

1. Carry the 'not very meaningful' names across from the code to the structure chart, so that it is easy to reference between the structure chart and the code, but the structure chart may not make much sense.
2. Call the modules and couples different names from those in the code, with a table showing correspondence, so that the structure chart is more meaningful, but more difficult to reference with the code.

The decision is yours.

13.5 CHECKING A STRUCTURE CHART

13.5.1 Checking for syntactic correctness

As the structure chart is a very simple diagram, there is hardly any syntax to check. One module can be connected to any other module via a module call, the arrow of which shows the direction of calling. The module call can have associated couples, either passed to or back from the module being called. There are no restrictions on the use of module calls or couples. However, remember that a particular programming language may not support everything that can be modelled in a structure chart.

13.5.2 Checking for clarity

Like all the other modelling tools, careful naming and partitioning will make the structure chart easy to understand.

13.5.2.1 *Structure chart naming*

As modules and couples are similar to data transformations and flows, the naming and partitioning will also be similar. Couples should have easily understood names which reflect the information they carry around the program. Modules should perform single conceptual functions and have easily understood names which reflect the functions they perform. Sometimes what a module actually does is not the same as what the module which calls it thinks it does. Consider 'validate teabag weight', called by 'monitor teabag' in the teabag boxing program. The code inside 'validate teabag weight' could be:

```
VALIDATE TEABAG WEIGHT (value : valid)
begin
 if min_range < value < max_range
  then invalid : = false
  else invalid : = true
end
```

'Validate teabag weight' checks that the value it has been given is within a certain range — only 'monitor teabag' knows that it is validating a teabag weight. However, calling it 'validate value in range', would not be as meaningful as 'validate teabag weight'.

A well-structured system has a balanced structure chart, like the one shown in Figure 13.14. This has control at the top, high level (or essential) functionality and data in the middle and low level (or implementation) functionality and data at the bottom.

At the top of the structure chart, names are more essential and therefore more meaningful with respect to the application. If we cut off the top two levels of the structure chart given in Figure 13.14, and consider just the modules at the bottom, they could describe just about any system. However, if we cut off the bottom modules of this structure chart, and examine just the top modules, these still describe the application. The names at the top of the structure chart are more meaningful than those at the bottom. Therefore, modules should be named by what their calling module thinks they do, not by what they actually do.

This may not always be possible, as the same procedure called to do 'different jobs' by different high level modules. For example, the module 'compare string' may be called by one module to 'validate login', and by another to 'check

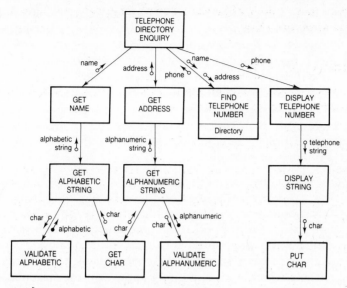

Figure 13.14   Balanced structure chart.

spelling'. Even though the module would have to be called 'compare string', we can still use the couple names to show what the higher level module thinks the lower level module does. If 'compare string' were validating a login it would be passed 'input login' and 'valid login', if it were checking spelling it would be passed 'input word' and 'correct word'.

The balance of a structure chart can also be considered in terms of control. Low level modules do the work, while higher level modules ensure that they are called in the right order. Therefore, you should find more control at the top of the structure chart.

13.5.2.2 *Structure chart partitioning*

There is sometimes a difference between modules which are theoretically well partitioned and a structure chart partitioned to produce a workable piece of code. Most of the time theoretical and practical partitioning lead to the same conclusion, but occasionally, theoretical good structure can be taken to a point where an impractical program is produced. These ideas are discussed more fully in the following sections.

Cohesion

A good module has a single conceptual function which it does each time it is called, no matter where it is called from. The cohesion of a module defines how many different things it does, and is a theoretical measure of good partitioning. Imagine the module 'produce radar display', which is passed the data couple 'radars'. The cohesion of this module is good, as it performs a single function. Imagine another module 'calculate tax, insurance or pension', passed three data couples 'salary', 'tax-code' and 'pension-code' and a control couple 'which calculation', which returns three data couples 'tax', 'insurance' and 'pension'. The cohesion of this module is bad, as it performs many different functions and is unable to do anything unless passed a flag by the calling module defining which of its jobs to do. This is irrespective of the fact that 'produce radar display' may contain much more code than 'calculate tax, insurance or pension' — it is concerned with conceptual functionality. Modules with bad cohesion are undesirable for a number of reasons:

1. If a module does a number of different things, it is difficult to find a name which clearly describes everything it does. Modules with bad cohesion usually have meaningless, or, worse still, misleading names. For example, if a module spends 95 per cent of its time doing X, and 5 per cent of its time doing Y, the temptation is to name the module 'do X' — this will make the structure chart and the code difficult to understand:
   (a) the module which does Y will not appear on the structure chart;
   (b) If we modify 'do X', we will be mystified by the 5 per cent of unrelated code.
2. A module which does bits of different functions suggests that a single function is spread across several modules within the structure chart. To modify that single function, all the modules which perform parts of it must be identified and modified. This is more difficult and dangerous than modifying a single module which performs the whole function.
3. Functions which are to be performed at the same time are often grouped within a single module. Imagine a program which required a module to 'calculate and display square-root'. Somewhere else in the application might require to 'calculate square-root'; however, this module also 'displays square-root'. If the original module had been written as two modules 'calculate square-root' and 'display square-root', these could be used at any time within the rest of the application. Modules with good cohesion are more likely to be reusable.

In a real program, you can take cohesion too far. A single module for every single different function in the program may create other problems. Imagine a program which draws red, green and blue circles on a screen. You can either write a single module, 'draw circle' or three modules, 'draw red circle', 'draw green circle' and 'draw blue circle'. Although the function 'draw circle' has to be passed a couple specifying the circle colour, the other solution involves creating three modules containing almost the same code. Using three similar modules instead of a single module implies more development effort, more code in the finished program and more difficulties in maintenance, as changes to circle drawing will affect three modules, not just one.

Whenever a module is created, consider whether similar functions are required elsewhere in the program. Strike a balance between modules which do not do enough and modules which do too much. Modules should be generally useful, but should never do things which are not required, and should always have good cohesion.

The measure of how 'useful' a module is is called 'fan-in'. In the teabag boxing structure chart, shown in Figure 13.1, 'send to operator interface' has a fan-in of 2, as it is called by two higher level modules. A module with high fan-in and bad cohesion is called by many different modules as it does many different jobs, and will suffer from all the problems discussed above. A module with high fan-in and good cohesion is likely to be reusable, i.e. a good candidate for a library routine. A module should always have good cohesion — with high fan-in it has the added benefit of a single area of work used from many areas which is developed and written once. Also, under maintenance, rather than changing many small areas in the code, only a single module need be changed.

Coupling

The amount of information shared between modules is called their coupling. Modules which are tightly coupled pass many parameters or share much data. The loosest coupling of all is between modules which share or pass no data. Loose coupling has a number of advantages:

1. To understand a module, it helps to understand all the data passed to that module. The less data passed, the less there is to consider and the easier the module is to understand.
2. Modules which share a lot of data tend to be very dependent on one another. This implies that it will not be easy to use or understand one module without the other.
3. The more data passed between modules, the more modules have access to a given piece of data and the more chances there are for the data to be corrupted. Also, if the data does get corrupted, there are more places where the corruption may have occurred.
4. The more modules a data item passes through, the more modules will have to be modified if that data item changes.

Module coupling can be seen from the structure chart, and although there will probably have to be some data movement for a system to do anything, loose coupling between modules is desirable. Avoid 'tramp data', i.e. information passed through a module which does not use it, just to get from one part of the program to another, as shown by 'robot arm error' in Figure 13.15. Tramp data can be removed by restructuring the code, shown later in this chapter.

There are two schools of thought on whether it is better to pass data as parameters or via shared data. As mentioned in Chapter 12, more bugs are caused by 'global' data than anything else; therefore passing parameters is much safer. However, if modules pass large numbers of parameters, it is also easy to make mistakes in module calls. If you use shared data areas, you should also use some method of keeping the data secure (e.g. an access layer as discussed in Chapter 12), and organize the data within the shared area in an understandable way.

Control couples are generally less desirable than data couples. Control couples fall into two groups:

1. Those giving status information, such as the 'wrong weight' flag returned from 'validate teabag weight'.
2. Those giving orders, such as the 'which calculation' flag passed to 'calculate tax, insurance or pension'.

Those giving status information are justifiable; however, those giving orders are normally an indication that the program is badly structured. Orders moving down the structure chart imply that the module receiving them has to be told which of its many jobs to do, and so has bad cohesion.

Orders moving up the structure chart imply that the controlling module is being told what to do by the lower level module. This implies that there is too much control in the lower levels of the structure chart for it to be balanced, and is often the result of a 'decision split'. Here a decision is made in one module, but the results of the decision are implemented within another module, as shown by Figure 13.15.

Decision splits are undesirable, as they make the structure chart and the code difficult to understand. Imagine reading a piece of code which sets a flag, and then having to trace the flag though several layers of procedure calls before anything is done with it. Alternatively, imagine coming to a procedure which examines a flag with no idea of where that flag had been set. In many cases, decision splits can be cured by restructuring, to place the decision as close to the resulting action as possible. In Figure 13.15, 'produce error message' could be called directly from 'remove teabag'.

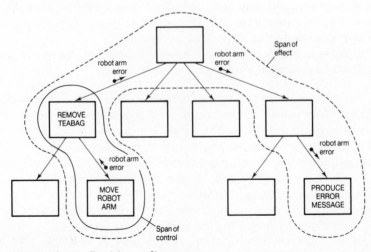

Figure 13.15   Decision split.

The span of control of a module is the area of modules that a module directly controls. The span of effect of a module is the area of modules that a module indirectly controls, by making a decision which affects those modules. Figure 13.15 shows the span of effect and the span of control of 'remove teabag'. While this module is in direct control of the modules beneath it, it also indirectly affects many other modules by passing on the 'robot arm error' flag.

A span of effect greater than the span of control indicates a decision split, and so it is desirable that the span of effect be no greater than the span of control.

13.5.3 Checking the implementation

Cohesion and coupling are theoretical measures of system structure, and are the technical terms which describe the idea of 'partitioning to minimize interfaces' discussed since the beginning of the analysis phase. With real code, we also have to consider the actual size of the modules. If modules contain too much code, they become complicated and difficult to understand; whereas if they are too small, the program that contains them is complicated, as it has to call many modules to get anything done. Also, as procedure calls represent an overhead in processing time, many very small modules may give an unreasonably slow implementation.

Somebody looking at a module for the first time should be able to follow its logic in their head. It is not just the amount of code that matters but the complexity and the type of constructs being used. Consider these extracts from two modules:

Module 1

```
1  x := largest
2  y := smallest
3  total := largest + smallest
4  medium := total DIV 2
5  if value > medium
6    then over := over + 1
7    else under := under + 1
```

Module 2

```
   if x > 5
2    then for z := 1 to x
3      a := lookup_table (z) - 42
4    else if y < 10 or flag = false
5      then c := x mod 5
6      else if flag = true
7        then c := 0
```

Although they have the same number of lines of code, module 1 is much easier to understand than module 2.

Fan-out helps to measure module complexity, by defining the number of lower level modules that a module calls. In the teabag boxing system structure chart, shown in Figure 13.1, the fan-out of 'monitor teabags' is 3. To understand fully what a module does, we should know what subordinate modules do. Earlier, the limit of human perception was defined as seven. If a module calls more than seven lower level modules, we cannot consider everything it does at the same time — so we cannot fully understand the module. A module which calls more than seven lower level modules may also be too large and complicated. If a module is too large or too complex it should be broken down by top-down decomposition — sometimes called factoring.

Originally, 'monitor teabag' was a single module. To perform its function it had to get teabag weight, validate teabag weight and store teabag weight. Therefore, 'monitor teabag' was factored to call lower level modules 'get teabag weight', 'validate teabag weight' and 'store teabag weight'. This gives smaller, less complex modules, and more detail on the structure chart, making the program easier to understand. Modules with smaller functional areas will also tend to be reusable.

13.6 SUMMARY

Since the structure chart is used to generate the code:

1. It should be well structured.
2. It should describe a sensible implementation.

Sometimes you will have to balance between the theoretical and the practical when producing your structure chart. At the end of the development, the system has to work, and if that involves making the code more efficient at the expense of some of its structure, you have no option but to destroy some program structure. However, this should only be considered if the code is too slow or too big. Efficiency for its own sake benefits nobody. Any structure destroyed in the name of efficiency will cost later in maintenance and ease of understanding.

Although unstructured code is not necessarily faster and smaller than well-structured code, well-structured code tends to be larger and slower than it needs to be, as it contains no tricky shortcuts and more code to help you understand what is going on. This means that it is actually easier to optimize than unstructured code, as there are more obvious places to optimize. Therefore, you should always start with structured code, and if you find that it is too slow, or too large, you can optimize it.

13.7 EXERCISES

In all of the following exercises, work backwards from the given pseudo-code to the structure chart that models the code.

1.　　RADAR RECEIVER
　　　begin
　　　GET RADAR SIGNAL (:radar_signal)
　　　FILTER RADAR (radar_signal:radar)
　　　IDENTIFY RADAR (radar:radar_id,identified)
　　　if identified = true then
　　　　DISPLAY RADAR (radar_id)
　　　end

　　　IDENTIFY RADAR (radar:radar_id, identified)
　　　begin
　　　radar_band : = radar.band
　　　MATCH BAND (radar_band:match_list)
　　　radar_freq : = radar.frequency
　　　MATCH FREQUENCY (radar_freq, match_list:match_list)

　　　* match routines may be called to match against all radars, or with a
　　　'match_list' of radars to be matched against *

　　　radar_pulse : = radar.pulse_width
　　　MATCH PULSE (radar_pulse, match_list:radar_id)
　　　end

2.　　DRAW GRAPH (x_axis, y_axis, point_array, no_of_points)
　　　begin
　　　DRAW X-AXIS (x_axis.end, x_axis.start)
　　　DRAW Y-AXIS (y_axis.end, y_axis.start)

　　　point_1 : = point_array (1)
　　　DRAW STAR (point_1);
　　　for next_point : = 2 to no_of_points do
　　　　begin
　　　　point_2 : = point_array (next_point)
　　　　DRAW STAR (point_2)
　　　　CONNECT (point_1, point_2)
　　　　point_ : = point_2
　　　　end
　　　end

In this example, the routines:

　　　DRAW X-AXIS
　　　DRAW Y-AXIS
　　　DRAW STAR
　　　CONNECT

are all provided by the software architecture.

```
3.    ACCEPT ORDER (: new order)
      begin
      READ CUSTOMER NAME (:customer name)
      READ CUSTOMER ADDRESS (:customer address)
      READ ORDER CODE (:order code)
      new order : = customer name + customer address + order code
      end

      READ CUSTOMER NAME (:name)
      begin
      repeat
       WRITE TO SCREEN ('Please insert customer name :')
       name : = null
       repeat
         READ CHAR (:name char)
         if name char = ALPHABETIC then
           name : = name + name char
        until name char <> ALPHABETIC
        VALIDATE NAME (name:valid name)
      until valid name = true
      end

      READ CUSTOMER ADDRESS (:address)
      begin
      repeat
       WRITE TO SCREEN ('Please insert customer address :')
       address : = null
       repeat
         READ CHAR (:address char)
         if address char = ALPHANUMERIC then
           address : = customer address + address char
        until address char <> ALPHANUMERIC
        VALIDATE ADDRESS (address:valid address)
      until valid address = true
      end

      READ ORDER CODE (:order code)
      begin
      repeat
       WRITE TO SCREEN ('Please insert order code :')
       order code : = null
       repeat
         READ CHAR (:order char)
         if order char = NUMERIC then
           order code : = order code + order char
```

```
    until order char <> NUMERIC
     VALIDATE ORDER CODE (order code:valid order code)
   until valid order code = true
   end
```

CHAPTER FOURTEEN

Code organization modelling

14.1 INTRODUCTION

Code organization modelling (COM) involves the following:

1. Translating each execution unit produced in SEM into a preliminary structure chart.
2. Refining the preliminary structure chart such that a well-structured, implementable program can be written from it.

A DFD cannot be mapped directly into a program, as it lacks the hierarchy of most programming languages. In COM we introduce a hierarchy into the existing models, using the structure chart as documentation. If the SEM is correct and well structured, COM will be almost an automatic procedure. The only part of COM which requires intelligence is refinement of the preliminary structure charts.

During COM, we concentrate on the DFD and STD. The ERD only describes the organization of data, and this has already been considered during SEM.

So far we have modelled the system using network diagrams. The difference between a hierarchy and a network is that different levels of control exist within a hierarchy. In a structure chart, the 'main program' controls lower level modules, which in turn control lower level modules. In a network there is no hierarchy of control, so although data transformations pass data to other data transformations, they do not control each other — all data transformations within a DFD are at the same level of control. To impose a hierarchy on the network, elements of the diagram must control other elements of the diagram, in addition to providing the functionality required of them.

A DFD with a control process already has some natural structure, as the control process is controlling the other data transformations in the diagram. Therefore, we concentrate initially on the control process and translate the DFD into a structure chart via the STD. A DFD without a control process will be searched for suitable candidates to control lower level modules. In this case, we translate the DFD into a structure chart directly.

14.2 TRANSLATION OF EXECUTION UNIT INTO PRELIMINARY STRUCTURE CHART

14.2.1 Translation of STD into preliminary structure chart

A control process controls the data transformations within the DFD, and therefore becomes the module at the top of the structure chart. In practice the control process becomes the main program. There are two methods of translating the STD into a structure chart. Both give well-structured programs, although they have different advantages and disadvantages.

The first method involves state transition tables (STTs). Here the STD is translated into a 'program readable' form and embedded into the main program. The program is able to animate the STD, giving code which works exactly the same as the original STD. The closeness of the code to the original STD gives easy traceability and maintenance.

However, it may sometimes be simpler and more efficient to use a more direct approach. The second method also involves coding the STD logic within the main program, but here the STD code is generated 'manually' by examination of the STD.

Deriving the basic structure chart is the same in both cases, it is what goes on inside the main program module that will be different.

14.2.1.1 *STD conversion*

Translating the STD into the structure chart is a simple procedure, and the initial steps of developing the structure chart are the same in both cases. We will translate the DFD and associated STD which defines the teabag boxing execution unit of the teabag boxing processor, given in Figure 12.16.

First, the basic structure chart is built from the STD and DFD by inspection. The STD/control process becomes the main program module, named to describe the function of the entire program. In this case 'teabag boxing control' becomes the module 'box teabags'.

In a well-balanced structure chart, the top module should only contain the program logic, i.e. the STD logic. All the work of the STD (i.e. all the actions and evaluation of conditions) should be done in the lower levels of the structure chart. Therefore, every action in the STD becomes a module. In this example, the STD has the following actions:

1. Check teabag weight.
2. Check for box full.
3. Send 'changing box'.
4. Replace box.
5. Send 'new box'.
6. Remove teabag.
7. Suspend (a call to the operating system).

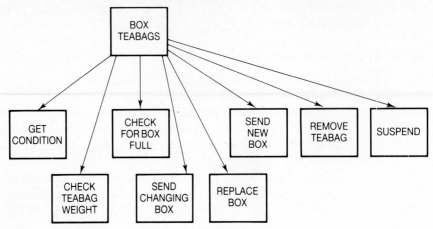

Figure 14.1   Basic teabag boxing structure chart.

These give the structure chart shown in Figure 14.1. We also introduce a module which will recognize conditions for the STD, 'get condition'.

Not all lower level modules correspond to DFD data transformations. For example, this structure chart has a module 'suspend'. An STD with action 'raise:too hot' would generate a module 'raise too hot'.

Information on coupling is taken from the DFD. In this example, 'check teabag weight' accesses the shared data stores 'teabag count', teabag weight' and 'required teabag weight'. Also, 'check teabag weight' and 'check for box full' produce flags (i.e. control couples) 'wrong weight' and 'box full'.

Finally, the module specifications can be generated from the data transformation specifications. For example, the module specification for the 'check teabag weight' module will be a version of the data transformation specification for 'check teabag weight', with more implementation detail. The module specification for the main program module, 'box teabags', is provided by the STD, teabag boxing control. This can be implemented in two different ways.

14.2.1.2 *State transition tables*

If the logic inside the STD is not trivial, and your programming language allows it, you should consider using state transitions tables (STTs) to implement the main program module. After building the preliminary structure chart, the STD is translated into an STT. Working from the SEM STD we turn any transitory states into real states; as in real technology, everything takes time. From the teabag boxing execution unit STD, we produce the STD shown in Figure 14.2.

Next we build a table, with all the STD conditions along the top and all the STD states down the side — so that each condition has a column and each state has a row in the table. In this STD we have five states:

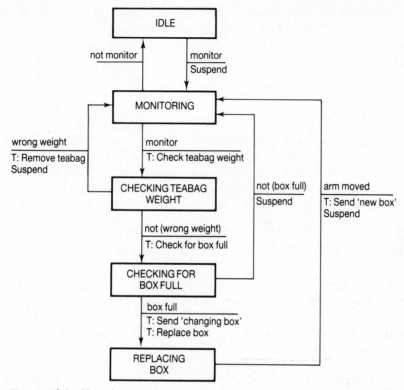

Figure 14.2   Translation of transitory states.

1. Idle.
2. Monitoring.
3. Checking teabag weight.
4. Checking for box full.
5. Replacing box.

Thus we need five rows, and we have seven conditions:

1. Monitor.
2. Not monitor.
3. Wrong weight.
4. Not wrong weight.
5. Box full.
6. Not box full.
7. Arm moved.

Thus we need seven columns. The cells in the STT are filled by the STD transitions. If the program is in a certain state and a certain condition occurs, it needs to know what actions to take and the new state which those actions take it into.

For example, if the STD is in the 'checking teabag weight' state, and it receives the 'wrong weight' condition, it will 'remove teabag' and suspend itself — moving back to the 'monitoring' state. This gives an entry in the table shown by Figure 14.3.

In the 'checking teabag weight' state there is also the possibility of a 'not wrong weight' condition, which gives another entry in the 'checking teabag weight' row. None of the other cells in this row will have entries, as 'checking teabag weight' only waits for the conditions 'wrong weight' and 'not wrong weight'. Translating all the transitions into cells gives the STT shown in Table 14.1.

The STT is converted into a pair of arrays, the action table and the transition table, which are embedded in the main program module. When the action table is passed a condition and state, it returns the actions to perform, and when the transition table is passed a condition and state, it returns the new state. If a given condition is not recognized in a given state, this will cause no change of state or actions. This results in null entries in the action table and entries of the current state in the state table. This results in a main program loop:

```
BEGIN
state := idle
FOREVER DO
 BEGIN
 CALL get condition (:condition)
 action := action-table(state,condition)
 state := state-table(state,condition)
 CASE action OF
 suspend : CALL suspend
 check weight : CALL check teabag weight
 remove : CALL remove teabag
         CALL suspend
 check box : CALL check for full box
 replace : CALL send changing box
          CALL replace box
 new box : CALL send new box
          CALL suspend
 0 : * do nothing *
 END CASE
 END
END
```

Initially 'state' is set to idle (the initial state of the STD). 'Get condition' is called to find the current condition. We use these two pieces of information to access the arrays which specify the actions to perform and what state that takes the system into. The case statement performs the appropriate action by calling the

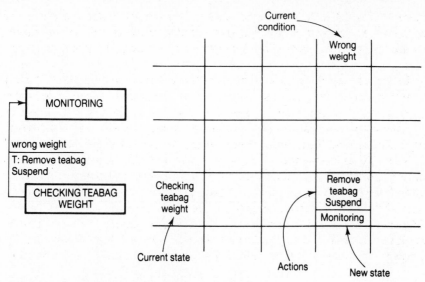

Figure 14.3   STT: checking teabag weight state.

appropriate procedure. When the procedure has finished, it returns control to the main program, where the next current condition is collected. This and the current state are used to access the tables, and call the appropriate lower level modules again.

In this example, the first condition expected in the 'idle' state is 'monitor'. Using this to access the action and state array:

```
action-table(idle,monitor) = suspend
state-table(idle,monitor) = monitoring
```

The program would then CALL suspend, and once unsuspended, by the arrival of teabag weight data, would return round the 'forever do' loop to CALL 'get condition', which would return 'monitor':

```
action-table(monitoring,monitor) = check weight
state-table(monitoring,monitor) = checking teabag weight
```

From here the program would CALL check teabag weight, and so on through the STD sequence.

Using this method, the main program has the same basic structure for all STDs, although there is no need to implement the arrays and case statement exactly as shown.

In this system, some of the conditions are returned by modules called from the case statement. Therefore, if the code is to work, some modifications should be made. Rather than 'check for box full' and 'check teabag weight' returning flags directly to the main program, they could set flags in a shared data area, examined by 'get condition'. Alternatively, we could modify the main program loop, such that 'get condition' was not called after 'check for full box'

Table 14.1 *State transition table*

	Monitor	Not monitor	Wrong weight	Not wrong weight	Box full	Not box full	Arm moved
Idle	Suspend						
	Monitoring						
Monitoring	Check teabag weight						
	Checking teabag weight	Idle					
Checking teabag weight			Remove teabag Suspend	Check for box full			
			Monitoring	Checking for box full			
Checking for box full					Send 'changing box' Replace box	Suspend	
					Replacing box	Monitoring	
Replacing Box							Send 'new box' Suspend
							Monitoring

and 'monitor teabag', when 'condition' was set from the flags returned to the main program.

Within the development STD we assume things happen only when we want them to, i.e. conditions occur only during states which wait for them. For example, we would not expect to get an 'arm moved' condition in the 'idle' state. Although this would be a mistake, you should consider whether it may actually happen and what you would do about it. Should you ignore it, send an error message or perform some diagnostics on the robot arm? You should ensure the system does not collapse whenever something unexpected happens. At this stage you should consider all the error conditions suppressed up until now. The table has a cell for every condition occurring in every state, and so explicitly points out all the unexpected circumstances.

You could also consider writing the 'get condition' module such that it only examines for certain conditions in certain states. For example, it would not make sense to look for the 'not wrong weight' condition in the 'idle' state, as it could never occur.

This is also a good time to include error conditions likely to happen at any time. Imagine changing this STD to cope with a power failure. Even for a very simple recovery procedure, the STD would become much more complicated, as the condition 'power failure' would add an extra transition to every state. It is much simpler to add an extra column to the table, which copes with 'power failure' occurring in any state.

As the STT is just a tabular form of the STD, and contains exactly the same information, it can be used during the essential modelling, if the complexity of the control warrants it. Imagine using an STD to define the operation of a complex communications system, with 20 states and 50 conditions, most of which could occur in nearly all of the states — the STD would be very complicated.

If the logic within the STD is very simple, the overheads involved in building, storing and using the table may make the next method of encoding more attractive.

14.2.1.3 *Direct coding*

An STD with very simple logic can be easily coded manually. The STD of Figure 14.4 shows the control of the 'receive operator interface' execution unit of the teabag boxing processor. It specifies that we should wait for incoming data, examine that data, and do one of three actions depending on the content of the data. Therefore our main program module will contain the following code:

```
FOREVER DO
BEGIN
CALL check incoming data (:data-type)
CASE data-type OF
  start : monitor := true
```

```
stop : monitor : = false
teabag weight : CALL receive new teabag weight
END CASE
CALL suspend
END
```

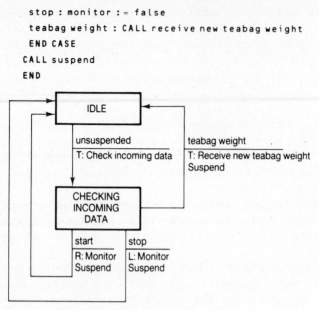

Figure 14.4 STD with simple logic.

The logic within the teabag boxing control STD would translate to the following code, which is much more complicated:

```
BEGIN
FOREVER DO
 BEGIN
 IF monitor = true THEN
  BEGIN
  CALL suspend
  CALL check teabag weight
  IF wrong weight = false THEN
   BEGIN
   CALL check for box full
   IF box full = true THEN
    BEGIN
    CALL send changing box
    CALL replace box
    CALL send new box
    END
   END
  ELSE CALL remove teabag
  END
 END
END
```

There are a number of problems associated with using this method if the logic in the STD is anything but trivial.

1. The more complex the logic, the easier it will be to make mistakes when translating the logic into code.
2. It is much more difficult to trace between this code and the original STD than between the STT and the STD. This has more relevance during maintenance. A modification to the STD during maintenance is easily reflected in an STT.
3. Unexpected conditions, i.e. error handling, are not explicitly considered in this method, which makes them much easier to forget about, and more difficult to handle.

Finally, let us consider STDs with long action lists, such as the one shown in Figure 14.5. Converting directly into a structure chart gives a main program module 'telephone directory', with lower level modules:

- accept chars
- check alphabetic
- print chars
- check alphanumeric
- find telephone number

This structure chart is missing an intermediate level. It shows the overall purpose of the program, and all the low level areas of work that are used to produce the required functionality, but not how those low level areas of work will be used.

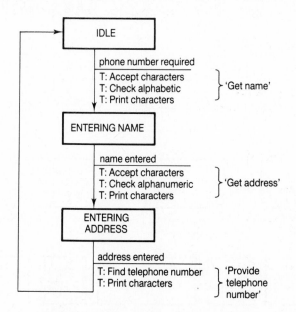

Figure 14.5   STD with long action lists.

Also, the main program module will be quite large and complicated, doing low level, rather than essential, areas of work.

The groups of actions defined on the STD can be named, as shown by Figure 14.5. These groups then be incorporated into a structure chart hierarchy, as shown in Figure 14.6, giving a more meaningful structure chart, and a main program module which only has to deal with essential areas of work.

14.2.2 Translation of DFD into preliminary structure chart

If the DFD does not contain a control process, there is no obvious candidate for the 'main program' module. Here, the DFD is searched for a data transformation which is either controlling or aware of what other data transformations in the DFD are doing. This data transformation becomes the 'main program', and the structure chart hierarchy is built around it.

DFDs will either be transform-centred, as shown in Figure 14.7(a), or transaction-centred, as shown in Figure 14.7(b). In a transform-centred DFD, low level data enter data transformations at the input edge of the DFD and become more processed and 'essential' as they reach the centre of the DFD. The essential function of the DFD is performed by the central data transformations, which produce essential output. This becomes more low level and implementation-dependent as it moves towards data transformations on the output edge of the DFD. Here, transform analysis is used to find the 'main program' data transformation.

In a transaction-centred DFD, input consists of data which is interpreted by a receiving data transformation, which decides on the data's path through the DFD. Here, transaction analysis is used to find the 'main program' data transformation.

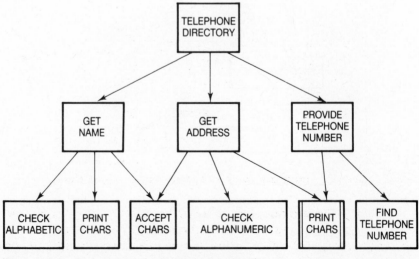

Figure 14.6   Structure chart with intermediate level.

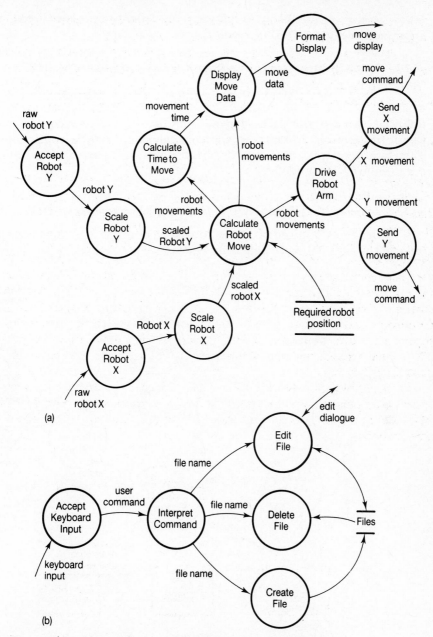

(a)

(b)

Figure 14.7 (a) transform- and (b) transaction-centred DFDs.

Most DFDs are not exactly transform-centred or exactly transaction-centred, but will veer towards one or the other. If a DFD seems to be a bit of both, it does not matter which method is used — either will yield the same result. In both cases, once the 'main program' data transformation is identified, the following steps are the same. As it is generally easier to introduce hierarchy into a transaction-centred DFD, we will consider that first.

14.2.2.1 *Introducing hierarchy into a transaction-centred DFD*

We will introduce a hierarchy into the transaction-centred DFD shown in Figure 14.7(b), by identifying a controlling data transformation. The path followed through the DFD depends on the user command, so the data transformation which interprets the command must be the controlling DFD. Therefore, 'interpret command' becomes the controlling data transformation, i.e. the main program module.

14.2.2.2 *Introducing hierarchy into a transform-centred DFD*

In a transform-centred DFD, low level inputs become high level inputs, followed by essential processing, after which high level outputs become low level

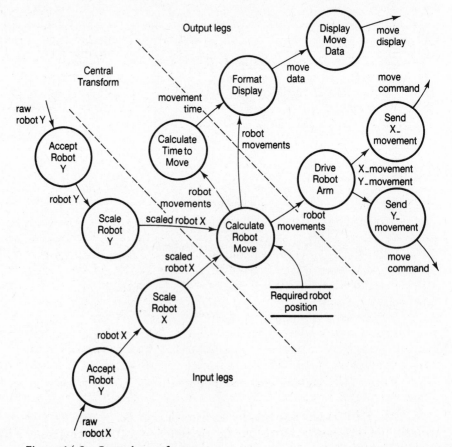

Figure 14.8   Central transform.

outputs. To produce a balanced structure chart, we look for the controlling data transformation somewhere in the centre of the structure chart, as that is where all the decision making and essential processing is done.

We will introduce hierarchy into the transform-centred DFD shown in Figure 14.7(a). Initially the centre of the DFD is identified, as this contains the controlling data transformation. This is achieved by removing all data transformations concerned with converting low level input into high level input, and high level output into low level output. The remaining DFD, called the central transform, is shown in Figure 14.8.

Next, we examine all the data transformations within the central transform to decide which is the 'highest level' transformation, i.e. which is dealing with the highest level of data and doing the most control. In this example, 'calculate robot move' appears to be doing most control and dealing with highest level data, and therefore becomes the controlling data transformation.

Sometimes, removal of input and output data transformations leaves a single data transformation, which automatically becomes the controlling data transformation. Occasionally, it is impossible to find a suitable data transformation to control the DFD, so one has to be created. Imagine a simple DFD with two data transformations. 'Collect data' receives input 'radar data', which is passed directly to 'display data'. This produces the output 'radar display'. Both data transformations are concerned with either input or output, and neither could be said to be any more 'in control' than the other. In this case, we insert a new data transformation 'control radar display', which accepts 'radar data' from 'collect data' and passes it to 'display data'.

14.2.2.3 *DFD conversion*

Once the controlling data transformation has been identified, creating the preliminary structure chart is very simple. Imagine the DFD loosely jointed and flexible. Pull the controlling data transformation to the top of the diagram and let the rest of the data transformations hang down from it. This has been done with the DFD of Figure 14.8 to give the DFD shown in Figure 14.9. This gives the basic form of the preliminary structure chart. The conversion from DFD to structure chart is completed by translating data transformations into modules and data flows into module calls with associated data couples.

While the couple names stay the same as the flow names, the data transformation names will probably have to be modified to become module names. The modules may do more work than the data transformations, as they may have to control modules beneath them. Also modules are named by what their calling module thinks they do rather than what they think they are doing themselves. This gives the preliminary structure chart shown in Figure 14.10.

At this stage, you may have to sort out knots in the structure chart, where a lower level module is called by more than one higher level module. Imagine two high level modules 'get name' and 'get address', which both call a lower

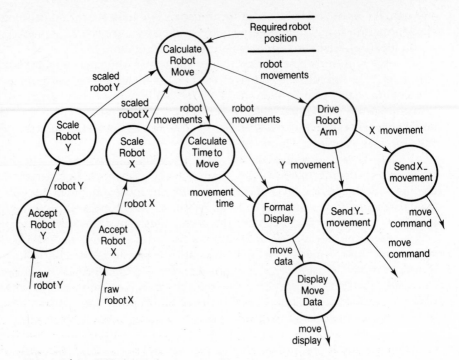

Figure 14.9   DFD hung from controlling data transformation.

level module 'accept char' to get characters from a keyboard. This will not cause a problem as, whoever calls it, 'accept char' will simply accept characters.

On the other hand, in Figure 14.10, 'display move data' is called by both 'move robot arm' and 'display time to move' before it can fulfil its function, as we wish to display 'robot movements' and 'movement time' in the same formatted display. 'Display move data' needs enough intelligence to expect to be called by different modules in sequence, and to remember by whom it has been called. This implies a lot of logic in a lower level module, and a lot of scope for error. For example, if 'display move data' is called by 'move robot arm' twice in a row without being called by 'display time to move', what will it do?

The module will be overly complicated, making it difficult to write, test and maintain. The structure chart could be restructured so the module was only called once with both pieces of information it needs by inserting a new controlling module. Both module calls into 'display move data' are now routed through the new module, as shown in Figure 14.11.

In the transform-centred DFD, 'calculate robot move' became the controlling transformation. Consider what would have happened if we had chosen the wrong data transformation. Choosing 'format display' to be the controlling data transformation, gives the structure chart shown in Figure 14.12.

This leaves the knot around 'calculate move time', which is now more

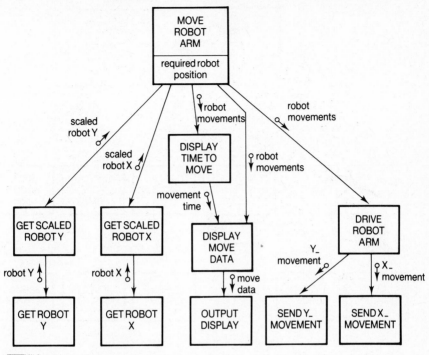

Figure 14.10 Preliminary structure chart.

serious, as it is called by 'calculate robot move' to do a calculation, the result of which is returned to 'move robot arm'. This problem can be easily remedied by removing the call to 'calculate move time' from 'calculate robot move' and passing the 'robot movements' data to 'calculate move time' directly from 'move robot arm'. However, the structure chart is unbalanced, since the data and functionality at the top of the structure chart are not as essential as those in lower level modules. Choosing a controlling data transformation from the input or output legs of the DFD will always result in an unbalanced structure chart.

14.2.3 Translating execution unit hierarchy into a preliminary structure chart

An execution unit is often described by more than a single DFD. Figure 14.13 shows the hierarchy of DFDs within the operator interface execution unit of the operator interface processor within the teabag boxing system, together with the structure charts that they produce.

Within a DFD hierarchy, all DFDs are converted into structure charts, which are connected into a single structure chart for the whole execution unit. In this example, data transformation '1.1.3 change teabag weight' decomposes

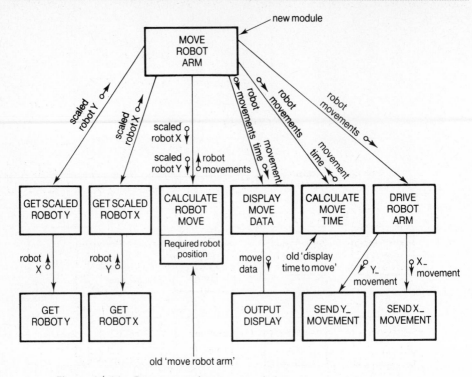

Figure 14.11   Restructured structure chart.

into a lower level DFD which describes its complete functionality. The structure chart generated by this lower level DFD therefore provides the complete functionality of the module 'change teabag weight'. This structure chart can replace the 'change teabag weight' module to give the complete structure chart shown in Figure 14.14.

During COM, the traceability table should be maintained, giving traceability from the system requirements to the code. The operator interface execution unit has the traceability table shown in Table 14.2.

There are two things to notice about this table:

1. The modules do not have numbers, as the subroutines within the code will not have numbers.
2. Only data transformations at the bottom of the DFD hierarchy and control processes produce modules. Data transformations with lower level DFDs do not produce modules, as they only group lower level modules for ease of understanding.

14.3 STRUCTURE CHART REFINEMENT

Structure charts generated directly from the DFD have a generally good structure, but may not make very good programs. Until now we have only

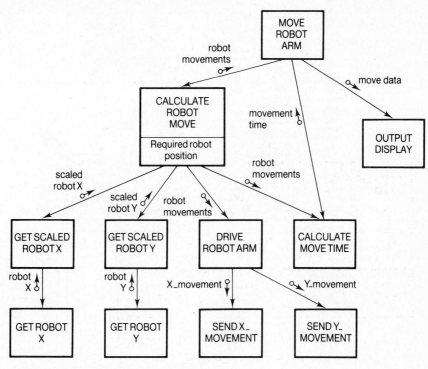

Figure 14.12 Controller from output leg.

Table 14.2

Software environment model		Code organization model
1.1.1	Control operator interface	Operator interface
1.1.2	Accept operator choice	Accept operator choice
1.1.3.1	Control updating of teabag weight	Change teabag weight
1.1.3.2	Provide new weight form	Provide new weight form
1.1.3.3	Accept new weight fields	Accept new weight fields
1.1.3.4	Verify new weight fields⁎	Verify new weight fields
1.1.3.5	Update required teabag weight	Update required teabag weight
1.1.4	Provide statistics report	Provide statistics report

considered conceptual functionality, so a single data transformation may have 2 or 2000 lines of code. As discussed in Chapter 13, modules should not be too big, too small or too complex.

Also, low level implementation detail has not been considered, and many

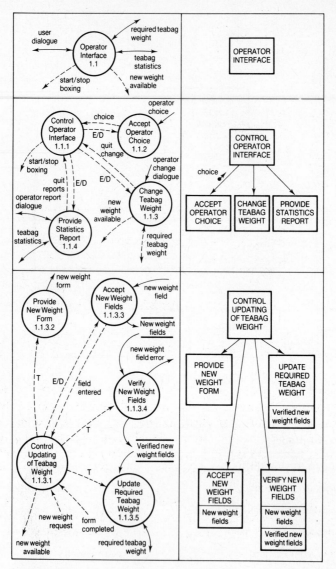

Figure 14.13 Execution unit DFD and structure chart hierarchy.

modules are likely to perform small areas of similar, or even identical, work. Again, as discussed in Chapter 13, it is not desirable to have many modules performing almost the same function — and these areas of work should be merged together.

Once the DFD has been converted into a preliminary structure chart, this should be refined to become well structured and a good program. As the main problem is module size, the first step will be to factor the modules within the

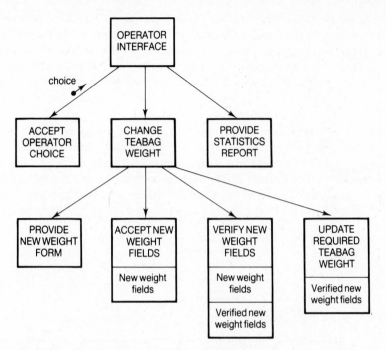

Figure 14.14   Structure chart for execution unit.

structure chart. Factoring will expose the lower level areas of work which can then be shared between higher level modules. At the other end of the scale, modules which are too small may be absorbed into their calling modules. Splitting and merging within the structure chart may result in the destruction of some of the initial good structure. Therefore, the final step involves checking the cohesion and coupling of the modules, and the balance of the structure chart, restructuring where necessary.

Let us refine the preliminary structure chart for the teabag boxing execution unit, produced in Section 14.2. Firstly, we factor those modules which are either too large or complex, or share areas of functionality, making the following modifications:

1. 'Check teabag weight' becomes 'monitor teabag', which calls 'get teabag weight', 'validate teabag weight' and 'store teabag weight'.
2. The common work of interfacing to the operator processor is pulled out of 'send change box' and 'send new box'. This gives two higher level modules 'send box changing message' and 'send new box message', which both call the lower level module 'send to operator interface'.
3. The common work of moving the robot arm is pulled out of 'remove teabag' and 'replace box', which both now call the lower level module 'move robot arm'.

The modules appear to have good coupling and cohesion; however, 'box teabags' is too busy, with a fan-out of 8. This can be remedied by restructuring around 'send changing box', 'replace box' and 'send new box message' to give the structure chart shown in Figure 14.15. 'Get condition' has been absorbed into 'box teabags', as all it does is check the 'monitor' flag. Also, the 'suspend' system call is no longer shown, as it does not make the structure chart any clearer (although the call is still made from 'box teabags').

Finally, the structure chart contains a small decision split. 'Monitor teabags' decides that the teabag is at the 'wrong weight'; however, nothing is done about this until the flag 'wrong weight' reaches 'box teabags'. The decision split could be removed by calling 'validate teabag weight' from 'box teabags' rather than 'monitor teabags'; however, this would make 'box teabags' too busy.

It is often impossible to produce a structure chart which is absolutely

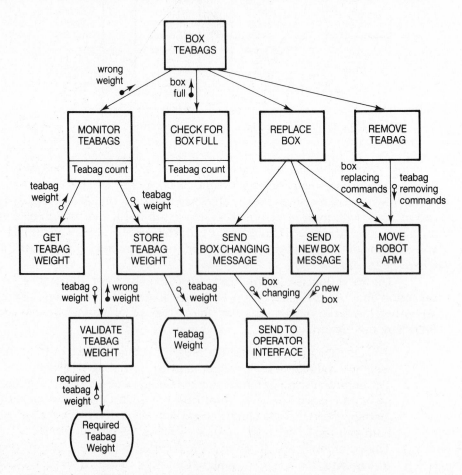

Figure 14.15 Teabag boxing structure chart.

perfect in all areas of structure — sometimes solving a problem in one aspect of the structure will cause problems in other aspects of the structure. At times such as these, you should use the solution that makes the structure chart easiest to understand.

14.4 SUMMARY

Translating the execution units from the teabag boxing system into structure charts will give the series of structure charts shown in Figure 14.16. The operator interface processor contains a single execution unit 'operator interface', shown in Figure 14.16(a). The teabag boxing processor contains four execution units:

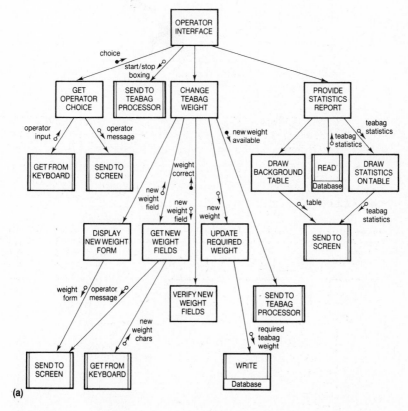

(a)

Figure 14.16   Structure charts for teabag boxing system: (a) operator interface processor — operator interface execution unit; (b) teabag boxing processor — receive operator interface execution unit; (c) teabag boxing processor — teabag boxing execution unit; (d) teabag boxing processor — send teabag weight.

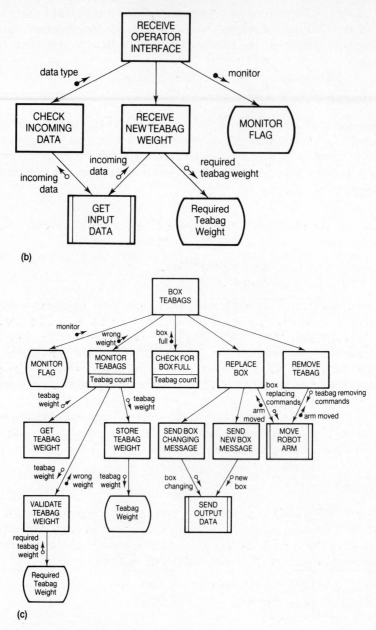

Figure 14.16 (*continued*)

1. Receive operator interface (Figure 14.16(b)).
2. Teabag boxing (Figure 14.16(c)).
3. Send teabag weight (Figure 14.16(d))
4. I/O package : this is really part of the software architecture that happens

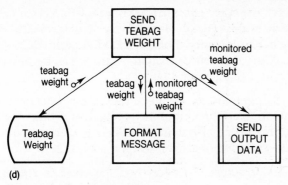

(d)

Figure 14.16 (*continued*)

to be written by the developer, rather than provided. It will contain just two routines:

(a) send output data (output data);
(b) get input data (input data).

All the structure charts shown have undergone some refinement from the preliminary structure chart, although further refinement would be possible.

These structure charts, together with their module specifications, can be used to write the code for the teabag boxing system. After that the software environment model documentation can be used to integrate those programs with the software architecture within each processor, after which they become the program documentation.

Finally, the processor environment model documentation can be used to integrate the processors within the system, to give a working, well-structured and fully documented development.

14.5 EXERCISES

1.   Using the method of state transition tables, produce a preliminary structure chart and state transition table for the washer control execution unit, described in exercise 1 of Chapter 12. As stated in Chapter 12, the software architecture for this implementation provide the following facilities:

(a) For communication with the washing machine:
    PUT (port-no, command)
    GET (port-no, data)
(b) For communication with the operator interface processor:
    SEND (command)
    RECEIVE (command)
(c) WAIT (number of milliseconds)

To compare the two methods, now build the code for the 'main program' module using the method of direct coding.

2. Produce a preliminary structure chart for the operator interface execution unit of the base processor in the missile control system, described in exercise 4 of Chapter 12. Remember to include all of the DFD hierarchy describing the execution unit when building the structure chart — these can be found in the answers to exercises 3 and 4 of Chapter 11.

3. Using the method of direct coding, produce a preliminary structure chart for the temperature control execution unit of the temperature control processor of the greenhouse atmosphere control system, described in exercise 2 of Chapter 12. Also produce pseudo-code for the 'main program' module.

4. Produce a preliminary structure chart for the DFD given in Figure 14.17.

5. Produce a preliminary structure chart for the DFD given in Figure 14.18.

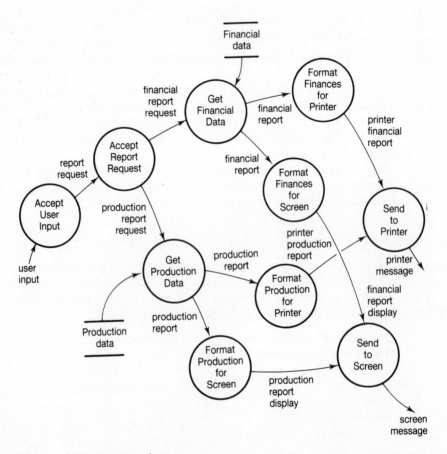

Figure 14.17   Exercise 4.

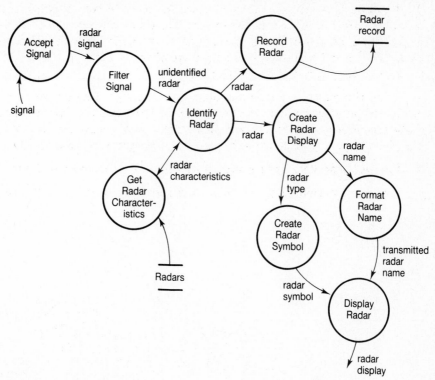

Figure 14.18 Exercise 5.

PART FOUR

Summary

CHAPTER FIFTEEN

Summary

15.1 INTRODUCTION

The previous chapters have described all the steps involved in a complete real-time development:

1. Analyze your system requirements — build the context diagram and event list, from which it should be possible to build the essential behavioural model.
2. Build the processor environment model — model the details of the human−computer interface and, if there is more than a single processor in the system, split the system behaviour between available processors.
3. Build the software environment model — design the program configuration, based on the facilities available to you.
4. Build the code organization model — internal program design.

Step-by-step guides to all these stages are available in the appendixes. However, before you start any development, you should decide which facets of structured analysis and design you will be using, and how these will fit with your current way of working. In Section 1.1.3, I said that real-time applications are all very different and in order to cater for everything, there are tools or stages in the modelling that may not be relevant in all developments. I also said that you should try to integrate all the valuable experience that you already have of software development into your use of the software development techniques.

It is not a good idea to start using structured analysis and design on a huge, new, critical project just because it is so confusing that you know traditional development methods will fail. There is a learning curve associated with the use of structured development, and inexperience in this area will not facilitate the smooth running of a project. It is better to use structured development initially on a small pilot project, and learn through experience which bits of the method to use and how to approach the development. A pilot project will allow you to produce a set of guidelines for others in your environment, such that when structured development is used in a critical situation, it will be used with the hindsight of previous experience.

It is also important to review any development at regular intervals. Using structured development techniques will only be of benefit to you if the models you produce are syntactically correct, meaningful and describe the correct requirements.

An automated CASE tool may help with syntactic checks, as we will discuss in Section 15.3; however, the meaning and functional correctness of the model can only be checked by human review.

The techniques describe an iterative and flexible approach. Throughout the book, I may have given the impression that you will completely finish one stage of the development before you start the next. Theoretically, and in an ideal world, that would be the approach to take. However, in the real world, this approach often proves unworkable. For example, to develop the processor environment model, you have to decide whether defined behaviour will fit within the storage and processing capacity of the chosen processor. You may only be able to do this if you have done some of the lower level design first to give you a better idea of how much storage and processing capacity a particular area of behaviour requires.

In practice, you may build a 'preliminary' processor environment model from the essential model, on the basis of which you could build parts of the software environment model. Discoveries from the building of the SEM could then be fed back into the development of the final PEM.

Modifications made in later stages of the development should ripple through the models only up to the stage of the development model that they affect. For example, a change to the SEM may describe a different implementation of a particular system requirement. If the functionality of the requirement remained the same, this would not necessarily ripple all the way through the essential model.

15.2 PROJECT MANAGEMENT AND AUDITING

For those involved in auditing or control of projects, the following points should be considered.

15.2.1 General points

Within a given company or department, standards should be produced defining how real-time structured development will be used. These standards should, if possible, be based on previous use of real-time structured development within the company. Ideally real-time structured development should be 'tested out' on a pilot project, rather than used on a full-scale project which is time- or budget-critical.

15.2.2 Milestones

Development models should be checked at the end of each development phase, otherwise much time may be wasted trying to evolve from models which are incorrect. Milestones can be seen as the end of the following stages:

1. Essential environmental modelling.
2. Essential behavioural modelling.
3. Processor environmental modelling.
4. Software environmental modelling.
5. Code organization modelling.

These checkpoints are really a minimum set of milestones and, depending on the size of the project, intermediate milestones may be introduced.

Note that it is not always necessary to complete the whole of one development stage before moving on to the next one. For instance, once the PEM has been completed it is possible to carry out the SEM and COM for just one processor without designing the internals of the other processors.

15.2.3 What to watch for in reviews

1. Overspecification. Especially in the early development phases, engineers have a tendency to overspecify. This will inflate the size of the early models, and ultimately the overall development time. It is also an indication that design decisions are being made too early in the development. Only specify down to a level at which you feel you understand what is going on, and can express what is happening adequately in the textual backup.
2. Failure to complete the data dictionary. Without textual specification the model cannot be checked or implemented.
3. A model is only correct if it passes all the automated toolkit checks, it is understandable, it reflects the customer's requirement and (in the design phases only) it is implementable.

15.2.4 Testing

Testing within a development is a very large area, and not one that I plan to examine in any depth at this stage. There are three levels of testing:

15.2.4.1 *Unit testing*

Unit testing can be defined as testing that the individual pieces of the system do what they were designed to do.

Unit testing should be performed against the relevant piece of the implementation model. You may be testing that a processor, an execution unit or a module functions as it was designed to. Unit test specifications can be held in the supporting specifications for the data transformations or modules in the appropriate part of the model.

15.2.4.2 *Integration testing*

The COM (code organization model) allows you to see how all the modules within a single execution unit interface to each other. Therefore, once the individual modules are proved correct, the structure charts of the COM can be used to integrate the modules in the correct order, and to verify the interfaces between them. The top level DFD of the SEM (software environment model) shows the interfaces between each execution unit and the software architecture. Therefore, once the individual execution units are proved correct, the SEM can be used to integrate the execution units and the software architecture within a single processor, and to verify their interfaces. The top level DFD of the PEM (processor environment model) shows the interfaces between processors within the system. Therefore, once the individual processors are proved correct, the PEM can be used to integrate processors within the systems and to verify their interfaces.

This integration testing path, back through the stages of the development, will to a certain extent help to isolate integration problems by linking them to particular development stages. It will also ensure that the integration is carried out according to the original development decisions. It is not uncommon to concentrate so much on the actual code towards the end of a development, that you forget why you decided to implement parts of the code in a certain way. This sometimes leads to large areas of the code being reimplemented in a way that is incompatible with the rest of the system, whilst trying to overcome integration problems.

15.2.4.3 *Acceptance testing*

Acceptance testing can be defined as testing that the overall system does what the customer wanted it to. Acceptance testing should be performed against the essential model, as this defines the customer requirements. Therefore, acceptance test specifications can be held in the transformation specifications of the essential model data transformations. If each data transformation of the essential model has an associated test specification, you will be testing each of the system's requirements.

15.3 CASE TOOLS

At the time of writing, there are many software packages available which will aid structured analysis and design. The main aims of these packages are the following:

1. To provide graphics facilities for drawing and presentation of the various models.
2. To provide facilities for the production of a project dictionary.
3. To provide automatic syntax checking of the models produced.
4. To support model hierarchies and ease maintenance of the models within those hierarchies.

There is a vast difference in the capabilities of the various packages available, ranging from those which are little more than drawing packages to those which integrate with other software development tools to provide an overall development environment.

Although it is possible to develop a system by hand, development of a large project involving a number of engineers is better attempted with the help of a toolkit. Even if there is only a single person involved in a development, developing by hand has its pitfalls. It can be very tedious redrawing a whole diagram, just to incorporate a small change. This becomes worse if you change an external data flow, which may ripple through the whole model hierarchy. Many of the simple consistency checks applied to the model, such as vertical balancing, are very boring to carry out, and as such are very easy to make mistakes in. These are just the kind of things that machines are very good at.

If you decide to use a toolkit, think about how you will use the techniques and investigate a number of toolkits to find one that matches your requirements. You will find that some toolkits are very strong in certain areas but weaker in others. For example, a toolkit many be very strong in configuration management, but may not perform all the required checks for balancing an STD against the corresponding DFD.

There follows a brief summary of the desirable features to look for when evaluating CASE tools for use within development.

15.3.1 Graphics

It is desirable that the CASE tool will allow you to draw all the prescribed diagrams:

1. Context diagram.
2. Data flow diagram.
3. State transition diagram.
4. Entity relationship diagram.
5. Structure chart.

It does not matter too much if some of the symbols are slightly different from those described within this book, providing the whole symbol set is covered. As long as you appreciate the difference in symbols this should not make any difference to your development.

15.3.2 Non-graphics

Check that the CASE tool allows description, within the project/data dictionary, for all the defined graphic symbols.

Check that there is some way of covering the non-graphic bits of the development, such as the event list in the analysis phase, and the traceability table in the design phase, even if the toolkit does not directly support them.

15.3.3 Checking

This is the major area in which an automated toolkit should help you — unfortunately the checking done by most CASE tools at the moment is fairly unsophisticated. There are three levels of checking which you should look for:

1. Syntax checking — within a given diagram, does the machine check that you are using the symbols correctly, i.e. will it allow you to send data into a control process, directly link stores, etc?
2. Diagram checking — again, within a given diagram, will it check that the rules of the diagram have not been violated, i.e. a context diagram should have only one data transformation, transformations should have at least one input and at least one output, etc? At a more sophisticated level, can you check
   (a) in the DFD for conservation of data;
   (b) in the STD for behavioural equivalence?
3. Project checking — for a given set of ERD/DFD/STD that define a project, will it check
   (a) balancing of STD against DFD;
   (b) balancing of DFD against ERD;
   (c) balancing of all levels of the DFD against one another?

Also worth considering is the flexibility of the checks it allows you to carry out. For example, will it force you always to check the whole of the essential model hierarchy, or will it allow you to check just a part of the hierarchy?

15.3.4 Human—computer interface

This is obviously a very subjective area, but do examine the ability to move easily between diagrams and supporting text within the dictionary. In some systems you cannot access the dictionary directly from the diagrams, and this will often make using the toolkit time-consuming and frustrating.

15.3.5 Support of real-time design

While most toolkits support the diagram hierarchy needed for the analysis (i.e. a direct DFD hierarchy down from the context diagram), few will support the 'matrix' structure needed within the design. This will mean that although you can check the various models within each stage of development (essential, processor environment, software environment, code organization), you may not be able to check across the *entire* development.

15.3.6 Configuration management

In a large project with a number of different people involved, a degree of configuration management is desirable, to keep the development under control.

Some toolkits offer almost nothing in the way of configuration management, while others are very sophisticated in this area. However, be on the lookout for toolkits which offer a great deal in configuration management, but are very basic in their support of the actual development process. These are likely to have started out as configuration management packages, and have the minimum bolted on to make them look like structured development toolkits.

15.3.7 Practical considerations

1. What hardware will it run on?
2. How many people will it support?
3. How quickly does it go?
4. Will it interface to any other packages on site?
5. Will it produce documentation in the right form?
6. How much does it cost?
7. What kind of support does the vendor provide?
8. Is it a mature tool?
9. Is there anybody within the development team with experience of it?

15.4 USE OF STRUCTURED DEVELOPMENT WITH OTHER TECHNIQUES

In order to develop a complex system effectively, you should use any tools that will make the development run smoother and help you to produce a better system. You should not consider structured development as one way of doing things and other development methods as completely different ways. Most techniques have areas where they are strong and areas where they are weaker — using an integration of different techniques will allow you to cover the weaknesses of one method with the strengths of another. Let us consider two other development techniques which are often seen as 'alternatives' to structured development.

15.4.1 Object oriented development

Within structured development, we group functional areas of the system together in units called data transformations. Within object-oriented development (OOD), areas of data and the functions that are applied to that data are grouped together into units called objects. (An OOD object is much more complex than an ERD object — you can think of an OOD object as containing an ERD object and all the functions that are performed on that object.) OOD objects should be structured with minimal dependencies between them, thus making them 'stand alone' units which can easily be used in other environments.

The most common argument in favour of the use of OOD is that it produces reusable code. However, most practitioners agree that in many real-time systems, the vast differences between processors and software architectures available at the moment make this a little unrealistic.

The main advantage of using OOD in a real-time system is that the minimization of object dependencies leads to a system consisting of independent objects — thus making the system easier to maintain. Looking at this in an abstract way, it is maximizing the benefits of coupling and cohesion, and in this respect OOD and structured analysis and design are very similar. In OOD, you strive to cut down on object dependencies, while in structured analysis and design you 'partition to minimize interfaces'. Both methods aim to produce units with good cohesion and coupling, which can be used independently.

At the moment, I see three potential stumbling blocks for the use of OOD in a real-time development:

1. The method of generating a set of objects from a set of system requirements seems to be unclear. The analysis consists of examining the system requirements and just 'deciding' what the objects will be. Also, there are no defined steps for design, such as the PEM, SEM and COM available within structured development.
2. Processors and software architectures are, on the whole, function-based. At the moment there are very few object-based processors and software architectures available. Organizing the system into objects at the analysis stage, which will then, for practical reasons, have to be split across processors and software architectures will only make the development more complicated. However, there are a number of object oriented programming languages which can be used to good advantage from an object oriented design.
3. There is no well-defined method of modelling control within OOD.

All of these stumbling blocks can be attributed to the fact that OOD has not yet had time to mature for as long as structured development. In the future, none of these problems may exist.

There are people already successfully using OOD in real-time development, by providing their own solutions to these problems. My solution to these problems would be to use the two techniques of OOD and structured development in parallel, using the methods of analysis and design to overcome problems 1 and 2, and the control aspects of structured development to overcome problem 3, to produce an object oriented system. This has already been discussed briefly in Section 6.2.3. Let us review what was suggested there and carry those ideas a little further.

Objects can be recognized in the analysis or design phases from the DFDs, by grouping data transformations around common data stores or terminators. Imagine a banking system DFD with four data transformations, 'check balance', 'add customer', 'withdraw money' and 'delete customer', all accessing the same store 'bank accounts'. As all of these data transformations are dependent on the same store, we can group all the functions and the data store together into an object. This would give us the 'bank account' object, with the following operations:

1. Check balance.
2. Add customer.
3. Withdraw money.
4. Delete customer.

In some cases, you may need to reorganize a function-based design to make it object oriented. Imagine the data transformation 'transfer funds', which moves data from the 'deposit account' into the 'current account' store. If we wanted to create a 'current account' object and a 'deposit account' object, we would have to split the data transformation in two, allowing us to see the separate object operations. 'Deposit money' would use the 'current account' store, and 'withdraw money' would use the 'deposit account' store. There is also information on using the DFD to help define objects in Section 6.2.3.

Objects could be shown as execution units forming part of the software architecture within the SEM, and calls to objects could be shown as calls to library routines within the COM. For example, to use the 'add customer' operation of the 'bank account' object, we would show a call to the library module 'bank account.add customer'.

15.4.2 Formal techniques

Within structured development a system is modelled as a hierarchy of network diagrams, which can be easily understood and checked for syntactic correctness. However, there is an amount of flexibility within structured development which means that it is not foolproof. Using a formal method (such as Z or VDM — Vienna Development Method), a system is modelled not in terms of diagrams, but in terms of mathematics and logic. A mathematical model can be rigorously checked for correctness and consistency throughout the process of analysis and design — which gives a way of producing code that is totally reliable (assuming that the initial requirements were captured correctly).

However, at the moment there a number of problems associated with using a formal technique in the development of a real-time system:

1. Formal techniques are not very user friendly. It would be unreasonable to expect a customer to be able to verify a formally specified system. Even engineers find it difficult to produce and understand formal specifications.
2. There is no 'method' for generating a formal specification from a set of system requirements, and no structured steps to take the initial specification through the equivalents of PEM, SEM and COM. Formal specifications are normally refined straight to code, with no structured consideration of the processors and software architectures that they will be running under.

3. There are no well-defined methods of modelling and refining control within formal techniques.

These are all problems which structured development could be used to solve. Structured development could be used to build an essential model (which would be user friendly), from which the formal specification could be generated. The steps of structured development could be followed until structure charts were produced, and reorganizations within the models could be reflected and verified by the formal specification. The formal specification could be used to check that the refinement to the design was being carried out correctly, whilst the structured development models could be used as the user friendly documentation of the design. This scenario could easily be achieved by populating all the specifications within the project dictionary with formal specifications, as the ERD provides the abstract data model around which most formal techniques revolve.

Here we have examined just two of the many development techniques that are available. There are also many more specialized techniques in areas such as testing, documentation, project management and quality assurance. The flexibility of structured development should make it possible to integrate all the techniques you require to develop your system in the best possible way.

Appendixes

Appendixes

Exercise answers

Do not expect to get exactly the same answer as given here. There are a number of factors which may make your answer look different from mine, but that does not necessarily mean that your answer is wrong:

1.   Interpretation — no matter how careful the specifier is, textual specifications sometimes tend to be woolly and open to different interpretations. If you have interpreted the initial text of the question differently from me, you are bound to get a different model. This is not a problem with the method or your use of the method, but with the vagueness of the English language and textual specification in general.

2.   Level of detail — as you are probably an engineer, you are probably used to worrying about detail and how things will work. However, if you put too much detail into initial models you may be making assumptions about the implementation. You are also complicating the model by putting in detail which may not be necessary at an early stage. Try to reflect the amount of detail given in the text. If your answers seem to have many more data transformations than mine, try joining them together into higher level transformations and see if you then end up with the same as me.

3.   If your models look different from mine, use your initiative!

If a DFD is syntactically correct, it is going to be understood by the person who is going to read it and reflects the specification that generated it, then it is right.

CHAPTER TWO

1. Washing clothes — see Figure A.1.

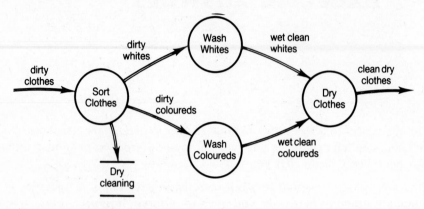

Figure A.1   Chapter 2, Exercise 1.

2. Joining a club — see Figure A.2.

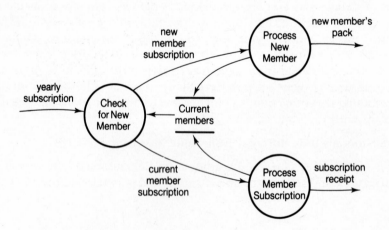

Figure A.2   Chapter 2, Exercise 2.

3. Making meringues — see Figure A.3.

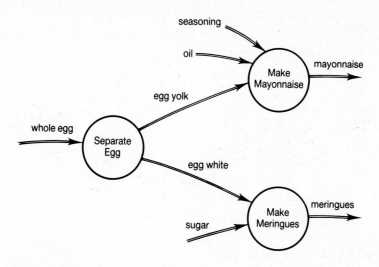

Figure A.3   Chapter 2, Exercise 3.

4. Weather data collection — see Figure A.4.

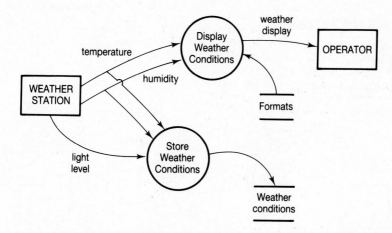

Figure A.4   Chapter 2, Exercise 4.

5. Conservation of data examples — see Figure A.5.

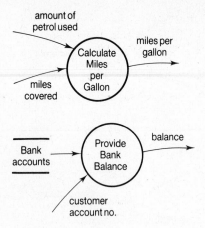

Figure A.5   Chapter 2, Exercise 5.

In the second part, another option would have been to extend 'bank account', such that:

bank account = account no. + customer name + balance

CHAPTER THREE

1. See Figure A.6

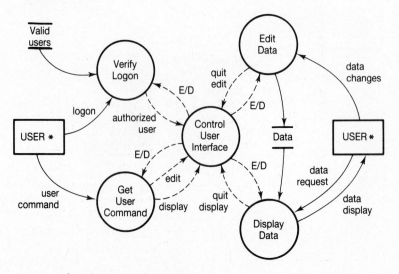

Figure A.6   Chapter 3, Exercise 1.

2. **Legal states**: 'Idle + operator idle'
   'Idle + analyzing'
   'Idle + changing parameters'
   'Initializing equipment + operator idle'
   'Initializing equipment + analyzing'
   'Reaction in progress + operator idle'
   'Reaction in progress + analyzing'
   'Reaction in progress + displaying current experiment'
   See Figure A.7.

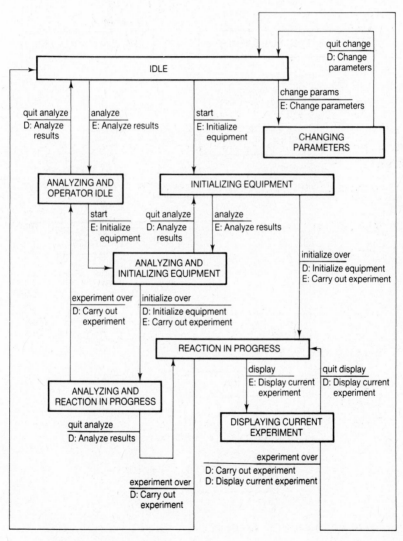

Figure A.7   Chapter 3, Exercise 2.

3. See Figure A.8.

State transition diagram for current experiment functionality

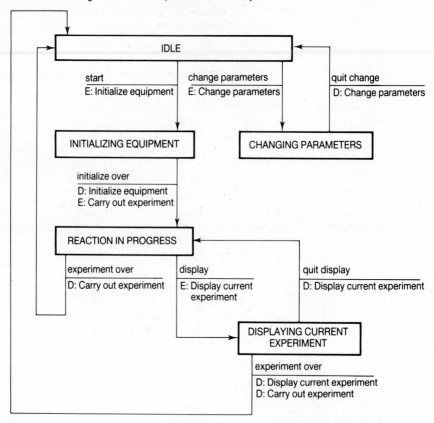

State transition diagram for analyzing results

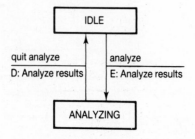

Figure A.8   Chapter 3, Exercise 3.

4. See Figure A.9.

Correct STD for lift control system

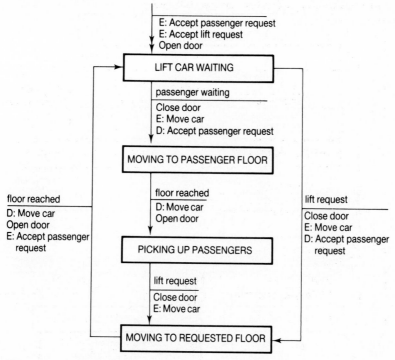

Figure A.9   Chapter 3, Exercise 4.

5. See Figure A.10.

STD for washing machine sequence

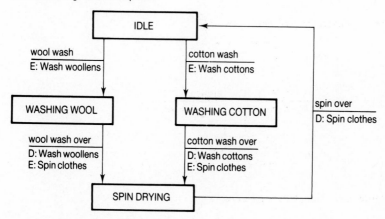

Figure A.10   Chapter 3, Exercise 5.

6. See Figure A.11.

STD for vending machine

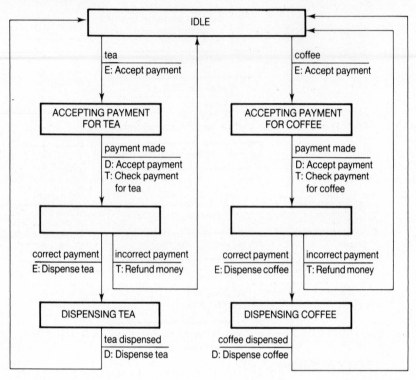

Figure A.11   Chapter 3, Exercise 6.

7. See Figure A.12.

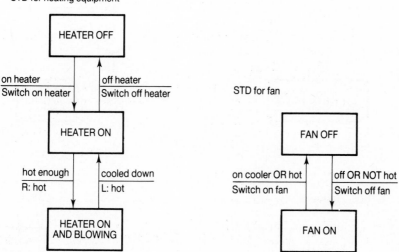

STDs to control fan heater

STD for heating equipment

STD for fan

Figure A.12   Chapter 3, Exercise 7.

CHAPTER FOUR

1. ERD (a) states that there is a relationship between a florist and flowers, which gives rise to a bouquet. Although this is true, and so the ERD is not wrong, the 'flowers' object will not allow us to specify the different information that we might want to keep about real and artificial flowers. Also, it is debatable whether the florist is something that we would want to store information about — and so perhaps the florist should not be an object.

   ERD (b) states that a single bouquet is made from many flowers, and that those flowers may be either real or artificial. The 'bouquet' object allows us to specify all the different types of bouquet, the 'is made from' relationship allows us to show which bouquets can be made from which flowers, and the subtype/supertype 'flowers' object allows us to specify different information for real and artificial flowers.

   ERD (c) states that there is a three way relationship between bouquet, real flowers and artificial flowers. This is not strictly true, as a single bouquet will either be made entirely from real flowers or entirely from artificial flowers.

2. See Figure A.13

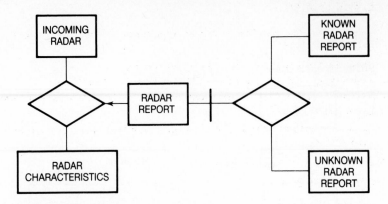

Figure A.13   Chapter 4, Exercise 2.

3. See Figure A.14.

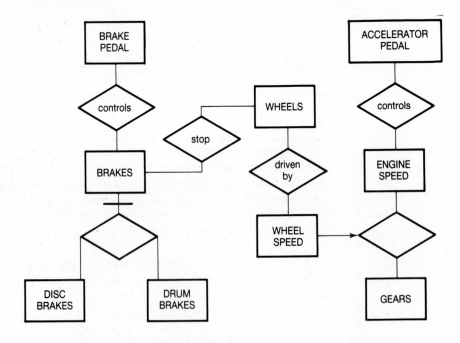

Figure A.14   Chapter 4, Exercise 3.

CHAPTER FIVE

1. Radar characteristics = radar frequency + radar strength + radar direction
2. Mayonnaise = {egg yolk} + oil + seasoning
3. Seasoning = [salt / pepper / salt + pepper] + (mustard)
4. Customer request = account number + [withdrawal + amount / deposit + amount / balance]
5. Car = 4{wheel}4 + 3{door}5 + [electric windows / manual windows] + (boot lid)

CHAPTER SIX

1. See Figure A.15.

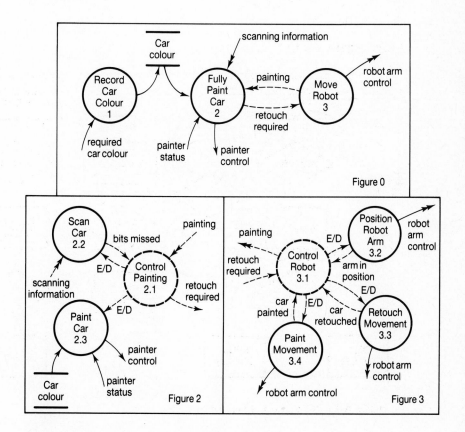

Figure A.15   Chapter 6, Exercise 1.

2. See Figure A.16.

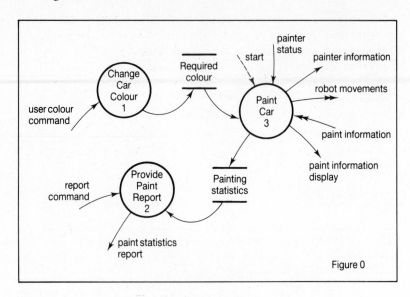

Figure 0

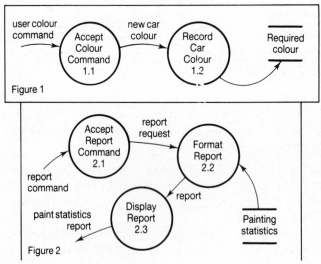

Figure 1

Figure 2

Figure A.16   Chapter 6, Exercise 2.

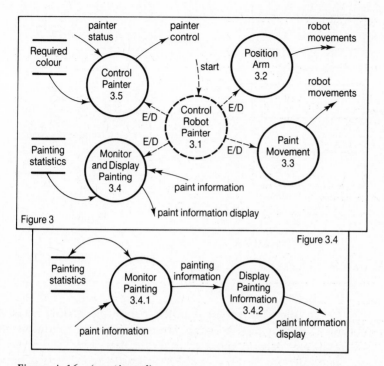

Figure 3

Figure 3.4

Figure A.16 (*continued*)

3. Figure A.17 shows only the modifications that need to be made to the DFD/STD to balance them. The STD and DFD given in the exercise were not in balance because of the following:

(a) The STD waited for conditions 'start' and 'stop', not shown on the DFD control process. These conditions have been added to the DFD control process, shown as input event flows — they probably come from a 'user' terminator.

(b) The STD has an action 'flash friendly lamp', not shown on the DFD control process. This action has been added to the DFD control process, as an output event flow — probably going to a 'lamp' terminator.

(c) The STD has an action 'T: display hostile radar', while the DFD data transformation is called 'display radar'. The STD does not wait for the condition 'unknown', although it is produced as an event flow entering the DFD control process by 'check radar type'. We have assumed that 'display radar' is the correct name for the data transformation, which will display both hostile and unknown radars.

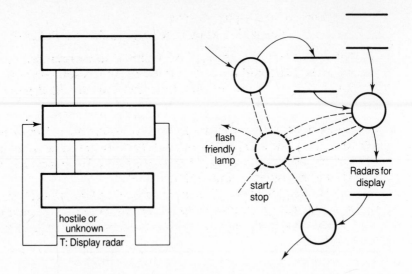

Figure A.17   Chapter 6, Exercise 3.

On the STD, rather than the condition 'hostile' causing the action 'T: display hostile radar', we now have the condition 'hostile or unknown' causing the action 'T: display radar'.

4. Diagrammatically the DFD and the ERD appear to be in balance; however, the project dictionary shows a number of discrepancies. Modifications in this case have only been made to the project dictionary.

(a) The relationship between 'captured radar' and 'known radar' described by the associative object 'identified radar', is that both the 'captured radar frequency' and the 'captured radar pulse width' lie within the bands identified for 'known radar'.

However, this relationship is not used in 'check radar type', where the 'captured radar' and 'known radar' are only matched on frequency. Furthermore, the 'captured radar' does not contain any pulse width information to match the relationship on.

The project dictionary will be modified such that:

captured radar = frequency + pulse width + strength
+ direction

The check at the beginning of 'check radar type' becomes:

if (captured radar frequency
     lies within known radar (x) frequency band AND

captured radar pulse width
lies within known radar (x) pulse width band)

(b) The 'captured radar strength' information does not appear to be used anywhere. It could either be removed from 'captured radar', or it could be kept as part of the information in identified radar.

5. See Figure A.18. 'Radar display' and 'radar display string' are data flows which are equivalent once decomposed. For this reason, we have decided to remove 'radar display string' from the project dictionary, and replace it with 'radar display' on the DFD.

   Although both the 'display radar' and its lower level DFD access the store 'identified radars', conservation of data on '1.3 build display radar' shows that it should be accessing the 'radar chars' field of the store.

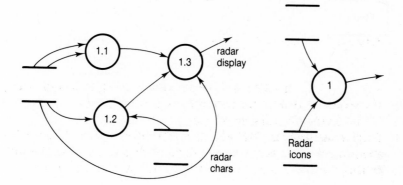

Figure A.18   Chapter 6, Exercise 5.

6. See Figure A.19.

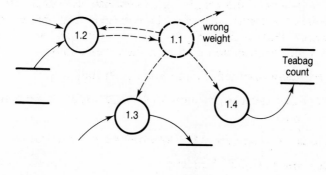

Figure A.19   Chapter 6, Exercise 6.

CHAPTER SEVEN

1. The best representation of the 'missile' terminator is option B, where 'directional data' represents the directional information sent from the control system, and the 'detonate' event flow represents the detonate command from the control system. It is assumed that the missile is tracked by another terminator attached to the control system.

2. See Figure A.20.

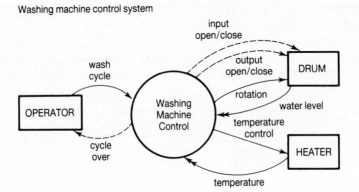

Washing machine control system

Figure A.20   Chapter 7, Exercise 2.

3. See Figure A.21.

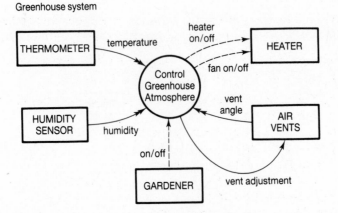

Greenhouse system

Figure A.21   Chapter 7, Exercise 3.

4. See Figure A.22.

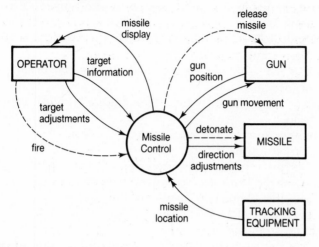

Missile control system

Figure A.22   Chapter 7, Exercise 4.

CHAPTER EIGHT

In these exercise answers, do not worry too much if you have not got exactly the same event list as here. There are a number of reasons for coming up with something different, and a different event list does not necessarily mean it is wrong:

1. You may have built the event list in more or less detail than here.
2. You may have seen the system working in a slightly different way.

As you will see from comments made in some of the exercises, two different event lists will often generate the same ultimate behavioural model.

1. For something to be an external event, the answer must be 'yes' to the following three questions:
   Q1: Does it happen in the system's environment?
   Q2: Does the system respond to it?
   Q3: Can it be localized to a point in time?
   (a) Operator enters wash cycle is an external event.
   Q1: Yes, from the operator.
   Q2: Yes, by starting the wash cycle.
   Q3: Yes, at the point when the 'wash cycle' data flow arrives.
   (b) Start washing according to wash cycle is not an external event.

Q1: No, this happens inside the system.
(c) Water temperature rises is not an external event.
Q1: Yes, from the heater.
Q2: No, the system will only respond when the temperature reaches a certain level.
(d) Water temperature reaches correct level for cycle is an external event.
Q1: Yes, from the heater.
Q2: Yes, by stopping heating and starting the drum rotation sequence.
Q3: Yes, at the point when 'temperature' reaches the correct value.
(e) Water temperature falls is not an external event.
Q1: Yes, from the heater.
Q2: No, the system is not interested in the temperature falling.
(f) Send 'cycle over' indication to operator is not an external event.
Q1: No, this happens from within the system.
(g) Water level reached is an external event.
Q1: Yes, from the drum.
Q2: Yes, by stopping filling the drum and starting to heat the water.
Q3: Yes, at the point when 'water level' shows the drum to be full.

2. Event 1: C/D
Change of state from 'idle' to 'filling drum with water'.
Data transformation required to store wash cycle.

Event 2: C/D
Change of state from 'filling drum with water' to 'heating water'.
Data transformation required to heat water.

Event 3: C/D
Change of state from 'heating water' to 'washing'.
Data transformation required to rotate drum during washing.

Event 4: C or C/D
Change of state from 'washing' to 'emptying drum of water'. If you assume that you will also start monitoring the water level at this point, it will be C/D, otherwise as emptying the drum of water is effected by the event flow 'input valve open', no data transformation is required. The data transformation will then be introduced as an event-recognizing data transformation whilst building the preliminary transformation diagram. Either way, the result of C or C/D will ultimately be the same. This also applies in event 1.

Event 5: C
Change of state from 'emptying drum of water' to 'idle'.
'Cycle over' is produced as an event flow, so no data transformation is required.

3. Table A.1 shows the event list for the greenhouse control system. The classification of responses concerned with raising and lowering temperature is control, as the temperature is raised or lowered by switching on and off the heater and the fan — both of which are done by event flows, and so a data transformation is not required.

Table A.1

Event	Response	Classification
1. Operator switches system on	Start monitoring temperature and humidity	C/D
2. Temperature gets too high	Start lowering temperature	C
3. Temperature correct	Stop lowering or raising temperature	C
4. Temperature gets too low	Start raising temperature	C
5. Humidity incorrect	Adjust vent and stop monitoring humidity for 5 minutes	C/D
6. Time to start monitoring humidity	Start monitoring humidity	TC/D
7. Operator switches system off	Stop monitoring temperature and humidity	C/D

4. Table A.2 shows the event list for the missile control system

Table A.2

Event	Response	Classification
1. Operator enters target information	Calculate where and when to fire missile	D
2. Time to start positioning gun	Start positioning gun	TC/D
3. Gun aimed	Stop positioning gun Release missile Start tracking and displaying missile Start accepting target adjustments	C/D
4. Operator requests fire	Send 'detonate' to missile	C
5. Operator enters target	Accept target adjustments	D
6. Tracker indicates missile fired	Stop tracking and displaying missile Stop accepting target adjustments	C

5. Table A.3 shows the event list for the telephone.

Table A.3

Event	Response	Classification
1. Receiver lifted	Produce 'line alive' tone Start sending input digits to exchange	C/D
2. Receiver replaced	If during call, inform exchange, otherwise stop sending digits to exchange Stop producing current tone	C
3. Exchange informs called line engaged	Produce 'engaged' tone Stop sending digits to exchange	C
4. Exchange informs called line free	Produce 'ringing' tone Stop sending digits to exchange	C
5. Exchange informs connected	Cease 'ringing' tone	C
6. Exchange informs disconnected	Produce 'line alive' tone	C

CHAPTER NINE

1. See Figure A.23.

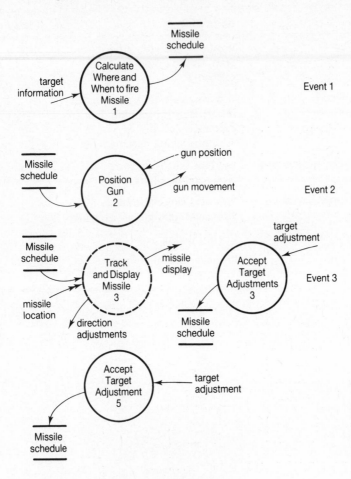

Figure A.23 Chapter 9, Exercise 1.

2. See Figure A.24.

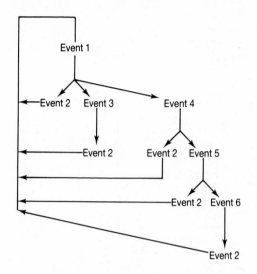

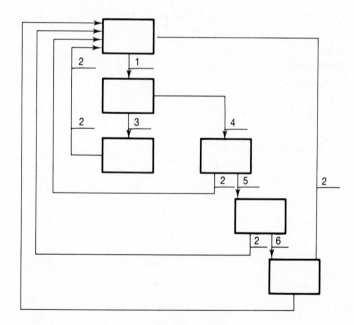

Figure A.24   Chapter 9, Exercise 2.

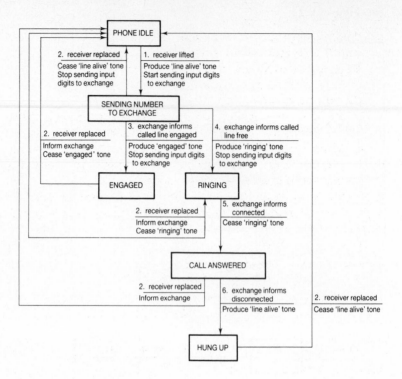

Figure A.24 *(continued)*

3. See Figure A.25. Comments:
   (a) Preliminary STD, event number 1:
       Event: Operator enters wash cycle
       Response: Start filling drum with water
                   Store wash cycle
       Classification: C/D
       Notice that the transition on the STD does not refer to 'store wash cycle'. This is because we have a compound event response, and the C classification refers only to 'start' filling drum with water.
   (b) In the preliminary transformation diagram, the event recognizer 'monitor water level' has been added.
   (c) In the levelled model, the STD conditions and actions have been refined from the preliminary model, to reflect what is shown on the DFD.

Preliminary STD: Control type events 1, 2, 3, 4, 5
                 Event sequence for washing machine controls

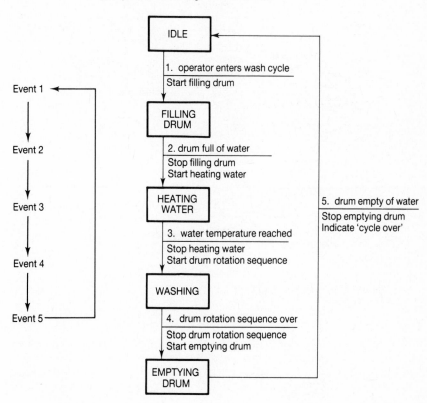

Figure A.25   Chapter 9, Exercise 3.

Preliminary DFD: Data type events 1, 2, 3

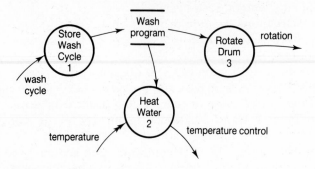

Preliminary transformation diagram

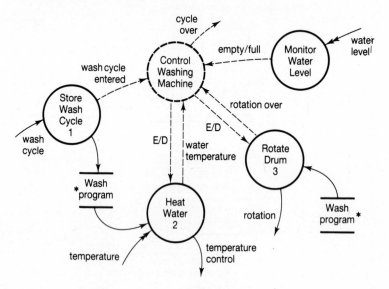

Figure A.25 *(continued)*

Levelled model

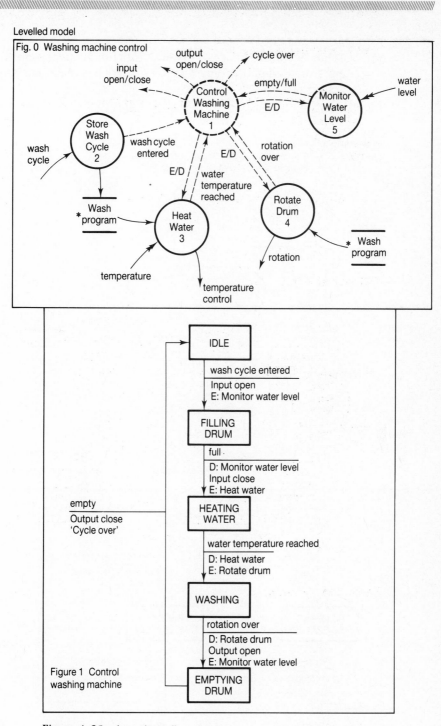

Fig. 0 Washing machine control

Figure 1 Control washing machine

Figure A.25 (*continued*)

4. See Figure A.26. Comments:
   (a) As there seem to be two distinct functional areas, controlling temperature and controlling humidity, these have been modelled in separate STDs.
   (b) In the preliminary model, notice that the two functional areas of

Greenhouse control system
Preliminary STD: Control type events 1,2,3,4,5,6,7
Event sequence for temperature control

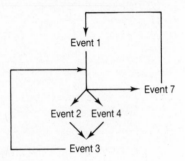

Generates the temperature control STD

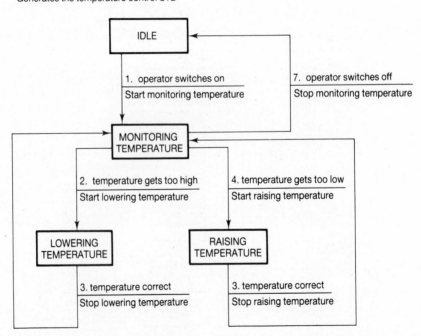

Figure A.26   Chapter 9, Exercise 4.

Event sequence for humidity control

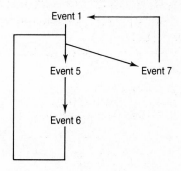

Generates the humidity control STD

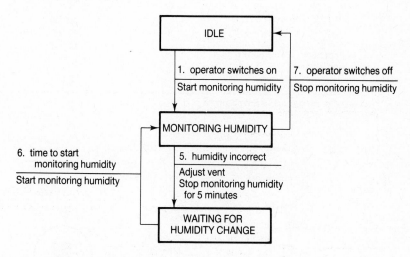

Preliminary DFD Data type events 1, 5, 6

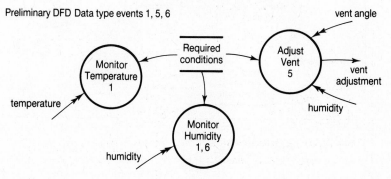

Figure A.26 (*continued*)

Preliminary transformation diagram

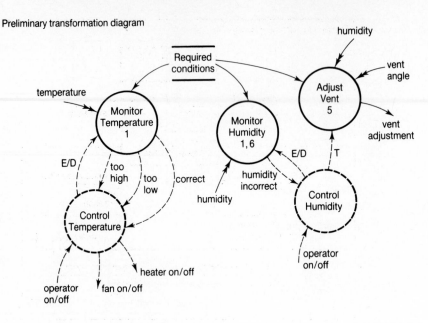

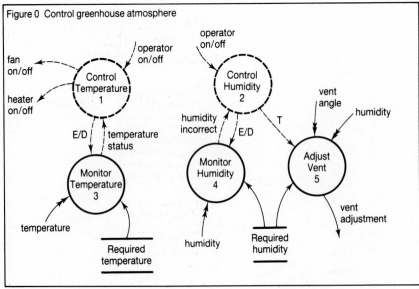

Figure 0 Control greenhouse atmosphere

Figure A.26 (*continued*)

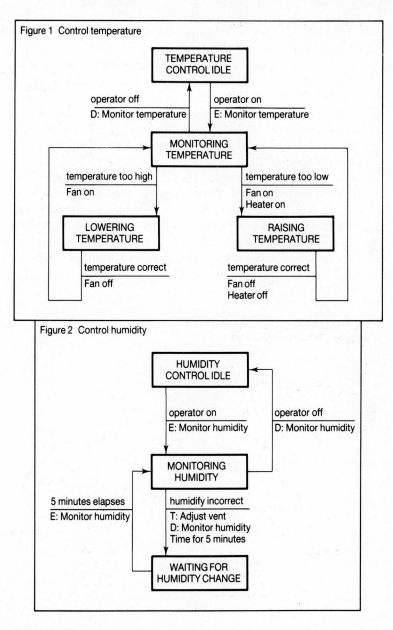

Figure 1 Control temperature

Figure 2 Control humidity

Figure A.26 (*continued*)

raising and lowering temperature are achieved not via a data transformation, but by switching on the heater and fan by event flows directly from the STD.

I have made a decision to 'hide' the 5 minute wait to start monitoring humidity within the STD, although I could also have shown this as a 'timer' data transformation on the DFD.

(c) In the levelled model, I could have levelled up to just two data transformations, 'control temperature' and 'control humidity'; however, I decided that five transformations were not too many for the top level DFD.

The event flows 'too hot', 'too cold' and 'correct' have been levelled into the single flow 'temperature status'.

The STD conditions and actions have been modified from the preliminary model, to reflect what is shown on the DFD.

The 'required conditions' store has been broken down into the 'required temperature' and 'required humidity' stores.

5. See Figure A.27. Comments:
   (a) In the preliminary STD, the 'missile in flight' state could have been broken into two: 'missile in flight' and 'missile about to detonate', where the 'operator requests fire' would have moved us from 'missile in flight' to 'missile about to detonate'.

   As in both states we are waiting for the same condition, 'tracker indicates missile fired', and in both states the missile is in flight, I decided that it was clearer simply to have a single state.
   (b) In the preliminary DFD I have introduced the 'schedule missile' event recognizer, which is comparing the current time against a time given in the 'missile schedule'.
   (c) The levelled model contains three high level data transformations.

Missile control system
Preliminary DFD: Data type events 1, 2, 3, 5

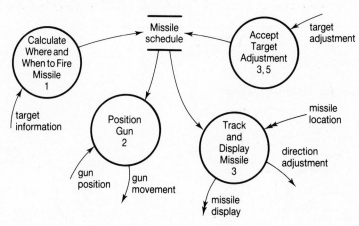

Preliminary STD: Control type events 2, 3, 4, 6

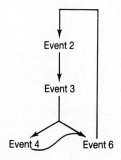

Figure A.27   Chapter 9, Exercise 5.

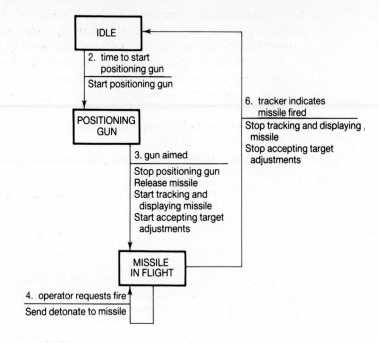

Preliminary transformation diagram

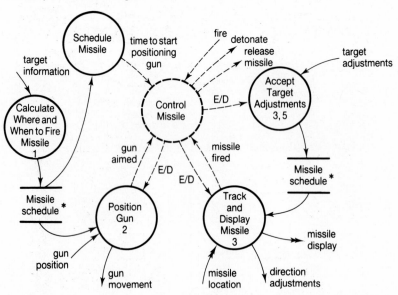

Figure A.27 (*continued*)

Initially, I decided that there were too many data transformations on the preliminary transformation diagram for the top level DFD, therefore some levelling would have to be done.

Levelling around the preliminary 'control missile' gave a top level DFD with two data transformations:

(i)   calculate missile schedule (from calculate where and when to fire missile);

(ii) missile control (everything else).

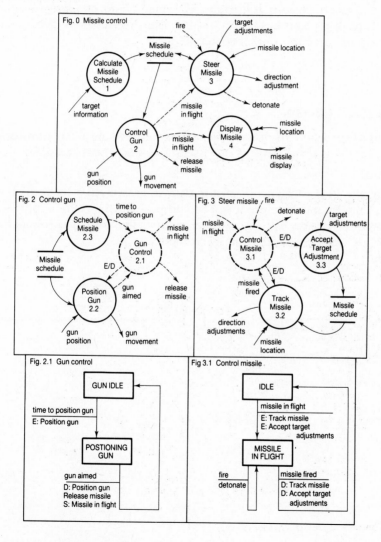

Figure A.27   (*continued*)

However, this gave a top level DFD which was almost too simple, and the lower level DFD of 'missile control' was almost as complicated as the one I started off with.

Therefore I decided to split the 'missile control' control process/STD into two, with respect to
(i) things controlling the gun;
(ii) things controlling the actual missile.
Also 'track and display missile' has been split into two separate data transformations, as it contains two different conceptual functions (one concerned with controlling the missile and one with producing a display). This has led to the data transformation '4 display missile'. This gave the final levelled model.

CHAPTER TEN

In places where the lower level diagram describing a data transformation or control process is the same as the essential model, the diagram has not been redrawn.

1. In the PEM of Figure A.28 the data transformation to be held on the cashpoint machine processor would probably be refined into two data transformations 'accept customer request' and 'display customer balance' with a control process between them.

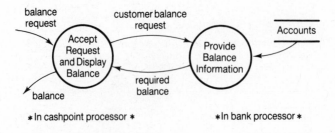

Figure A.28   Chapter 10, Exercise 1.

2. See Figure A.29.

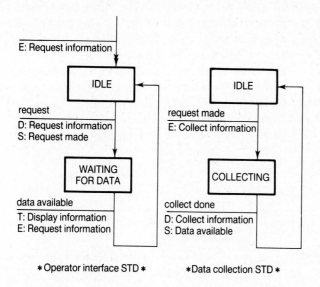

Figure A.29   Chapter 10, Exercise 2.

3. See Figure A.30. Notice that the HCI processor receives 'temperature' and 'humidity' directly from the temperature and humidity sensors, rather than via the temperature control and humidity control processors.

   This is a design decision that I have made. As far as I know (i.e. there is no specification that suggests otherwise), there is no reason why the HCI processor cannot communicate directly with the temperature and humidity sensor — this way the gardener will still get temperature and humidity reading even if there is something wrong with the temperature or humidity control processors.

   On the other hand, it would be an equally good design to have

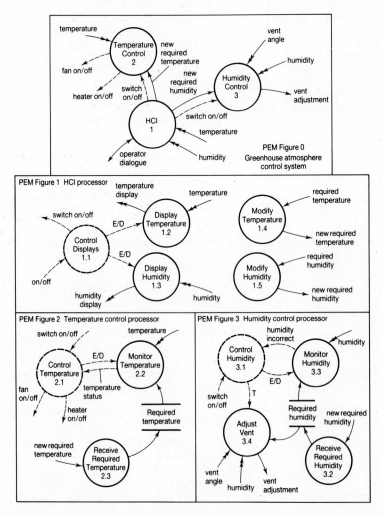

Figure A.30   Chapter 10, Exercise 3.

the temperature and humidity routed through the temperature and humidity control processors — that way the gardener may be more aware of problems with the temperature and humidity control processors. The traceability table is given in Table A.4.

Table A.4

Essential model	Processor environment model
1.1 Control temperature	2.1 Control temperature
	1.1 Control displays (part)
1.2 Display temperature	1.2 Display temperature
1.3 Monitor temperature	2.2 Monitor temperature
2.1 Control humidity	3.1 Control humidity
	1.1 Control displays (part)
2.2 Display humidity	1.3 Display humidity
2.3 Monitor humidity	3.3 Monitor humidity
2.4 Adjust humidity	3.4 Adjust humidity
3. Modify temperature	1.4 Modify temperature
	2.3 Receive required temperature
4. Modify humidity	1.5 Modify humidity
	3.2 Receive required humidity
Required temperature	Required temperature (temperature control)
Required humidity	Required humidity (humidity control)

4. The allocation table is given in Table A.5. See Figure A.31.

Table A5

Processor	Essential behaviour
Human–computer interface	1 Control washing machine (part)
	2 Store wash cycle (part)
Washing machine control	1 Control washing machine (part)
	2 Store wash cycle (part)
	3 Heat water
	4 Rotate drum
	5 Monitor water level
	Wash cycle

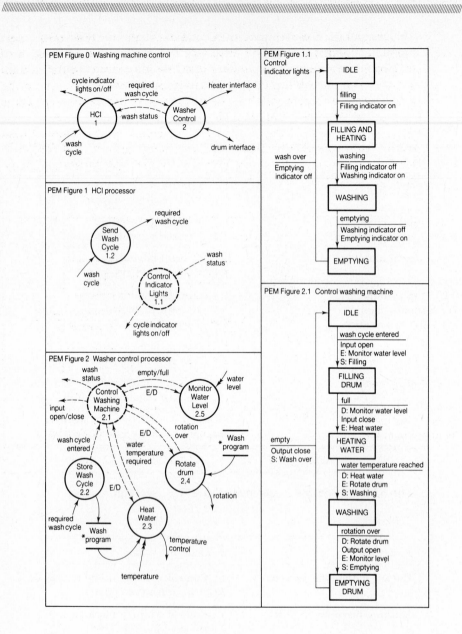

Figure A.31   Chapter 10, Exercise 4.

5. See Figure A.32, the allocation table (Table A.6) and the traceability table (Table A.7). For this exercise, version 1 of the answer to Exercise 4 of Chapter 11 has been used. If you have used the model produced in version 2, you will see that integrating the HCI with the essential model has made processor allocation more difficult. This will normally be the case, as the HCI will tend to be positioned all on the same processor.

Note that as I have allocated the single data transformation '3 steer missile' to the single processor 'missile control', and as '3 steer missile' has no lower level DFD, there is no lower level DFD for the 'missile control' processor within the PEM.

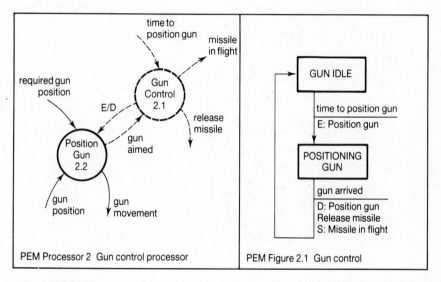

Figure A.32 Chapter 10, Exercise 5.

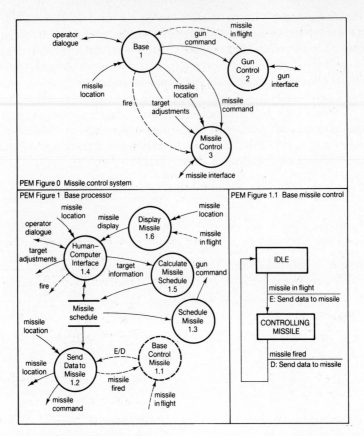

PEM Figure 0 Missile control system

PEM Figure 1 Base processor

PEM Figure 1.1 Base missile control

Figure A.32 (*continued*)

Table A.6

Processor	Essential behaviour	
Gun control	2.1	Control gun
	2.2	Position gun
Missile control	3	Steer missile
Human−computer	1	Calculate missile schedule
	2.3	Schedule missile
	4	Human−computer interface
	Missile schedule	

Table A.7

Essential model		Processor environment model	
1	Calculate missile schedule	1.5	Calculate missile schedule
2.1	Control gun	2.1	Control gun
2.2	Position gun	2.2	Position gun
2.3	Schedule missile	1.3	Schedule missile
3	Steer missile	3	Missile control
4	Human−computer interface	1.4	Human−computer interface
5	Display missile	1.6	Display missile
Missile schedule		Missile schedule (base)	
		1.2	Send data to missile
		1.1	Base control missile

CHAPTER ELEVEN

1. See Figure A.33. Comments:
   (a) On the context diagram and top level DFD, the event flows which would switch on and off the individual lights have been levelled into the single event flow 'cycle indicator lights on/off'. I have done this because I do not think it is any less clear than having three individual event flows, one for each light.
   (b) In the STD, I did not know whether it would be better to call the event flows being produced by the light colours:
      • red light on/off
      • yellow light on/off
      • green light on/off
      or by names showing what the lights were indicating:
      • filling indicator on/off
      • washing indicator on/off
      • emptying indicator on/off
      Although I felt that the names were more generally meaningful, I did not know whether it would be better to show the light colours, as they would prove to my customer that I understood the required interface.

      In this case, it would depend on what you thought would be more meaningful to the customer, and although I finally went for the 'names', using the light colours would be equally valid.

      The original 'cycle over' indicator has been 'implemented' by the lights, as all the lights out indicates that the cycle is over.

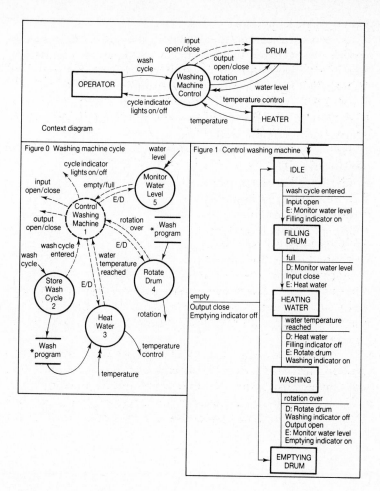

Figure A.33   Chapter 11, Exercise 1.

2. See Figure A.34. Comments:
   (a) In the context diagram, the original terminators 'thermometer' and 'heater' have been merged into 'temperature regulation', and 'humidity sensor' and 'air vents' have been merged into 'humidity regulation'. I have done this on the assumption that we are now most interested in the details of the HCI, and therefore showing the regulation equipment in too much detail would make the diagram unnecessarily complicated.
   (b) The top level DFD has been levelled, as the addition of the new data transformations
   - modify required temperature
   - modify required humidity
   - display humidity
   - display temperature
   made the original DFD too large.

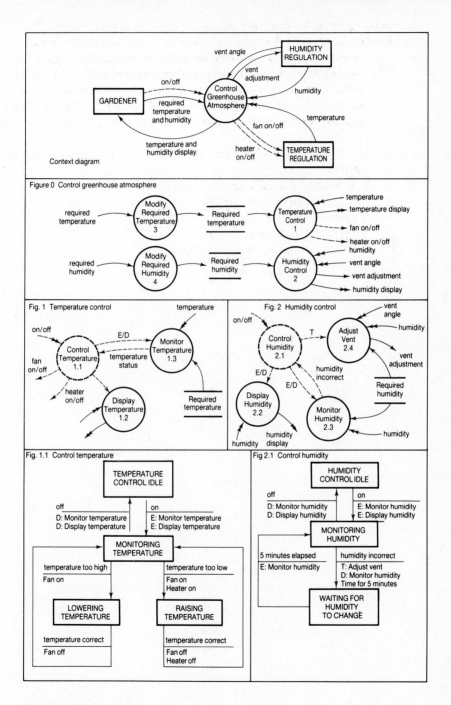

Figure A.34   Chapter 11, Exercise 2.

3. (a) I attempted this exercise using the context diagram (Figure A.35) and event list method (Table A.8).

     The preliminary and behavioural models for the HCI, shown by Figure A.35(b), were generated directly from the context diagram and event list. These models actually describe what is happening inside the original data transformation '3.3 accept target adjustments'. Therefore, what has been provisionally labelled 'Figure 0 preliminary

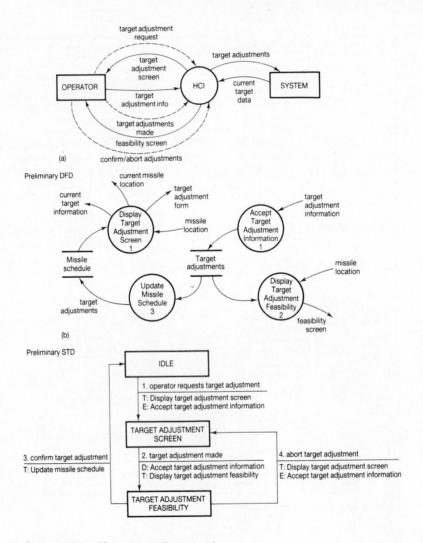

Figure A.35   Chapter 11, Exercise 3.

accept target adjustments HCI' is actually 'Figure 3.3 accept target adjustments', thus **Figure 5** of the HCI becomes Figure 3.3.5, within 'accept target adjustments'.

The essential HCI was suppressed within '3.3 accept target adjustments' of the missile control essential model.

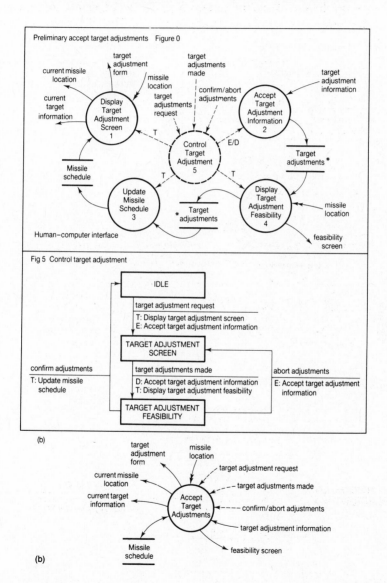

Figure A.35 *(continued)*

(b) **Version 1: Here, the whole of the HCI has been hidden inside '3.3 accept target adjustments'. This means that Figure 3 of the new model looks the same as the essential model, except that there is more input and output to '3.3 accept target adjustments', to fulfil the data requirements of the HCI.**

In this case, the lower level DFD describing 'accept target

Version 1 Figure 3 Steer missile

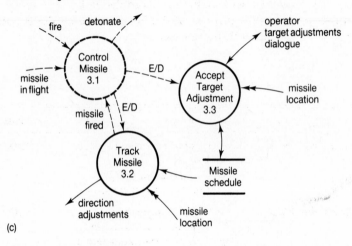

(c)

Version 2 Figure 3 Steer missile

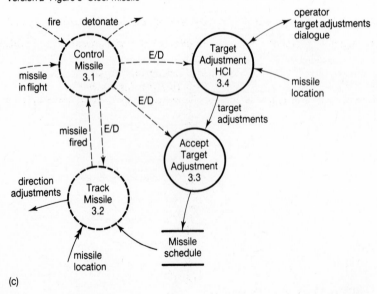

(c)

Figure A.35 (*continued*)

adjustments' is given by the behavioural model shown in Figure A.35(b).

Version 2: Here, the HCI has been decoupled from the original functionality of '3.3 accept target adjustments'. This means that Figure 3 of the new model has the added data transformation '3.4 target adjustment HCI', while the original data transformation '3.3 accept target adjustments' remains unchanged.

In this case, from the behavioural model given in Figure A.35(b), 'update missile schedule' is replaced by '3.3 accept target adjustments', whilst the rest of the behavioural model is contained within '3.4 target adjustment HCI'.

Table A.8

Event	Response	Classification
1. Operator requests target adjustment	Display target adjustment screen Start accepting target adjustment information	C/D
2. Target adjustments made	Stop accepting target adjustment information Display target adjustment feasibility	C/D
3. Confirm target adjustment	Update missile schedule	C/D
4. Abort target adjustment	Display target adjustment screen Start accepting target adjustment information	C/D

4. See Figure A.36. To arrive at the STD/DFD given by Figure A.36(b), each 'screen' that would have been produced as part of the HCI has been translated into a state on the STD. User inputs have become conditions, and the system's response to those user inputs have become actions.

Notice that I have built the hierarchy of the STD/DFD models to match the hierarchy of the menu structure — not only was this the easiest thing to do, but also it will make maintenance easier as there is direct traceability between the model and the actual HCI.

Version 1: Here, the HCI has been decoupled for the original

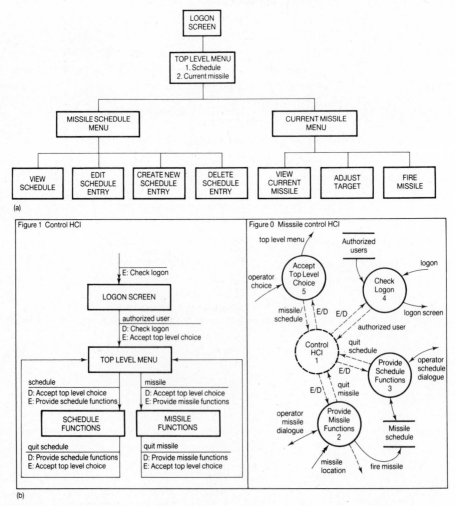

Figure A.36   Chapter 11, Exercise 4.

model, and the only change to the original data transformations is that interfaces with the operator have been replaced by interfaces with the 'human—computer interface' data transformation.

The lower levels of '4 human—computer interface' are given by the DFD hierarchy of Figure A.36(b) except that

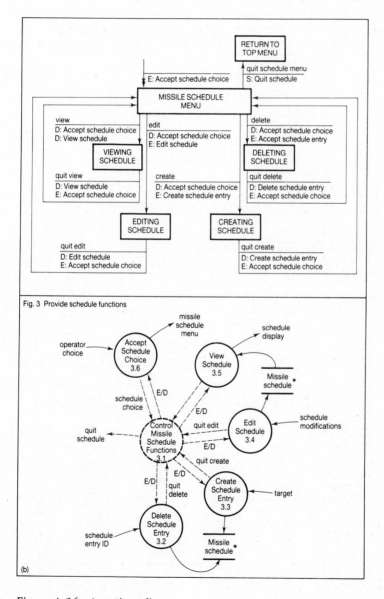

Figure A.36 (*continued*)

452 *Appendixes*

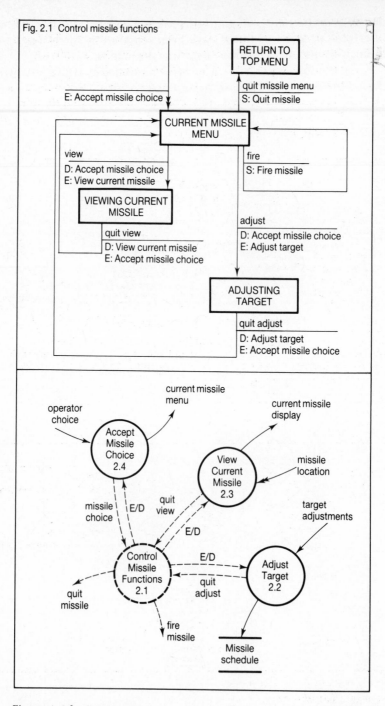

Fig. 2.1 Control missile functions

RETURN TO TOP MENU

quit missile menu
S: Quit missile

E: Accept missile choice

CURRENT MISSILE MENU

view
D: Accept missile choice
E: View current missile

fire
S: Fire missile

VIEWING CURRENT MISSILE

quit view
D: View current missile
E: Accept missile choice

adjust
D: Accept missile choice
E: Adjust target

ADJUSTING TARGET

quit adjust
D: Adjust target
E: Accept missile choice

operator choice

current missile menu

current missile display

Accept Missile Choice 2.4

View Current Missile 2.3

missile location

missile choice · E/D

quit view

E/D

target adjustments

Control Missile Functions 2.1

E/D

Adjust Target 2.2

quit missile

quit adjust

fire missile

Missile schedule

Figure A.36 (*continued*)

- '3.3 create schedule entry' is replaced by '1 calculate missile schedule'
- '2.2 adjust target' is replaced by '3.3 accept target adjustments'
- '2.3 view current missile' is replaced by '5 display missile'
- 'fire missile' is replaced by '3.1 control missile'

Version 2: Here, the essential model has been restructured so that the HCI has been fully integrated with the original functionality.

The lower levels of '1 human−computer interface' are given by the DFD hierarchy of Figure A.36(b).

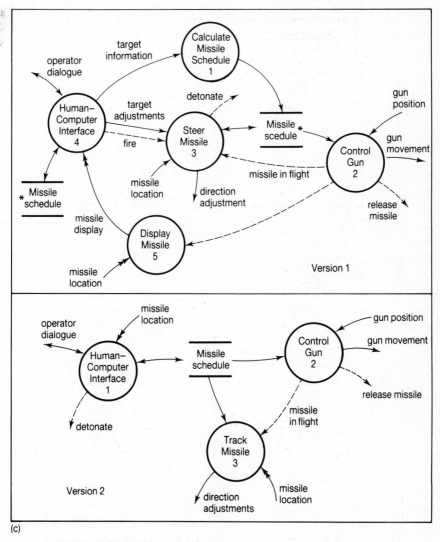

(c)

Figure A.36   (*continued*)

- '3.3 create schedule entry' replaces '1 calculate missile schedule'
- '2.2 adjust target' replaces '3.3 accept target adjustments'
- '2.3 view current missile' replaces '4 display missile'
- 'Fire missile' replaces '3.1 control missile'

CHAPTER TWELVE

1. See Figure A.37. At the top level I have decided not to show the part of the software architecture which provides the 'wait' facility, as I felt that it did not make the documentation of the design any clearer.

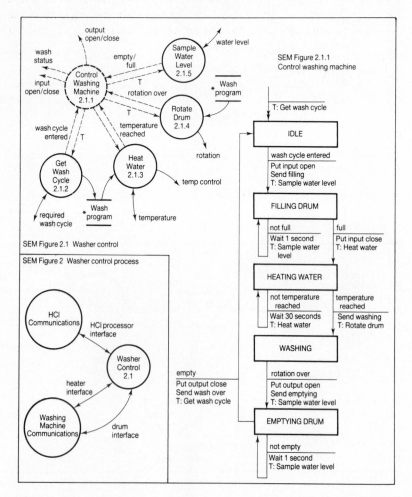

Figure A.37   Chapter 12, Exercise 1.

(a) The 'put' and 'get' facilities for ports 1–6 have been represented by the 'washing machine communications' package.
(b) The 'send' and 'receive' facilities for the operator interface processor have been represented by the 'HCI communications' package.

    The lower level DFD and STD are very similar to the PEM, except for the following:

(a) The direct communications with other processors/pieces of equipment have been replaced by calls to communications packages.
(b) The two data transformations which formerly acted on continuous inputs (monitor water level and heat water), are now triggered at an appropriate sample interval, rather than enabled and left to run.
(c) The PEM transformation 'store wash cycle' which ran independently is now controlled by the control process (remember, there can only be a single thread of control within an execution unit), and its name has been changed to reflect this.

2. See Figure A.38. There will be two interrupt handlers:
(a) 'Interrupt' 'switch on' 'handler' will set the 'temperature control' task to runnable, and set the 'off' flag to false.
(b) 'Interrupt' 'switch off' 'handler' will set the 'off' flag to true.
The 'temperature control' execution unit will be given a higher priority than the 'receive required temperature' execution unit, which will be able to run during the many 'suspends' of the 'temperature control' execution unit.

Comments:

(a) As no I/O facilities with the HCI processor have been defined, it is assumed that these will be written as part of the 'receive required temperature' execution unit.

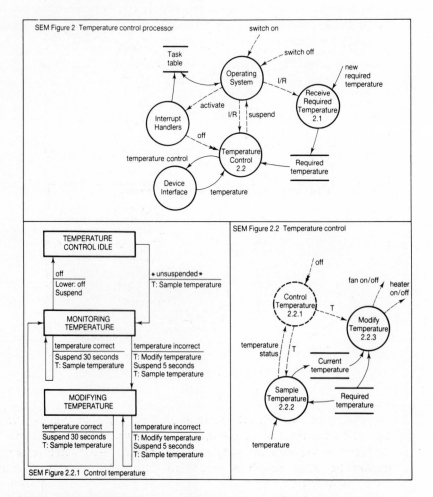

Figure A.38 Chapter 12, Exercise 2.

(b) The 'current temperature' store has been added within the 'temperature control' execution unit, as it seems wasteful for both 'sample temperature' and 'modify temperature' to read the same temperature value in.

3. See Figure A.39. There will be two interrupt handlers:
(a) 'Interrupt' 'switch on' 'handler' will set the 'humidity control' task to runnable, and the 'off' flag to false.

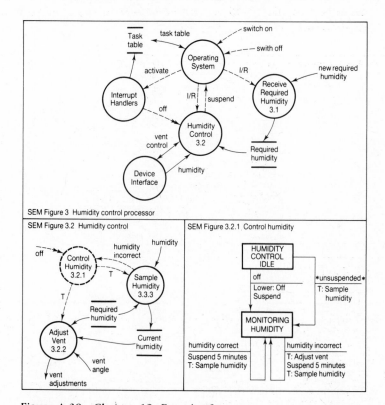

Figure A.39   Chapter 12, Exercise 3.

(b) 'Interrupt' 'switch off' 'handler' will set the 'off' flag to true. The 'humidity control' execution unit will be given a higher priority than the 'receive required humidity' execution unit, which will be able to run during the many 'suspends' of the 'humidity control' execution unit.

Comments:

(a) As no I/O facilities with the HCI processor have been defined, it is assumed that these will be written as part of the 'receive required humidity' execution unit.

(b) The 'current humidity' store has been added within the 'humidity control' execution unit, as it seems wasteful for both 'sample humidity' and 'modify humidity' to read the same humidity value in.

4. See Figure A.40.
   (a) Only one execution unit has been shown, although there may be many execution units.

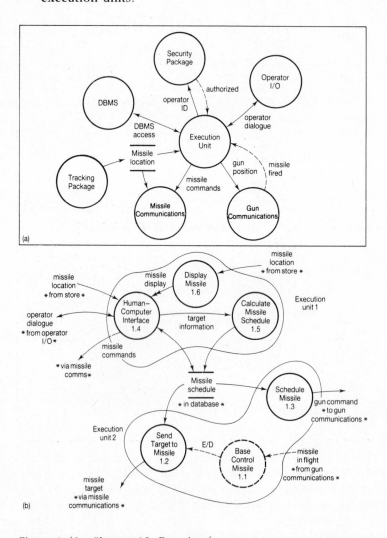

Figure A.40   Chapter 12, Exercise 4.

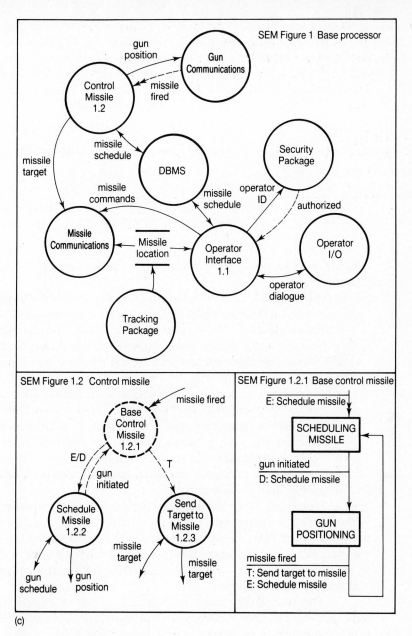

SEM Figure 1 Base processor

gun position

Gun Communications

missile fired

Control Missile 1.2

missile schedule

missile target

DBMS

Security Package

missile commands

missile schedule

operator ID

authorized

Missile Communications

Missile location

Operator Interface 1.1

Operator I/O

operator dialogue

Tracking Package

SEM Figure 1.2 Control missile

missile fired

Base Control Missile 1.2.1

E/D

gun initiated

T

Schedule Missile 1.2.2

Send Target to Missile 1.2.3

missile target

missile target

gun schedule

gun position

SEM Figure 1.2.1 Base control missile

E: Schedule missile

SCHEDULING MISSILE

gun initiated

D: Schedule missile

GUN POSITIONING

missile fired

T: Send target to missile

E: Schedule missile

(c)

Figure A.40 (*continued*)

Table A.9

Software architecture	PEM component
DBMS	Missile schedule
Security package	1.4.4 Check logon (part)
Missile communications	1.2 Send data to missile (part)
Gun communications	Interface: 1.3 Schedule missile
Operator I/O	Interface: 1.4 HCI
Tracking package	Interface: 1.4 HCI
	Interface: 1.2 Send data to missile

(b) Allocation to software architecture is shown in Table A.9.

(c) Comments:

    (i) Execution unit 1: as there is no concurrency within the human–computer interface, this will all be inside the same execution unit. 'Calculate missile schedule' and 'display missile' are also part of the human–computer interface sequence (as shown by the direct data flow), and therefore is also kept within the execution unit.

    (ii) Execution unit 2: although the two groups of behaviour within this execution unit seem at first glance to be asynchronous, examination reveals that the 'missile in flight' event flow will always follow a 'gun command' being sent by 'schedule missile' — therefore the two groups of behaviour are sequential and should be within the same execution unit.

(d) The internal DFD of execution unit 2 has been shown, as this differs from the PEM that generated it.

    However, the only difference between the SEM and the PEM in the case of execution unit 1 is that external interfaces are now via packages rather than direct, the missile schedule has to be accessed via the DBMS, and the authorization part of 'check logon' is done by the security package. Therefore the internal DFD of this execution unit has not been redrawn.

    The traceability table is shown in Table A.10. All other packages within the software architecture are concerned with providing external interfaces.

Table A.10

Processor environment model	Software environment model
1.1 Base control missile	1.2.1 Base control missile
1.2 Send data to missile	1.2.3 Send target to missile *Missile communications* (part)
1.3 Schedule missile	1.2.2 Schedule missile
1.4 HCI	1.1.1 HCI *Security package*
1.5 Calculate missile schedule	1.1.2 Calculate missile schedule
1.6 Display missile	1.1.3 Display missile
Missile schedule	DBMS

CHAPTER THIRTEEN

1. See Figure A.41.

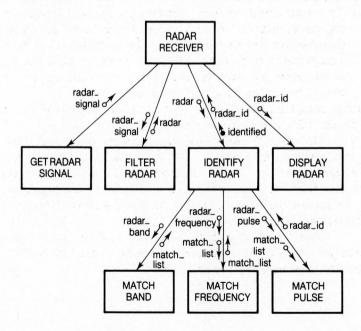

Figure A.41   Chapter 13, Exercise 1.

2. See Figure A.42. Notice that as 'draw star' is called with both 'point_1' and 'point_2' at different times in the program, I have compromised and called it with 'point'.

      I have shown the variables nested within records, such as x_axis.end, as purely x_end on the module called. If you imagine deeply nested records, the module calls could get very crowded if all the nesting were included.

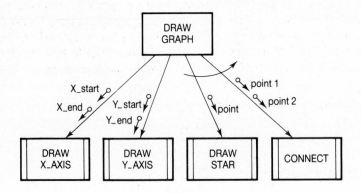

Figure A.42   Chapter 13, Exercise 2.

3. See Figure A.43. I have assumed that 'write to screen' and 'read char' are not provided, and are to be written as part of the code at a lower level. However, it was difficult to join them to all the higher level modules that called them. I have used the library symbol in repeat calls of these modules, although you could have used the connector symbol.

I have called the 'write to screen' module with 'name request', 'address request' and 'code request', as I did not want to write the actual character strings passed to the module on the structure chart.

I have not shown a 'repeat' symbol around the whole of the modules called from within 'read customer name', as they will only be repeated if the 'customer name' is invalid. As this is unlikely to be the norm, repetition shown around these modules would be misleading. Similarly for 'read customer address' and 'read order code'.

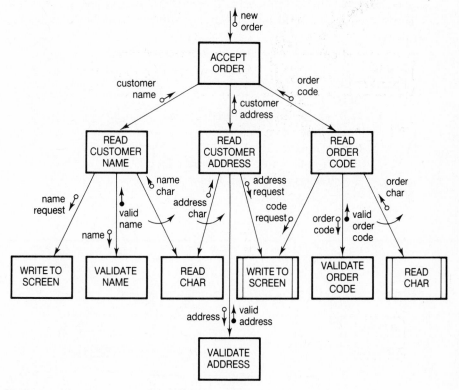

Figure A.43   Chapter 13, Exercise 3.

CHAPTER FOURTEEN

As you probably have experience of writing 'sensible' code, you may find yourself making refinements to the preliminary structure charts as you go along; for example, it is very obvious sometimes that a module will be too small, or that two modules are actually performing the same function. For this reason, do not worry too much if your own answers appear to be a more reasonable way of implementing the program than the preliminary structure charts in the set answers. Also, as mentioned at the beginning of Chapter 14, the extent of symbols used on the structure chart is often a matter of style. In these answers, I have tended not to use the iteration or selection symbols, even when they are appropriate, as I feel they clutter the diagram and prefer to investigate the module specification if I am interested in the module algorithm.

1. See Figure A.44 and Table A.11. This example requires no 'get condition' module, as the conditions are always provided by the modules being called.

    Pseudo-code for control washing machine

Begin

Forever Do

        Begin

        Call get wash cycle (:wash cycle)

        Put (input valve, open)

        Send (filling)

        Call sample water level (:water level)

        If water level < > full then

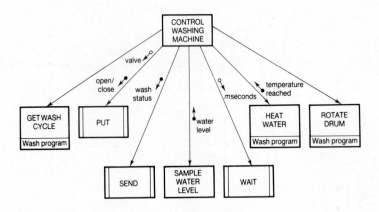

Figure A.44   Chapter 14, Exercise 1.

Table A.11

	Wash cycle entered	Not full	Full	Not temperature reached	Temperature reached	Rotation over	Not empty	Empty
Idle	Put input open Send filling Sample water level Filling drum							
Filling drum		Wait 1 second Sample water level Filling drum	Put input close Heat water Heating water					
Heating water				Wait 30 seconds Heat water Heating water	Send washing Rotate drum Washing			
Washing						Put output open Send emptying Sample water level Emptying drum		
Emptying drum							Wait 1 second Sample water level Emptying drum	Put output close Send wash over Get wash cycle Idle

```
            Repeat
                    Wait (1000)
                    Call sample water level (:water level)
            Until water level = full
    Put (input valve, close)
    Call heat water (:temperature reached)
    Repeat
                    Wait (30000)
                    Call heat water (:temperature reached)
    Until temperature reached = true
    Send (washing)
    Call rotate drum
    Put (output valve, open)
    Send (emptying)
    Call sample water level (:water level)
    If water level < > empty then
                    Repeat
                            Wait (1000)
                            Call sample water level (:water level)
                    Until water level = empty
    Put (output valve, close)
    Send (wash over)
    End
End
```

2. See Figure A.45.

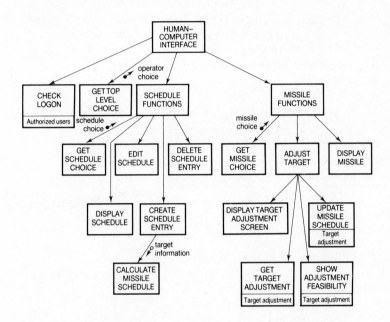

Figure A.45 Chapter 14, Exercise 2.

3. See Figure A.46.

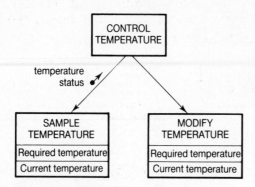

Figure A.46   Chapter 14, Exercise 3.

```
        Pseudo-code for control temperature
Begin
Forever Do
        If not (OFF) Then
                Begin
                Call sample temperature (temp-status);
                If temp-status = correct Then
                        Call suspend (30)
                Else Begin
                        Call modify temperature
                        Call suspend (5)
                        End
                End
        Else Call suspend ()
    End
```

4. See Figure A.47. This answer was obtained using transaction analysis, choosing 'accept report request' as the controlling module. Notice that although 'send to printer' and 'send to screen' are called by more than one higher level module, there is no problem here, as they are expected to do the same, whoever calls them.

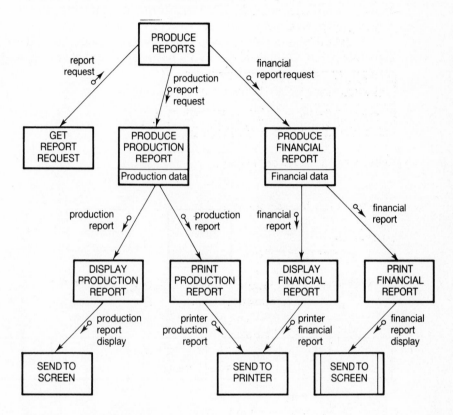

Figure A.47   Chapter 14, Exercise 4.

5. See Figure A.48. This answer was obtained by transform analysis. Initially 'identify radar', 'create radar display' and 'record radar' were included in the central transform, as they are connected by the essential data 'radar'.

However, by examination, although I very nearly chose 'identify radar' to be the controlling data transformation, I decided to introduce a new controlling module to the structure chart.

There was initially a knot in this structure chart, around the data transformation 'display radar'. This has been cured by reorganization around the 'display radar' module.

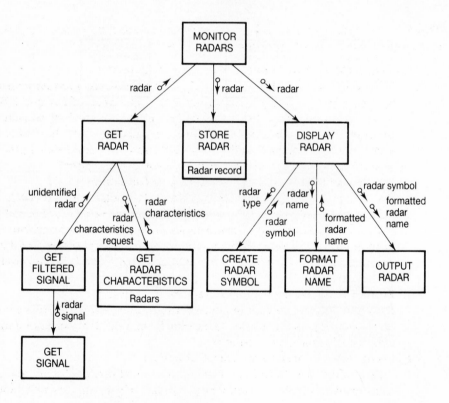

Figure A.48 Chapter 14, Exercise 5.

Connections within a data flow diagram

This appendix gives examples of connections between data flow diagram symbols, stating their validity and meaning.

1. Discrete data flow between data transformations.
   DA produces X which flows directly to DB and is accepted immediately by DB. X is effectively synchronizing the operation of DA and DB, as it carries not only data, but a stimulation. If DB is controlled by a control process, DB must be 'enabled' before it can accept X. If DB is 'disabled' when X arrives, then X will be lost. DB must be a continuous process, as only continuous processes can wait for discrete data.

2. Continuous data flow between data transformations.
   DA is continually producing X, which is continually accepted and processed by DB. As in (1), X will synchronize the actions of DA and DB. Only a continuous data transformation may produce a continuous data flow. If DB is controlled by a control process (it may be either continuous or one-shot), any data values of X which arrive while it is not activated will be lost.

3. Prompt between data transformations.   INVALID
   Data transformations cannot control one another. Even if there is a lower level control process inside a data transformation, it should not control data transformations outside itself.

4. Event flows between data transformations.
   This implies that there is a lower level control process inside one data transformation which is monitoring the state of something which another data transformation is doing, via an event flow.

5. Discrete data flow from data transformation to terminator.
   A data transformation will produce X, which is sent directly to a terminator, but the terminator can choose to ignore X. As the terminator is outside our perfect technology, we have no control over it.

6. Continuous data flow from data transformation to terminator.
   Control aspects as (5). The data transformation must be continuous and X will be continually available to the terminator.

7. Discrete data flow from terminator to data transformation.

   X is sent from the terminator, when it wants to send it. If the data transformation is controlled by a control process and is enabled, or is not controlled by a control process, it will accept X. If the data transformation is controlled by a control process and is disabled, X will be lost.

8. Continuous data flow from terminator to data transformation.

   Control aspects as (7). X is continually available to the data transformation — in most cases this will mean that the data transformation is continuous.

9. Prompts between terminator and data transformation.   INVALID

   A terminator may not send or receive enable/disable or trigger, as it is not part of the system's perfect technology.

10. Event flows from terminator to data transformation.

    The terminator is either making a request or reporting its status to the system.

11. Event flows from data transformation to terminator.

    The data transformation is either making a request, or reporting the status of the system to the terminator.

12. Discrete data flow from data store to data transformation.

    X is always available to the data transformation from the store, but as the store is a passive device which cannot 'send' the data, the data transformation must 'collect' the data when it needs it. A data store between data transformations implies that there is no synchronization between them.

13. Continuous data from a store.   INVALID

    The concept of continuous data coming from a store is not really applicable. Continuous data is always available, because it is always being sent (and therefore has the potential to be continually changing). Data in a store is continuously available, but is not always being sent and will therefore maintain its value.

14. Discrete data flow from data transformation to store.

    A data transformation may place discrete or continuous data in a store; however, data must be placed into the store discretely. If continuous data is continuously placed in a store, the implication is that the data is continually being updated in the store — in which case a store is not required, as that is the characteristic of a continuous data flow.

15. Event flow between data transformation and data store. ⎫
    Event flow between terminator and data store.   ⎬ INVALID
    Event flow between control process and data store.   ⎭

    Data stores can only hold data; event flows will either be held in event stores, or converted into data to be held in a data store.

16. Data flow between data transformation and control process. INVALID
    Dataflow between terminator and control process.

    It is illegal for the control process to produce or accept any data, because of the desire to separate control and data in the system. If the control process needs to know the value of a piece of data, it must first be converted into an event flow by a data transformation.

17. Discrete event flow from data transformation to control process.
    Discrete event flow from terminator to control process.
    Either a data transformation recognizes an event XC and signals this to a control process, or a terminator reports a status or makes a request of the control process, via XD. If the control process is in a state where it is waiting for the condition XC or XD, it will be accepted, otherwise it will be ignored and lost.

18. Continuous event flow from data transformation to control process.
    Continuous event flow from terminator to control process.
    In this case the events can be visualized as flags which can be examined at any time by the control process. In this case if the flags are set in a state where the control process is not waiting for that condition, they will still be set it enters into a state where it is waiting for that condition.

19. Prompt from control process to data transformation.
    A control process will only tell a a data transformation to enable/disable or trigger. As data transformations are meant to be single function units which do the same thing every time they are called, no other event flow should be needed.

20. Event flow from data transformation to event store.
    Event flow from terminator to event store.
    In both these cases the event will be caught by the event store. For the reasons stated in (13), event stores will only accept discrete events.

21. Event flow from event store to data transformation.
    This implies a lower level control process inside the data transformation, which is using the event store.

22. Event flow from event store to terminator.
    As the reading of an event store is a state transition diagram mechanism, it does not make sense to show a terminator reading an event store.

23. Data flow between terminator and data store.
    A terminator may access a data store which is *outside* the context bubble boundary; it may not directly access a store inside the system. This implies two things:
    (a) The data within the store is shared between the system and the terminator.
    (b) As between two data transformations, a direct data flow implies an element of synchronization which is not implied by a data store.

24. Discrete event flow between two control processes.
    A control process may make requests or pass status information to another control process via an event flow. The reaction of the receiving control process will be the same as if the event had come from anywhere else.

25. Continuous event flow between control processes.

This can be visualized as a flag between two control processes — see (18).

26. Communication between stores.   INVALID

    There is no direct communication between stores, as they are passive devices. The movement of data between stores must be achieved using a data transformation (data stores) or a control process (event stores).

27. Event flow from event store to control process.

    The way in which a control process uses an event store is discussed fully in Chapter 3.

28. Flows between terminators.   INVALID

    As flows between terminators must take place outside our system, they are of no interest to us, and so should not be shown.

Step-by-step guide to analysis

1. To start, you need a full appreciation of your system requirements, gathered from:
   (a) discussion with your customer;
   (b) studying any relevant documentation;
   (c) studying systems with a similar purpose to your own.
2. Build the *essential environmental model*, comprising
   (a) context diagram (Figure A.49);

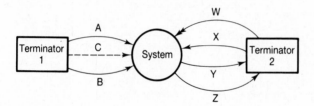

Figure A.49   Context diagram.

   (b) event list (Table A.12).

Table A.12

Event	Response	Classification
1. Event C	Start monitoring W	C/D
2. Event (2) from W	Start transforming X into Y	C/D
3. Event (3) from W	Start transforming X into Z	C/D
4. Event from B	Stop transforming X into Y	C
5. Event from A	Stop transforming X into Z	C
6. Time to stop	Stop monitoring W	C

These can be built in any order, or in parallel.
3. Generate the *essential behavioural model*, comprising

    DFDs

    STDs

    ERDs

from the context diagram and the event list.

(a) From the classification column of the event list, decide which diagram to build first.

       [In this case, we have six control type events and three data type events; therefore we will start with the STD.]

(b) Starting with the diagram indicated by step 3(a), build preliminary DFD, STDs and ERD directly from the event list and context diagram (Figure A.50).

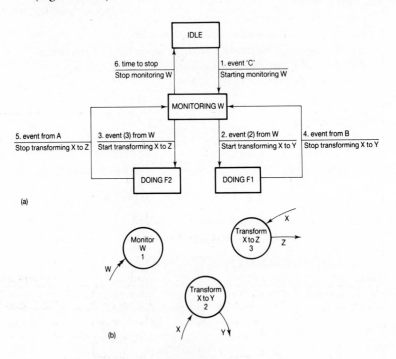

Figure A.50   Preliminary models: (a) STD, (b) DFD.

(c) Level and refine the preliminary models into a DFD hierarchy, creating event-recognizing data transformations where necessary (Figure A.51).
4. Complete entries in the project dictionary for all models components.

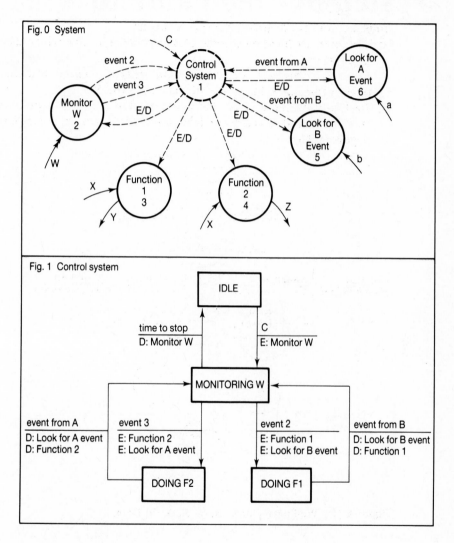

Figure A.51 Levelled model.

Step-by-step guide to processor allocation

1. To start you need:
   (a) the essential model;
   (b) the proposed processor configuration (Figure A.52).

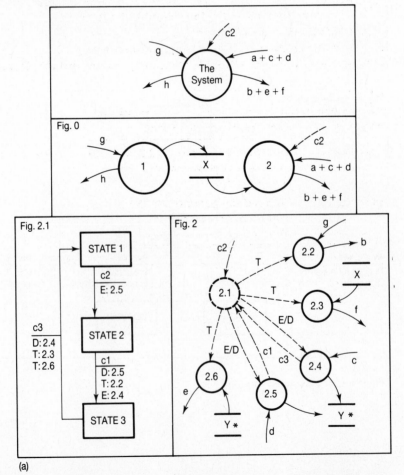

Fig. 0

Fig. 2.1

Fig. 2

(a)

Figure A.52 (a) Essential model and (b) processor configuration.

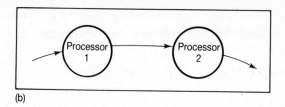

(b)

Figure A.52 *(continued)*

2. Allocate behaviour from as high up the essential model hierarchy as possible, allocating according to the following:
   (a) Why you picked the processor in the first place, i.e. if you have a processor with graphics capabilities, all the graphics behaviour should reside on it; if you have a processor to provide the user interface, all the user interface behaviour should reside on it.
   (b) Minimization of processor interfaces.
   (c) Any restrictions caused by required concurrency.
3. Build an allocation table (Table A.13) to help you record the allocation.

Table A.13

Processor	Essential model component
Processor 1	Data transformations: 1, 2.2, 2.3, 2.6 Control processes: part of 2.1 Data stores: X, Y
Processor 2	Data transformations: 2.4, 2.5 Control processes: part of 2.1 Data stores: Y

4. Based on the table entries for each processor, build the lower level diagrams that reflect the behaviour required on each processor, adding extra behaviour as appropriate (Figure A.53).

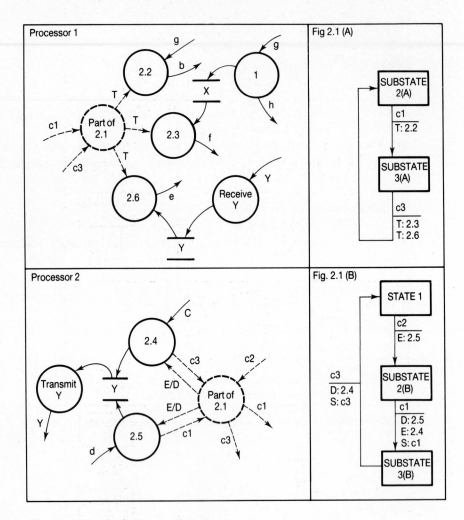

Figure A.53 Preliminary allocation.

5. Draw boundaries around each processor DFD to generate the top level processor data transformation, and renumber diagram components to reflect the new organization (Figure A.54).

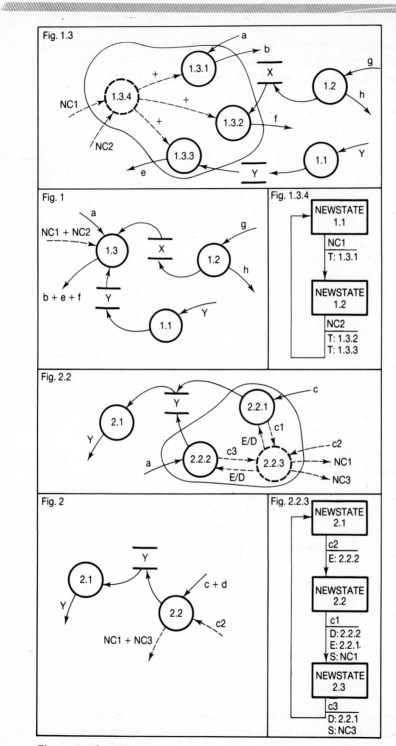

Figure A.54   PEM lower levels.

6. Join all the top level processor data transformations together to generate the top level PEM DFD (Figure A.55).
7. Complete supporting specifications within the project dictionary for all PEM components.

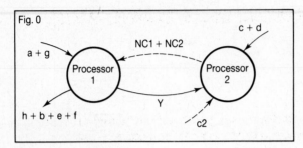

Figure A.55   PEM Figure 0

//

Step-by-step guide to software environment modelling

1. To start, for each processor, you need the following:
   (a) The processor environment model (Figure A.56).
   (b) Implementation details.

   > [For this system, we have the following implementation details:
   (i)   X, Y arrive one after the other, every 5 seconds. Collection of a single X or Y value takes in the order of milliseconds.
   (ii) Create reports will run for a period in the order of tens of seconds.
   (iii) Values of X and Y entering the system should always be collected.]

   (c) The proposed software architecture.

   > [The software architecture here consists of:
   (i)   A fairly sophisticated operating system, which allows up to 32 execution units. Execution units should be allocated a priority, and the operating system will run execution units on an interrupt/resume (I/R) mechanism, always running the highest priority execution unit. Execution units may communicate via shared data areas, and may suspend themselves for specified periods of time, allowing lower priority execution units to be run.

   > The operating system also provides a number of I/O routines which can be used for terminal I/O.
   (ii) An arithmetic package, which when passed a set of figures, carries out a mathematical analysis on those figures, returning the result of the analysis.

   The software architecture can be modelled by Figure A.56(b).]

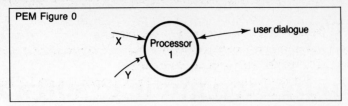

PEM Figure 0

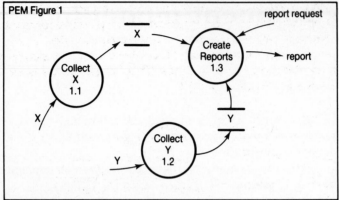

PEM Figure 1

(a) Processor environment model.

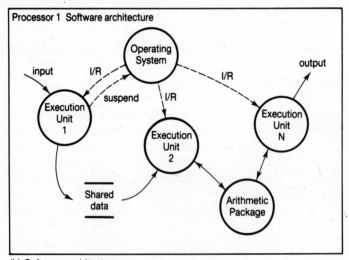

Processor 1 Software architecture

(b) Software architecture.

Figure A.56

2. Allocate behaviour to the software architecture:
   (a) By examining the PEM behaviour with respect to the functions provided by the software architecture.

   [In this example part of '1.3 create reports' has been allocated to the arithmetic package, shown by Figure A.57(a).]

   (b) Remove common processing by considering the implementation of PEM behaviour and merging common areas of processing such that the same behaviour will not be implemented twice.

   [In this example both '1.1 collect X' and '1.2 collect Y' will contain the same input routines. This behaviour has been merged, as shown by Figure A.57(b).]

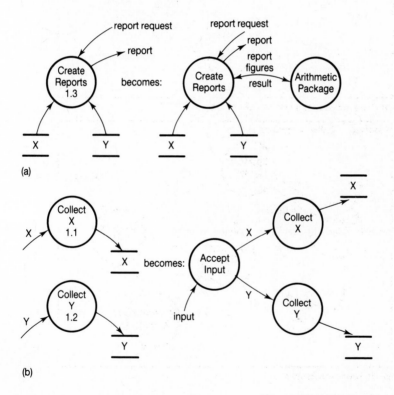

Figure A.57　(a) Allocation to software architecture; (b) removal of common processing.

3. Allocate remaining behaviour to execution units (Figure A.58), according to: concurrent activities and the minimization of execution interfaces.

[As they are all connected by stores, 'collect X', 'collect Y' and 'create reports' are all essentially asynchronous. However, the implementation details specify that X and Y will always arrive one after the other. Therefore, we have decided to 'collect X' and 'collect Y' in sequence, and so put them in the same execution unit.]

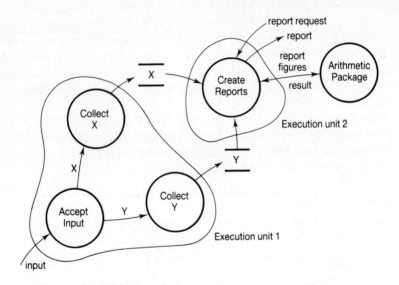

Figure A.58   Allocation to execution units.

4. If you have more than one execution unit, work out how to ensure that the execution units are activated in the correct sequence, by examination of the following:
   (a) The operating system.
   (b) The implementation details.
   (c) The PEM requirements.

   [The implementation details specify that values of X and Y arrive every 5 seconds, and must be collected, and that the amount of time that it takes to 'create reports' may interfere with this collection. Therefore we will give 'collect X and Y' a higher priority than 'create reports', so that it will always be able to collect the data. We are also told that data should be collected every 5 seconds, therefore after each data collection 'collect X and Y' will suspend itself for (5 seconds − collection time), so 'create reports' can run.]
5. Model the resulting design (Figure A.59). The top level DFD of the SEM will always resemble the model of the software architecture produced in step 1 (Figure A.56(b)), but flows, stores and data transformations should now have meaningful names.

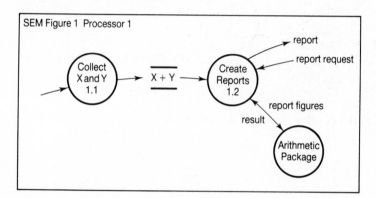

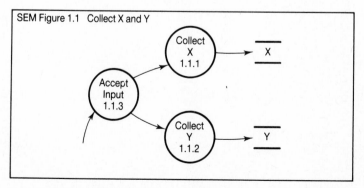

Figure A.59   Software environment model.

6. Complete the traceability table for the allocation (Table A.14).
7. Complete supporting specifications in project dictionary for SEM model components.

Table A.14

Processor environment model	Software environment model
1.1 Collect X	1.1.1 Collect X 1.1.3 Accept input (part)
1.2 Collect Y	1.1.2 Collect Y 1.1.3 Accept input (part)
1.3 Create reports	1.2 Create reports *Arithmetic package*
Data store: X	X (shared)
Data store: Y	Y (shared)

Step-by-step guide to code organization modelling

1. To start, the following are needed for each execution unit:
   (a) The software environment model (Figure A.60).
   (b) A knowledge of the programming language being used to implement the code.

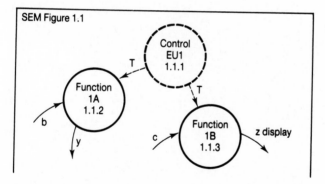

Figure A.60   SEM hierarchy for single execution unit.

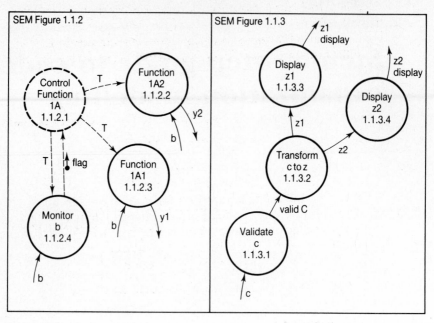

Figure A.60 (*continued*)

2. Translate each DFD from the SEM into a preliminary structure chart (Figure A.61).

       If the DFD has a control process, translate via the STD, otherwise use either transform or transaction analysis, depending on the type of DFD.

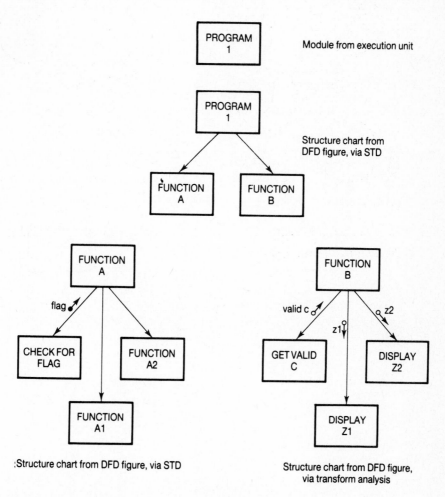

Figure A.61   Structure chart hierarchy from execution unit.

3. Form the preliminary structure charts into a single preliminary hierarchy, based on the hierarchy of the DFDs within the execution unit (Figure A.62).

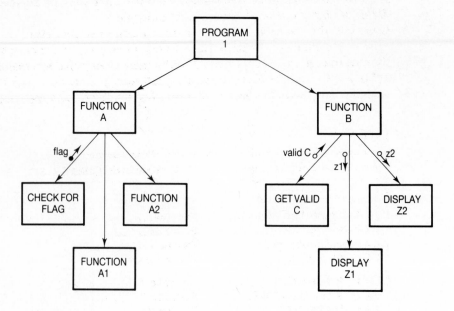

Figure A.62   Preliminary structure chart.

4. Refine the preliminary structure chart such that it will give an implementable, well-structured program.

> [This has not been attempted, since to do it sensibly, we would need to have a good idea of what all the modules were to do in some detail, which we do not have in this example.]

5. Complete the traceability table for the allocation to modules.

> [As we have not done the refinement step (4), we cannot show the true traceability table, as the allocation may change under refinement. Table A.15 shows traceability to the preliminary structure chart.]

6. Complete entries in the project dictionaries for all modules and couples.

Table A.15

Software environment model		Code organization model
1.1.1	Control EUI	Program 1
1.1.2.1	Control Function 1A	Function A
1.1.2.2	Function 1A2	Function A2
1.1.2.3	Function 1A1	Function A1
1.1.2.4	Monitor B	Check for flag
1.1.3.1	Validate C	Get valid C
1.1.3.2	Transform C to Z	Function B
1.1.3.3	Display Z1	Display Z1
1.1.3.4	Display Z2	Display Z2

Glossary

Action An action is a component of a state transition diagram which specifies what the system will do when certain conditions are true within the system.

Balancing Balancing a model involves carrying out a number of checks on that model to ensure that it is consistent. A model can be balanced either vertically or horizontally:

1. *Vertically*, i.e. each transformation has the same inputs and outputs as the lower level diagram which describes it.
2. *Horizontally*, i.e. entity relationship diagrams correspond with data flow diagrams, which correspond with state transition diagrams.

Behavioural model The behavioural model comprises:

- data flow diagrams
- state transition diagrams
- entity relationship diagrams
- supporting specifications

which completely describe the requirements of a system.

Condition A condition is a component of a state transition diagram which specifies what has to be true in a certain state of the system before certain actions can occur.

Continuous With respect to components of the essential model, a continuous flow will be available over a period of time, a continuous transformation will be active over a period of time.

Code organization model This model shows the programs within the system as a hierarchy of modules, it consists of:

structure charts
project/data dictionary

Context diagram The context diagram shows the following:

1. Anything in its environment which the system interfaces to (terminators).

494

2. Any interfaces between the system and its terminators.

Control process   The control process transforms input event flows (showing the status of the system) into output event flows, in order to control the system. The control process is a 'shorthand' form of the state transition diagram, used to show control on the data flow diagram.

Data dictionary/project dictionary   The project dictionary holds the supporting specification (usually in textual terms) of all the diagram components (including process and module specifications) within the model. It is important for holding lower level specifications, which cannot easily be shown on the model, and which allow the model to be checked.

Data flow   A data flow is used to carry information around a data flow diagram.

Data flow diagram (DFD)   The DFD represents the functions of a system as a network of circles (data transformations) linked by data flows and data stores. The data transformations may be further defined by lower level DFDs or by transformation specifications.

Data store   A data store is used to hold information within a data flow diagram.

Data transformation   A data transformation is used to transform input flows into output flows, and thereby show the functionality of a system.

Disable   Perfect technology mechanism for switching off a continuous data transformation, sometime after it has been switched on (enabled).

Discrete   With respect to components of the essential model, a discrete flow is only available at a point in time, and a discrete transformation will be active at a point in time (i.e. it will perform its function instantaneously).

Enable   Perfect technology mechanism for switching on a continuous data transformation, which will later be switched off (disabled).

Entity relationship diagram (ERD)   The entity relationship diagram represents the structure of information within the system. System entities are represented as a network of rectangles (objects) linked by diamonds (relationships).

Essential model   The product of analysis is the essential model — an implementation-free documentation of the system consisting of the following:

1. Statement of purpose.
2. The environmental model:
   (a) context diagram;
   (b) event list.
3. The behavioural model:
   (a) data flow diagrams;
   (b) state transition diagrams;
   (c) entity relationship diagrams.
4. Supporting data/project dictionary.

The aim of this model is to document the structured analysis phase, and thereby describe the customer requirements.

Event flow   The event flow is used to carry status information around the data flow diagram.

Event list   The event list is part of the environmental model, and consists of a table holding the following:

1. Events — all external stimuli to which the system reacts.
2. Responses — the reaction of the system to external stimuli.
3. A classification of the event and response, which ease the building of an essential behavioural model.

Event recognizer   An event recognizer is a special class of data transformation which is used to transform data into event flows.

Event store   The event store is used to store status and control information in the data flow diagram.

Implementation model   The product of design is the implementation model, which shows how a system will be implemented and documents decisions made throughout the design process, consisting of the following:

1. The processor environment model
   (a) data flow diagrams;
   (b) state transition diagrams;
   (c) entity relationship diagrams;
   (d) project/data dictionary.
2. The software environment model:
   (a) data flow diagrams;
   (b) state transition diagrams;
   (c) entity relationship diagrams;
   (d) project/data dictionary.
3. The code organization model:
   (a) structure charts;
   (b) project/data dictionary.

Levelling   Levelling a model involves partitioning a complex model into a hierarchy of understandable pieces.

Lower   Perfect technology mechanism for producing a continuous event flow (flag) between two control processes/STDs. Lower will set the flag to false, and raise will set the flag to true.

Module   A module is the unit used on a structure chart (which describes a program) to describe a subroutine, procedure or function within that program.

Object   An object is a component of an entity relationship diagram which represents something which plays a functional role in the system, and about which data will be stored.

Processor environment model (PEM)   The processor environment model defines the allocation of essential model components to real-world

⌐processors, and shows the details of the human—computer interface. The processor environment model consists of:

- data flow diagrams
- state transition diagrams
- entity relationship diagrams
- project/data dictionary

Project dictionary — see Data dictionary.

Prompt   A prompt is a special class of event flow, which can only be produced by a control process and is used exclusively to switch on and off data transformations. Enable/disable and trigger are prompts.

Raise   Perfect technology mechanism for producing a continuous event flow (flag) between two control processes/STDs. Raise will set the flag to true, and lower will set the flag to false.

Relationship   A relationship is a component of an entity relationship diagram which represents an association or mapping between objects within the system.

Signal   Perfect technology mechanism for producing a discrete event flow between two control processes/STDs.

Software environment model   The software environment model shows how the processes defined in the essential model have been organized into execution units (tasks) with respect to the processor software architecture, scheduling and running constraints.

The software environment model consists of:

- data flow diagrams
- state transition diagrams
- entity relationship diagrams
- project/data dictionary

State   A state is a component of a state transition diagram which represents an observable mode of system behaviour which persists over time.

Statement of purpose   An overview description of the system, which precedes the essential environmental model.

State transition diagram (STD)   The state transition diagram shows the control and sequencing within a system over time. The sequence of behaviour within the system is represented by a network of rectangles (states) connected by transitions.

Structure chart   The structure chart shows the internal structure of a program in terms of a hierarchy of modules (procedures, functions, subroutines).

Structured analysis   A collection of tools and associated techniques used to establish exactly *what* the customer requirements for a system are. Structured analysis provides a model which can be elaborated and reorganized to reflect decisions made during structured design.

Structured design   A series of tools and techniques that allow developers to develop the model produced in structured analysis through the various phases of design, showing *how* the customer's requirements will be implemented.

Transformation specification   A description of what is happening inside a data transformation — the aim is to show what happens in order to transform the inputs of the data transformation into the outputs in a clear and unambiguous way.

Transition   A transition is a component of an STD which represents the movement of the system from one STD state to another. Transitions have associated conditions which specify what has to be true before the transition will be made, and actions, which specify what must be done to effect the transition into the next state.

Transitory state   A transitory state is a component of an STD which represents the system evaluating internal data in order to decide what conditions are true. Transitory states are unnamed as they do not represent true system states.

Trigger   Perfect technology mechanism for activating a discrete one-shot data transformation, which does not need to be switched off, as it performs its function instantaneously.

Bibliography

Allen, C.P. (1991) *Effective Structured Techniques*, Prentice Hall, Hemel Hempstead.

Boehm, B.W. (1981) *Software Engineering Economics*, Prentice Hall, Hemel Hempstead.

Coad, P. and E. Yourdon (1990) *Object Oriented Analysis*, Prentice Hall (Yourdon Press), Hemel Hempstead.

De Marco, T. (1978) *Structured Analysis and System Specification*, Prentice Hall (Yourdon Press), Hemel Hempstead.

(1989) *Concise Notes on Software Engineering*, Prentice Hall (Yourdon Press), Hemel Hempstead.

Hatley, D.J. and I.A. Pirbhai (1987) *Strategies for Real-time System Specification*, Dorset House, New York.

Jones, C. (1980) *Software Development: A rigorous approach*, Prentice Hall, Hemel Hempstead.

McMenamin, S.M. and J.F. Palmer (1984) *Essential Systems Analysis*, Prentice Hall (Yourdon Press), Hemel Hempstead.

Page-Jones, M. (1988) *The Practical Guide to Structured Systems Design*, Prentice Hall (Yourdon Press), Hemel Hempstead.

Ward, P.T. and S.J. Mellor (1985) *Structured Development for Real Time Systems*, Prentice Hall (Yourdon Press), Hemel Hempstead.

Yourdon, E. (1985) *Structured Walkthroughs*, Prentice Hall (Yourdon Press), Hemel Hempstead.

Yourdon, E. (1989) *Modern Structured Analysis*, Prentice Hall (Yourdon Press), Hemel Hempstead.

Index